THE AUTHOR WISHES

TO EXPRESS HIS HEARTFELT THANKS TO ALL THE JOURNALISTS AND REPORTERS FROM EVERY COUNTRY, WHO SPENT THEIR LIVES WITNESSING AND CHRONICLING THE WARS OF THE TWENTIETH CENTURY.

WHITE STAR PUBLISHERS

1
Kuwait, Operation Desert Storm 1991,this Marine's blue eyes display force and determination, but also anguish at having to confront the terrible experience of war.

2-3
Ypres, April 22, 1915: a British soldier dies suffocated by the mustard-gas thrown by the Germans violating all war regulations. So it begins the chemical war, one of the most terrible chapters of WWI.

4-5
Phnom Penh, capital of Cambodia, 1974: women and children flee in a hurricane of iron and fire. The Khmer Rouge have just begun their attack on the capital, in which over 1 million people had sought shelter.

7
A wounded Russian soldier wanders on the battlefield during the resistance against the German troops, which penetrated Soviet territory on June 21, 1941.

8-9
Khe Sanh, Vietnam, 1968: an ammunition warehouse blows up next to a group of marines, who try desperately to find shelter.

TEXT BY
LUCIANO GARIBALDI

PROJECT MANAGER AND EDITORIAL DIRECTOR
VALERIA MANFERTO DE FABIANIS

GRAPHIC DESIGN
CLARA ZANOTTI

EDITORIAL COORDINATION
FABIO BOURBON
CRISTINA LENZI
MARIA VALERIA URBANI GRECCHI

TRANSLATION BY
GLOBE / STUDIO VECCHIA

TRANSLATION EDITOR
PETER SKINNER

CONTENTS

Introduction

The twentieth century was by far the bloodiest period in human history—two world wars and so many other deadly "regional" conflicts. Unfortunately, the 21st century did not start off much better. The terror attacks of September 11, 2001 were ominous. The wars in Iraq and Afghanistan have been bloody. The carnage we still see in various parts of Africa, including in Darfur and Congo, has been awful.

Still, it was the twentieth century that saw genocide take on an incredible new dimension, complete with highly efficient, state-of-the-art technology. I refer here, in part, to the Holocaust, which remains the single most destructive act of genocide ever. But despite pleas of "Never Again," genocide continued throughout the century. It was also a century that saw the development—and, more frighteningly, the use—of nuclear weapons by the United States to end the war with Japan.

When asked to write this introduction, I was immediately responsive. The wars of the century, after all, had shaped my generation. Born after World War II, I was one of those self-indulgent baby boomers who could only read and hear stories of the war. My grandparents on both sides had lived through World War I in Europe, only to die in the Holocaust. My parents survived, and, like so many other refugees both before and after them, wound up in the United States where they prospered in a multitude of ways. In sharing their personal stories, they always instilled within me a rock-solid hatred of war and a reverence for freedom.

Growing up in the 1950s and 1960s, I was also shaped by the Cold War. But the first actual fighting war that I had to confront personally was the Vietnam War. That war threatened to engulf me in 1970, when I graduated from college and my draft status automatically became 1-A. But that was also the year when the government began using a lottery system for the draft. I was lucky. My lottery number was high enough to put me beyond the possibility of becoming one of the draftees. I was spared. I could attend graduate school without worry. But many of my friends could not. Some paid the ultimate price for their service during that war. I think of them often when I visit the Wall at the Vietnam War Memorial in Washington D.C.

The 1967 Six-Day War in the Middle East also had a dramatic impact on my thinking, even though I was growing up in upstate New York, thousands of miles away. I can still remember coming home from a summer job in the Catskill Mountains one particular June day to find my mother crying in the kitchen. She was convinced the Jews of Israel were about to meet the same fate that the Jews of Europe had met only two decades earlier. That, of course, did not occur. But the image of her and her terrible anxiety remains clear in my mind.

As a reporter now for more than three decades, I've covered several so-called high-intensity and low-intensity wars. I was in Beirut in 1981 during the Israeli invasion, and reported on countless terrorist incidents in the Middle East. I was CNN's military affairs correspondent at the Pentagon during the Persian Gulf War—when most of you probably first heard my name. That was a unique moment because, for the first time, parts of a war were brought to you live. But the Pentagon maintained a fairly sophisticated hand in shaping which parts we all would see. Theirs was, as has been widely acknowledged, a highly sanitized version of the war. As impressive as those gun-camera videotapes were, they gave us, of course, only a small piece of the story.

The more recent war in Iraq in this new century has been covered much more thoroughly, bringing the awful guts of warfare to an international audience.

Over the years, I was an eyewitness to the devastating results of many wars that I did not actually cover. It sounds like a cliché, but when I traveled to Africa with President Clinton in 1998 and saw the Hutu and Tutsi survivors of the earlier slaughter in Rwanda and Burundi, I could still smell death in the air. At a ceremony commemorating the more than half a million people killed during that war, I recall needing to put a handkerchief over my mouth. It is shocking to be reminded of how many people in different parts of the globe have been slaughtered. Think of the two million people who were killed by the Khmer Rouge in Cambodia, or the million Biafrans killed in Africa. Sadly, such brutality continues today. I often have wondered how it was possible that so many had been killed so recently. One would have thought that once the cold ugliness of war was brought into living rooms around the globe, the killing should surely have stopped.

On the other hand, I was very fortunate to cover some very hopeful events of the twentieth century, too. I was in Moscow in December 1991 when the Red Flag went down for the last time from over the Kremlin, ending the seventy-four year Communist regime of the Soviet Union. That marked the real end of the Cold War. I was also fortunate to cover the signing of the Israeli-Egyptian peace treaty at the White House in March 1979, which marked the first real peace between Israel and an Arab neighbor—though peace in that part of the world still, unfortunately, remains elusive.

I hope this book will have an enlightening effect on its readers. I hope that when the reader sees these incredible pictures and absorbs the accompanying text, he or she will step back and remember that evil can begin with one person and can spread from there. I also hope that as a new generation of young people become exposed to this "Century of War," they will come to recognize that we each have a personal responsibility to do what we can to avoid war. But we should have no illusions that our efforts will meet with anything remotely resembling immediate success.

For many of you, looking at these pictures will be painful. Some of them are very ugly. But having seen the "real" thing first-hand, I can tell you that these images are nothing. Death up close is so much worse. Read *Century of War*. Share it with your children and grandchildren. If you lived through war, tell them your stories, so they will better understand this bloodiest century in history. We need to keep a record so that we might actually learn from the tragic blunders of the past.

Wolf Blitzer
Washington, D.C.

1899
1902

THE ANGLO-BOER WAR

THE 20TH CENTURY BEGAN WITH THE OMINOUS SIGNS OF WAR BETWEEN EUROPEANS FOUGHT IN A DISTANT REGION OF THE WORLD, IN SOUTH AFRICA.

The Dutch (or Boer) Republics of the Orange Free State and the Transvaal, and the British colonies of Natal and the Cape, subject to Queen Victoria became a battleground for colonists, killing each other, 6300 miles away from their homeland. The Dutch word Boeren means "colonial." The Boers were farmers who during the first half of the 18th century had emigrated to South Africa to seek their fortune. They had colonized a large part of these immense territories, establishing farms and breeding cattle. Above all, they began exploiting the rich deposits of gold and diamonds.

Grudges between the two communities dated back to an act of British imperialism. In 1880, Britain had annexed the Transvaal but was then forced to retreat after losing the battle of Majuba Hill (1881). Shortly thereafter, enormous lodes of gold were discovered in the Transvaal and the gold rush began, bringing in British subjects from the Cape and Natal. Thousands of Britons came to settle in the region, requesting--but not obtaining--the right to vote and equalization of taxes. As a result, the situation had become increasingly strained.

In Pretoria, the Transvaal's capital city, the Boer president Kruger was uncompromising; in Cape Town, the Cape colony's capital city, the governor, Sir Alfred Milner (1st Viscount Milner), responded with a series of provocations and attacks. In essence, the English could not tolerate the Afrikaander (the conservative Dutch settler) nationalism. Above all else, the Afrikaander goal was to gain control of the gold mines. The protracted showdown culminated in an ultimatum that President Kruger issued to Sir Alfred Milner on October 9, 1899. Milner rejected the ultimatum, and fighting broke out on October 12. During the first phase of the war (until January 1900), the Boers, who had mobilized an army of 40,000 men, were on the offensive. After defeating the English troops, numbering 20,000 men, they besieged the colonial cities of Ladysmith, Kimberley, and Mafeking.

The last week of 1899 was a demoralizing one for the British: the London papers called it "the black week" and the European press made the defeat of the British in

10
The uniforms and arms of British (top and bottom) and Boer (center) soldiers during the war's first phase. The war's primary cause was that both the Boers and the British settlers in the Cape and Natal colonies wanted to control the gold and diamond mines of the Transvaal.

11
A British ambush for Boer troops during the war's second phase, which began in October 1899. The conflict turned ferocious and bloody after London sent 60,000 men to the area. Lord Roberts and Lord Kitchener, both experienced in fighting colonial wars, were in command.

THE ANGLO-BOER WAR
1899-1902

South Africa the news of the hour for. Her Majesty's government had to react. Queen Victoria demanded it. London placed two seasoned colonials in charge of its expeditionary force: Lord Roberts as commander and Lord Kitchener as his chief of staff. In the meantime, reinforcements arrived: 60,000 British soldiers landed at Cape Town, Elizabeth, and East London. On February 28, leading 26,000 men, General Buller liberated Ladysmith. On March 31, it was Kimberley's turn: Lord French's Army Corps marched on the city with 40,000 men, led by the cavalry back from the overwhelming charge on Bloemfontein. The Orange Free State was annexed to Great Britain and Pretoria finally fell on June 5, with the Transvaal close behind. But victory was elusive. Guerrilla warfare began, with two long years of brutal assaults, repression, and devastation at the expense of civilians. Following the defeat of the Boer army on the battlefield, President Kruger, old and disheartened, left for Europe; as a result, power was equally divided between Vice President Burger and the "generalissimo" Botha. The latter never accepted defeat and launched violent, decisive actions to wreak havoc, with quick forays by a battle-hardened mounted infantry that moved about carrying its own rations and supplies. The British response was ruthless. First, Lord Roberts began burning down the farmsteads and destroying crops, but he was called back to London at the beginning of 1901. Lord Kitchener took over command of the troops; he was eager to end the war because he had no intention of losing his posting as supreme commander in India. Consequently, Kitchener set up enormous concentration camps where thousands of women and children prisoners were struck down by epidemics. He also ordered summary executions of prisoners and enlisted 10,000 African natives, although at the onset of hostilities the Boers and English had solemnly pledged to leave the indigenous populations out of the conflict.

The outcome was that the Boers shot natives who were bearing arms when captured. In retaliation, Kitchener had the Boers responsible for the executions shot when they were captured. An endless spiral of violence flared, at whose end no fewer than 30,000 civilian victims were counted, not to mention the difficult-to-calculate military losses. The ruthlessness of British repression was so great that it drew criticism against Great Britain from the entire civilized world. But as long as Queen Victoria was on the throne, Lord Kitchener could show no mercy in South Africa. Only with the eighty-two-year-old sovereign's death on January 22, 1901 and her son Edward VII's accession to the throne was it possible to loosen the grip of repression.

British troops in South Africa numbered 250,000 by this time. They were battling against 30,000 rebels, who succumbed on May 31st, the day the Boers were forced to sign the Treaty of Unification in Pretoria. The document demanded that the defeated population acknowledge themselves as British subjects in exchange for permission to retain their Dutch language and traditions.

12
Two Boer soldiers (one showing his state's flag) resist the British offensive. The British succeeded in overcoming the Dutch colonies' resistance, first conquering the Orange Free State, and then, on June 5, 1900, the Transvaal and its capital, Pretoria.

13
Fierce Boer resistance in the Transvaal. Artillery (above) and gun-carrying units (below) confront Lord Kitchener's advance. After the end of the open conflict, two years of guerrilla war began, during which more than 30,000 civilians were killed. The British used a total of 250,000 soldiers in the war. One of them was the young officer Winston Spencer Churchill, the future victor of the Second World War.

1899

1900

THE

BOXER WAR

ALTHOUGH KNOWN TO HISTORY AS THE "BOXER REBELLION," THE SERIES OF BLOODY CONFLICTS THAT TOOK PLACE IN CHINA DURING THE FIRST YEAR OF THE 20TH CENTURY ACTUALLY AMOUNTED TO AN AUTHENTIC WAR; IT INVOLVED EIGHT GREAT POWERS AGAINST THE PRECARIOUS MANCHU EMPIRE, SUSTAINED BY THE DOWAGER EMPRESS-TZU-HSI.

The elderly, temperamental Empress surrounded herself at court with eunuchs and sages. She was a fanatical protector of animals, refusing to walk in the imperial gardens for fear of trampling on the ants. Above all, she was fiercely opposed to modern technology in all its forms and had banned modern "deviltries" such as the telephone and the bicycle within the Forbidden City (the imperial citadel in Peking). With good reason she hated the meddling of Westerners who, although rivals, had formed alliances to share the spoils of the empire, taking advantage of its weakened state. China had lost two wars in the second half of the nineteenth century, one against the British and one against the Japanese. Through the system of "territorial concessions" Japan had annexed Formosa (Taiwan) and Korea, and Russia had annexed Port Arthur and Manchuria. Great Britain controlled the Yangtze river's estuary and Germany the mines of Shantung.

With this territorial expansionism came widespread proliferation of Catholic and Protestant mssions. These were established throughout China, which in 1900 had a population of 340 million. The missions had thousands of followers, dividing loyalties and creating friction within communities.

The third source of conflict was Western racism, at times so excessive as to sanction the posting of signs reading "No dogs or Chinese allowed" at the entrances to the European quarters of Shanghai and other cities of the empire. This Western aggression resulted in the creation and consolidation of several nationalist groups. The most militant of these was the society of the "Righteous and Harmonious Fists," whose members were drawn mainly from the peasants in the north, although noblemen and courtiers of the Empress also joined these groups. Their enthusiasm for boxing led the British to dub them the "Boxers." Their first victims were the Chinese converts to Christianity. Wearing outlandish headgear and long red tunics, armed with revolvers and sabers, the "boxers" attacked the missions and massacred the converts to cries of "Sha! Sha!" ("Kill! Kill!").

The turning point came on December 31, 1899. Until then,

14
The Great Powers' offensive has just begun. This followed the murder of the German ambassador by a Boxer rebel in Peking on June 9, 1900. Tientsin was first city the Powers captured. Top left and below: French and Japanese trenches. Top right: devastation done by Chinese in Peking's embassy district.

15
Bodies of dead Chinese soldiers, loyal to the Empress Tzu-hsi are lying along Peking's walls. The International Expeditionary Corps, commanded by the German General von Waldersee, captured Peking.

THE BOXER WAR
1899-1900

the Boxers had not dared to raise their weapons against any Western missionary, but on that day the first white Catholic missionary was killed in Peking. This was only the beginning: within a couple of months the zealots in the red tunics had murdered 200 priests and nuns. Five hundred foreigners, comprising diplomats and embassy employees with their families, lived in the Legation quarter of Peking. They were nationals of eleven countries: the United States, Japan, Germany, France, Great Britain, Italy, Belgium, Austria-Hungary, the Netherlands, Russia, and Spain. The Europeans' situation was becoming ever more perilous. The Boxers hated the railways and telegraph poles because they offended the *feng shui*, the spirits of wind and water, and so the railway stations around the capital were burned down one after another. On June 9, 1900 a bomb went off at the racetrack, destroying the stands. On June 13 the German ambassador Von Ketteler was on his way to the Ministry of Foreign Affairs in a sedan chair carried by two servants when a Chinese soldier approached, lifted the curtain, and shot him in the head. Panic swept through the Legation quarter, and soldiers were called in to defend the various offices.

In response to the situation the meantime, in Tientsin, where the Great Powers' battleships were anchored, an international expeditionary force was formed, composed of 2,129 seamen and their officers under the command of a British general, Edward Seymour. Twenty five miles from Peking the troops confronted Chinese soldiers. The battle ended with 62 dead and hundreds of wounded. Some sailors went ahead to open up the road and fought their way into the Legation quarter to give support to the American, European, and Japanese soldiers defending the area. During July, the foreign powers had finally reached an agreement. Eight of them, the United States, Austria-Hungary, Great Britain, France, Germany, Italy, Japan, and Russia, declared war on China. The battleships steamed at full speed for Tientsin. In Peking, the Boxers burned down all the embassy buildings except the British Embassy, inside which members of the other delegations barricaded themselves. The siege lasted 55 days -- 55 days of privation and horror. There were no provisions and the besieged had to kill their animals to feed themselves: first the horses, then the dogs and cats. Any Westerner who was captured was decapitated.

Finally, an international army of 20,000 men set out from Tientsin in five divisions. The German general in command, Alfred von Waldersee, had only one order: Be ruthless! Journalists from the most prestigious newspapers followed his forces. The Indian Sikhs of the British division were the first troops to enter Peking, scaling the walls on August 12, 1900. The Sikhs fought street by street. During the night of August 15, the American general Adna Chaffee, a veteran of operations against the American Indians, attacked the Forbidden City, which the Empress Tzu hsi had fled just in time, after having had her son's favorite thrown into a well because she had refused to obey the Empress's orders. And so began the acts of revenge, the plundering and raping, while entire Chinese families committed suicide, the only way out of the shame they had suffered. The journalists were shocked, as the reports in *Le Figaro* and *Corriere della Sera* testify.

The Boxers were hunted down until Christmas Day, 1900, when the allied troops marched in triumph through the streets of Peking. Hundreds of Boxers were killed. They were beheaded, and their heads were put into wooden cages where they remained on show for days in the squares and streets. The Empress had to stand by while her most faithful subjects were called "war criminals" (the first time in the 20th century that the term was used) and then allow them to be punished. Dozens of court dignitaries were executed, foreshadowing what was to happen at the international Nuremberg trials. Dozens more were forced to take their own lives. The Empress was also forced to exile her minister of foreign affairs, Prince Tuan, to offer her formal apologies to Germany, to erect monuments in the foreign cemeteries desecrated by the Boxers, but above all to pay an enormous sum in reparation--£67 million, the equivalent of about $10 billion in 2000, although the payment was spread over 40 years.

The intention was that China would never rise again after such a blow. On the death of Tzu hsi, her nephew Pu Yi succeeded her as the last emperor of the Manchu dynasty. He was deposed in 1911 by the political leader of modern China, Sun Yat-sen, who proclaimed China a republic. Pu Yi became emperor of Manchukuo, a puppet state of Japan. At the end of World War II, he was sent to a Communist work camp. Hatred of foreigners--and above all of missionaries and bishops--then lay dormant for sixty years, only to resurface violently with Mao Tse-tung and the Cultural Revolution of the 1960s.

17
The vendetta. Top: Japanese soldiers decapitate Boxer rebels in front of an Indian contingent of the British Expeditionary Force and Chinese government army soldiers. Center: Boxer prisoners awaiting execution. Bottom: A condemned prisoner about to be executed. Boxer rebels committed serious crimes against the foreign community, especially against Christian missionaries and their converts.

1899
1900

THE

RUSSIAN-JAPANESE WAR

AT THE END OF THE BOXER REBELLION, RUSSIA OCCUPIED MANCHURIA, BUILT A RAILWAY TO GET SUPPLIES TO THE NAVAL BASE OF PORT ARTHUR, AND PENETRATED KOREA.

Russian expansionism worried Tokyo, which had never tried to hide its centuries-old designs on Korea. The Russian viceroy of Manchuria, the despotic Prince Yevgeny Alekseyev, was an element in increasing tension. Alekseyev, the natural son of Tsar Alexander II, felt he had been given a sacred mission to render Russia invincible in the Far East.

The friction finally surfaced in a diplomatic note of October 3, 1903, in which Alekseyev asked the Emperor of Japan to recognize Russian interests in North Korea above the 39th parallel. Tokyo replied politely but firmly: no recognition of Russian interests. This was only the start of a struggle involving various offenses and provocations given and received, including a few Japanese landings in South Korea. Finally, on February 6, 1904, the Japanese ambassador in St. Petersburg closed the embassy, broke off diplomatic relations with the Tsar, and returned to Japan.

This was a warning signal, but in spite of it, the Russians were caught unprepared. Two days later, on February 8, a Japanese steamship entered Port Arthur and in view of thousands of Russian sailors, who were watching from the battleships at anchor, took aboard Japanese subjects resident in the city, who had only just left their homes. Among them was a secret agent who had marked on a map the exact position of the Russian ships at anchor--there were thirteen cruisers and battleships along with four destroyers. The destroyers, however, were out on the high seas on a military exercise, at the end of which they were to proceed to the port of Dalny. The orders had come directly from the viceroy, bypassing the commander of the fleet, Admiral Stark.

This decision, which was to have tragic consequences, was later seen as an enormous blunder. On the night of February 9, the Russian sailors on watch thought the silhouettes of the warships on the horizon were the destroyers returning to base. Foreshadowing what was to happen on December 7, 1941 at Pearl Harbor when the Japanese attacked the US fleet, they proved to be three groups of Japanese destroyers, which torpedoed and sank the battleships *Tsarevich* and *Retvizan*, and the cruiser *Pallada*. The Russian guns blazed fiercely, but it was dark and the Japanese ships were only slightly damaged.

18

Top: Japanese troops crossing a river in Manchuria, near Motien hill. The Japanese invasion of Manchuria, considered by Russia to be Russian territory, began on February 9, 1904 with a Japanese attack on the Russian military base of Port Arthur, followed by a series of troop landings.

Bottom: Japanese soldiers burning the bodies of comrades killed fighting against the Russians. The photo was taken on August 26, 1904, during the long Japanese siege of the Russian base at Port Arthur, defended by General Stössel. Port Arthur fell on January 1, 1905.

19

A Russian trench during the battle of Mukden (February 20 to March 10, 1905). The battle, which was won by the Japanese, cost thousands of lives. By the time of this battle, General Stössel had already been recalled from the front and condemned to 10 years in prison for his surrender of Port Arthur to the Japanese.

THE RUSSIAN-JAPANESE WAR
1904-1905

At dawn a large component of the Japanese fleet appeared offshore and opened fire. For the Russian sailors it was a massacre: for historians it was the first slaughter of the 20th century. At the same time, nine Japanese battalions attacked and sank two Russian cruisers in the Korean port of Chemui Po, while three Japanese armies, which had landed at Kuantung in Korea, invaded Manchuria.

It was full-fledged war. Viceroy Alekseyev was transferred to Mukden and Admiral Makarov, much loved by the sailors, came as quickly as he could from St. Petersburg to replace him as commander-in-chief. However, the flagship he had only just boarded, the battleship *Petropavlosk*, hit a Japanese mine. The ammunition hold exploded and the battleship sank like a stone with Makarov and all men on board. In this moment of misfortune, as Admiral Togo maintained the blockade and successfully repulsed all Russian attempts to break through it, Japan's armies inflicted heavy losses on the Tsar's soldiers in a series of battles that continued until October. In Port Arthur the besieged Russians prepared to resist General Nogi's army to the last man. After digging trenches and shelters around the perimeter of the city, the men of the garrison fought with their bayonets against the enemy's attempts to break through the land defenses. The situation had become a true war of position, a foretaste of what was to happen on the European fronts during World War I. Indeed, the Russian-Japanese conflict can be seen as a bloody experiment in new weapons and assault-and-defense techniques, a preparation for the even more devastating conflict to come.

Port Arthur fell on January 1, 1905, when the Russian General Stössel was forced to surrender. When he returned home he paid for his "cowardice before the enemy" with ten years imprisonment, while the victor, General Nogi, overcome with remorse for having sent hundreds of his soldiers to their death in the bayonet attacks, committed suicide.

The war came to an end in two bloody battles, the land battle of Mukden, fought on land from February 20 to March 10, 1905, and the naval battle of Tsushima. In a desperate attempt to reverse the outcome of the conflict, the Tsar had ordered the Baltic fleet to go to the aid of its countrymen. Under the command of Admiral Rozhestvensky, 34 warships set sail and reached the Far East after months at sea. They were ambushed on May 27, 1905 off the island of Tsushima, where Admiral Togo emerged victorious from what may have been the greatest naval victory of all time. Of the Russian ships, 22 were sunk, six captured, and a further six fled the battle scene. For the Russians, this was the end.

The peace treaty, mediated by President Theodore Roosevelt , was signed on September 5 in Portsmouth, New Hampshire. Japan was given a free hand in Korea, Russia gave Port Arthur back to the Chinese, and Manchuria was forced to cede the island of Sakhalin to Japan. The Mikado's island nation had become a great power on the world stage.

20
Japanese troops enter Port Arthur after the Russian surrender. General Nogi, the Japanese commander, was to face a much more dramatic fate than General Stössel, his Russian counterpart. Regretful that he had sent hundreds of his soldiers to their deaths on Russian bayonets, General Nogi committed harakiri.

21
Photographs of the historic naval battle of Tsushima (May 27, 1905), which marked Japan's definitive victory over Russia. Of the Russian fleet, 22 ships were sunk, six captured and the remaining six escaped. Top: the Russian cruiser Orel. Center: Japanese ships ready to intercept the Czarist fleet. Bottom: the remains of Russian ships sunk at Tsushima.

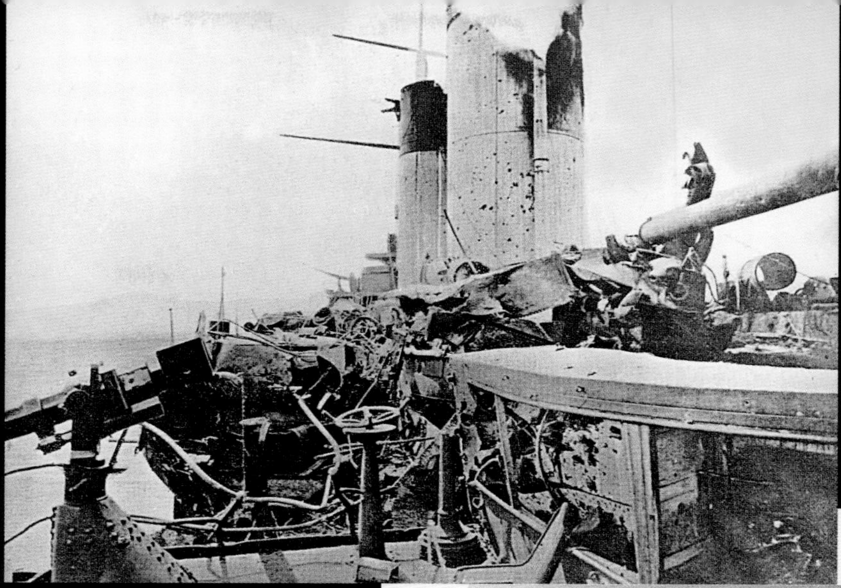

1904
1905

1911
1912

THE

ITALIAN-TURKISH WAR

IN ITALY IT WAS CALLED THE "LIBYAN UNDERTAKING" AND WAS THE SUBJECT OF OPERETTAS, SONGS, AND MUCH RHETORIC. IT WAS A LONG-AWAITED COLONIALIST VICTORY FOR THE YOUNG MEDITERRANEAN NATION AFTER THE DEFEATS SUFFERED AT ADOWA IN EAST AFRICA AT THE END OF THE 19TH CENTURY.

The Italians had watched from the sidelines the constant expansion of other European powers in the Mediterranean and the Balkans. Having taken possession of Tunisia and Algeria, France was now moving into Morocco, while Great Britain controlled Cyprus, Egypt, and the Suez. Occupation of Tripolitania, formally under Turkish sovereignty, was therefore the only possible way - according to the forceful Italian nationalist movements - of re-establishing equilibrium in the Mediterranean. But there had to be a reason for such action, some pretext, even a dubious one. As a result, on September 27, 1911, the Italian government, headed by the liberal Giovanni Giolitti, sent an ultimatum to Sultan Mehmet V inviting him to cooperate peacefully with the occupation of Tripoli by the Italian Army, to be sent to protect the local Italian community, which was threatened by the Muslim Berbers. Istanbul did not reject the ultimatum, and the Turkish Government limited itself to asking Italy to respect formal Turkish sovereignty. This request was refused, and at 2:30 p.m. on September 29, Italy declared war on Turkey.

In the days leading up to the declaration of war, Italian military dispatches and the nationalist press had talked unceasingly of a "military rout." It did not turn out quite like that. The 20,000 Italian troops landed at Tripoli in two stages on October 10 and 12, under General Caneva. They met fierce resistance from the Turkish contingent of 4,000 men, in particular from the Berber cavalry. During the landing at Beng-

22
Three key events in the military campaign in Libya. Top: Italian aviators at Tobruk. Center: a scene from the battle for the Khufra oasis, which preceded the Italian troops' conquest of Tripoli. Below: Berber guerrillas hanged in Tripoli after the Italian victory. Apart from 8000 Turkish soldiers based in Cyrenaica and Tripolitania, no fewer than 20,000 irregular indigenous troops (the Berbers) paid heavily for opposing the invading Italians, whose air force conferred superiority. Overall, Italy deployed 100,000 soldiers in this war.

23
Italian dirigibles bomb Turkish positions on Libyan territory. The Italian-Turkish war of 1911-1912 was the first in history in which air attacks (carried out here by dirigible airships) determined the outcome.

THE ITALIAN-TURKISH WAR
1911-1912

hazi, a fierce battle took place during which 600 Italian soldiers were killed. The invading army quickly grew to 100,000 soldiers, against 20,000 Libyans and 8,000 Turks.

For the first time in history, aviation was used in a conflict. Italian aircraft based in Sicily bombed the enemy. While the fighting on land became a war of attrition, in April 1912 the Italians executed a lightning naval attack: five destroyers managed to get through the Strait of the Dardanelles, while an expeditionary force commanded by Admiral Millo occupied Rhodes and twelve other Turkish islands in the Aegean Sea (since then called the Dodecanese islands). Such operations alarmed Vienna, which protested to Italy, fearing repercussions on the fragile balance in the Balkans. Austria's fears turned out to be well-founded, as on October 8, 1912, Montenegro, closely followed by Bulgaria, Serbia, and Greece, declared war on Turkey, giving rise to the "First Balkan War."

Fearing further developments, the great powers put pressure on Rome and Constantinople to end their war, and on October 18, 1912, the Treaty of Lausanne was signed. Turkey kept its formal sovereignty, conceding administrative and political autonomy to Libya - in other words to Italy - and maintained its judicial powers through the cadï (judges) appointed by the Sultan. For Italy, however, Libya (consisting of Tripolitania and Cyrenaica) did not turn out to be an easily managed acquisition. Skirmishes continued to affect the military and civilian population until Libya was finally defeated in 1931 by General Rodolfo Graziani.

24
Inhabitants of Tripoli look on as Italian Granatieri march into the Libyan capital. On October 10 and 12, 1911, Italian troops landed in North Africa and the government of Giovanni Giolitti presented a declaration of war to Sultan Mehmet V. The Berbers fiercely resisted the Italian assaults, which followed air attacks on their positions. During the landing at Benghazi, 600 Italian soldiers were killed.

25
Two photographs of the Italian landing in Tripolitania. While the fighting in Libya went on, Admiral Millo conquered Rhodes and 12 smaller islands in the Aegean Sea (April 1912), henceforth called the Dodecanese. The Italian-Turkish war ended on October 18, 1912, with the peace of Lausanne. Turkey maintained formal sovereignty over Libya, while Tripolitania and Cyrenaica were placed under Italian administration.

THE

BALKAN WARS

THE DYING SUBLIME PORTE

The two Balkan Wars of 1912 and 1913 sealed the fate of the declining Ottoman Empire. The decline that had begun at the end of the 16th century with the battle of Lepanto and had continued with the Turks' defeat at the gates of Vienna by the Christian armies commanded by Prince Eugene of Savoy. The background to events was the war between the Sublime Porte and Russia, centuries-old enemies. This war ended in 1878 with the advance of the Tsarist troops into the Caucasus and the Balkans. The Treaty of Berlin, which ended the hostilities, also marked a geopolitical cataclysm, similar, though on a smaller scale, to the one that overwhelmed Europe when the USSR collapsed in 1991. From the remains of Ottoman Empire's former Balkan territories new states arose: Serbia, Montenegro, Bosnia and Herzegovina, Bulgaria, and Romania, all firmly under Russian influence. All that remained in Turkish hands of the Balkans was Macedonia, Northern Greece around Salonika, and the southern part of the Serbian territory.

The Balkans had experienced further upheaval in 1908, when Austria-Hungary, concerned by Serbian expansionism, had annexed Bosnia and Herzegovina in a political and military move, the outcome of which was to further reinforce Serbia's dependence on Russia. It was therefore a much weakened Turkey that Italy attacked in 1911, her battleships having sailed through the Dardanelles, penetrated the Bosporus, and conquered the Dodecanese Islands. This last affront had repercussions on Turkey's domestic politics. It forced the "Young Turks" party--which had only just come to power, headed by Enver Pasha, and in whose ranks Mustafa Kemal, the future "Atatürk," was already emerging--to adopt highly nationalistic positions.

26
Top: the capture and imprisonment of Turkish soldiers at Florena, Macedonia, during the First Balkan war; Turkish farmers arrive at the gates Istanbul while Sultan Mehmet V's troops find themselves mired in a military disaster.

27
The top two photos document the conquest of Thessalonika by Greek troops after a bloody siege; the army of the Sublime Porte, who had already fought against Italian troops on the Libyan front, this time was unprepared.

The First Balkan War

The change in the political climate effected by the Turkish government alarmed Russia, which feared possible Turkish revenge for the defeat of 1878. Through the diplomatic maneuverings of Hartwig, the Russian representative, in Belgrade, an alliance was brokered between Serbia and Bulgaria in order to oust Turkey once and for all from the Balkans and undermine its primacy in the Bosphorus. The alliance was extended to include Montenegro and Greece, and on October 8, 1912, while still at war with Italy, Sultan Mehmet V received a declaration of war from the four Balkan nations. The campaign was swift and disastrous for the Turkish army. While the Greeks besieged Salonika and forced Hassan Pasha into defeat, the Serbs, commanded by Prince Alexander, faced Zekki Pasha north of Monastir. Three days of fighting followed, ending in a Turkish defeat with 17,000 dead and wounded and 10,000 prisoners. But the most outstanding victories were achieved by the Bulgarians, who overcame the Turkish troops on the Vadar River at Kirk-Kilisse and Lulebugaz. The Treaty of London, signed on May 30, 1913, ended the war. Turkey lost Salonika, Uskub, Janina, Shkodër, and Adrianople and had to give up definitively all hope of holding territory in the Balkans.

THE BALKAN WARS
1912-1913

The Second Balkan War

The conclusion of the first Balkan War had left all parties discontented. Serbia, which wanted an outlet to the Adriatic, had been unable to obtain one because of the fierce opposition of Austria and Italy. Greece protested Italy's annexation of the Dodecanese. Bulgaria, above all, having sustained the greater part of the military action, felt it had lost out to Serbia in the division of the territories decided in the course of the Conference of London, and sought help and support from Vienna, which had long been hostile to Belgrade.

Thus, while the settlement was still being discussed and argued about in London, barely a month after the conclusion of the previous conflict, Bulgaria attacked Serbia. Romania, Greece, Montenegro, and Turkey immediately sided with Serbia and declared war on Bulgaria, which found itself completely isolated. The Austro-Hungarian Empire, on the other hand, on whose support the powers in Sofia were counting, was careful not to intervene.

The Bulgarians were defeated and forced to sign the humiliating Treaty of Bucharest (August 10, 1913). Southern Dobruja and Silistra were handed over to Romania; Macedonia was almost totally annexed to Serbia; Turkey regained Adrianople; Crete and Salonika were definitively assigned to Greece; finally, Albania's independence and its three main cities, Shkodër, Durrës, and Vlorë were recognized, and Prince William of Wied became its first king.

Not even the second Balkan War managed to resolve the discord in the region. A discontented Serbia continued to represent a threat, mainly to the neighboring Austro-Hungarian Empire, and the spark that was to set off World War I arose from this friction.

28
A Bulgarian cannon firing on Adrianople. The Second Balkan War broke out less than a month after the Peace of London (30 May 1913), which concluded the conflict. Bulgaria was not satisfied and attacked Serbia. Bulgaria soon it found itself isolated and had to face Turkey and all the other Balkan nations.

29
Top: civilians fleeing from Adrianople, besieged by the Bulgarians. Bottom: Bulgarian forces waiting to commence their assault on Adrianople. The Peace of Bucharest (August 10, 1913) did not reward Bulgaria's blood sacrifice. It returned Adrianople to the Turks and created an independent Albania. Leaving Serbia unsatisfied, the peace thus created the basis for the World War I.

World War I

IN AUGUST 1907 FRANCE, RUSSIA, AND GREAT BRITAIN DREW UP THE "TRIPLE ENTENTE,". IN DECEMBER 1912 ITALY, GERMANY, AND AUSTRIA-HUNGARY RENEWED THE "TRIPLE ALLIANCE".

Europe was thus divided into two blocs of approximately equal powers, a situation that seemed to the diplomatic world of the time to be a good way of ensuring the ongoing stability. Few stopped to consider the blatant contradictions that characterized both treaties:
- Italy was a long-standing enemy of Austria-Hungary, but no one asked how these two nations were supposed to get along with each other;
- Russia, also from a dynastic point of view (the Tsarina was German and the Tsar a cousin of the Kaiser), clearly had more in common politically with Germany than with Great Britain, a historic ally of Japan, which the Russians considered their bitterest enemy;
- The hostility between France and England that came to a head in the Napoleonic period was no secret; the two powers had also clashed more recently over colonial interests.

Italy and Britain were therefore the weak links in the two alliances. Indeed, in neither treaty was were there any automatic intervention clauses regarding Great Britain or Italy: both nations would be able to make their reservations heard in the case of a conflict involving their respective allies. As events turned out, only Italy was to take advantage of this opportunity. The first sign of an independent stance with respect to the foreign policy of the Triple Alliance came from Italy at the end of 1913, when the situation in the Balkans was again becoming critical. Serbia crossed the border established by the London Conference at the end of the Balkan Wars and occupied Albanian territory. Austria reacted by sending an ultimatum to Belgrade, but Italy was quick to distance itself. As the Serbian army withdrew from Albanian territory, there was no need for the Entente Cordiale to resort to force, but the episode confirmed that the Balkans were still the tinderbox of Europe. At the heart of the Balkan question was Serbia's aggressiveness, a factor that could blow the Habsburg empire apart. Vienna took countermeasures, occupying and annexing Bosnia-Herzegovina. Not only did this experience not serve as a lesson to Serbia, instead it increased its hatred for the neighboring empire, which it saw as vulnerable due to the dynastic crisis in its ruling family. The elderly Emperor Franz Joseph (1830-1916) was overwhelmed by a series of painful family tragedies: the firing squad execution of his brother Maximilian, Emperor of Mexico; the suicide of his own son and heir to the throne, Archduke Rudolph, with his mistress, Maria Vetsera, in Mayerling; and the assassination of his wife, the Empress Elizabeth, in Geneva by an Italian anarchist. With no direct heir, Franz Joseph saw the title of archduke pass to his nephew Franz Ferdinand (1863-1914), whose three sons by his morganatic wife, the Bohemian Sophie von Chotek, were excluded from the succession. The Habsburg-Lorraine line would therefore die out, and with this event the Austro-Hungarian Empire would break up. In the meantime, the Second Socialist International had united all the European socialist parties, and, adhering to Marxist doctrine, undertook never to fight a war against the workers. The socialist parties were in fact to oppose their respective governments with strikes, sabotage, and finally by the workers' refusal to take up arms. It turned out to be a complete failure. French and German workers soon forgot their solemn promises made in the name of the working class

1914

1918

30
Desolation in the Plezzo valley: an Italian trench filled with soldiers killed by poison gas. This scene symbolizes what Pope Benedict XV called "the useless slaughter."

World war I
1914-1918

June 28, 1914: Sarajevo!

Once the great maneuvers of the Austro-Hungarian army in Bosnia were completed, Archduke Franz Ferdinand paid an official visit to Sarajevo accompanied by field marshal Franz Conrad von Hötzendorf, the chief of staff. The news in the Belgrade and Sarajevo newspapers, filled the Bosnian Serb nationalists with anger and disgust, the more so as June 28, the date set for the imperial parade, was the day of Vidovdan, the feast of St. Vito, sacred to the Serbs' Orthodox faith. It was the day on which, 525 years earlier, the Serbs had suffered a crushing defeat in Kosovo at the hands of the Turks. The Serbs had been forced to give up all hope of sovereignty and independence from 1389 until the end of the Balkan Wars, when Serbia had then regained Kosovo and the feast of St. Vito once again become a day of great religious celebration and national pride. But in Sarajevo there was to be neither celebration nor gatherings. On the contrary, the Austro-Hungarian oppressors had chosen that sacred day for the archduke's visit and military parade. This was a provocation, an offense that required a bloody response. At least this was the opinion of a small group of Bosnian Serb extremists headed by Danilo Illic. The group had two young followers, Gavrilo Princip, a 19-year-old student, and Nedjelko Cabrinovic, a 21-year-old printer, ready to do whatever was necessary.

On the morning of June 28, 1914, the hills around Sarajevo echoed to the sound of artillery fire. It was a military salute to Archduke Franz Ferdinand, who wanted a parade and the cheering crowds to compensate his "Soph" (as he called his wife) for the humiliations she had suffered in Vienna. In Sarajevo, she was not the "Bohemian Chotek" or "the Duchess of Hohenburg," the titles the more tolerant courtiers at Schönbrunn had given her. Here she was "Her Imperial Highness." The procession went through the streets of Sarajevo, packed with people--some exultant, some just curious. The imperial couple was in the third car. Franz Ferdinand sat straight as a ramrod in his white uniform, a green feather in his hat. The crowd applauded. Suddenly a grenade was thrown over the heads of the couple, exploding under the wheels of the car behind. Shouts, uproar, and general confusion followed; some people had been wounded. "Carry on!" ordered the archduke, rising to his feet in order to take charge of the situation. He affectionately squeezed Sophie's shoulder. The vehicles reached the town hall, where a brief reception was held. The atmosphere was tense, with constant interruptions and reports from the military police. The archduke soon received news that the attacker had been found: his name was Cabrinovic, he was a printer. After throwing the bomb he had jumped into the Miljacka River. He had on him a cyanide pill to take rather than be captured: either he did not have time or his courage failed him.

The procession started. Now it was up to Gavrilo Princip, who had witnessed his companion's failure, to strike. He positioned himself on the Latino Bridge. The vehicles approached. Franz Ferdinand's car led, he wanted to arrive first at the hospital where he intended to visit the wounded. Princip pulled out his pistol and fired two shots. Sophie slumped forward. Her husband barely had time to shout "Sterbe nicht!" ("Don't die!") before he fell across her. Blood trickled from his mouth. By the time the car reached the governor's residence, Sophie was dead. There was barely time to administer the last rites to the archduke. The Austro-Hungarian Empire had received a mortal blow. The days following the Sarajevo tragedy highlighted the limitations and contradictions of the great Austro-Hungarian empire, now in rapid decline. The police managed to catch both anarchists but were unable to get to the bottom of the plot. Was it the isolated action of nationalist fanatics, as the two young men insisted (with Princip adding that he was sorry for having accidentally hit the archduchess), or was it a plot hatched at the highest levels in Belgrade? Emperor Franz Joseph, who was summering at Bad Ischl, received the terrible news from Count Paar, his aide-de-camp. The emperor seemed undecided as to what he should do. On the other hand, Austria was caught up in a wave of anti-Serbian protests and riots, with student demonstrations and wildcat strikes by workers. Students, workers, and the press all demanded severe reprisals against Serbia. At the ministry of foreign affairs in the Ballhausplatz, the general feeling was that the sooner action was taken against Belgrade, the better. Conrad von Hötzendorf, the chief of staff, was in full agreement. He saw no serious risk for the Austro-Hungarian troops; it was a question of carrying out a punitive expedition. As to the reactions of the other European powers, he was certain that they would be limited to a few protests, with no further action taken. The Emperor was by no means as certain, as shown by the four weeks he let pass from the day of the assassination until ever more insistent and indignant public opinion forced him to take action. It was not until July 23, 1914, that Cout Giesl, the Austrian ambassador in Belgrade, handed King Peter Karageorgevitch's government the Austrian ultimatum. It demanded that all Serbian patriotic associations be dissolved, that the "material and moral" perpetrators of the assassination be handed over, and that any teachers who dared talk to their pupils of Serbian territory subject to Austria be dismissed from the schools in the kingdom. Finally, the Austrian police were to be allowed to intervene in Serbia to find and punish the perpetrators of the attack. Serbia was given 48 hours to accept or reject the ultimatum.

World war I
1914-1918

World War I, the bloodiest of all wars, was also the most absurd, unexpected, and paradoxical of all. Nobody really believed in the inevitability of such a war, no government really wanted to declare it, and even up to a few hours before it was declared, no ruler thought that it would really happen. The events immediately prior to the conflict involved the countries of Europe in a fatal dance more suited to the theatre of the absurd than to the initiation of one of the greatest tragedies in the history of mankind. When the Austrian ambassador in Belgrade left his residence at 6 p.m. on July 23, 1914, to deliver the ultimatum to the Serbian government, he directed his driver to take him to the Ministry of Finance rather than to the prime minister's offices. In fact, the finance minister was the only government member to be found that day in the Serbian capital. The prime minister, Pasic, was in the middle of an election campaign; the other ministers, including the minister for Foreign Affairs, were on vacation. The remaining unfortunate minister read the ultimatum, turned pale with fear, and managed to stutter that it was impossible to convene the Council of Ministers in 48 hours because they were all out of the city. But Giesl was unmoved: "We live in the age of the telephone, the train, and the car. You'll manage it." The Austrian ambassador to Berlin found a similar climate on July 5, when he was instructed to deliver Emperor Franz Joseph's message to the Kaiser. In it, the emperor confidentially informed his ally of the plan--soon to become common knowledge in the corridors of power in Vienna-to re-appraise Serbia's sovereignty. Most key government members were away on vacation. Chancellor Bethmann-Hollweg was already installed in his country house, keeping in touch by telephone, and the secretary of state, given the basically calm situation, had just married and gone off on his honeymoon. Kaiser Wilhelm--convinced that if there was any war at all it would be a small skirmish on his doorstep to be resolved, as usual, with a few shots fired in the Balkans--formally confirmed his loyalty to the Alliance. He then left eagerly for a planned cruise in the North Sea aboard his yacht. Moreover, the Kaiser was convinced that the Tsar would never become involved in a war to defend the Serbs, who had assassinated an heir to the throne. Wilhelm II and Nicholas II were cousins; they wrote to each other in very friendly terms, using the intimate "du" form of address, with Wilhelm signing himself "Willy" and Nicholas "Nicky." No, Russia and Germany would never go to war over the Sarajevo assassination. Nor would the other signatories to the Entente intervene. Wilhelm II was a nephew of Edward VII, and first cousin of the reigning George V. But did sovereigns carry as much weight as they once had? Or was real power, the power to decide peace or war, life or death, now in the hands of the so-called "representatives of the people"? Who carried more weight, a king or a president of a republic? On July 20, Poincaré, president of the French Republic, arrived in St. Petersburg. Three days of talks served to strengthen the alliance between Russia and France. The Russian ministers and generals swore that Russia would not stand by while Serbia was bullied. As to France, could it have forgotten the still painful humiliation of Sedan? Definitely not. If Germany dared help Austria-Hungary to repress Serbia, it would find it had taken on more than it could handle. The will to go to war, which would later characterize the outbreak of World War II, was absent here. On the 23rd, Austria delivered its ultimatum to Serbia. Forty-eight hours later came the apparently conciliatory reply, but three hours before replying Belgrade had given the order for general mobilization. Telephones rang non-stop, newspapers throughout the world published the news, and Europe held its breath.

On July 27, France recalled its troops from Algeria and Morocco. On July 28, Austria-Hungary declared war on Serbia, and France gave the order for general mobilization. The next day, July 29, the Tsar ordered general mobilization, followed almost immediately by an earnest appeal from the Kaiser, his dear cousin "Willy," who had interrupted his sailing trip in the North Sea: "Don't do anything rash, I beg you." Moved by this message, Nicholas II revoked his order, maintaining partial mobilization in respect of Austria-Hungary. On the same day, the Kaiser's other cousin, George V, ordered the British fleet, the most powerful in the world, to prepare for battle. The days that followed were terrible. On July 30, as a result of threats to Serbia, Russia reinstated the order for general mobilization. The Triple Alliance's reply was not long in coming: on July 31, Vienna ordered the general mobilization of the imperial troops; Berlin, delivered two ultimatums, one to Russia and one to France. In its ultimatum to Russia, Germany asked that the order for general mobilization be revoked "within twelve hours of receiving this document." The ultimatum to France asked Paris to declare "within eighteen hours" its neutrality in the event of a war between Russia and Germany, and by way of guarantee to cede the fortresses of Toul and Verdun to Germany. Russia did not even deign to answer. France replied tersely that "it would act in keeping with its own interests." At this stage, Germany had no way out: on August 1, 1914, declared war on Russia, followed August 3 by a declaration of war on France. Italy, aware of the provisions of the Triple Alliance, hastened to declare its neutrality. On August 3, Germany invaded Belgium, which had refused to allow the Kaiser's troops to cross its territory. As a result, on the next day, August 4, England sent Germany an ultimatum in which it reminded

World war I
1914-1918

the Germans of Belgian neutrality. "The treaties are pieces of paper," was Chancellor Bethmann-Hollweg's famous scornful reply. London responded with a declaration of war. World War I had begun.

Despite Georges Clemenceau's famous maxim "War is far too important an affair to be left to generals," it is undeniable that military commanders made a major contribution to the war's outbreak. The end of the 19th century and the beginning of the 20th saw a new generation of commanders, mostly of middle-class background, which was to become ever more important in both the military and the ministries. In the German army's general staff alone, in the fifty years between 1860 and 1910, those who were members of the nobility dropped from 60 to 30 percent. The rising stars were more pragmatic and less romantic than the blue-blooded commanders. Without exception they admired Napoleon and supported the theory that the best solution to a military problem was to attack. Such an approach brought them brilliant success in the war games, the trust of rulers and politicians, as well as the support of the great war industry. Defensive strategies were in effect relegated to the background, as the "Schlieffen Plan" demonstrated. The German army had adopted this plan as a model for ensuring uniform action of the armed forces in a conflict. Alfred von Schlieffen, the Kaiser's chief of staff from 1891 to 1905, using all the most aggressive means at his disposal, brought the French army to the verge of defeat in a matter of weeks. Once the French were defeated, he would then be free to deal with Russia and thus victoriously free his country from the vise-like grip of war on two fronts, which Germany, by reason of its geographical position, could not avoid. The great power of the "new military class" was directly linked to conscription. Enormous offensives could only be achieved by having vast numbers of men ready (or forced) to die. Without military conscription, neither a First nor Second World War could have been launched. Clearly, the 20th century's great massacres represented the most terrible fruits of the new forces introduced into society by the French Revolution. Military service was first adopted by the Convention in Robespierre's time: it became more widespread and standardized in Napoleon Bonaparte's time. He introduced conscription in the nations that he conquered (Italy, Belgium, and Spain). Soon other countries adopted it: Austria in 1805, after the defeat at Austerlitz; Prussia in 1806, after the defeat at Jena. Great Britain was the exception, not introducing conscription until 1916. From Napoleon's time on, compulsory enlistment was responsible for the proliferation of wars. Until then, even the bitterest of wars ended with a few thousand dead. For a brief period in the mid-19th century France introduced purchased exemptions from military service, a system Russia and the the newly formed nation of Italy also adopted. But after the defeat of Sedan, France abolished this system, which favored the affluent. The Russian and Italian generals agreed with the French generals that Germany had won the 1870 war thanks to conscription. So it was widely reintroduced. From the late 19th century until the eve of World War I, compulsory military service had also helped fuel the great emigrations from Europe to America, since the New World countries (in particular the United States), followed Great Britain in forgoing compulsory military service. Flight from conscription became such a problem that some European nations passed laws prohibiting men of military service age from emigrating. On the eve of World War I, conscription, an indirect product of the French Revolution, enabled Europe's political and military powers to plan endless battlefields. The conscripts most directly affected were strong, healthy men classed as "able" at their physicals, and who came from +rural backgrounds, the sons of peasant farmers or small-holders. These were the lambs and ressels sent to the slaughter:

- Russia: 5,500,000 men, 124 ships
- Germany: 4,500,000 men, 331 ships
- Austria-Hungary: 3,700,000 men, 120 ships
- France: 3,500,000 men, 395 ships
- England (volunteer army): 700,000 men, 590 ships
- Serbia: 400,000 men, no ships.

35

Departing for the front the youth of Europe leaves home to be massacred because of the military leaders' intransigence. The soldiers leave with a smile, like these British sailors embarking for the Continent (top) or conscripts from the French provinces arriving with their bundles at the Gare du Nord, Paris (bottom). The picture in the center was taken after that Germany had declared war on Russia: in Berlin the masses streamed into the streets to cheer under the portrait of Franz Josef, the Austro-Hungarian emperor.

1914
1918

36

On August 3, 1914, Germany invaded Belgium, which had refused to let the Kaiser's troops cross its territory: Belgian barricades at Malines in a strenuous attempt at defense (top); Belgian infantry at the front (center) prepares to counter the German attack. Belgian resistance was soon overcome. Bottom: Brussels has been captured and the victorious German troops march through the municipal square. The German High Command's Schlieffen Plan anticipated violation of Belgian neutrality; it incorporated German attacks on France from both the east (German border) and the north.

THE INVASION OF BELGIUM
1914

The Schlieffen Plan's key point was this: To breach the fortified barrier France had erected after 1870 along its frontier with Germany, the German invasion of Belgium would require 36 armed corps (a total of 70 divisions) and, fanning out from Metz, a pincer action that would force the French army towards the Swiss border, surrounding and trapping them. The risk of the French breaking through towards Alsace-Lorraine had been calculated: The Blitzkrieg, or crack land forces of the German right flank, would move faster than the French.

Although Helmuth von Moltke, since 1906 the chief of staff of the German army, had adopted the Schlieffen Plan, he decided to reduce the size of the units that would attack Belgium, and thus the French left flank. Von Schlieffen's 36 armed corps (calculated to a man!) were reduced to 26, and the defense of Alsace-Lorraine was reinforced; two changes were seen as the cause of the Plan's failure.

At 7 a.m. on August 2, 1914, the German Sixteenth Division entered the Grand Duchy of Luxembourg. At 7 p.m., the German ambassador in Brussels delivered an ultimatum to Belgium: King Albert was to allow the German troops to cross his territory. Belgium was given twelve hours to answer yes or no. Belgian premier Brocqueville called a cabinet meeting that night. The government decided to resist "to save the honor of Belgium." The King was in agreement. At 8 a.m. on August 4, German troops invaded Belgium. Until that moment, the great game of strategy that had all the world holding its breath seemed like a bad dream unfolding on a colossal chessboard. Now it had become reality, a reality made of blood fear, heroism, and death.

Moltke's first objective was the fortress city of Liége; with its twelve forts it blocked the route to the Meuse valley. General von Emmich attacked with 25,000 men, 8,000 cavalry and 124 cannon. The Belgian garrison had 6,000 men, but reinforcements arrived on the night of August 4, bringing the numbers up to 30,000 soldiers commanded by General Léman. The German order to surrender was ignored and the battle began. Something the Germans could never have foreseen occurred: the civilian population fought alongside the soldiers. The Germans died in their thousands under Belgian machine-gun fire.

At an early stage Emmich was replaced by General Erich Ludendorff, a young officer and favorite of the chief of staff. He attacked villages and houses. His ferocity was such that the British, French, American, and Russian war correspondents at the front invented the legend of the "Belgian children" who had their hands bitten off by the fierce "Boches." It was a lie, the first of many that would become an endless resource in the psychological war. This particular news item aroused such horror among the English that thousands of young men joined up to "teach the Germans a lesson"; but it also roused much anti-German feeling in neutral Italy.

In a short time all the Belgian the forts had fallen. On August 16, the battle of Liége was over. The Germans, having won in spite of heroic Belgian resistance, advanced towards Brussels.

Meantime in France the military staff were planning to mount an offensive in the direction of Alsace and Lorraine, the two German regions on France's northeastern frontier. The 1st French Army attacked on August 7 and advanced as far as Mulhouse but was immediately forced to retreat. They were held in check again on August 19 and 20, while other French forces were defeated in the battles of Morange and Saarbrücken and chased back across the border. During these same days the German right flank advanced inexorably across Belgium. King Albert's army was forced to withdraw to Antwerp. On August 20, the Kaiser's troops entered Brussels.

Finally the French understood the true purpose of the German right-flank advance towards the Franco-Belgian border. At this stage Joseph Jacques Joffre, the chief of staff, ordered the 3rd, 4th and 5th Armies, plus the British Expeditionary Force, to converge on the Belgian border. The enemy forces engaged battle on August 21. For two days and two nights the bloody "frontier battles" were fought, at the end of which both the French and the British retreated. On August 23, at the close of the battle of Charleroi, the Germans set fire to more than 150 houses whose inhabitants had fired at them. At this point two German armed corps had to be sent to the eastern front, where the Russians had just won a victory at Gumbinnen. Moltke removed two corps from the right flank rather than from the Alsatian front as he was obsessed with making sure that the borders were defended and that the French could not invade the Fatherland. This is generally seen as Moltke's second fatal mistake. He directed operations from his headquarters in Luxembourg while Joffre, his French counterpart, was always traveling up and down the front, seeing what was happening. Nevertheless, the German forces were undeniably superior to the French, partly due to the iron discipline that was imposed on the men, who could be shot for cowardice or simply for insubordination. Battle casualties were scattered all over the Champagne area. The Germans advanced inexorably and occupied Lille, Amiens, Reims. They were aiming for Paris.

THE BATTLE OF THE MARNE: PARIS IS SAFE

1914

The seemingy unstoppable German advance caused panic in Paris, where minister of war Millerand wrote to Joffre ordering him to have cowardly commanders court-martialed "and condemned to death as in 1793." Joffre refused to copy Carnot, who in 1783, would have not hesitated to condemn Dumouriez, the hero of Valmy and Jemappes, to death, but in the space of a few days he dismissed 48 of his 200 closest colleagues.

On September 2, the government fled to Bordeaux. Two and a half million men were on the move. Everything depended on the commanders, their prestige, their sang-froid, and their global view of military events, rather than on their resources. Joffre maneuvered shrewdly, moving units from the right flank to the left flank. He convinced Sir John French, the British commander, to collaborate, not an easy task given his impulsive character and his known reservations regarding the French. After the disastrous battles of Mons and Le Cateau, Sir John had retreated towards the Channel to lick his wounds, with the intention of embarking his men for home. In the meantime, from Bordeaux, the government had called General Gallieni out of retirement on the Côte d'Azur and made him military commander and governor of Paris with full powers. Joffre had placed the 6th Army at his disposal.

On the other side of the front, Moltke realized from his small number of prisoners that the French army was evading his pincer action. Moltke was 67, an old-style general, a chief of staff who did not go to the front lines but gave his orders by telephone after listening to his commanders' reports. This meant that in practice every commander in the army ended up acting according to his own personal criteria. There was no overall view of the situation at the German army's highest level; only a strong central command such as Joffre's could provide this.

While Moltke ordered his armies to proceed in a southeasterly direction, thus lengthening the encircling right flank, but also weakening the offensive force of the army's attack. General von Kluck, commander of the 1st Army, mounted a frontal attack in the direction of Paris. This led the French to believe that the entire invading army's true objective of the was Paris. Gallieni therefore decided to mount a counter-offensive and managed to get a reluctant Joffre to follow him. They were to fight on the Marne.

Between September 5 and 10, the 5th and 9th French Armies and the British forces stopped the German advance. General Gallieni requistioned 700 taxis in Paris to carry an entire division to the front, each taxi making two trips. News of episodes of patriotism and valor abounded. Eighteen hundred French cavalry soldiers crossed the Betz Forest to take the 1st German Army from behind. The 3rd French Army heroically defended Verdun, where thousands of lives were sacrificed. The 9th Army, commanded by Foch, achieved legendary status in the accounts of the war correspondents, where it was known as "the army that always attacks."

On the evening of September 9, the German troops received the unexpected order to retreat. The astonished commanders had no idea why Moltke had made such a decision, but they obeyed. Moltke had, in fact, received disastrous but false information about the resistance being put up by some of the French armies. Incredulous but enthusiastic, the French watched the withdrawal of the Germans. Paris was safe. The Battle of the Marne had saved the capital..

Within one month, 500,000 French and British troops were either killed, wounded, or taken prisoner. The German army lost 300,000 . The mobile defense was over. From now on, it was to be a terrible war of static defense. The great massacre was about to start, what Pope Benedict XV called in a letter to the leaders of the warring countries, "the useless slaughter."

39

Mountains of corpses: bayonet and machine guns leave thousands dead in the trenches. The body of a French soldier killed by a bomb lies in the mud, his now useless canteen next to him.

1914

40-41
In these two pages more dramatic images of the battle of the Marne. Top left: between Sovain and Tahire, dozens of French corpses lie in the mud. Bottom: French artillery try to stop Kaiser's troops. Right: German troops leave their trenches to attack at Montdidier-Noyon.

43
Entangled corpses in a French trench near Flanders. These soldiers belonged to the British Expeditionary Force, commanded by Sir John French, an officer who showed little inclination to take orders from Joffre. After defeats at Mons and Le Cateau, the British field marshal retreated toward the Channel, intending to take his men back to the UK. In the end Joffre convinced him to keep fighting--and proved to be right.

THE EASTERN AND WESTERN FRONTS: FOUR YEARS OF WAR

1914-1917

1914

On the western front, after the assassination at Sarajevo, the general mobilization, and the declarations of war, Belgium was attacked, followed by the Battle of the Marne and the beginning of the war of static defense. On the eastern front, after their defeat by Russian forces at Gumbinnen, the German troops commanded by Marshal Hindenburg won the Battles of Tannenberg and the Masurian Lakes. In Galicia (in southern Poland) the Austro-Hungarian army was defeated in the two battles of Lvov (August-September 1914). Having lost eastern Galicia, the Austrian imperial army continued fighting in the Carpathian passes. Hindenburg came to the aid of the army, which had been flattened by the Russian "steamroller," and mounted a counteroffensive with the 9th German Army, commanded by Mackensen. This maneuver of enormous scope started on November 11 and ended shortly before Christmas at Limanova, in a serious defeat for the Russians.

1915

On the western front, following the French armies' failed attempt to break through the lines (the winter offensive of Champagne), the battle of Ypres commenced, and was fought from April 22 to May 25, 1915. For the first time poison gas was widely used. The Franco-British attacks between May and July, known as the "battle of Nôtre Dame de Lorette," were in vain. The German autumn offensive in Champagne also failed. On the eastern front, German action led to the second battle of the Masurian Lakes (February 4-22, 1915), at the end of which they took 100,000 Russian prisoners and recovered East Prussia. But things did not go so well for the Central Powers in the confrontation in the Carpathians, where the Russians launched an offensive in January and, after three months of fighting, crossed into Hungary. The Austrians counterattacked in early May and defeated the Russians in the Battle of Tarnovo, taking Galicia and Bukovina. In the meantime, the Germans moved out of reconquered East Prussia to occupy Lithuania. On July 1, 1915, Austro-German armies unleashed an offensive along the entire front from the Baltic to the Carpathians. The Central Powers took Warsaw, Brest-Litovsk, and Vilnius. The Battle of Tarnapol, from September 6 to 8, effectively halted the Austro-German advance. There was a truce in the winter of 1915-16. On the Balkan front Franz Joseph's troops took Belgrade and Budapest.

1916

On the western front, the battle – or rather the massacre – of Verdun took place from February 21 to July 21. In the early weeks of the offensive the Germans had the upper hand, capturing Hill 364, Fort Douaumont and Fort Vaux. But victory was to remain out of reach. The losses on both sides were incalculable. The massacre of Verdun led to a change of military leadership for both the Germans and the French. Hindenburg and his "shadow" Ludendorff, who had been victorious in the East, replaced the German field marshal Erich von Falkenhayn. In November, Robert Nivelle took over from Joseph Joffre at the end of the French debâcle in the battle of the Somme, fought between June 24 and November 26. Nivelle bolstered the morale of his men and successfully led them in the recapture of the forts of Verdun. On the eastern front, Tsarist General Aleksey Brusilov, commander of the Russian 8th Army, launched an offensive and gained ground in Galicia, but at the cost of heavy losses. The first signs of the collapse of the Russian army appeared during this offensive, with numerous episodes of insubordination and the refusal of whole fighting units to carry out their officers' orders. During Brusilov's battles, Alexander Kerensky, Russia's minister of war, first came to the fore because of his rousing speeches to the troops, inciting them to victory against the Germans. This was to win him nomination as prime minister (on July 27, 1917), but also the eternal hatred of the Bolshevik party.

1917

On the western front, the French began their advance on February 22, forcing the Germans to withdraw to the "Siegfried line" (Arras-Soissons). On April 2, the British attacked Arras but the offensive failed. The French offensive then came to an end with the battles of Aisne and Champagne (April 6 and May 27, 1917). Some serious acts of mutiny occurred among the French troops during this battle. The outcome was the replacement on May 15 of Nivelle by Philippe Pétain. He put down the rebellion harshly; those responsible were sentenced to death and executed by firing squad. He wanted to avoid any possible involvement with the workers' protests on the home front (as was happening in Russia). During the battles of Aisne and Cambray, British tanks were used on a large scale, although the effectiveness of this new weapon initially fell far short of expectations. During the battle of Flanders, the heavy German artillery proved more successful than the tanks. In Paris, on November 16, 1917, Parliament's vote of confidence went to Georges Clemenceau, who swept away all defeatism and prepared the ground for victory. On the eastern front, there was a series of Austro-German military successes while discontent and rebellion increased among the Russians. In September and October they captured Riga and the Baltic islands.

791

THE GREAT MASSACRES: TANNENBERG

1914

It took only two days — August 19 and 20, 1914 — to seal the fate of East Prussia. In these two days the Russian army, under the command of General Zilinskij, inflicted a heavy defeat on the German 8th Army led by General Max von Prittwitz. The battle was fought at Gumbinnen, where the Germans were truly routed, abandoning East Prussia as far as the Vistula to enemy hands. Whether defeat was Prittwitz's fault or that of headquarters, which had sent only one army against the Russians, who had two, is difficult to judge. Certainly, headquarters accepted no blame, since Prittwitz was replaced by a Baron Paul von Beneckendorff und von Hindenburg, a 67-year-old retired general who was later to become President of the Weimar Republic and make Adolf Hitler his chancellor. Hindenburg was never alone; Erich Ludendorff, his 49-year-old chief of staff, was always at his side, destined like Hindenburg to become a legend. The inseparable team revitalized and reorganized the ranks of the 8th Army and on August 26 pitted them against the Russians at Tannenberg, a fatal site in German history. It was there that in 1410 King Ladislas II of Poland defeated the Teutonic knights, commanded by Erich von Plauen.

The Russians easily outnumbered the Germans, with 21 infantry divisions against the Germans' 11 divisions. But everything seemed to conspire to cancel out this advantage. For example, the Russian 2nd Army (General Samsonov) was unable to decode its messages and so the chief of staff was forced to send out unencoded orders. The Germans intercepted them and were thus able to forestall every enemy movement. It was a disaster; the Russian Army was destroyed, and 500 cannon and 50,000 men fell into German hands. Samsonov committed suicide.

After four days of fierce hand-to-hand fighting, the German 8th Army won an overwhelming victory over the Russians under Samsonov's command. This victory redeemed the 8th Army's record and revenged it on the Russians, who left 93,000 prisoners in Hindenburg's hands. Russian losses were heavy (40,000 men killed and wounded); German losses were not small (10,000 men). On November 1, 1914, on the strength of his victory at Tannenberg and the German 9th Army's decisive support in turning around the Austro-Hungarian armies' shaky fortunes in Galicia, Hindenburg was nominated commander-in-chief of Alliance's troops on the eastern front, with Emperor Franz Joseph's full approval.

In the meantime, the "old" general, now field marshal, repeated his success at Tannenberg. This occurred at the Masurian Lakes, where the Germans faced General Rennenkampf's Russian troops. Bitter fighting occurred around the lakes from September 7 to 9. On the 9th, the German cavalry attacked the Russians on their flank, in the Goldap region. On the 10th the Russian commander ordered a general retreat. Hindenburg was thus able to advance a further 62 miles along the whole front, recapturing East Prussia.

44-45
Photographs of the Battle of Tannenberg, the eastern front's bloodiest, fought between Germany and Russia right after the outbreak of hostilities. The Germans, commanded by Field Marshal von Hindenburg and his chief of staff, General Ludendorff won the battle. Top left: Tannenberg is destroyed--August 30, 1914, exactly one month after war started. Bottom: endless lines of Russian prisoners of war at Augustów-Tannenberg. Right: German soldiers in a ruined house await the enemy.

46-47
Left: French troops in their trenches, attack the enemy with a weapon invented just before the beginning of the war: the flamethrower. Top right: German soldiers observe the scene before the gas attack from their trench. Center right: after the Ypres' attack the French also fought wearing gas masks; bottom right: Australian troops collecting bricks in the ruins of Ypres to build fortifications to protect the railway lines.

THE GREAT MASSACRES: YPRES

1915

At Ypres in Belgium on April 22, 1915, the French defenders saw a greenish-yellow cloud about 7 feet high advancing towards them. As it came closer the cloud rose up like a tidal wave, like a wall of mist. At first the soldiers thought the wave was a smoke screen, and they readied themselves to meet the Germans who were sure to advance from it. But what awaited them was a terrible death. Soon the trenches and surrounding fields were full of crazed soldiers running in all directions, tearing the collars off their shirts and greatcoats, shouting and begging for water, spitting blood, and rolling around on the ground trying in vain to breathe.The French called it yprite, the Germans *Gelbkreuzkampfstoff* (yellow cross combat material), and the British mustard gas. There had been a precedent; in October 1914 the French had fired canisters of tear gas for the first time. The Germans, however, had replied with asphyxiating gas, in total violation of the Hague Convention. Germany practically had a monopoly on mustard gas, produced in the BASF factory in Ludwigshafen.The attack at Ypres killed five thousand soldiers, and ten thousand were disfigured or blinded. The "*poilus*" (the nickname given to French soldiers) were terrorized; the world had turned ugly, and the press in Paris thought defeat was inevitable. Two days later, confirming the most pessimistic predictions, the Germans repeated the massacre east of Ypres, against Canadian troops. Another five thousand died. But the German high command affirmed that they had only wanted to carry out "an experiment," and after further attacks in the Ypres area throughout May, orders were given that only tear gas, such as the French used in the past, should be used. Was this an acknowledgment of error? No. The fact was that an Anglo-French team had developed a gas mask that used sodium carbonate and potassium carbonate to neutralize the effects of the mustard gas. Moreover, news had also spread that some British engineers were perfecting a machine (called a Livens, after the man who invented it) capable of avenging the shocking attacks at Ypres. It was a steel tube fitted with an electrical firing device, and inside was a bomb containing gas. By setting them in the ground at an angle of 45 degrees, a hundred Livens tubes could produce results every bit as appalling as those at Ypres. The British made great use of Livens tubes the following year, 1916, at the Somme. As for the Germans, BASF developed a blinding liquid that had a strong garlic smell. It was scattered over enemy terrain in 1917, causing sores, blindness, and death from blood poisoning due to the liquid's vapors entering the venous system through the lungs. The British counted 3,000 casualties, either dead, wounded, or blinded. The Germans continued to use this gas. In June 1918, the French took take their revenge. They fired gas bombs at the German lines, which by this stage were retreating, and killed thousands of German soldiers.

1915

48-49

This image shows one of the most dramatic moments of the war: it's April 2, 1915 French soldiers await for the enemy in their trenches. Germans soldiers, wearing masks, move toward them in a yellowish-green cloud that moves like an raging sea: this event is the beginning of chemical warfare. French soldiers, incredulous and unaware, die horribly, with no way out.

THE GREAT MASSACRES VERDUN
1916

The attack at Verdun on February 21, 1916 was the first in the history of war to be preceded by heavy artillery bombing (a practice that was to become standard during World War II). The bombing was designed destroy the enemy, causing death in the trenches, in the gun emplacements, and between the wire barricades. It was also the first attack that involved large use of the air force for observation and to direct artillery fire.

By this stage in the war, the French army had suffered losses amounting to 994,000 dead or taken prisoner, and over 1.5 million wounded. This was slaughter, pure and simple, although the German commander-in-chief, Erich von Falkenhayn, had not yet had enough of it. He had decided that he would not bother with small territorial advances (experience had shown they had no weakening effect on enemy resistance) but would focus on inflicting the greatest possible number of losses on the enemy--in other words, on a war of pure extermination.

Before starting the pre-attack bombardment, Falkenhayn ordered sham preparations to deceive Joffre into thinking he was going to attack Alsace, in the direction of Artois. But he had no intention of undertaking this attack. Once he was sure this maneuver had thrown the French off balance, he opened fire. At dawn on February 21, two million 380-mm and 420-mm shells fell on a front of only 2.5 miles. The Germans placed heavy cannons every 72 feet and light cannons every 58 feet. The bombardment lasted for nine hours. Verdun was almost completely destroyed; the civilian population was annihilated and the surrounding countryside was nothing but a carnage scene with thousands of smoking craters.

The infantry was given the order to attack at 4 p.m. The German soldiers advanced in waves, preceded by flame-throwing divisions. The French, already decimated by the cannon fire, were bayoneted or burned alive. The enemy broke through at least 2 miles of the front and three lines of defense. On February 24, Fort Douaumont, which had been considered impregnable, fell. The premier, Aristide Briand, sent Joffre an angry message: "If you lose Verdun you are cowards!" and appointed Philippe Pétain commander of the Verdun front.

Pétain knew that he could not use the two railway lines (they had fallen into German hands) to get supplies to his men, so he put all his resources into vehicle and roads which he flattened and widened. In a short time he had masses of artillery being transported along the eastern bank of the Meuse. He then brought in six divisions to replace the twenty divisions decimated by the Germans. The 30th Armed Corps alone suffered 680 dead and 3,200 wounded in a week, while 16,500 were taken prisoner.

Between February 27 and March 6, a total of 190,000 men and 23,000 tons of ammunition were brought in 3,900 trucks along the road from Bar-le-Duc to the front at Verdun. From then on the French called this road *la voie sacrée*, "*the sacred way*." Once the fighting units had been made up, the fighting started again. Both sides made much use of flame-throwers and poison gas. The forts of Douaumont and Vaux were lost, recaptured, and occupied several times, with heavy losses on both sides. By the end of June the figures were chilling. French losses were 179,000 men dead or taken prisoner, with 279,000 wounded. By the middle of December when the battle of Verdun came to an end, 500,000 had died in the field, 20 every hour for every mile of the front. There was mourning and tears for millions of families, and glory for two French officers who distinguished themselves for their courage and ability: Robert Nivelle and Charles de Gaulle.

51
Top: the photo captures a moment of the tragic attack of the French army near Verdun, which can be seen in the photo on the bottom, partly destroyed by the heavy bombings it was subjected to by the Germans.

52-53
Scenes from the terrible trench warfare characteristic of the first world conflict. At Verdun, a group of French soldiers cutting a barbed wire barrier, on which they found the body of one of their comrades.

54-55
More images of the battle of Verdun. Left: a French cannon in action, while (right) a group of French soldiers in a trench, close to the wooden crosses that mark the improvised burial site of their killed comrades; bottom left: French troops past a convoy of carts loaded with the corpses of their fallen comrades. Bottom right: a French colonial infantry company (Zouaves) in the woods near Caures. Between February 27 and March 6, 3900 lorries transported 190,000 men and 23,000 tons of munitions to the Verdun battle lines. The French now call the road they took la Voie sacrée, *the Sacred Way.*

56-57
At the Somme, summer of 1916. Left: imperial troops in their trenches shell the enemy with their machine-guns; right: English troops prepare to storm out of their trench to launch a man-to-man attack.

THE GREAT MASSACRES: THE SOMME
1916

As the battle of Verdun was at its height, the French and British launched the Somme offensive. The two high commanders, Joseph Joffre and Douglas Haig, had planned this maneuver at the Franco-British summit at Chantilly during the previous December. It was to take place in parallel with similar offensives on the Italian and Russian fronts. Foch was in charge of operations involving the British 4th and the French 6th armies. This was the plan, but by the time of the attack the Verdun situation had decimated French troops, as ever more men were poured into that inferno.

The principal thrust thus fell to the British; 13 British and 5 French divisions carried out the attack, which the two chiefs of staff had calculated would force Germany to call a halt to the war by the end of 1916. The Somme offensive was the most classic of what were called "artillery battles." The estimated five days of preparatory bombardment (along the lines of the Verdun attack) were to become seven. The artillery storm was unleashed on June 24, 1916. In the first day the British, who had 1,532 cannons and 316 mortars, fired 1.8 million shells, amounting to 32,000 tons of iron and lead; the French, who had 465 cannons and 300 mortars, fired 380,000 shells. The artillery had to rest periodically to give the gun muzzles time to cool down. The iron raining down on the trenches would bury the enemy, obliterate all trace of the communication trenches, annihilate the machine-gun nests, flatten the lookouts, and above all kill as many of them as possible.

But two factors would force the attacking armies to lower their expectations. The first, which became known as "Falkenhayn's trick," deprived the Franco-British operation of its principal target, the enemy soldiers. Having foreseen an attack, Falkenhayn had had shelters built very deep below ground, up to the equivalent of two floors down, where the soldiers hid protected from the artillery storm that swept away only those few soldiers who chose (willingly or unwillingly) to make the supreme sacrifice. The second factor also resulted from lack of information among the French and British commands. They thought the Germans had set up only two lines of defense, but Falkenhayn had set up three.

On July 1, 1916, the Franco-British troops launched four successive attack waves. Every British infantryman (all volunteers) had a steel helmet, a spade, a blanket roll over his shoulder, and two gas masks. In his haversack he had cutlery, soap, socks, and emergency food rations; in his jacket pocket was a first-aid kit; in his bandolier he carried 220 rifle cartridges; and in a pouch over his shoulder two hand grenades. The total weight of this equipment was 66 pounds, plus his Enfield rifle. In addition some had to carry pickaxes, shovels, and wire-cutters. Such equipment was a serious encumbrance that slowed them down, though their commanding officers had assumed that the "Tommies" would find only dead bodies in the enemy trenches.

The Tommies passed the first line of defense (between 1640 and 3280 feet from the enemy positions) and reached the second (up to 3 miles and more beyond the first lines). Confident that they would not run into the enemy at this stage, they found themselves facing the German units that had surfaced from their underground passages practically unharmed, ready to machine-gun anything and everything that moved.

The British army's left flank and the center were forced back with heavy losses. The right flank, together with the French contingent, got through the second line, but then ran into the third line, still perfectly intact. By the end of July 1, 1916, the first day of the advance, 20,000 British soldiers had been killed.

The fighting continued along the Somme throughout July and August, producing no result other than cartloads of dead. On September 15 the British sent their first tanks into battle (so-called because they were supposed to look like gasoline tanks), but of the 49 tanks used at the Somme only nine were able to give cover to the advancing infantry, and they were finally put out of action by the enemy artillery. By its end, the battle of the Somme, an unrivalled disaster for the British volunteers, cost both sides more than a million men.

58-59
This series of photos again shows the bloody battle of Somme: to the left, top and center, British soldiers come out from under cover to face the enemy on open ground; bottom: at the end of a battle between British tanks and German tanks, during which the latter came out worse. Right: howitzers of the British corps shoot on enemy lines.

The Somme
1916

60
Italy entered the war on May 24, 1915, when its infantry crossed the Piave river. The Italians faced the Austro-Hungarian military. Between June and November 1915, the Italians fought the first four battles of the Isonzo. Top left Italian weaponry crosses the Isonzo; center: Austrian unit is firing machine guns from above against an Italian position; bottom: Italian Alpini troops marching in deep snow.

1916

Italy at war
1915-1918

The Italian government, headed by the liberal Antonio Salandra, declared its neutrality on August 3, 1914. It justified its position by saying that Austria-Hungary had clearly violated the terms of the Triple Alliance by failing to consult Italy before declaring war. In fact, after the assassination at Sarajevo, Vienna had kept Berlin informed of its every move and every intention, but had kept Rome completely in the dark. Perhaps this was unavoidable. There was long-standing antipathy, even decades outright hatred, between the Austrians and the Italians. At the Conference of Vienna in 1814, Metternich had declared that Italy did not exist, it was merely a "geographic expression," and Garibaldi, in 1848, had ordered his men, who were retreating from Rome, to shoot the hated Austrian "white shirts" on sight. Further, Italy had recently made friendly overtures to Serbia, which had become the bitterest enemy of the Austro-Hungarian Empire.

Together with the Catholic Church and the vast majority of the population, the liberal government and the opposition parties, including Catholics and Socialists, all Italian factions declared themselves in favor of a negotiated neutrality. But many others were fanning the flames of war, urging the government to take advantage of the situation to conclude the Risorgimento and the unification of Italy by annexing the territories still under Austrian sovereignty. They included nationalists, irredentists (political extremists now exiles in Italy from Italian territories subject to Austria, such as Trentino and Venezia Giulia), and members of the trade union movement with ties to the Socialist Party. Filippo Corridoni, a major figure among the trade unionists, signed up as a volunteer and was killed during an attack on the "Frasche trench." Of the 218 trade-union officials who followed his example, 70 were killed in action, Also pro-war were members of the lively intellectual groups that published literary reviews and were involved in the Futurist movement founded by Filippo Tomaso Marinetti. One of Italy's brightest young journalists, Benito Mussolini, editor of the Socialist daily *Avanti!*, unexpectedly sided with the interventionists. Turning his back on the Socialist Second International's commitment to neutrality and refusal to fight as well as on his own pacifist past, he founded the daily *Il Popolo d'Italia*, which quickly became a success and later made him the leader of the Fascist Movement.

Moreover, the interventionists had been involved in the war right from the early days. In August 1914, Peppino Garibaldi, nephew of the great Italian hero, had founded an "Italian Legion," which four thousand young volunteers had joined. They left for France where they fought the Germans in the Argonne campaign. Two of Garibaldi's descendants, Bruno and Costante, lost their lives during the fighting in France.

Using a strong dose of political opportunism to manipulate the ever more rancorous demonstrations of the nationalists, the Salandra government made some discreet overtures to Austria-Hungary, leading Vienna to believe that Italy was sorely tempted to join the Entente Cordiale (Russia, France, and Great Britain), but that it could be persuaded not to if Vienna were prepared to return to Italy the regions that Austria had seized: the province of Trent, the provinces of Udine and Gorizia (Friuli), and the provinces of Trieste, Pola, and Fiume (Venezia Giulia). Vienna's reply was curt: "Don't even think about it, we will never give them back."

At this point, there was nothing more to prevent Italy from responding to the Entente's ever more insistent offers of friendship and alliance. On April 26, 1915, the British and Italian foreign ministers signed the secret London Pact. In exchange for declaring war by the end of May, Rome would obtain a series of territories that included all those sought from Austria, plus the Austrian South Tyrol as far as the Brenner Pass, the Istrian peninsula in the Adriatic, Dalmatia, Vlorë in Albania, and (in the case of an Allied victory), a few areas deriving from the breakup of the German colonial empire in Africa.

This London Pact moment marked the beginning of Italy's headlong rush into war. On May 3, 1915, the government spoke out against the Triple Alliance. On May 5--the anniversary of the departure of Garibaldi's Thousand to take the Kingdom of the Two Sicilies in 1860--Gabriele D'Annunzio, the most popular Italian poet of his time, made a rousing speech in Genoa, in which he exhorted King Victor Emmanuel III to declare war on Austria-Hungary. Wild demonstrations in Genoa and other Italian cities greeted the poet's inflammatory words. On May 24, Italy declared war on the Empire and the infantry crossed the Piave River, which marked the frontier. The Royal Army's chief commander was Luigi Cadorna, the son of General Raffaele Cadorna who in 1870 led the Bersaglieri in holding Rome against Pope Pius IX's Swiss troops.

Unfortunately, Italy was far from ready to throw itself into the inferno of the world war, which had already proved to have an insatiable appetite for human life. The 1.5 million conscripts were not properly equipped to fight. The Italian army had very few cannon, enough machine guns for two regiments, no hand grenades at all, and even rifles ("model 91") were in short supply--and most dated from 1870. Many officers had to buy their pistols with their own money. Even helmets were lacking and had to be supplied by France, bearing the letters RF (République Française). Having neither gelignite nor even wire cutters, the Italian soldiers had to use garden shears to cut through barbed wire.

These problems did not affect the morale of the soldiers, conscripts though they were, and they threw themselves into battle with great fighting spirit. The Italian front went from the Tridentine Alps (with Trent in the center) to the Carnic Alps (with Gorizia marking the center). It was 435 miles long and was the most challeging of all World War I fronts. The first bloody battles took place at Carso, the arid land made up of rocks, gorges, caves, and military fortifications that lies above Trieste. Though the most Italian of cities, it was also Austria-Hungary's principal military port. From June to November 1915, the first four battles of the Isonzo were fought. The enemy used the strategy that had become standard on other fronts: the frontal attack, which led to the slaughter of Italian soldiers caught in Austrian machine-gun fire.

Meanwhile the Italian Alpini, specialists in mountain warfare, moved in to attack on the west, on the Passo del Tonale and on the Adamello and Presena glaciers. The Italians' courage was praised by David Lloyd George, who less than a year later was to become prime minister of Great Britain. He stated: "Only courageous men, supremely courageous men, could have attempted to capture these gigantic fortresses while being fired on by Austrian cannons and rifles, and once they had reached the top, face the Austrian bayonets held by proud, well-trained soldiers commanded by able generals."

After the short winter truce (March 11 to 19, 1916), the fifth battle of Isonzo was joined, as part of the counteroffensive that Pétain had launched in France in defense of Verdun. But it soon became clear that the battle was not going well for the Italians: they were forced to retreat after very heavy losses (60,000 dead and 170,000 wounded). The Austrian commander, Franz Conrad von Hötzendorf, took advantage of the Italian troops' demoralized state to launch a "punitive expedition" (May 15 to 24). But fierce Italian resistance at Pasubio, Passo Buole, and the Altipiano di Asiago prevented the Austrians from advancing into the Padana valley.

On June 9, after heated debate in parliament, the Salandra government fell and Paolo Boselli was elected prime minister. A government with a strong nationalist component replaced a government that had been seen as lethargic and passive. Shortly afterwards, on August 6, 1916, the sixth battle of the Isonzo began. It lasted until September 16 and ended with the taking of Gorizia by the 3rd Army, commanded by the Duke of Aosta. Then came the seventh, eighth and ninth battles of the Isonzo. The Boselli government, acting on information from the front that German soldiers were fighting alongside the Austrian imperial troops, declared war on Germany on August 28, 1916. The government now stood firm in its decision to fight the war come what may, without hesitation or fear. It therefore rejected the peace offer that Emperor Charles I (who had succeeded his great-uncle Franz Joseph) had proffered during his visit to the front at San Giovanni di Mariana.

Italy's political decision to fight on had the effect of making the fighting harsher. Austria gave orders to start air bombardments of the cities of the Veneto and even Milan: it was a foretaste of the terrible slaughter of civilians that became a feature of World War II. The only way to defend cities and towns from this new threat in the skies was to send up Italian planes to fight them. Italy was second to none in this field, having a squadron of courageous pilots, including Francesco Baracca.He had successfully completed 34 attacks on enemy planes before his plane was hit by the Austrians on June 19, 1917. It crashed on the Montello, killing Baracca.

This aerial warfare was ongoing during the tenth battle of the Isonzo, when the Alpini took Ortigara. General Cadorna gave the order to attack on June 10, 1917. He had 74 battalions (of which 20 were Alpini and 6 were Bersaglieri) and 1500 cannons along a 8.6-mile front. The Italians advanced until the 24th, when the Austrians launched a violent counterattack making heavy use of flame-throwers, mustard gas, and brutal clubs spiked with nails to smash the skulls of soldiers writhing on the ground from the effects of the gas. The Italians were slaughtered.

The eleventh battle of the Isonzo ended in even greater disaster for the Italians, in spite of the 5000 cannon, 1700 mortars, and reconnaissance and fighting planes that Cadorna had mustered. On the morning of September 19, 1917, 45 Italian divisions attacked the Austro-German positions (Germany had sent the formidable Alpenkorps to fight alongside their ally). After a week the Italians lost the battle; 143,000 Italian soldiers were dead or wounded, and 110,000 Austrian and German soldiers suffered the same fate. The Italians won two small victories: they captured Bainsizza and Monte Santo.

Germany's destruction of the Russian army enabled it to

send heavy reinforcements to the ever more exhausted imperial Austro-Hungarian army on the Italian front. Among the young German officers of the Alpenkorps was one destined to become famous, Erwin Rommel. He commanded the Alpine battalions of Württemberg. Otto von Below's newly formed 14th Army, 15 divisions strong, was also there.

On October 24, 1917, the highly organized Austro-German offensive suddenly broke through the Italian lines at Caporetto, in Friuli. The Italian 2nd Army disintegrated and its units retreated in disorder to cries of "every man for himself," scrambling down the Alpine valleys almost to Venice. The Austrians were hot in pursuit; they now saw themselves celebrating their victory in gondolas on the Grand Canal. The Itaian 3rd Army managed to retreat in good order, in a sort of strategic withdrawal, to the banks of the Piave and Monte Grappa, where, between November 10 and 26, 1917, they fought to hold back the enemy forces. It was in these circumstances that the volunteer corps, such as the Caimani del Piave and the Arditi, came to the fore. These battalions were made up mostly of young men, many of them students, for whom the war was a question of national pride, or refugees from the irredentist areas who knew only too well that if captured by the enemy they would be hanged.

These young Italian volunteers were inspired and encouraged by the sacrifice of so many of their countrymen who had already given their lives. These heroes included the brothers Carlo and Giovanni Stuparich from Trieste; Cesare Battisti, a renowned journalist from Trento (he had represented minority Italian-speaking groups in the Viennese parliament and was hanged on July 12, 1916, in the castle of Buon Consiglio); the Istrian Fabio Filzi; Nazario Sauro, a submariner; and Damiano Chiesa, an artillery officer. In all, five medals for valor in action.

The Caporetto debâcle and the "holding battle" on the Piave cost the Italians 40,000 dead and 300,000 prisoners and wounded. A further 300,000 soldiers of the 2nd Army threw off their uniforms and fled home to their wives, children, and parents, pursued and hunted down by the Carabinieri. Some were even found in the Abruzzi mountains.

The military collapse cost prime minister Paolo Boselli his job. He resigned on October 26, the day after the defeat of Caporetto, while the Allies were considering abandoning Italy to its fate. At the meeting at Peschiera (November 8, 1917) between Victor Emmanuel III; the British prime minister, Lloyd George; and the French chief of staff, Nivelle, the king refused to retreat to the Mincio and managed to convince the Allies to send reinforcements of men, arms, and airplanes.

The new Italian premier was Vittorio Emmanuele Orlando and the new chief of staff General Armando Diaz. The king also managed to obtain agreement that Diaz should be in command of the allied forces, six French and four British divisions. The front having been re-established, the Italians and allied forces counterattacked. New forces arrived at the front: They were the "ragazzi del '99", young men born in the last year of the 19th century called up at nineteen, who fought fearlessly. The Italian navy also fought courageously. Luigi Rizzo, who fought at sea with the MAS (the destroyers that Gabriele D'Annunzio had renamed *Memento audere semper*, "remember always to be daring,") had already helped to sink the Austrian battleship *Wien*. With the MAS, he sank the *St Stephen*, the pride of the imperial Austrian navy, on June 10, 1918. At the same time D'Annunzio, with an air squadron based at Aviano (from where NATO bombers took off for Serbia in 1999), flew over Vienna dropping not bombs but leaflets extolling the superiority of the Italians and inviting the Austrians to surrender. It was an incident that resonated throughout the world.

On June 15, the decisive battle of the Piave began. The Austrians attacked with 59 divisions, 7500 cannons, and 600 airplanes. Diaz met them with 40 divisions, 9500 cannons, and 900 airplanes. The Austrians managed to set up many bridgeheads on the right bank of the river, but on June 19, the Italians counterattacked. On June 23, after four days of furious hand-to-hand combat, the Austrians were forced to retreat while the footbridges and pontoons were destroyed with explosives and the occupied areas west of the Piave became death traps for the Austrians.

On October 24, exactly one year after the Caporetto defeat, Diaz launched the final offensive. The Italian army crossed the Piave in many places; the Austrians fled towards the mountains pursued by the Italians, who defeated them in the decisive battle of Vittorio Veneto. On November 4, the plenipotentiaries of Italy and Austria signed the armistice at Villa Giusti. Italy obtained Trent and Trieste, where to the joy of the people, soldiers arrived on November 5, waving the Italian flag. In World War I, out of a total of 5,200,000 soldiers mobilized, Italy lost a total of 680,000 (600,000 soldiers and 80,000 civilians), and over one million others were wounded and maimed.

66-67

Top left, long lines of Austrian prisoners marching towards assembly camps following the final battle of Vittorio Veneto (November 4, 1918), won by the Italians. Bottom: the Royal Army occupying Trento. Right, a photo showing the Italian withdrawal from Caporetto (October 1917), which marked, for the army of Victor Emmanuel III, the most dramatic and humiliating chapter of the conflict.

64

Top left: Italian soldiers moving through communication trenches dug in Mount Podgora during operations for the seizing of Gorizia. The city was taken on September 16, 1916 by infantrymen of the Third Army, under the command of the Duke of Aosta. Top right: Italian troops engaged in a difficult climb to reach a position dug in the mountain, from where they will aim their artillery at the Austrians. Bottom: Italian infantrymen attacking the Austrian positions in the Carso, in 1917.

65

Italian mountaineers troops, known as "Alpini" lift with difficulty a cannon up to a mountain top; the "Alpini" specialists in mountain warfare, also attacked the Austrians from the west, in the Tonale pass and on the Adamello and Presena glaciers.

1918

THE WAR IN THE BALKANS

1915-1918

In the Balkans, a part of Europe that would long remain a source of conflict, a sort of third local war continued. In mid-August Austria sent a "punitive expedition" into Serbia in revenge for the assassination of Archduke Franz Ferdinand and his wife. On November 6, 1914, the imperial troops entered Belgrade, but were then beaten back with heavy losses on December 12. From this moment, and for many months, the Balkan front was neglected because Franz Joseph's army was busy trying to foil Russian attempts to penetrate imperial territory through the Carpathian mountains.

On October 6, 1915, Bulgaria joined the war, fighting alongside Germany and Austria-Hungary. The decision was made 24 hours after the Allies had launched a plan to liberate Serbia. On October 5 (the day before) two British divisions supported by French units had landed at Salonika in order to prevent the Bulgarians from attacking the Allied army from the east. But the plan failed. The Bulgarian army was more than ready for the Allied troops and forced them back to the sea, inflicting very heavy losses.

At the same time the Prussian general, August von Mackensen, ordered a massive Austro-German offensive against the Serbs, who suffered a total defeat. The remains of King Peter Karageorgevitch's army fled through Albania in the depths of the winter of 1915-16 in an attempt to reach the sea, pursued and exterminated by the Austro-German troops. The survivors were rescued by Italian boats and taken to Corfu, which was under French occupation.

Italy also joined the conflict: On August 21, 1915, it declared war on Turkey and on October 19 it declared war on Bulgaria. In January 1916 Austria invaded Montenegro, the Allies' base, and eliminated the small nation from the war. Romania, which had entered the war in August 1916 on the Entente's side, was beaten within a month by the Austrians and Bulgarians.

On June 27, 1917, it was Greece's turn to join the Entente in the war. Not until September 1918, however, did the Allies manage to get the better of the fierce and tenacious Bulgarians. Until then they had managed to repel all attacks from the sea and from the air base at Salonika. On September 29, 1918, Bulgaria signed an armistice with the Allied powers, preceding Austria-Hungary by a month.

68-69
Left: Romanian soldiers marching toward the front to the sound of violins; bottom: Austro-Hungarian troops during a reconnaissance; right: Serb civilians fleeing during the Serb army's retreat toward Macedonia.

70-71
Here on the Turkish front, during the landing in Gallipoli, April 1915; left: a British unit is attacking immediately after leaving the boats; right French soldiers shooting from behind a protective sand barrier.

THE WAR IN THE MIDDLE EAST

1915-1918

The true commander of the Turkish armies in World War I was a German, the Prussian General Otto Liman von Sanders. Formally titled "inspector general," he directed operations and gave the Allies a lot of trouble. The commander of the British forces in the Mediterranean was Sir Ian Hamilton, who had already made a name for himself as a general in the Boer War. He decided to launch an attack on Turkey, forcing a passage through the Dardanelles and landing at Gallipoli. This town was at the northern end of the peninsula that flanked the western shore of the Dardanelles. Sir Ian's plan was simple: to occupy the strait

and then take Istanbul, thus making it possible to re-establish a supply route and communications between Russia and the Mediterranean through the Bosporus.

Winston Churchill, First Lord of the Admiralty, gave his full approval to the plan and supervised landing plans. British, French, Australian, and New Zealand forces took part. The Australian Imperial Force (the AIF) sent 330,000 volunteers to Europe, out of a population of five million subjects of the British Crown. New Zealand was no less generous, sending 220,000 volunteers. By the end of the operation 59,000 Australians and 17,000 New Zealanders had lost their lives.

The landing area was poorly chosen: the men came ashore on a narrow sandy stretch dominated by steep cliffs, from the top of which the Turks massacred the soldiers as soon as they hit the beach. Among the Turkish officers in charge of the firing, following Sanders' orders, was the young colonel Mustafa Kemal, the future Atatürk, father of the modern Turkish Republic. New landings on August 6 resulted in further massacres. In November, the Allies finally admitted the operation had been a failure. It cost the lives of 200,000 soldiers and was to go down in history as "the Gallipoli disaster."

Also in November 1915 the British, who had attempted to advance from Kuwait along the Tigris into Mesopotamia, were driven back by the Turks and annihilated. Turkey was attacked on a third front by the Russians in the Caucasus and along the Black Sea. Here things did not go well for the Turks; in the first months of 1916 they lost the cities of Erzurum and Trabzon.

In August 1916, starting in Suez, the British attacked the Turks and drove them back as far as Palestine. This marked the beginning of the "Palestine campaign" for Aqaba and Jerusalem. Thomas Edward Lawrence, a British Arabist who was working for the British secret services, became a key figure in the Arab revolt against Turkish domination. The first result of Lawrence of Arabia's activities was Emir Hussein's attack on the Turkish fortress of Medina on June 5, 1916. Hussein then proclaimed himself King of Arabia, and in December, Great Britain officially recognized him.

In the meantime Lawrence had undertaken daring guerrilla operations in the desert. The most spectacular, carried out in July 1917, involved the capture of the port of Aqaba on the Red Sea. From then on the Arab tribes supported the British advance, first in Palestine with the taking of Jerusalem, then in Syria, and finally with the capture of Damascus. At the end of the war, Lawrence, who was also an archaeologist and writer, joined the RAF as an enlisted airman, preferring to keep quiet about his glorious past as a combatant. He wrote about the Arab Revolt in *The Seven Pillars of Wisdom*, one of the great works of 20th-century English literature. He died in 1935, aged 47.

72-73

The Allied landing, involving mainly British, French and Anzac troops at Gallipoli. Right: British warships firing on Turkish positions near Gallipoli; bottom: a British battery in action on the cliffs; of the eight pieces of heavy artillery that were brought ashore, seven were immediately destroyed.

75

Photos of the war at sea. The Germans in particular used a submarine fleet (U-boats) for a hit-and-run campaign. Top: a German fleet on their way to the North Sea in a battle formation; center: British heavy guns firing in open seas; bottom: the German fleet in the port of Kiel.

THE WAR AT SEA
1915-1918

The first skirmishes on the high seas occurred at the end of August 1914 in the Bay of Heligoland (North Sea) when a small British squadron sank four German ships: 1200 sailors lost their lives. Then on September 22 a German U-boat in the North Sea torpedoed three British cruisers, and on October 27 a German mine destroyed the battleship *Audacious* off the Irish coast. From the start of hostilities the Allies had put a naval blockade in place against the Central Powers. The British fleet patrolled the North Sea, the English Channel, and the Mediterranean to stop Germany and Austria-Hungary from obtaining supplies. British warships constantly stopped the merchant ships of neutral countries, threaten with sinking if they sought any German port in the North Sea or the Baltic, or any Austrian port in the Adriatic. The German reaction was twofold. They mined the British and Irish coasts (considered war zones) and waged a bitter submarine war against Great Britain. On May 7, 1915, the most dramatic and cruel episode of this marine war occurred: the sinking of the *Lusitania*. It was one of Britain's largest ocean liners, sailing between Liverpool and New York. U-boat U-20, commanded by Captain Schweiger, intercepted the Lusitania off Cape Kinsale on the south coast of Ireland, and fired two torpedoes. The liner overturned and sank in twenty minutes. The passengers were all civilians, and 1,198 lost their lives, including 291 women and 20 children. Among the dead were 128 Americans. This fact provoked strong protests throughout the world. America was indignant; Washington sent a strongly worded protest to Berlin threatening reprisal. But the Lusitania had in fact been carrying war equipment.

On August 19 the German U-24 torpedoed and sank the British passenger ship *Arabic*, on which three Americans had been traveling. This time Washington sent an ultimatum and Germany was forced to withdraw its U-boats from the Irish coast and the English Channel and to guarantee that no further ships would be sunk without warning and without provision for rescuing the civilians.

The German naval offensive then concentrated on the ocean, hunting down enemies flying the Union Jack. Just off Coronel on the Chilean coast, the German East Asiatic Squadron (under Admiral Graf von Spee), which had crossed the Pacific, sank two British cruisers. On rounding Cape Horn, Spee then decided to make an incursion to Port Stanley in the Falkland Islands, the British base in the Atlantic, 373 miles off the coast of Argentina. But the cruisers *Inflexible* and *Invincible* were waiting for him. The German squadron was destroyed except for one ship, which was sunk a few months later.

The Atlantic and the Pacific were the theaters of a fierce naval war the Germans waged with small fast cruisers such as the *Dresden* and the *Königsberg*. Another of these small cruisers, the *Emden*, ran into the coral reef protecting the Cocos Islands in the Indian Ocean and sank. Closer to home, the most memorable encounter took place in the North Sea, off the Jutland peninsula, for which the battle is named. The British were in a position of clear superiority. They had two squadrons of battleships and battle cruisers protected by light cruisers and destroyers. At the end of May 1916 the entire British fleet weighed anchor from its base in Scotland to meet a German fleet that had left Cuxhaven and whose signals been intercepted by radio. Contact occurred on May 31 off Jutland. At the onset, the Germans sank two British ships and with a diversionary tactic tried to draw part of the enemy fleet southwards. The British in turn pretended to retreat, followed by the German fleet, which sank a third battle cruiser. At the last moment, however, the Germans realized it was a trap and avoided it (the British were lying in wait for them close to their base). They turned about and made full steam ahead for home, pursued, fired on, and several times hit by the British.

The German promise not to sink any more British merchant ships without warning was only good for a few months. In March 1916 there was a heightening of tension as a result of the naval blockade. The German chief of staff ordered his U-boats to sink without warning any British ship that was not a passenger vessel. But on March 24, U-boat 29 torpedoed the ocean liner *Sussex* without warning; once again a number of American passengers died. The United States protested once more, and again a counter-order was issued to the submarines. Finally on February 3, 1917, after further attacks and further American victims, the United States broke off diplomatic relations and on April 6, declared war on Germany. Just a few months prior to this, on February 1, 1917, Germany had declared indiscriminate submarine war: all merchant ships, even those sailing under neutral flags, headed for any Allied port would be sunk without warning.

In the war at sea, the attacks of the Italian Navy's assault teams on the Austro-Hungarian Navy deserve note. Luigi Rizzo, in command of a motor torpedo boat, sank the battleship *St. Stephen* in Premuda on June 10, 1918. Six months before, having entered the port of Trieste in the same vessel, he had sunk the battleship *Wien*. The deadly weapon that guaranteed the success of these missions was the guided torpedo (father of the future World War II model), developed by Major Raffaele Rossetti, a skilled naval engineer. The guided torpedo was fitted with an electromagnetic explosive charge. The assault team placed it on the keel of the enemy ship before diving into the

1914
1918

4

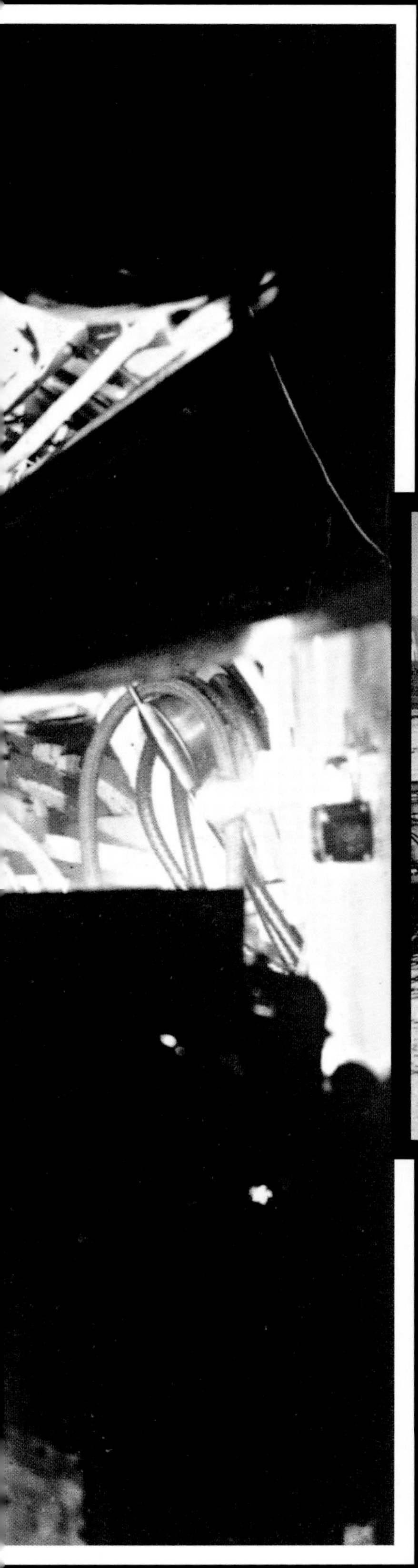

76-77
More images of the war at sea. Left: a sailor on a U-boat loading a cannon; top right: a U-boat has just aimed at a British torpedo. Bottom right: U-boat fleet at the Bremen ship yards.

sea and swimming to safety. Italian assault teams successfully carried out other missions using this torpedo in the Austrian base at Pola and in the Kvarner islands in the Adriatic. Then, on October 31, 1918, a small convoy commanded by Costanzo Ciano came out of the canals of Venice and sank the *Viribus Unitis*, the flagship of the Austro-Hungarian fleet. Although taken prisoner, the Italians were liberated four days later by their comrades, after the surrender of Austria.

At the end of the war the German fleet, which had been trapped at Scapa Flow in the Orkney Islands, scuttled its own ships so that they could not be divided up among the victors.

THE WAR IN THE SKY

1915-1918

When World War I started the airplane had been in existence for a mere eleven years. The only previous use of the new flying machine during armed hostilities occurred during the Italo-Turkish War in 1911, when Italian planes had taken off from Sicily to bombard the Turko-Libyan troops during the Italian landing at Tripoli.

The major powers thought that the small, fragile planes of the period would be useful mainly for reconnaissance, to keep an eye on enemy movements and positions. But this new weapon was soon to undergo unimagined developments and be used in air raids. This was made possible by increasing the capacity of the fuel tanks, thus increasing flying time and range. For example, the seven airplanes of D'Annunzio's pamphlet drop on Vienna flew for more than 621.4 miles without landing.

Britain created the Royal Air Force (RAF) as an independent force, the third after the Navy and the Army. The other warring nations integrated their air forces into their respective armies and navies. Since World War I was essentially a war of position, a war fought in the trenches, the airplane was basically used for reconnaissance and (given the limited protection offered by a necessarily lightweight fuselage) to a lesser extent for machine-gun attacks. Famous air aces were indeed shot down, after achieving incredible victories in aerial duels, by single infantrymen who managed to pierce the fuselage (and often mortally wound the pilot) with a single shot, as if shooting a pigeon. By the end of the war a total of 177,000 airplanes had been used (Italy had built 6,000 of them) and 50,000 pilots had been killed. Among these were several legendary aces. Baron Manfred von Richthofen (called the "Red Baron" because of the color of his plane), was hit and killed by a novice English infantry after having engaged and shot down 80 enemy aircraft. The Italians Francesco Baracca (34 victories) and Silvio Scaroni (26 victories); the French René Fonck (75 victories) and Georges Guynemer (54 victories); the Briton Edward Mannock (73 victories); the Canadian Billy Bishop (72 victories); the American, Edward Rickenbaker (26 victories).

78-79
War in the skies. Left: a duel between a British SE-5 (top) and a German L.V.G. CI. Right: though the picture is an old photomontage, it gives a good idea of how dramatic the aerial duels of World War I were.

1916

THE IRISH QUESTION
1916

With the aim of diverting the greatest possible number of British troops from the front, the German secret service contacted Sinn Fein ("We Ourselves"), the Irish separatist movement that has continued fighting for Ireland's complete independence from Great Britain. Secret agreements were made and the steamship *Aud* was dispatched, camouflaged as a Norwegian cargo ship and laden with weapons (including 20,000 rifles). The British warship *Bluebell* intercepted the Aud off Ireland's south coast and sank it. When the reason for the captured survivors' mission was discovered, it caused a scandal that put a stop to further plotting between Germany and the Sinn Fein. However, it did not stop the Irish nationalists, who planned to take advantage of the British military forces' involvement in the war and organize an armed uprising.

One of the movement's main figures, Sir Roger Casement (who had been made a baronet for his diplomatic services to the Crown) secretly organized a trip to Germany. His aim was to form an Irish brigade from prisoners held in the German concentration camps. (The Russian General Vlasov made the same mistake in World War II when he assembled the Third Reich's Cossacks into an army to launch against the USSR). But a humiliating checkmate awaited Sir Roger: instead of the hoped-for three thousand men, less than fifty signed up. All the other Irish prisoners contacted hated the Germans more than they did their English "stepbrothers," whose language they spoke and with whom they had more in common in the way of culture and customs.

By this time, the German military command considered that the Irish independence movement was only a bluff and abandoned Sinn Fein to its destiny. But Sinn Fein did not give up. At 10 a.m. on April 24, 1916, the Easter Rising started in Dublin. Groups of armed insurgents commanded by Patrick Henry Pearse attacked the police stations and public buildings of Dublin and set up their command in the Post Office building on O'Connell Street, the city's main street. The rebellion spread throughout the country and the leaders of the uprising thought they had won. They were sure that London would not leave the front undefended to take back a few Irish cities.

The British government took drastic action. Field marshall French was recalled from the front line to repress the uprising. A storm of fire descended on Dublin, where the cruiser *HMS Helga* sailed up the Liffey, destroying the historic center of the city with its cannons. Two hundred fifty buildings were reduced to rubble. The uprising was ruthlessly put down throughout Ireland; the barricades erected by the insurgents were destroyed by cannon fire at point-blank range. There were thousands of civilian victims. All the uprising's leaders were captured and condemned to death, either to be shot or hanged (in the case of government employees). The Republican cause's finest supporters thus lost their lives, watched by an indifferent Germany, which seemed farther away than ever from Dublin. Together with Patrick Henry Pearse, Thomas McDonagh and Thomas Clarke were shot.

After a long, humiliating trial, Sir Roger Casement was found guilty of high treason and hanged. General Maxwell, an Englishman who had been sent to Dublin as special governor, was in charge of overseeing the hanging.

But Sinn Fein did not die. It won the elections in 1918 and the following year its 73 members of Parliament, with Eamon De Valera, the father of modern Ireland, as their leader, proclaimed the independent Republic of Ireland. The first civil war between anti- and pro-British Irish followed in 1919-1921, with the country being split between Eire (capital Dublin) and Ulster (capital Belfast). A second civil war (1921-23) ended with Eire finally obtaining independence from the British.

80

Dramatic photo documentation of the Irish Rebellion. In April 1916, the Irish refused to fight with Britain against Germany. Top left: the famous statue of Nelson, blown up by insurgents in O'Connell Street, downtown Dublin. Right: Dublin streets in turmoil during a general strike. Bottom: Paddy (Patrick), a young Irish resistance hero seen in the Sackville Street battle, where Irish Liberation Army volunteers were fighting. The uprising was crushed by Field Marshal French, who had been recalled from the European front. The uprising's leaders were all caught, sentenced to death and executed.

AMERICA IN THE WAR
1917-1918

Public opinion in America, already aroused by the sinking of the transatlantic liner *Lusitania* on May 7, 1916 by a German submarine, became ever more hostile and resentful towards Germany. This reaction was caused by the constant U-boat attacks on British merchant ships with American passengers on board. One hundred eighty American civilians died in this way. Ever more hostile letters of protest to the German government put President Woodrow Wilson's pacifism to the test. In February of that same year, he had sent Colonel House as his special representative to talk to the governments of London, Paris, Berlin, Rome, and Petrograd in an effort to bring about peace.

82
1917: the USA takes up arms. On April 2, 1917, the United States war declared war on Germany, and December 7 on Austria. The 1st US Division, commanded by General Pershing, lands in France at the end of June 1917. The image show scenes of US infantry men attacking enemy trenches in St. Mihiel.

On November 21, 1916, Emperor Franz Joseph died; his successor, Charles I, was in favor of peace. The German chancellor Bethmann-Hollweg was not averse to considering the American proposals, and on December 12, 1916, the German Reich officially invited the United States to undertake a peace mission to sound out the countries of the Entente. But the replies from Rome, Paris, London, and the other Allied governments were negative. Wilson insisted. On December 21, he sent a letter to the warring countries exhorting them to try to come to some peaceful agreement. The countries of the Alliance were in favor, but those of the Entente were not.

On January 9, 1917, in response to the suffocating Allied naval blockade, the Germans decided to wage an all-out submarine war. From that date all ships flying the Union Jack, whether military or merchant vessels (excluding passenger ships), would be sunk without warning. The Germans were true to their word, and more Americans traveling on British steamships lost their lives. This aroused fury in the United States. On March 3, 1917, Washington broke off diplomatic relations with Germany, after the secret service had intercepted coded anti-American messages passing between German battleships and the Mexican maritime authorities. America declared war on Germany on April 6, 1917 (followed by a declaration of war on

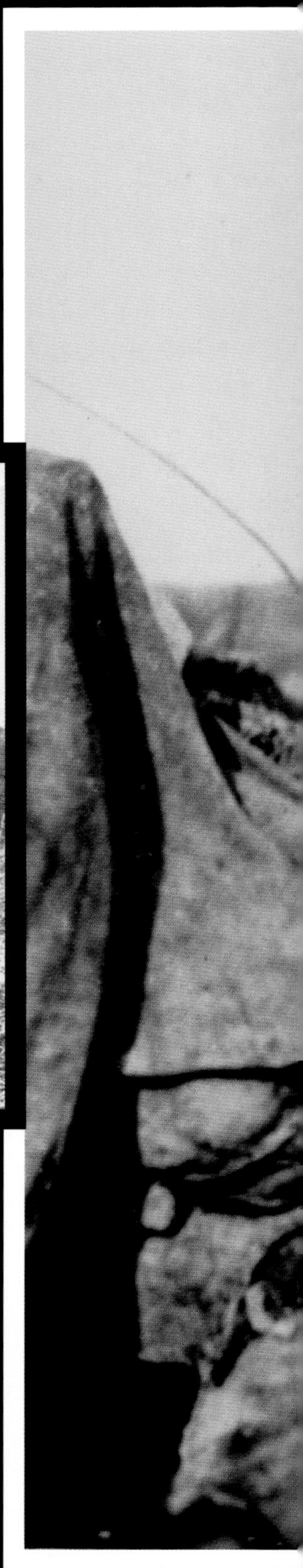

83
A US soldiers of the First Division launching hand grenades on the Aneauville front, France. American armymen were dressed and equipped like their comrades in British Army.

Austria-Hungary on December 7). The only person left to plead for peace at this stage was Pope Benedict XV, who was therefore seen by the Italian government and nationalist movements as having Austrian leanings.

The United States started pouring men, cannons, planes, trucks, munitions, and thousands of tons of supplies of all kinds into the western front and, via Alaska, into Russia. The supplies to Russia stopped, however, with the Bolshevik revolution. On January 8, 1918, Wilson disseminated his "Fourteen Points." This act was in preparation for the much-hoped-for end to the war, out of which should be created a League of Nations (the precursor of the United Nations). Wilson's principal points were as follows:

- secret agreements between states should be prohibited;
- there should be complete commercial freedom throughout the world;
- foreign troops should leave Russia (thus clearing the way for the Bolsheviks in October 1917);
- Alsace and Lorraine should be handed back to France;
- Italian-speaking territories should be given back to Italy (which also managed to get the South Tyrol);
- the Balkan states should be provided with some guarantee of stability;
- the creation of an independent Poland should be supported.

Wilson's "Fourteen Points" were inspired by a Realpolitik as well as by vision and unquestionable wisdom, and were for the most part accepted at the Versailles peace conference. In the meantime, since the Americans found themselves fighting a war, they decided to do it properly. Because they only had a small volunteer army, Congress immediately passed a law regarding conscription. The US Army was thus increased thirtyfold, and soon four million men were ready to embark and be thrown into the inferno of the war. Of these four million, 90 percent were sent to France, to reinforce the British Expeditionary Force, although 8 percent of the conscripts did not speak English but only Spanish. Then there was problem of the black Americans. There were 10,000 black Americans in the volunteer army, but given the racial prejudice of their white fellow soldiers, they were put in separate units with officers of their own color. But how would these 200,000 black conscripts be received at the front?

The fears were quickly dissipated: the French soldiers welcomed the black soldiers from across the ocean as comrades on an equal footing. They brought jazz music with them, which was popular among the French soldiers. In particular, the performances given in the area behind the front by the band of the 15th New Yorker Regiment were a great success. In October 1917 the Americans, white and black, moved up to the front line and started to suffer casualties. They proved to be brave soldiers. Commanded by General John Pershing, they had a fundamental role to play in the Allied counteroffensive in July-August 1918. A total of more than 100,000 American soldiers men died. Officers who would later have glorious military careers gained their first experience of war in the trenches of Champagne. Among them were Douglas MacArthur and George Patton. In general, the optimism and courage of the Americans boosted the morale of the men at the front, exhausted after four years of battles and killing. American soldiers also fought on the Italian front. Among them was Ernest Hemingway, who was an ambulance driver, then an infantryman in the Italian infantry. He wrote two novels based on his military service in the Veneto, *Across the River and Into the Trees* and *A Farewell to Arms*.

84
Above, American machine-gunners of the 23rd Infantry Regiment in action in the French woodlands; below, a French Renault tank protecting the American advance.

85
Infantrymen from the 18th Regiment of the American First Division resting amidst the bombed remains of St. Mihiel, after a long, exhausting march.

THE PUTSCH OF LENIN
1917

The Russian rebellion in March 1917 took the governments at war by surprise. There were strikes in the factories, mutinies at the front and behind the front, and soldiers who refused to repress the turmoil in the capital, Petrograd. Discontent had been simmering for a long time before it finally exploded. The soldiers at the front were demoralized by the terrible massacres that swept through them. In addition to the nearly 2 million who died, 3 million were wounded and 2.5 million had been taken prisoner. In the major cities essential food was in short supply as the young peasant farmers and field-workers called to arms had to abandon their crops. There was risk of famine. The riots that culminated on March 8 with the Petrograd uprising forced the government led by Golitsin to resign. Prince Lvov replaced him; his first action was to suggest that the Tsar abdicate. But nobody in the imperial family was willing to take up the Tsar's heavy burden and so Russia remained without a head of state, while executive power passed to the Duma (the parliament) in Petrograd. Lvov's government was also of short duration. He decided to resign and was succeeded by Alexander Kerensky, a lawyer and famous political orator who, since he belonged to the Revolutionary Socialist Party, pleased the working class. He had served as minister of war in Lvov's government. In spite of his party's name, Kerensky was not a defeatist; on the contrary, he was an ardent patriot, and his government' goal was to re-enter the war against Germany and drive the enemy out of Russian territory once and for all. He therefore undertook an exhausting but successful series of visits to the front, making ardent speeches to the troops. While the members of his party and those of the Democratic Constitutional Party (KD: the Cadet Party) gave him their full support, the pacifist elements in the Social Democratic Party disagreed with him. First in Petrograd and then in the other major cities of Russia, the Social Democrats set up "councils of workers and soldiers," in favor of peace at any price. Two former leaders of the Marxist revolution of 1905, Vladimir Ulyanov (Lenin) and Lev Davidovich Bronstein (Trotsky), who were in exile, agreed to join the "Councils" or "Soviets." They had both fled to escape death sentences the Tsar imposed after the disturbances of 1905. Lenin was living in exile in Switzerland, after spending much time in Italy; Trotsky was in the United States. Of the two men, Lenin had the higher standing, given his following among the extremists on the revolutionary movement's fringes. What better opportunity could the Germans have asked for than to create confusion among the enemy ranks? They contacted him and organized and financed his return to Petrograd in a special train. Here he began his political agitation, writing newspaper articles, holding assemblies in the factories, and taking an active part in the meetings of the Soviets of workers and soldiers in Petrograd. The Soviets' membership had split into two: the Mensheviks ("the majority") and the Bolsheviks ("the minority," to which Lenin belonged). Lenin was therefore an agitator with a limited following who preached violence. His thesis can be summarized in four points: • immediate end to the war with surrender to Germany, which organized and paid for his return to Russia; • abolition of the Duma, to be replaced by representatives elected by the Soviets (therefore, only soldiers and workers could vote); • nationalization of the land and the banks (therefore, the abolition of privately owned real estate (including that of small-holders), introduction of the "kolkhoz" (collective farm), and end of private finance), and abolition of the army, to be replaced by a "people's militia." It was a plan that appealed only to a very few fanatics. However, two events that occurred within a few weeks of each other were to alter the situation in his favor. The first was the Social Democrat Party's failure to convince their fellow parties in the various warring countries to take part in an international conference to be held in Stockholm. The conference's goal was to discuss solidarity among the workers of the world and pressure the powers to end the war. But the Social Democrats' plan failed: no social democrat party was prepared to go to the conference; national interests were more important than Marx's utopian ideas. The second event was the General Kornilov's putsch. In September 1917 he tried to return the Tsar to the throne. His attempt failed, although he did help Lenin to obtain a majority in the Petrograd Soviet. Secure in his new position of power, Lenin organized the attack on the Winter Palace on November 6, 1917 (October 25th, according to the Eastern Orthodox calendar). The palace was the seat of government. From the cruiser *Aurora*, which was moored close to the building, the sailors of the Soviet fired a few rounds while the "*Red Guards*" of the Soviet entered the courtyard, after overwhelming and forcing the military cadets on sentry duty into surrender. Kerensky fled and Lenin convened an all-Russian conference of workers' and soldiers' councils. The response, however, was considerably less than all-Russian: at the opening of the conference the participants were almost exclusively limited to those from Petrograd. Although this state of affairs should have facilitated Lenin's plans, he found himself once more without a majority, since the Menshevik and Social Revolutionary representatives refused to recognize the new all-Bolshevik government he had proposed. The Mensheviks and Social Revolutionary representatives abandoned the conference in protest. Trampling on every democratic rule, safe in the knowledge that his Red Guards were behind him, Lenin forced through his plan: Yakov Sverdlov was appointed president of the Republic, Lenin himself was

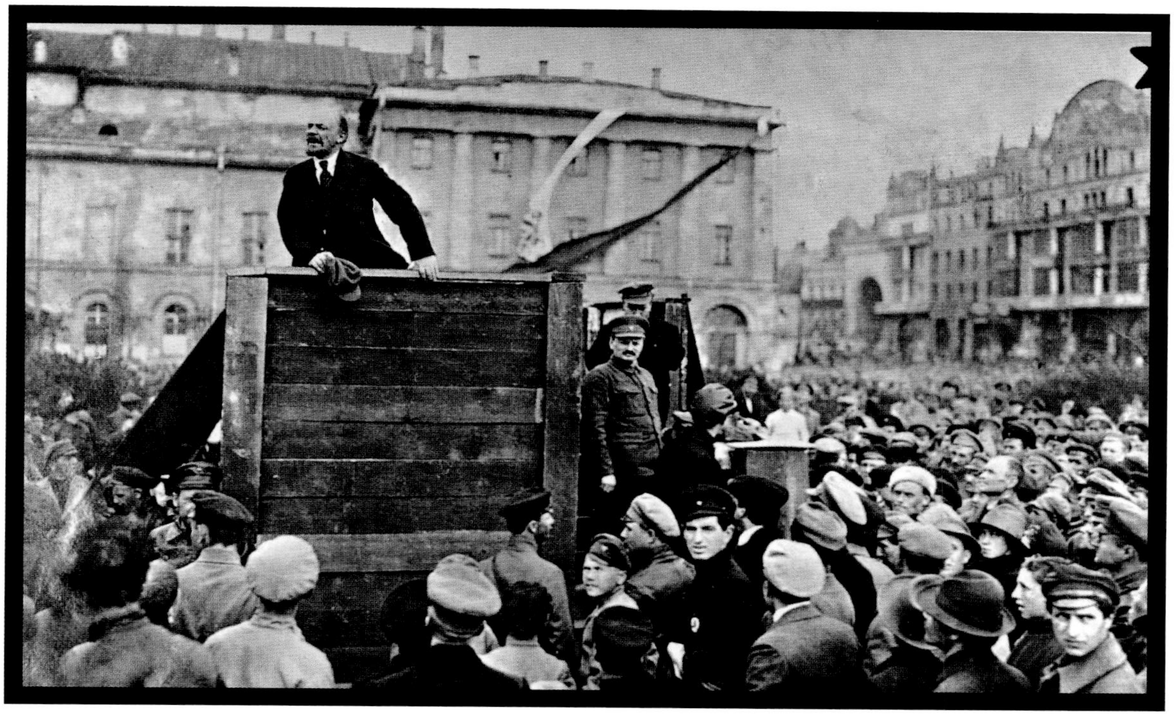

head of the government, and Leon Trotsky was minister of foreign affairs. The state's new name was to be the "Soviet Republic," later to become the "Union of Soviet Socialist Republics" (the USSR), which after years of bloodshed ceased to exist in 1991.The Soviet republic's reputation was tarnished in July 1918 by Petrograd's order for the assassination of the royal family at Yekaterinburg, where Tsar Nicholas, the Tsarina, and their children were held prisoner. The new régime fought and won a bloody civil war with the anti-communist White armies variously commanded by Kolchak, Denikin, Yudenich and Wrangel and supported by the victorious Allied coalition of World War I. But the USSR was not grateful to the true instigator of victory, Leon Trotsky, the head of the Red Army. Forced into exile in Mexico in 1927 after Stalin came to power, Trotsky was killed in 1940 by paid assassins sent by Moscow.

87
Photographs of the Bolshevik coup d'état under Lenin, which led to Russia's exit from the war. Top: Lenin, leader of the extremist (Bolshevik) faction of the Russian Socialist Party, is talking to the masses in Petrograd. On the right, on the stairs to the podium, is Leon Trotsky. Bottom: pictures were taken on November 7, 1917, during the assault on the Winter Palace.

"Cease Fire!"

1918

The Bolshevik coup d'état in October 1917, financed and supported by the German secret service to quash the Russian nationalist movements that gravitated around the Tsar, gave the Reich a comforting illusion. For a while Berlin believed Germany could still win the war, once freed from the nightmare of fighting on two fronts. On February 10, 1918, Trotsky, the Soviet Republic's newly appointed minister of foreign affairs, declared that Russia considered the war over and would therefore proceed to demobilize. It was a way of repaying the Germans for the help given to Lenin, but there was still a debt to pay. In fact, despite Trotsky's declarations, the Germans continued to advance from the point at which they had halted at the start of the Russian revolution. At this point the Soviet Republic was forced to yield to the enemy that was no longer an enemy in order to avoid the invasion of Moscow and Petrograd. On March 3, the Soviet Republic signed the Treaty of Brest-Litovsk. The new state accepted all of Germany's conditions: to give up Poland, Lithuania, and Estonia, and to recognize Finland and the Ukraine as autonomous and independent states. Germany, Austria-Hungary, Bulgaria, and Turkey signed the Treaty as victors.The German high command was now able to concentrate on its one western front. It still had 200 divisions with 3.5 million men, a force equal to that of the Allies before the United States started sending massive reinforcements. Four spring offensives were planned and carried out. The first offensive, launched on March 21 in Picardy, aimed to isolate the British Expeditionary Force and drive it back to the sea. But the maneuver failed, resulting in very heavy German losses and leaving 90,000 prisoners in enemy hands. The second, launched on April 9 in Lys, was more successful for the Germans, who managed a slow and exhausting advance into French territory. On May 27, the third offensive was launched between Soissons and Reims. The Germans captured the historic Chemin des Dames, crossed the Aisne and reached the Marne, where they were brought to a standstill. With the fourth offensive, begun on June 9, they did not manage to reach its target of Compiègne, which town, to underline the German defeat, was chosen as the place where the armistice was signed. Finally, on July 15, the German army launched a summer offensive on the Marne and in Champagne. But on July 18, generalissimo Ferdinand Foch, who in the interim had been named Allied commander-in-chief, launched a counteroffensive. Thanks to the rapid and constant flow of American troops and equipment and the heavy use of tanks, Foch was able to launch a series of uninterrupted counterattacks. By September he had forced the Germans to retreat to the Siegfried Line, the Reich's last line of resistance. The German soldiers stayed there without attacking until November 11 (when the armistice was signed at Compiègne). Twenty-two years later in the same forest of Compiègne, Hitler redeemed the shame of that day by forcing the French to sign their surrender to the Wehrmacht right there. On November 10 the day before the armistice was signed, Kaiser Wilhelm II fled to Holland, leaving Germany in a state of chaos. A few days previously, on November 4, Austria-Hungary had to sign the armistice with Italy. With Charles I's to exile in Switzerland on November 11, the Austro-Hungarian empire ceased to exist. Austria too was in a state of upheaval, with rioting and dissent. Hungary took advantage of the situation to declare itself an independent state. These events marked the end of the Triple Alliance and the Central Powers. World War I cost the lives of 9 million people, most of them under 30 years old. The Germans suffered the heaviest losses, with 2 million dead. The Russians followed with 1.7 million dead, then the French with 1.3 million, the Austro-Hungarians with 1.2 million, and finally the Italians with 600,000 dead. Hundreds of thousands of soldiers returned home mutilated, blinded by mustard gas, suffering from tuberculosis, or having lost their reason; they were broken in body and spirit. Their families received only very small war pensions. In Europe, monuments big and small were erected in memory of those who had died. Gigantic mausoleums were built in places like Verdun (France), Redipuglia (Italy), and Gallipoli (Turkey). They did not serve as an effective warning to future generations.

88
The picture captures the elation of the American troops on hearing the news that the war has ended, in November 1918.

89
War is over – a platoon of German soldiers makes one last, grief-stricken salute to fallen companions.

THE EUROPEAN REJECTION OF BOLSHEVISM

1918-1919

During 1917 the news from Petrograd resounded throughout Europe. First the March 1917 uprising and then Bolshevik putsch in October made headlines. This second event (which some cause-supporting newspapers erroneously called the "October revolution") directly contradicted the Second International's solemn but vain oath: "Never will a worker point a gun at another worker." But the European governments had nothing to fear. In Germany, Italy, and above all in France and England, the desire to crush the enemy was much stronger among the combatants than the desire for peace.

The situation changed as the war drew to a close. The first signs came from Germany. On October 29, 1918, units of the German Navy mutinied at Wilhelmshaven and, in imitation of events in Russia during the previous year, sailors set up a workers' and soldiers' council. As the situation at the front grew critical, a hundred revolutionary fires broke out within Germany. On November 7, an uprising broke out in Munich in which peasants from the Bavarian countryside joined the workers and soldiers. On November 9 it was Berlin's turn. Prince Max von Baden, the premier, resigned, realizing the city was in an uncontrollable state, with soldiers refusing to take orders from their officers. The Kaiser and the crown prince escaped to Holland; the few members of parliament who had reached the Reichstag declared the Republic, and Friedrich Ebert, president of the Social Democrats (Sozialistische Partei Deutschlands, SPD), formed a provisional government. However, there was nothing very Bolshevik about the plan. Ebert was in favor of a working class victory, but good German that he was, he first of all wanted order re-established.

It was to be expected. The Socialist movement's most extremist sections did not agree and set up in Berlin an "executive council of representatives of workers and soldiers," a sort of alternative government. The inspiration for the initiative came from the Spartacus League, whose leaders were Karl Liebknecht and Rosa Luxemburg. Karl Liebknecht (1871-1919), a social democratic member of parliament, wanted to keep faith with the decisions of the International. At the outbreak of war he had publicly denounced it and its supporters, and thus the Kaiser. He was arrested and spent four years in a labor camp. Released just when the front was beginning to collapse, he refused the post of minister in Ebert's government. Rosa Luxemburg (1870-1919) was a journalist of Polish origin who, at the beginning of the war, had incited the workers in rousing articles to strike in protest. She also was imprisoned; shortly after her release she founded and edited the weekly newspaper *Rote Fahne* (Red Flag).

On December 1, Rosa and Karl founded the German Communist Party. It was a combination of national sentiments and Russian rubles. On December 16, when members of the Spartacus League demonstrated for the first time in the streets of Berlin, they were confronted by government soldiers who shot directly into the crowd and killed sixteen people. After this deadly clash, Ebert hastened to form the Freikorps, units of ex-servicemen who had been left without jobs at the end of the war. They were given police work to do and were answerable to the minister for domestic affairs, the socialist Noske. For this reason Noske became known among Bolshevik supporters throughout the world as "Noske the traitor."

On December 23, the Wilhelmshaven sailors involved in November rebellion marched on the former Royal Palace in Berlin. At the head of the march were the Communist Party leaders. The sailors intended to arrest Ebert and put him on trial. But thirty of their number were killed by cannon fire from an artillery unit. The rebellion was reorganized, and on January 5, 1919, the members of the Spartacus League were once more ready to go into the streets and squares of the city, but this time they were armed. Violent and protracted fighting broke out. Ten days later (on January 15) Ebert put down the rebellion with the help of the Freikorps, who arrested and then tortured and killed the Communists in prison. Karl Liebknecht and Rosa Luxemburg were assassinated on the same day, January 15, after the Freikorps had destroyed and set fire to Communist Party headquarters.

In February, the Weimar Republic came into being, named after the town where the first assembly met. Ebert was elected president, and Philipp Scheidemann chancellor. Bolshevism was finished for good in Germany. It had no foothold at all in Hungary and Italy, at least up until the end of World War II. For a short while there was a coalition social democrat-communist government in Budapest, led by the Bolshevik Bela Kun. But domestic troubles, combined with an armed attack by Romanians and Czechs along the frontier, led him to resign. Admiral Miklos Horthy replaced him; he established a right-wing dictatorship. The Soviet attempt to found an Italian Communist party that might eventually come to power and act as a Russian fifth column

91
These pictures show the Spartacist revolt which flared up in Berlin after the German defeat. Top: crowds of demonstrators blocking one of the main thoroughfares of the city; bottom: the head of the pro-Soviet party, Karl Liebknecht, addressing the crowds.

92
The days of victory. Top: English folk in a festive mood, flying banners and flags on a double-decker bus in London; bottom: in Paris the US community celebrates victory.

in the West also failed. In 1921, Antonio Gramsci, Amadeo Bordiga, and Nicola Bombacci, all dissatisfied with the Socialist party, established the Italian Communist Party. They tried to bring the northern cities to a standstill through strikes and attacks on ex-servicemen and police forces. But they encountered violent opposition from Benito Mussolini's Fascist movement. The 1924 elections, which followed three years of civil war, brought the Fascists to power in their own right. Earlier (on October 28th) the party had joined a coalition government led by Mussolini. The Italian Communists were forced into exile in France or Russia. Exile proved bitter in the Russia of the faithful Palmiro Togliatti, the Russia of Stalin's persecutions. Several hundred Italian Communists were condemned as "deviationists" and killed in the Gulag, another bitter homage to the Communist tradition.

1919

THE TREATY OF VERSAILLES

1919

The post-World War I peace conference opened in Versailles on January 18, 1919. The representatives of the 32 victorious states participated; the defeated states were excluded. Among the nations "on trial" was Germany, whose delegation, headed by Count Brockdorff, was forced to remain outside the door and could only send in written notes. Among the "judges" were the so-called "Big Four": Woodrow Wilson for the United States, Georges Clemenceau for France, David Lloyd George for Great Britain, and Vittorio Emanuele Orlando for Italy, although Italy was not to have any decisive say in the proceedings. In essence France, Great Britain, and the United States made all the decisions. First, the conference formally accused Germany of causing the war: "The allied and associated governments declare--and Germany admits--that Germany and its allies are responsible for all the losses and damage suffered by the allied and associated governments as a result of the war that was forced on them by the aggression of Germany and its allies." This premise was necessary in order to be able to pass a judgment on the defeated power that required it to make reparation payments. These, the victors hoped, would reduce Germany to penury for at least 42 years--the period of time that Germany was granted to pay off the war debt in installments. It was an astronomical sum: 269 billion gold marks to be shared out as follows: 52% to France, 22% to Great Britain, 10% to Italy, 8% each to Belgium and the other Allies involved in the conflict. In addition, Germany had to hand over all its steamships over 1600 tons, half of those with a tonnage of between 1000 and 1600 tons, all the coal from its coal mines, all the herds produced on its farms and all butchered animals, and all its colonies. These territories were to be parceled out among France, Great Britain, and Japan (even though Japan, in that it had not sided with the Central Power, had nonetheless contributed minimally to the Allied victory). Italy, which had been promised a few crumbs from the German colonial empire, was left empty-handed. Furthermore, Germany was to lose Alsace and Lorraine, Poznan, East Prussia, Memel (Klaipeda), western Schleswig-Holstein, and some areas along the Belgian border, thus losing 13 per cent of its territory and 10 per cent of its population. In addition Germany had to give up Danzig (declared an open city), and was forced to demilitarize the west bank of the Rhine and demolish the military fortresses that had for centuries been its bastion. The army was dismembered and dissolved. Its armed forces, reduced to no more than 100,000 men, were to be called the "National defense army" (Reichswehr); it could not have tanks, submarines, or large-caliber artillery, and it was never to be commanded by a "General Staff." A few years later, Adolf Hitler was to disregard totally all these conference terms.

Although the principles of the peace conference were based on Woodrow Wilson's Fourteen Points, the clauses that Germany was forced to sign seem much more like revenge than justice. One clause (never implemented but successfully taken out and dusted off at the end of World War II) stated that the Kaiser and his generals should be handed over to an international court for the punishment of war crimes. For once Wilson's pacifist exhortations were listened to, and the League of Nations was founded, located in Geneva. Its members were to undertake never to go to war again to resolve their differences, and to set up an International Labor Organization with a mandate to pursue social justice and create humane working conditions. Clearly, the fear of a worldwide workers' revolution had given governments pause for thought.On June 28, 1919, five years after the Sarajevo assassination, the Treaty of Versailles was signed; it was followed by four other international treaties designed to resolve questions left unresolved at Versailles. The last of these treaties was signed in Lausanne on July 24, 1923. Among these treaties was one that established the reparation that Austria, now a republic, should make. Austria's army was to be limited to 30,000 men and the nation was not to unite with Germany (this explains why in 1938, in defiance of the Treaty of Versailles, Hitler called Germany's military occupation of Austria the "Anschluss" or union). Italy obtained more than it expected from Austria (not only the Italian province of Trent, but also the German-speaking South Tyrol), but less than it expected from the recently formed Yugoslavia; Italy was not allowed to annex the "Italianissimo" Istria and its capital Fiume. Austria-Hungary lost Slovakia to Prague; Croatia, Slovenia, and Bosnia to Yugoslavia; and Transylvania to Romania.The victors thus created a series of buffer states around Germany (Czechoslovakia, Austria, and Hungary) and, which was of more concern, around the Soviet Union (Finland, the Baltic republics, and a stronger Poland).The Ottoman Empire was the last of the four great empires (Turkey, Russia, Germany, Austria-Hungary) to be dismantled; in 1922 Turkey became a republic with Mustafa Kemal Atatürk as its leader. It lost vast territories, but they were not handed over to those who had a right to them (i.e., to the Arab people who had sided with the Allies and taken up arms against the Turks). The Turkish territories were divided, as territorial mandates, between Great Britain and France. Finally Rhodes and the Dodecanese were awarded to Italy; Cyprus and Egypt to Great Britain; the Aegean Islands and Smyrna to Greece. Armenia, whose people had been massacred by the Ottoman troops, finally became independent.

1920

THE

RUSSIAN-POLISH WAR

THE FACT THAT DURING WORLD WAR I POLES WERE FORCED TO FIGHT AMONG THEMSELVES RESULTED FROM THE PARTITIONS MADE IN THE LATE 18TH CENTURY. POLAND WAS DISMEMBERED THREE TIMES, AND ITS REMAINS ANNEXED TO THE THREE EMPIRES THAT WERE SUFFOCATING IT: THE TSARIST, THE AUSTRO-HUNGARIAN, AND THE PRUSSIAN.

As a result, the Austro-Hungarian army conscripted the Galicians of southern Poland (Galicia); the German army conscripted the young men of the Poznan region, and the Tsar's army took the Poles from the eastern regions.These young draftees, wearing three different uniforms, were flanked by units of Polish volunteers bent on taking up arms against the age-old German oppressor. One unit formed in by Polish expatriates in London was called the "English Legion." The second, formed in Russia, was named the "Russian Legion." But a third Polish Legion--composed entirely of volunteers--was established in Galicia by Jozef Pilsudski (1867-1935), a fifty-year-old revolutionary born in the Eastern territories. He exhorted his fellow citizens to fight to cast out the Russians. Pilsudski was also convinced that one day he would take up arms against the Germans and Austrians to free the Polish homeland once and for all from centuries of foreign domination.

The "Pilsudski Legion" was at the front lines from the beginning of the Galicia campaign and in combat was the first to penetrate the Russian regions. The Tsar's former prisoner (Pilsudski had been deported to Siberia in 1887 and was forced to perform hard labor until 1892) took his revenge for the hardships he had endured. But his rebellious spirit soon manifested itself again with his Austrian superiors, who had him arrested and interned. General Haller took up Pilsudski's torch, taking shelter in France with most of the Pilsudski Legion. These Poles, who fought against the Germans, just as the Anders Legion was destined to do during the Italian campaign in 1944-45 during World War II. When the two central European empires collapsed, the Polish population--which had regained the lands released by the Russians after the Treaty of Brest-Litovsk had no trouble disarming the Austrian and German troops, who had been left with neither orders nor an emperor. The Polish nation gave itself a single government, according to the terms established by the Versailles Conference. Not unexpectedly, the first president of the Polish Republic was Jozef Pilsudski. Having been oppressed for more than a century, the Poles were now seeking revenge through the military occupation of vast territories located beyond their border with Russia (now the USSR) that had been established by the Treaty of Brest-Litovsk. At the end of 1919, Chicherin, the Soviet foreign minister, made a proposal to Warsaw for reconciliation, and asked that the negotiations be carried out in a neutral city: London or Paris. But Pilsudski refused to believe that Russia had changed.

94
Marshal Jozef Pilsudski during a military parade. Pilsudski, a famous military leader and the first President of a free Poland, died in 1935. After the end of the World War I, Pilsudski formed a new, modern Poland, free and independent after more than a century of forced incorporation into Russia, Austria-Hungary and Germany.

95
A fallen Russian soldier at Bei Grodno in northeastern Poland during the advance of Pilsudski's troops, about to invade Kiev, capital of Ukraine. Pilsudski, who had spent five years as a prisoner in Siberia during the Czarist regime, attacked Bolshevik Russia on April 7, 1920.

THE RUSSIAN-POLISH WAR
1920

As far as Pilsudski was concerned, the Russians remained imperialists, even under the guise of Marxism. Having defeated the internal threat posed by the "white" armies of Kolchak, Denikin, and Yudenich, it was to be expected that, avid as always for booty, the Russians would then turn against Poland. He therefore decided to place at least two buffer countries between Polish and Soviet soil: White Russia (Byelorussia), whose capital was Minsk, and the Ukraine, whose capital was Kiev. But Poland could not succeed in a project of this scope could without first declaring war on Russia. Consequently, on April 7, 1920, Polish troops, backing the independent Cossacks led by Ataman Petlyura, marched on Kiev and conquered the city. This defeat stung the Russian. The appeal that the old Tsarist general Brusilov, hero of the Galicia offensive in 1914, had thrown at the Bolshevik soldiers to "win back Kiev" seemed to prove Pilsudski right: the Pole had never been duped by the scenario of "proletarian internationalism" preached by Lenin but detested by the Russian people. Kiev was recaptured by Budyenny's Cossack cavalry, the pride of the Red Army. Budyenny had already won dozens of battles against the Tsar's "white" avengers. And immediately after the re-capture of Kiev, this same cavalry, followed by the bulk of the Soviet army, set its sights on L'vov. Pilsudski waited in vain to receive supplies of arms and weapons from the West. His war had been painted by the mass media--always siding prejudicially with those who promise to liberate the exploited masses--as an "anti-proletarian war." As a result, German, English, French, and Italian workers, railwaymen, and sailors blocked the ships and trains heading for Poland. And it was no accident that the owners of those newspapers (namely, large-scale international financiers) were plotting with Lenin during those years, convinced that they could conquer new and more profitable markets for exploiting human resources. By August 13, 1920, the Russians were within sight of Warsaw. The foreign ambassadors fled and the only ones who remained at their headquarters were the papal nuncio, Monsignor Ratti (the future Pope Pius XI) and the Italian ambassador Tommasini. As the Russian cannons thundered on the outskirts of Warsaw, young farmers, students, and women hurried to enlist as volunteers, flinging themselves fervently against the invaders as trams loaded with the dead and wounded crossed the capital. Finally, Polish National Army began its the counteroffensive. General Sikorski, commanding the reserves, attacked the Red Army's right flank from the north, while Marshal Pilsudski, commanding the volunteers, attacked the left flank from the south. What the Poles continue even today to call "the miracle" came to pass: The Red Army dissolved and the Russians fled toward the border in disarray. During the Polish pursuit of the Russians, Sikorski penetrated Lithuania and occupied Vilnius. The armistice was signed in October. Pilsudski demanded territories much further east of the Curzon Line (adopted by the Versailles Conference as the Russian-Polish border). As a true victor, he annexed Volhynia, Polesie, and Podolia to Poland. The Conference of Ambassadors acknowledged the new boundaries in 1923. But Pilsudski's hopes of creating two vast buffer states (one in the Ukraine with 40 million inhabitants, the other in Byelorussia with 20 million) were dashed when the USSR annexed the two countries and transformed them into two "Soviet republics." Moreover, the regions incorporated by Pilsudski (who remained in power until his death in 1935) were to be a constant source of trouble for the Warsaw government. Disorders were fomented by the USSR, which thirsted for revenge--and obtained it when dividing up Poland with Hitler in late 1939.

96
A group of young Polish female volunteers being trained for the defense of Warsaw, under threat from General Budyenny, commander of the Cossack cavalry. Warsaw was saved by the "miracle" (as became known) of thousands of youths, students, girls and workers who with their makeshift forces heroically resisted the Russians.

97
Top: one of the few French tanks that reached Warsaw. Center: Polish volunteers marching. Bottom, on May 7, 1920 the Polish artillery entered Kiev, supporting the Ataman ("leader") Petlyura, who had rebelled against the Bolsheviks. The Russian-Polish war ended with the armistice of October 1920, which assigned to Poland large territories that had previously been Russian.

1920

THE

ITALIAN-ETHIOPIAN WAR

ON DECEMBER 5, 1935, ALONG THE BORDER BETWEEN THE ETHIOPIAN EMPIRE AND ITALIAN SOMALILAND, A RIFLE SHOT RANG OUT NEAR THE UAL-UAL WELLS. NO ONE WILL EVER KNOW EXACTLY WHO FIRST OPENED FIRE-THE ETHIOPIAN SOLDIERS OF THE NEGUS HAILE SELASSIE OR THE SOMALI "DUBATS" ENLISTED IN THE ITALIAN ARMY.

That rifle shot was following by a furious shootout with cannons and machine guns; when it was over, there were 137 bodies on the ground: 107 Ethiopians and 30 Dubats. For some time following the incident, responsibility for it was volleyed back and forth. Italy accused the Ethiopian troops of having attacked first. The Negus maintained exactly the opposite, and after futilely appealing to the "friendship pact" signed with Italy in 1928 and requesting international arbitration to settle the dispute, he turned to the League of Nations. Mussolini's response was an ultimatum to Haile Selassie: He had to hand over the responsible parties for punishment and reimburse Italy for damages. In 1935, Ras ("Prince") Tafari (the future Emperor Haile Selassie) was still the right-hand man of the Empress Zauditù. In 1923, he had succeeded in having Ethiopia admitted to the League of Nations. The following year, he made a triumphant tour of Europe with thirty servants, six lions, and four zebras. He visited Cairo, Marseilles, Rome, Paris, and London and had decided to transform Ethiopia into a modern nation. He built schools, hospitals, and roads, convincing the empress to abolish slavery with a decree that imposed the death penalty on anyone involved in trading slaves. On August 2, 1928, Ras Tafari signed a twenty-year friendship pact with Italy. When the empress died on April 3, 1930, he proclaimed himself "Negus Neghesti" ("king of kings"), taking the name of Haile Selassie ("Might of the Trinity"). Ambassadors from all over Europe attended his solemn coronation on November 2, 1930. Following Italy's ultimatum after the Ual-Ual incident, the showdown dragged on for ten months, giving Mussolini had all the time he needed to prepare his attack. He appointed General Emilio De Bono commander of operations and immediately started to send men and arms to Eritrea. During these ten months, 500 ships docked at Massowa bringing 200,000 Italian volunteers, 25,000 horses, 4200 vehicles, 600 cannons, 120 tanks, and an equal number of aircraft. Added to these forces were the 65,000 Eritrean "Askaris," who had long been faithful to Italy, and 100,000 Dubats from Italian Somaliland. In Italy, it was total mobilization: the radio, newspapers, magazines, movies, and newsreels spoke of nothing but East Africa. The stance taken by the League of Nations (which voted to adopt sanctions against Italy following the attack on Ethiopia, fatally pushing Mussolini toward Hitler) simply exasperated the Italian people's nationalist fervor. This objective was achieved on December 18, 1935--the day dedicated to "rings for the homeland." Even famous anti-Fascists like the philosopher Benedetto Croce donated their gold wedding rings. Mussolini and Fascism had never been so popular. On October 2, Il Duce stood on the balcony of the Palazzo Venezia in Rome to make one of his most famous speeches. The next day, Marshal De Bono crossed the Mareb, the river that marks the boundary between Eritrea and Ethiopia, while General Graziani attacked from Somaliland. In just a few days, the Italians conquered Adowa, Aksum, and Adigrat. Since De Bono refused to be flexible about instructions sent to him from

98
Italians advancing against Addis Ababa, the Ethiopian capital.

99
Haile Selassie with his bodyguards (above) abandons his capital to seek refuge in British-controlled territory.

THE ITALIAN-ETHIOPIAN WAR
1935-1936

Rome, Mussolini replaced him with Marshal Pietro Badoglio. For Fascist leaders, going off to fight in Ethiopia became an obligation. The air raids of the "Caproni" bombers multiplied. Members of the "La Disperata" squadron included Galeazzo Ciano (Mussolini's son-in law), Mussolini's sons Bruno and Vittorio, flying ace Ettore Muti, and poet Filippo Tomaso Marinetti, while the secretary of the Fascist Party, Achille Starace, commanded a motorized column.

The princes leading the Ethiopians, Ras Mulughietà, Ras Cassa, and Ras Immirù, resisted, for each had about 60 to 70 thousand men under them, and a total of 13 old airplanes but no tanks. In particular, Ras Immirù won back Sciré and entered Eritrea. At this point, the war turned violent and ruthless. The Italians used asphyxiating gas, despite the fact that the Geneva Convention banned such gas. The battle against Ras Immirù to regain Sciré was an extremely difficult one. Sixty Italian officials and 894 soldiers lost their lives. But the road to Addis Ababa was opened.The Italians' last battle was fought against the imperial guard at Mai-Ceu. The "Pusteria" Division of the Italian Alpine troops prevailed. On May 5, 1936, at 4 o'clock in the afternoon, Italian troops entered Addis Ababa. In Rome, Mussolini, alerted by telegram, appeared at the fateful balcony. The square was already crowded with people. "The war is over! Peace has returned! But it is a Roman peace!" announced Il Duce as the shouts of the crowd drowned out his words. To hear Mussolini's speech at 9:30 on the evening of May 9 over 30 million delirious people crowded city squares all over Italy, connected by radio to the Palazzo Venezia and equipped with cumbersome loudspeakers. The crowd went wild. Following his speech, Mussolini had to come back out onto the balcony 42 times! After the war, Italy finally had an enormous amount of territory at its disposal as an outlet for its rapidly growing population but only 3500 farming families (for a total of 30,000 people) moved to Ethiopia to reclaim and cultivate 120 thousand hectares of land of the 50 million available. A pittance! The true reason for this failure lay in the fact that Ethiopia was by no means a peaceful land. Instead, it was a country that fell prey to unending violent and bloody guerrilla warfare. The war had lasted seven months, with 2000 Italians and several thousand Ethiopians, Somali Dubats, and Eritrean Askaris among the among the dead. But the guerrilla warfare was destined to last five years, taking a far greater toll in human lives: 5000 Italians and an unknown number of Abyssinians. Following the conquest of Addis Ababa, "sciftà" (bandits) infested the country. In reality, Ras Immirù, Ras Cassa, and Ras Destà had 50,000 men armed under the their command. The towns of Goggiam, Gimma, Scioà, Galla Sidamo, and Harar were in the hands of the rebels. On May 22, 1936, General Badoglio passed the insoluble situation onto to his rival, General Rodolfo Graziani.The guerrilla actions and attacks were countless. On June 27, 1936, three hundred Ethiopians--former officer cadets--attacked an Italian barracks and killed the general of the air brigades, Vincenzo Magliocco, and eleven airmen. On July 28, Ras Cassa's two sons, Averà and Asfawossen, entered Addis Ababa with two thousand "sciftà" but were repelled. Graziani executed Alba Petros, the Abuna of Dessié and the brains behind the attack. General Tracchia captured the Ras' two sons and had them shot.On February 19, 1937, an attempt was made on General Graziani's life. This act was followed by harsh repressions. Surrounded by his faithful followers, Ras Destà went to Egià on February 24 and asked to speak to General Graziani. In response, he was shot in the back of the head.The new leader of the revolt was Abebe Aregai, former chief of the municipal guards in Addis Ababa, who two years later, in 1939, the exiled Negus would name commander-in-chief, as all the Ras were gone. On June 10, 1940, the guerrilla action turned into full-fledged war, which was quickly won by the Ethiopians thanks to the military aid of the English. Emperor Haile Selassie, the Negus now in exile, had fled Addis Ababa at dawn on May 2, 1936. He reached Djibouti, where the British cruiser "H.M.S. Enterprise" was waiting for him. This marked the beginning of his exile in England, as well as the deadly confrontation between Mussolini's government and Great Britain. During his five years in exile, which he spent on an estate in Bath, near London, Haile Selassie followed and guided the resistance of his faithful Ras against the Italians. When the League of Nations legitimized the Italian conquest of Ethiopia, he went to Geneva to protest, speaking before representatives from all over the world. Following the defeat of the Italians in East Africa during World War II, he chose the date of May 5, 1941 for his triumphant return to Addis Ababa--the anniversary of Badoglio's triumph in Ethiopia and Mussolini's in Rome.

101

Top, a death scene in a Somali village hit by Italian bombs (the Italians also dropped asphyxiating gas bombs). Center, Askaris on camels. Traditional enemies of the Ethiopians, they became allies of the Italian army. Bottom, a moment of victory: after the start of World War II, Ethiopian soldiers loyal to Haile Selassie cross the Omo river to regain Ethiopia.

1935
1936

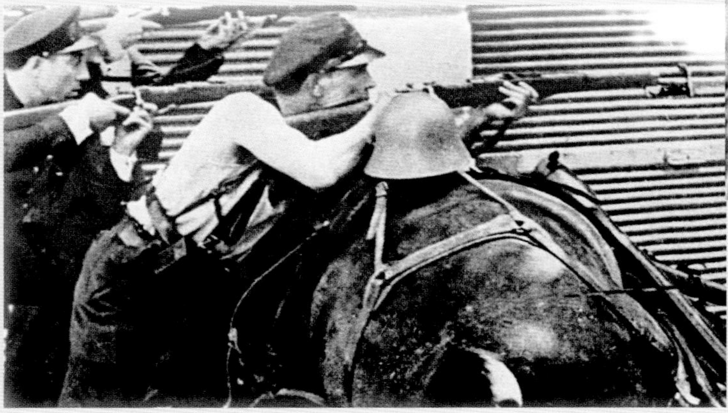

1936
1939

THE

SPANISH WAR

ALTHOUGH KNOWN IN HISTORY AS THE "SPANISH CIVIL WAR," THIS HARSH MILITARY CONFRONTATION, WHICH TOOK PLACE BETWEEN JULY 17, 1936, AND MARCH 31, 1939, IS BETTER DEFINED AS THE "SPANISH WAR." ACCORDING TO THE MOST AUTHORITATIVE HISTORIAN ON THE SUBJECT, THE ENGLISHMAN HUGH THOMAS, IT COST A MILLION LIVES.

Though the war was fought in Spain, the leading European powers sent in much weaponry and numerous combatants. In particular Stalin's USSR, Hitler's Germany, Mussolini's Italy, and Léon Blum's Popular Front coalition in France did so, divided as they were by profound ideological hatred, with Germany driven by the desire to avenge its defeat in World War I. It was essentially a war between Fascism and Communism, two opposing ideologies and two irreconcilable world views. From a military standpoint, it was the dress rehearsal for World War II, the ideological war par excellence, as never before seen in history.

Years of disorder and civil dissent preceded the outbreak of the war. In 1931, following General Miguel Primo de Rivera, Marquis of Estella's seven-year dictatorship, the Spanish people, as ordered by King Alfonso XIII, went to the polls. The Republican parties won a majority of the votes. The King deduced the consequences of this and went into exile. The republic was established, and it passed a socialist-style constitution that, among other restraining institutions, created a highly politicized police force, the "Asaltos." The right reacted on both the Monarchical-Catholic and the Fascist fronts. Among factions favoring the monarchy, the most combative ones were the Carlists, also known as the "requetés" (coined from the contraction of the ancient expression used by their forerunners in the Carlist war, who responded to the greeting "Todo bien?" by answering "Requetebién"--"Very well"). Among the Fascists, the most feared group was the Falangist group, founded in 1933 by José Antonio Primo de Rivera, son of the general who died in 1930. The Falangists went about armed and uniformed, like the Fascist squads in Italy in 1921-22. Their greeting was "Cáfe" ("Camaradas! Arriba Falange Española!"—"Comrades! Long live the Spanish Falange!"). The domestic situation, already unstable, came to a head with the political elections in February 1936. These resulted in the victory of the Popular Front coalition, encompassing all the left-wing parties. Manuel Azaña was elected president of the republic, with Quiroga as premier. In just over four months, there were 260 political murders, 70 party headquarters were devastated, 10 newspaper offices were destroyed, and 340 strikes blocked the nation's economic development. Monarchist José Calvo Sotelo, former minister of finance in Primo de Rivera's dictatorial government, launched into a harsh tirade in parliament against the Quiroga government. Communist deputy Dolores Ibárruri, "la Pasionaria," retorted, calling him a Fascist. His answer was heated: "Better dictatorship than chaos. I declare myself a Fascist!" The next day (July 12), unknown killers assassinated Lieutenant Castillo of the Asaltos. That night, a group of Asaltos knocked at the door of Calvo Sotelo, who vainly invoked parliamentary immunity. He was forced to get dressed and go with them "to be interrogated." He sat in the front seat of the car. During the trip, he was killed with two gunshots to the base of his skull, shot by police lieutenant Cuencas. His bloody body was thrown into a cemetery. On July 17, the nationalist military revolt broke out in Ceuta and in Melilla, Spanish Morocco. The "Tercio Extranjero," the Spanish Foreign Legion, occupied the public buildings. Any military official who opposed the revolt were shot. The password for all military headquarters in mainland Spain was broadcast by radio from Morocco: "Sin novedad" ("No news"). This was equivalent to an order for each command to take over in its own district. The plan had been prepared the year before by a very young general, Francisco Franco Bahamonde, immediately after he had been named

102

Top: Generalissimo Francisco Franco Bahamonde at the front; center: Communist militias exchanging fire with the enemy early in the Civil War, started with the Alzamiento (the uprising) of military units stationed in Morocco. Bottom: Attention! – Nationalist troops after the relief of the Alcazar in Toledo, on September 28, 1936.

commander-in-chief of the army as a reward for putting down a revolutionary insurrection in Asturias. Nevertheless, the "Alzamiento" (The Uprising) was not led by Franco but by 64-year-old General José Sanjurjo, who was in exile in Portugal. According to the insurrectionary plans, he was to take over the government leadership. Everyone awaited him. In the meantime, Seville fell: General Queipo de Llano, commander of the Carabiñeros, took the city after violent clashes in the streets against the Asaltos and armed workers, who had set eleven churches on fire. Two hundred thousand workers mobbed Madrid, addressed by Dolores Ibárruri. That day, "la Pasionaria" launched what would become the motto of the war: "No pasaran!" ("They shall not pass!"). The military commander of the capital sided with the workers, and 10,000 rifles were distributed to union organizations.On July 20, an airplane took off from a small airport outside Lisbon. On board was General Sanjurjo. Sanjurjo was killed on thatplane when it crashed, and leadership of the revolt was handed over to Franco. Franco was born in 1892 in El Ferrol, Galicia. At just twenty years of age he was an official in Morocco, where he put a bloody end to an Arab revolt. At the age of 33, he was the youngest general in the world. Ruthless in his actions against the Asturian miners in 1934, he was named commander-in-chief, but in February of 1936, President Azaña dismissed him and "exiled" him to the command of the Canary Islands garrison. After proclaiming a state of emergency and handing power over to the military throughout the country, Franco left the Canary Islands to take over the general headquarters in Ceuta.

The first generals to obey Franco's call to authority and fake power firmly into their own hands were General Mola in Pamplona and General Cabanellas in Saragossa. But Spain's internal clash immediately became an undeclared international war. As early as July 30, the first Italian and German planes landed in Morocco, bringing the help that Franco had requested. This occurred after the French government, composed of the Popular Front coalition (left-wing parties), had sent 30 military aircraft to Madrid with French crews. While Hitler authorized his airmen only to deliver the aircraft and then come home immediately, the Italian airmen arrived to fight the "Reds." The Italians were led by Colonel Ruggero Bonomi and air ace Ettore Muti, both returning from the recently ended Italo-Ethiopian War. This Italian participation strengthened relations between Rome and Berlin and cooled the older alliance between Italy on the one side and France and England on the other. At this point, Mussolini became Hitler's surest ally. To avoid triggering international diplomatic trouble, the Italian airmen enlisted in the "Tercio" as volunteers. They represented the vanguard of what was to become a substantial contribution to military airborne operations: the "Italian Legion" with 6000 airmen and 710 planes (Fiat fighters, Savoia-Marchetti bombers, and Breda combat planes). Soon Hitler also authorized the recruitment of 16,000 German volunteers (flying combat planes and driving tanks). Some 300 of them died in battle. The Republican side of the Spanish conflict received 260 airplanes from France, 60 from Great Britain, and 72 from the United States, all without crews. Soon, however, the USSR sent 2000 planes (the SB-2 Katiuska and the I-16, renamed the "Moscow"), flown by expert Soviet pilots. By the end of the war, 1900 "Republican" airplanes had been downed or destroyed on the ground, 210 managed to escape to France or French Algeria, and the remainder were captured by Franco's sympathizers. What pushed Stalin to get so involved in the Spanish War? First, it was a matter of prestige: he could not allow the only openly Marxist government to be formed in Western Europe to be suffocated by the Monarchist-Fascist reaction. Second, by helping Republican Spain to resist, he was pursing his goal of widening the gap that now divided the capitalist powers of the West--Italy and Germany on the one hand, and France and England on the other. Still, Stalin could not overdo any military commitment to the Republicans since he had participated in the "Non-intervention Committee" meeting held in London on September 9, 1936, which had the declared purpose of averting a worldwide conflagration. This need, which on the one hand restricted the USSR, gave rise to the formation of the International Brigades on the other.

Since the first onset of hostilities, the Comintern--the Communist International encompassing the ranks of the Moscow-funded European Communist parties - began to recruit volunteers. A propaganda campaign was launched in Europe and America. The main recruiting office was located in Paris and was run by Willy Münzenberg, a German Communist exiled in the USSR. Moscow sent the Italians Palmiro Togliatti ("Ercole Ercoli") and Vittorio Vidali ("Carlos Contreras") to Madrid as government "advisers." Many Italian expatriates in Paris, such as the Republican Randolfo Pacciardi and liberal Carlo Rosselli, founder of "Giustizia e Libertà"--while not Communists--joined the International Brigades. Italians were the leaders of the International Brigade's military forces. Chief among them was Luigi Longo ("Gallo"), who organized and trained foreign volunteers in Albacete, Spain. In December 1936, Longo became the inspector general for all the international brigades. During the Italian civil war from 1943-45, Longo headed the "Garibaldi" brigade and was later responsible for executing Mussolini. The Comintern did its job well. Idealists and libertarians of all types fought side by side, but the Communists were in command, and all the tactical and strategic decisions were made at the Russian embassy in the capital. The Spanish republic's military situation reflected its political one. Through the unity and discipline of its upper echelons, the Communist party by the end of the year monopolized nearly all military, public, and civil offices. The Party achieved this in part through its adroit adulation of the new government leader, Largo Caballero, praised as "the Spanish Lenin," and its motto: "Let's win the war first; we'll talk about our differences later." The man who imposed this line of action was party secretary José Diaz, but the person who invented and decided all this was Stalin's man in Madrid: Palmiro Togliatti, the future head of the Italian Communist Party. While the Italians were the brains behind the International Brigades, the fighters themselves were of all nationalities. They came from all over the world — 40,000 of them, as Franco himself admitted during a June 1927 discussion with Hitler's envoy. They fought honorably until the autumn of 1938, the date of the terrible battle of the Ebro. Enlisted alongside workers and intellectuals who had fled from Fascist Italy and Nazi Germany were artists, anarchists, and writers. These men of letters included George Orwell, poets such as W. H. Auden, and journalists and novelists such as André Malraux and Ernest Hemingway. The first foreign military formation one to enter the fray was the 11th International Brigade (led by General Lazar Stern, later by General Enrique Lister); it was involved in defending Madrid as early as November 1936. The 11th was followed by the legendary 12th, the Garibaldi Brigade, composed mainly of Italians led by Randolfo Pacciardi. (Several times in the post-World War II period, this unyielding anti-Communist served as a minister in Italian governments, together with Edgardo Sogno, a national hero of Italy's wartime Resistance.) Fighting as captain in the ranks of the Garibaldi was Pietro Nenni, Benito Mussolini's youthful companion in their early socialist struggles but now divided from him by profound enmity. The Garibaldi Brigade's Italians became the heroes of the defense of Madrid's University City area. While one Italian faction was the International Brigades' decisive core, another faction was Franco's leading ally, demonstrating the hatred between the Italian right and left wings, a hatred destined to last for decades. In July 1936, Mussolini had sent planes and tanks (and crews) to Spain by sea. In December, he sent the first officially sponsored infantry regiments. These were the "Frecce Nere" and "Frecce Azzurre" brigades, and they were followed by the "Littorio," "Fiamme Nere," and "23 Marzo" divisions. Of the foreign contingents involved in the Spanish War on the Nationalist side, the Italian were the most numerous and battle-hardened (with 50,000 regulars), then the Portuguese (20,000 men), the German (15,000), and the Irish (nearly 1,000 volunteers).

When the hostilities broke out, nearly 310,000 Republican fighters--who were undisciplined, poorly armed, not professionally trained, and often led by would-be commanders--faced 210,000 Nationalists. The government army, whose soldiers wore light-blue or gray uniforms with a red star pinned to their berets, was composed mainly of Spaniards (about 20,000 career military or enlisted men and nearly 300,000 volunteer militiamen). The Nationalist army was instead a multiethnic one in which were Italian Fascists and Primo de Rivera's Spanish Falangists. However, command was solidly in the hands of Francisco Franco, the "generalissimo" or "Caudillo". The Nationalist generals - Mola in the north and Queipo de Llano in the south - had highly professional and well-disciplined units at their disposal. They also had 15,000 Monarchist volunteers in the north, who marched into battle waving Carlist flags and saying the rosary, and the Falangist volunteers in the south, who were organized into 100-men units. Arriving from Africa were the Moroccan "Tabores" (troops on horseback) and the "Banderas" of the "Tercio," whose motto "Viva la muerte!" ("Long live death!") had been coined by General Millan Astray, a war hero worshipped by his men. During combat against the Moroccan rebels, he had lost an eye, an arm, and a leg. These men, who in just a matter of months took Cádiz, Córdoba, Granada, Badajoz, and Toledo, then began to lay siege to Madrid. After taking Granada, the Nationalists took revenge by killing the great poet García Lorca, who had taken refuge in his brother-in-law's house, the Socialist mayor of the city, who was also shot. Following the hard fight to conquer Talavera (September 4, 1936), the Nationalists hurried to liberate the Alcázar de Toledo, under attack by the Republicans. The Nationalist Colonel José Moscardo had barricaded himself with his men in the old military school. The colonel had refused to surrender, even after the Republicans let him talk by phone to his son --who had been taken prisoner--warning him that if he refused to lay down his arms, they would have his son shot. Moscardo refused to be blackmailed and the boy was killed before his very eyes. Led by General Varela, the Nationalists entered Toledo after defeating 5000 militiamen during the battle of Bargos. On September 28 they liberated the Alcázar. Moscardo became the national hero of the Spanish War. The Nationalist offensive against Madrid began on October 19. The city was defended by enormous Republican forces supplied by Russian ships at the ports of Barcelona, Cartagena, and Valencia. The Russians and the pro-Nationalist Italians had their first skirmish on October 29: the Soviet tanks had to retreat. The Republican air force--also Soviet-supplied--was unable to intervene in the battle; nearly all the airplanes, intercepted by Italian aircraft commanded by Ettore Muti, were downed. On November 4, Franco's columns were within sight of the capital. At the beginning of November, the divisions led by generals Mola and Varela entered the suburbs of Madrid, defended by 40,000 fighters under General Miaja (Asaltos, Anarchists, International Brigades, and regulars). The government fled to Valencia, while Azaña, the president of the republic, fled to the convent of Monserrat in Barcelona. Four Nationalist columns led the attack. "The fifth column," stated Mola, "is already in the city." But the Nationalists' "fifth column" was not the only one in the city. Alongside Miaja, the Russian generals Ivan Antonovich Berzin, head of the NKVD (the former OGPU and future KGB) and Jacob Smuckevic, commander of the Soviet air force, were planning the city's defense. In the government's stead was a "Junta de defensa" led by Italian Vittorio Vidali and Russian journalist Mikhail Koltsov, a personal friend of Stalin, who was directly in contact with the Soviet dictator. At the front lines, were two figures who were destined to become legends: Anarchist Buenaventura Durruti, who arrived from Catalonia at the head of 3500 Anarchists, and the Communist Valentin Gonzales, nicknamed "El Campesino" ("the Farmer"). He was indeed a farmer, a giant in stature with outstanding physical strength. His shadow was another mysterious Soviet agent known as "Medina," about whom nothing more was ever learned. One of the stars of the major battles--from Madrid to Guadalajara to Teruel--"El Campesino" was to escape to Russia, where he ended up as one of the dissidents persecuted by Stalin, who interned him in Vorkuta Gulag. From here, he managed to escape to France and finally returned to Spain following Franco's death. He was certainly not the only Communist fighter whose political faith led him to an unexpected fate. Things went much worse for his companion Durruti. On November 21, after he had clashed with the Russian "advisers," his body was found in the middle of the battle of Madrid. Hit by a stray bullet, recounted his closest comrades. Under the orders of Miaja and Gonzales, barricades were set up and the women's battalions, organized by "La Pasionaria," came to the front. The women were ready to pour boiling oil on the Nationalists from their windows. The arrest and shooting of suspected Falangists and their families was the order of the day. In Madrid's jails, the Communist guards slaughtered 600 political prisoners. The execution squads were led by the future Soviet marshal Konstantin Rokossovski (under the nom-de-guerre of "Miguel Martinez"). Another 400 prisoners met the same fate a few days later. The first head-on clash between the Nationalists and Republicans occurred at the University City, defended by the 11th and 12th International Brigades. The battle raged along the Manzanares river. Numerous Italian aircraft bombed the Republican trenches, while German airmen of Condor Legion bombed military targets in the city. At the beginning of December, the siege of Madrid was over. The Nationalists were forced to retreat to their starting position. After the month of fighting, the two sides counted 12,000 dead, mainly Nationalists. On February 5, 1937, the Italian pro-Nationalist divisions led the attack on Málaga and entered the city on February 8. The Republicans were pursued to Motril and thousands were captured. Exhilarated by this success, Mussolini was convinced that winning a few more battles like that of Málaga was all. He sent another division, the "Littorio," to Spain, and ordered General Mario Roatta to take command of all the Italian units (they numbered 30,000 men at that time) united in the VTC (Volunteer Troop Corps). The next Nationalist target was Guadalajara, north of Madrid. The battle commenced on March 8, 1937. Lined up of the defending side were 60,000 Republicans, including the Italians from the Garibaldi Brigade, with 60 Russian tanks. After two days the Fascists were forced to retreat to the Carretera de France. They left 500 dead behind, and 300 prisoners in Republican hands. A thousand men were wounded. The Republicans' losses were even higher: 5000 dead or wounded and 500 prisoners. It was a meager victory for the Republicans, who nevertheless exploited the "victory of Guadalajara" for anti-Fascist propaganda. The Garibaldi Brigade was to be avenged in August with the capture of Santander.

The explosion of hatred against the Catholic Church and its representatives during the Spanish War deserves its own chapter. There is a symbolic photograph of the war showing a platoon of militiamen as they "shoot" the statue of Christ the Redeemer at Cierro de los Angeles, during the siege of Madrid. By the end of the hostilities, 4184 clerics, had been assassinated, a total that included 14 bishops, 2365 friars, and 283 nuns. Some 150 churches were completely destroyed, while 4850 were devastated and desecrated. Never before in history had the Catholic Church been struck so savagely. Not even the later Romans had accomplished so much in three centuries. Some priests were crucified; others were cut to pieces or buried alive. The Communist militiamen tortured priests and nuns before bloodthirsty crowds. A crucifix was rammed down the throat of the mother of two priests; drunk militiamen donning religious habits made obscene gestures and committed other acts of turpitude inside churches; nuns were raped before being massacred with rifles run through their genitals. (After the Liberation, the French and Italian Communists perpetrated similar barbarities on women who had fought alongside the Nazis or Fascists.) The Anarchists in particular had "specialized" in digging up the bodies of saints and defecating on them. For their part, the government authorities were preoccupied only with preserving the works of art kept in the churches. After this, a semblance of legality took over, not in the sense that the religious were spared. They continued to be assassinated, but only after "due process" for "abetting the enemy." In the meantime, all the churches were transformed into warehouses and stalls, as had been done in Russia following Lenin's coup. The brutishness that the Anarchists showed toward the religious did not save them from a tragic day of reckoning with the Communists. The clash between the two most violent ideologies of the Spanish War was due to the ironclad centralizing will of the Communist leaders sent by Moscow. Harsh encounters had already occurred in Madrid during the siege (such as Durruti's mysterious death). Subsequently, the Communists had attributed the fall of Málaga to the inexperience and presumed cowardice of the Anarchist formations. The final reckoning came between May 3 and 7, 1937, in Barcelona, when the Communists assassinated four hundred Anarchists and other dissidents. Among the victims were Trotskyite Andres Nin and the Italian Camillo Berneri, the leader of the anti-Fascist Anarchist resistance. This fraternal bloodbath, which Orwell describes in his novel *Homage to Catalonia*, led to the resignation of Largo Caballero's government and the nomination of Juan Negrín (a man suggested by the Soviet advisers) as the new premier. The year 1937 began with the Nationalists, led by General Mola, launching a major attack on the Basque provinces. Some 60,000 men (including two Italian divisions) moved against 45,000 Basques led by General Llano de Encomienda. The Basques were by no means Communists—rather, they were conservatives and Catholic. But in the summer of 1936, taking advantage of Spain's political crisis, the Basque leaders had finally succeeded in getting Madrid's approval to establish an independent republic. They were well aware that if Franco were to win, they would irrevocably return under Spanish domination so they decided to fight and to fight alone, because they received no help from Valencia, the seat of the government. The Nationalists marked the beginning of their offensive with the terror-bombing of Guernica, a Basque city with a population of 7,000 located 19 miles from Bilbao, in the province of Vizcaya (Biscay). Guernica is a holy city. It was the ancient religious capital of the Basques, where under the large oak tree their kings swore to respect freedom. Because of this, the German Condor Legion targeted it for carpet-bombing--the first in history--on April 26, 1937. It was a Monday, market day, and the streets were crowded with people. Suddenly and without any warning, the German airforce's Heinkel 111s and Junker 52s swooped down on the people and houses in successive waves, one every twenty minutes. The inferno lasted for three hours leaving 1700 dead and 900 wounded: not a house was left standing. During the Nuremberg trials, Hermann Göring, the head of the Luftwaffe, said, "We wanted to test the effects of carpet-bombing on the morale of civilians." On June 3, Nationalist commander Mola died in a plane crash. On June 19, the Nationalist columns of General Dávila entered Bilbao. On August 26, 1937, it was the Italians' turn (the "Littorio," "23 Marzo," and "Fiamme Nere" divisions), who conquered Santander after devastating air bombing. On October 21, Franco took Gijon, in Asturias. At Christmas, 100,000 Republican militiamen marched against Teruel (east of Madrid) to draw Franco away from his hold on the capital. In the freezing weather, it became a massacre 60 days long, with the city taken and then recaptured until the Nationalists' final victory on February 22, 1938. Twenty thousands Republican militiamen were killed. Between July 25 and December 1938, the final and fateful contest between the Nationalists and the International Brigades played out along the River Ebro. The outcome was catastrophic for the latter, who forced to flee to hospitable France. While the Republicans organized their final resistance to defend Valencia, the seat of the government, Barcelona fell on January 26, 1939. In the city streets, the tanks led by Italian general Gastone Gambara encountered no resistance--only bodies. That same day, Mussolini began his triumphant speech to the crowd of 200,000 people in Rome's Piazza Venezia: "They said, 'No pasarán!' We passed!" After the capture of Barcelona, events moved rapidly. On February 9, 1939, Gerona and Figueras fell. On February 28, England and France recognized General Franco's government: the president of the Spanish Republic, Azaña, resigned and fled to Paris. While the Republican militiamen in Madrid fought their last desperate battle, the Communist leaders instead procured passports and visas so that they could reach safety. None of them lost their lives defending the University City. General Miaja took refuge in Oran (Mers-el-Kebir), Negrín in Paris, "la Pasionaria," "El Campesino," and General Barceló in Moscow. Left on the battlefield were the dead and those taken prisoner: 30,000. Franco--who was already thinking ahead to the pacification and to the memorial in the Valle de los Caídos, in the Sierra de Guadarrama, where he would bury the fallen of both sides--quickly freed them, with the exception of professional military officers, all whom were shot. Valencia, the last bastion, fell on March 30. Its defender, General Casado, who had proclaimed himself the head of the provisional government, set sail for England. On March 31, Pope Pius XII wrote to Generalissimo Franco: "Raising our heart to God, we thank Your Excellency for the victory of Catholic Spain."

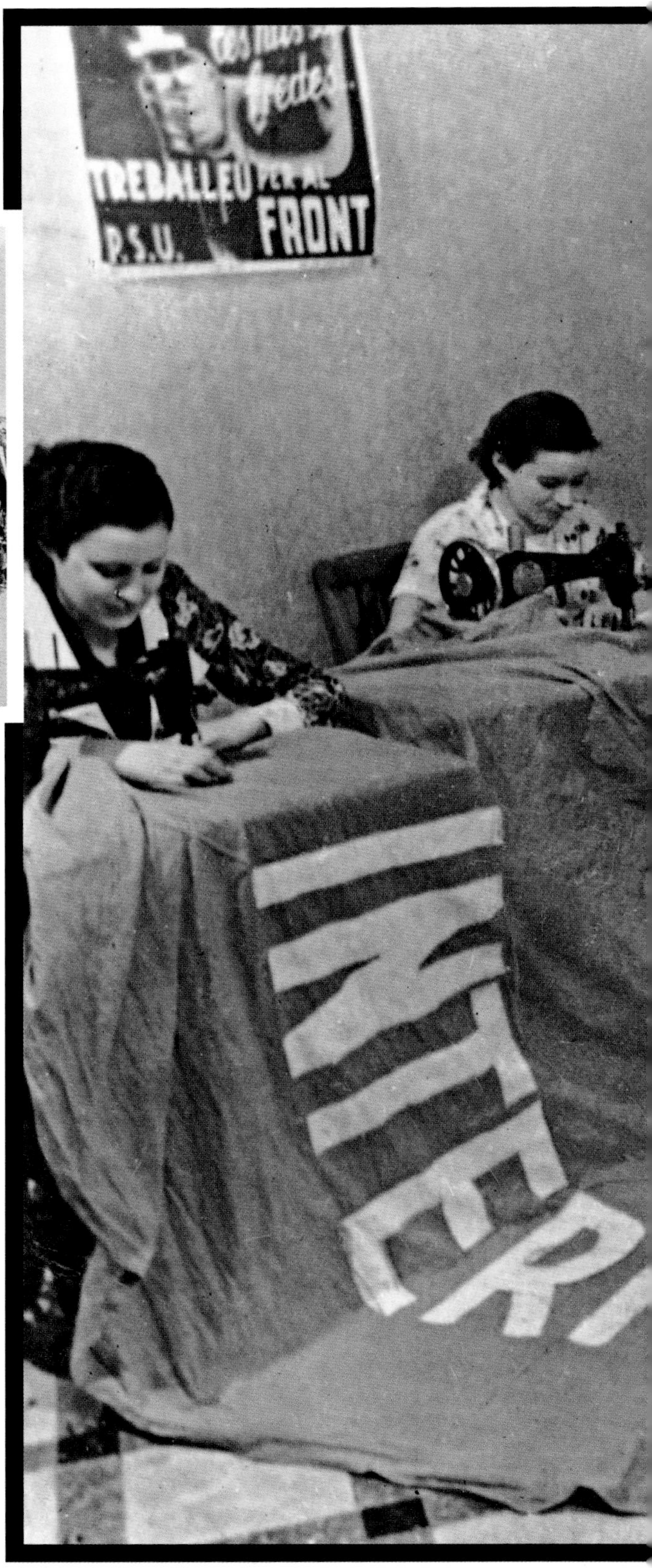

108

Above, the International Brigades march through the streets of Barcelona in October 1938. Center: Falange volunteers marching and making the Roman salute. The Falange was a fascist formation founded by José Antonio Primo de Rivera. The Falangistas admired Mussolini and were the Communists' fiercest enemies. Bottom: a female Communist militia member, holding her weapon, poses together with her comrades.

109
Left: seamstresses making a hammer-and-sickle banner for the International Brigades.
Top right: the Moroccan cavalry in the Tercio parades. During the first phase of the war, many Italian air force career officers enrolled in the Tercio Extranjero *(Spanish Foreign Legion). Thus Italian military intervention in support of the Nationalists remained covert.*

110

A Republican platoon (with a female militia member on the right) during the battle of the Ebro, October 1938. This was one the war's bloodiest fights, ranking with the battles for Madrid, Guadalajara and Santander.

111

Top left: Militia units from the International Brigades surrendering to Nationalists.On the right: Nationalist artillery in action in the Sierra de Guadarrama. Bottom: government soldiers fighting in Teruel, January 1938.

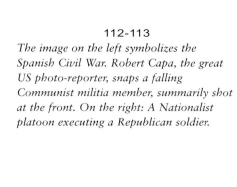

112-113
The image on the left symbolizes the Spanish Civil War. Robert Capa, the great US photo-reporter, snaps a falling Communist militia member, summarily shot at the front. On the right: A Nationalist platoon executing a Republican soldier.

1936 1939
the Spanish war

1936
1939

115
Top: Nationalist soldiers, after the capture of Teruel; center: a cannon firing from a Republican-held position during the battle for Madrid. Bottom: Guernica after the bombing. On April 26, 1937, Hitler's Luftwaffe "carpet bombed" this Basque town, totally destroying it.

114
Civil war is over: to escape the winners' revenge members of the International Brigades are forced to ask political asylum to neutral countries. In this image a group of communist volunteers is escorted into French territory.

THE

CHINESE-JAPANESE WAR

ON THE EVENING OF JULY 7, 1937, AT THE MARCO POLO BRIDGE IN PEKING THERE WAS A SKIRMISH AND SHOOTING BETWEEN THE JAPANESE GARRISON, BASED IN PEKING SINCE THE BOXER REBELLION, AND A GROUP OF CHINESE NATIONALISTS AND SUPPORTERS OF CHIANG KAI-SHEK'S GOVERNMENT, THEN BASED IN NANKING.

The event was a carefully worked-out act of provocation, and the Japanese government used it to justify its decision to invade China from Manchuria where it had its army bases. Manchuria was a Chinese region that Japan had occupied in 1931, following the "Mukden Incident." Mukden was a town in southern Manchuria where, on September 18, 1931, a bomb exploded on a Japanese train. It was never known whether the explosion was an act of terrorism or a provocation by the Japanese secret services. Nonetheless, the attack became the pretext for the Japanese to invade the vast region north of the Great Wall. Chiang Kai-shek's Nanking government put up so little resistance to the invasion that in just three months the Japanese army had occupied the whole of Manchuria. It also managed to take Shanghai, the biggest port on the southern Chinese coast, after crushing Shanghai's Chaipei neighborhood, a center of Chinese nationalist resistance. This required a fierce joint air and sea strike in which thousands of civilians died.

Having occupied Manchuria, the Japanese transferred the capital from Mukden to Chang Chung. They remained the region Manchukuo, and installed Henry Pu Yi as the head of their puppet government. Henry Pu Yi was the last emperor of China, and was driven out of Peking in 1924. When the Japanese accorded Manchukuo a pseudo-independent status, Henry Pu Yi became head of state.

In 1931, when these events were taking place in Manchuria and Shanghai, Chiang Kai-shek had been unwilling to undertake a war with Japan. But after the attack in July 1937 he decided to stand up to the Japanese. Even Mao Tse-tung's Communists, against whom he had been waging a bitter civil war since 1926, encouraged him to resist and agreed to temporarily suspend hostilities. China's honor was at stake here. But Japanese military and technical expertise was far superior. On July 29, 1937, only twenty days after the invasion, the university area of Peking-Tientsin, headquarters of the nationalist students, was bombed and reduced to a pile of rubble. Then in just four days the Japanese occupied Peking.

In August the war spread to the Yangtze Kiang valley, to the Yellow river, and almost as far as Shanghai, which Chiang Kai-shek had every intention of recapturing. He had in fact brought in from Nanking in the south his best divisions, commanded by German officers who had fought in the First World War and now cropped up all over the South America and the Far East as experts in military affairs. But the attack on Shanghai failed and Chiang Kai-shek lost 60 percent of his soldiers.

Another catastrophe oocurred at battle of Paoting, fought in September on the Peking-Hankow railway line. There 30,000 Japanese sacked the city and committed unprecedented acts of violence against the civilian population.

1937

1938

116
A Japanese unit controls access to a bridge leading to Shanghai's Kiewgwan sector. In 1937 (the year of the Chinese assault under Chiang Kai-shek), the city had been held by Japanese troops since 1932.

THE CHINESE-JAPANESE WAR
1937-1938

While Chiang Kai-shek transferred China's governmental capital to Hankow (310 miles west of Nanking) in September 1937, Mao Tse-tung organized his Eighth Army, called the "Peasants' Army." A division of this army commanded by Lin Piao joined battle with and destroyed a Japanese brigade in the mountains of Shansi, below the Great Wall. (Many years later, when Mao had become the Communist dictator of China, he had Lin Piao killed.). The Japanese suffered a second defeat at Ta-Her-Xuang, in Shantung, this time at the hands of the General von Falkenhausen, one of the German heroes of the First World War, and now Chiang's chief military adviser. During this battle the Japanese lost 16,000 men, 40 tanks, and 70 armored cars.

In the spring of 1938, after the inactivity of the winter, the Japanese army invaded the Keifeng region. The Chinese put up strenuous resistance and breached the dikes, flooding an area the size of Italy, in an attempt to stop the enemy advance. It was to no avail. The Japanese army advanced like a steamroller and at the end of the summer captured Chiang's capital, Hankow. On October 21 Canton was captured. The war was over, and the surviving units of Chiang's army took refuge in the impregnable mountains of Chungking.

The Communists continued to carry out anti-Japanese guerrilla attacks. In light of the rapprochement between Nazi Germany and Japan, Chiang dismissed the German generals he felt he could no longer trust, and at the same time dismissed a group of Italian air force officers, who were equally suspect in his eyes. He slowly replaced these cadres with American and British advisers.

After December 7, 1941 (the Japanese attack on Pearl Harbor) Chiang finally sided openly with the Allies and declared war on the Axis powers. He was not able to do much from his refuge in the mountains, but he sent an expeditionary corps to Burma to help the British under Japanese attack. The course of the Second World War in the Far East enabled the Chinese Nationalists to regroup their armed forces, and at the beginning of 1945 they once more attacked, capturing Kwangsi. But at this stage the fatal encounter took place with Mao Tse-tung's armies, which were much stronger and rooted in the peasant population: one million men armed with weaponry provided by the USSR. Immediately after Japan surrendered, Mao once more took up the civil war interrupted in 1937. This was to end three years later October 1, 1949, with all of China under the control of the Communist dictator.

The Chinese-Japanese 1937-1938

118-119
The conquest of Shanghai by Japanese "Blue Jackets" in 1932. This occurred after the Japanese occupied Manchuria and renamed it Manchukuo. Tensions between Japan and China had been growing steadily before open war erupted in 1937.

120-121
Left and center: the unstoppable Japanese advance through Chinese villages after Japan launched major military operations in July 1937. Top right: volunteers of Mao Tse-Tung's Chinese Popular Army prepare to defend the Great Wall against Japanese attacks. Mao suspended the civil war against Chiang, which had been going on since 1926. Bottom: Japanese troops parade inside the Forbidden City after capturing Peking July 28, 1937.

WORLD WAR II

FAILED DIPLOMACY AND THE RISE OF THE THIRD REICH

No more than 100 young men in the military, no commander-in-chief, no heavy artillery or military aircraft, no submarines or ships of over 9840 tons. These were the conditions the Treaty of Versailles imposed on Germany at the end of World War I. The idea was that Germany, punished for having dared to endanger the world, would never again present a military threat to any nation. Nor an economic or trade threat, given the economic crisis that defeat brought, with the collapse of the mark and widespread unemployment. But during the 1932 political elections, the National Socialist German Workers' Party ("National Sozialistische Deutsche Arbeiter Partei" or NSDAP) won 37% of the votes and Adolf Hitler, its Führer (leader), was named chancellor. He made no effort to conceal his plans and had in fact lucidly expounded them in his book, *Mein Kampf* (My Struggle), published in 1924. His program centered on the search for *Lebensraum* (living space) for the German people, to extend to the Urals at the expense of Europe's eastern nations; the return to military sovereignty; and a mortal struggle against the Jews.

With his rise to power, Hitler eliminated democracy. He took over the position of head of state and combined it with his post as chancellor, and required soldiers to swear loyalty to him personally. Most important, he contravened the terms of the Treaty of Versailles, by re-arming the Reichswehr (loosely, "the Reich Defense Force"), which he transformed into the Wehrmacht ("the Armed Forces"), remilitarizing the Rhineland. By 1934, the German army could count on 300,000 regulars, and the Navy began to build cruisers and submarines. Hermann Göring, the minister for the airforce, reorganized the Luftwaffe. In 1935, the Krupp factories began massive production of heavy weaponry, in March, Hitler reintroduced mandatory military service. The major powers and the League of Nations had only one alternative: to defeat Hitler through a military invasion of Germany. But France and Great Britain, frightened by the impressive military parades of the Third Reich, failed to speak up, and the United States, which had maneuvered the international Geneva agreement, retreated behind its isolationist policy. In addition, during the dramatic year of 1936, when the Italo-Ethiopian war broke out, France and Great Britain committed the tragic mistake of voting for sanctions against Italy, the only power that could have checked Hitler by military means. Italy had demonstrated this capacity in 1934, when the Nazis assassinated Austrian chancellor Engelbert Dolfuss. The unfortunate vote-for-sanctions decision pushed Italy fatally into Hitler's arms and laid the foundations for World War II. At the moment he started the war, Hitler could rely on 2,600,000 soldiers, 3200 tanks, 4000 aircraft (half of which were bombers), 3 battleships, 10 battle cruisers, and 57 submarines.

122
Taken in 1928 by his personal photographer, Heinrich Hoffmann, Adolf Hitler appears in his typical orator's attitude. Nineteen Twenty Eight was the year of the Munich Putsch, the failed "Beer Hall Putsch" that cost the Führer jail time in Landau prison, but which made him popular throughout Germany.

1939
1945

124-125
Left: saluted by the SA (Sturmabteilungen), Hitler ascends the steps of the Nuremberg stadium during the Parteitag (annual Nazi party congress) of 1934. Right, during a meeting of the Hitlerjugend (Hitler Youth) blond-haired, blue-eyed Aryan children meet the Führer. According to fanatical theories of "racial purity," they represented a "superior race."

S·D·A·P·

1939
1945

126
Top: in front of the German Reichstag Adolf Hitler responds to the appeal from the President Roosevelt to avoid the outbreak of a world war, repeating his demands: intransigence over Poland and demands for the Danzig "Corridor" (summer 1939).

Bottom: another spectacular picture of the Parteitag, which took place in Nuremberg in 1938. The historic city in Lower Bavaria that became one of the symbols of Hitler's power was chosen by the victors of the Second World War as the seat of the International War Crimes Tribunal.

World War II
1939-1945

127
The Führer salutes the Wehrmacht during the Nuremberg Party congress of 1937. These spectacular gatherings were the result of the genius of architect Albert Speer, Hitler's minister, who spent twenty years in Spandau Prison after the war and wrote the famous book, Inside the Third Reich.

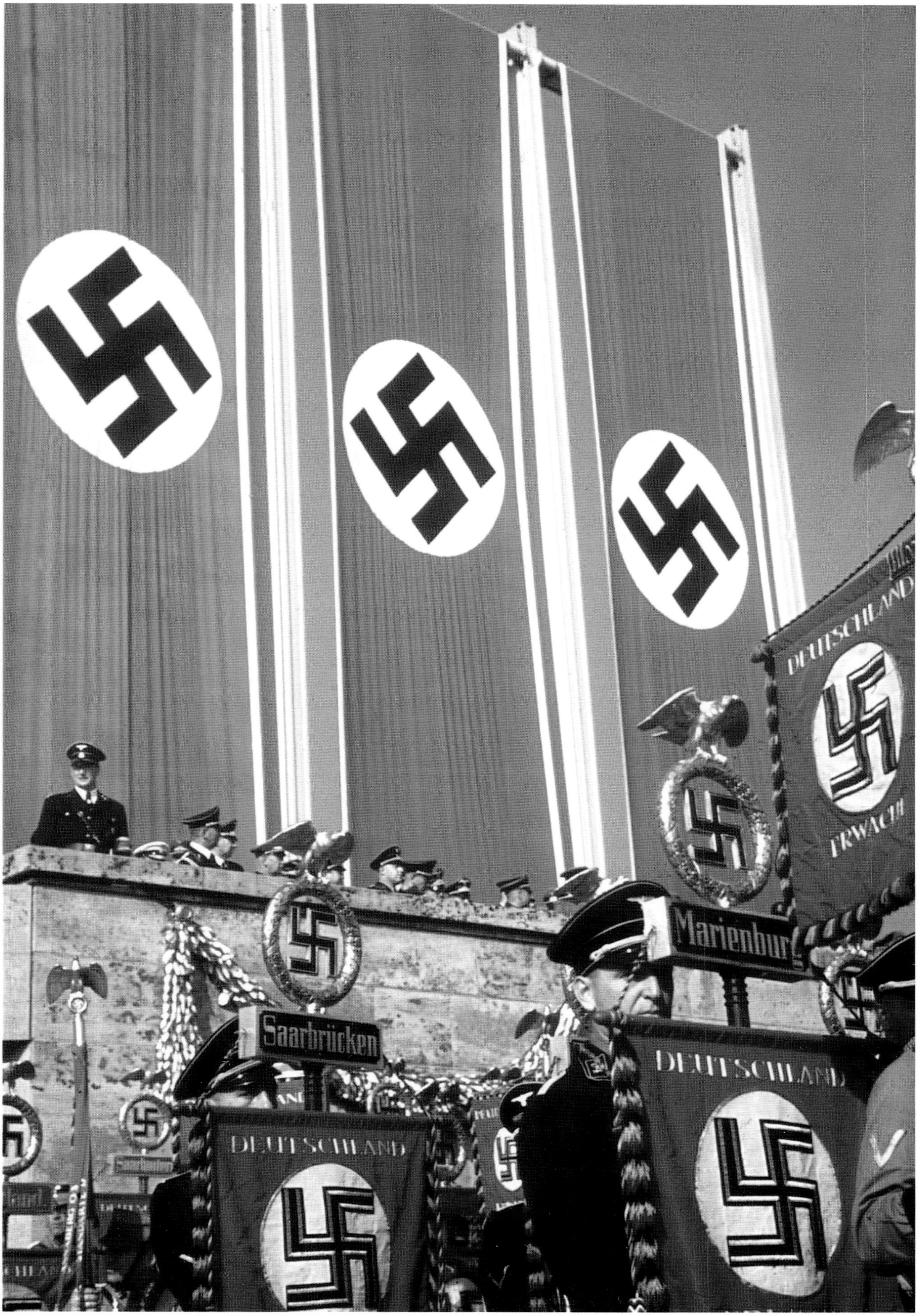
Saarbrücken
DEUTSCHLAND
DEUTSCHLAND

1938
1939

FROM THE ANSCHLUSS TO THE OUTBREAK OF WAR

1938-1939

One clause of the Versailles peace treaty banned the union (Anschluss) of Austria with Germany. In 1937, as a challenge to the treaty and an open provocation to the World War I victors, Hitler announced his plans for the Reich to annex all German-speaking territories in Europe (with the exception of Switzerland), and to create an Anschluss with Austria. This was Führer's native land; he was born in the town of Braunau-am-Inn, on April 29, 1889). At the time of Hitler's announcement, the Austrian chancellor was the conservative Kurt von Schuschnigg, who opposed Anschluss. On February 12, 1938, Hitler summoned Schuschnigg to a meeting at the Berghof, his mountain chalet in the Bavarian Alps. He accused Schuschnigg of fortifying the Austrian-German border. With a blow to the chancellor's mouth, Hitler rudely demanded that he put out his cigarette, hissing, "No one has ever dared smoke in my presence."

Discouraged but firm in his resolve to resist, Schuschnigg returned to Vienna and called for a referendum on March 13 to find out whether the Austrians truly wanted Anschluss. But Hitler was not about to take any risks. He mobilized the Austrian Nazi party, led by Arthur Seyss-Inquart, minister of the interior. Following a series of serious popular revolts fomented by the Nazis, Seyss-Inquart forced Wilhelm Miklas, the president of the Austrian Republic, to cancel the referendum and name him chancellor in Schuschnigg's stead. Once in power, Seyss-Inquart appealed for German troops to enter Austrian territory "to quell the disorder." At dawn on March 12, 1938, the Germans invaded. To placate Mussolini, Hitler announced that the Brenner Pass border would not be touched: the German-speaking South Tyrol would remain in Italian hands. During the early hours of the invasion, the SS arrested 79,000 opponents of Hitler and the Anschluss. Two days later, on March 14, Hitler made his triumphant entry into Vienna, before a delirious crowd of two million people. The first thing he did was to send Mussolini a telegram: "I will never forget this." A few days later, the Austrian cabinet issued a decree by which Austria became a province of the Reich the Ostmark (Eastern Border Region). The referendum held on April 10 ratified the Anschluss with yes-votes from 99% of the Austrian population. A similar referendum was held in Germany on April 18 with similar results. Kurt von Schuschnigg was taken prisoner and held in the Dachau concentration camp until 1945, when he went to the United States and became a professor at Columbia University in New York City. Three million German-speaking citizens lived in the Czechoslovak region known as the Sudetenland, one of the territories that Adolf Hitler had pledged in 1937 to annex to the Reich. In April 1938, Konrad Henlein, head of the German Sudeten party, rejected the proposals the Czech central government made, promising to protect the rights of the German minority. He asked for full autonomy for the Sudeten area, with the option of German inhabitants formulating their own policies and organizing the region on National Socialist principles. Prague rejected the request. The response from Berlin was swift: Hitler alerted the army and instructed it to be ready to "crush Czechoslovakia." Germany sent an ultimatum on September 26: Military occupation of Czechoslovakia if it refused to grant the right of self-determination to the Sudetenland. This was the moment to crush Hitler and eliminate him from politics and history, but no nation had the courage to take this step. In fact, Great Britain secretly pushed the Czechoslovak government to accept the Sudetenland's request for independence. When France, bound to Czechoslovakia by an alliance, had no choice but to order general mobilization on September 28, 1938, the British prime minister, Neville Chamberlain, telephoned Mussolini to beg him to intervene for the sake of peace. By this time, everyone knew that Hitler had scheduled his attack for October 1st. Mussolini wasted no time; in just a few hours, he convened a summit meeting for the next day in Munich.

On the morning of September 29, 1938, the leaders of the four major powers, Édouard Daladier, Neville Chamberlain, Benito Mussolini, and Adolf Hitler, arrived in Munich. The summit began at noon and ended at 1 a.m. on September 30. With the exception of Hitler, who could hardly wait, no one wanted war. Czechoslovakia, which did not participate in the meeting, was exhorted to accept the requests of Henlein's party. In exchange, Hitler promised that he would not dismember Czechoslovakia and would give the 800,000 Czechs living in the Sudetenland six months to decide whether to

128

Top left: Soldiers of the German Wehrmacht remove the sign that marks the border between Austria and Germany, implementing Hitler's Anschluss policy, the reunification of the two nations with German language and culture. Top right and bottom: the Führer makes a triumphal entrance in Vienna after the plebiscite that sanctioned the annexation of Austria to Nazi Germany.

stay or go. Czechoslovakia had to give up its fortifications in the mountains along the German border. Even a "declaration of Anglo-German friendship" was signed. Upon their return home, Chamberlain and Mussolini were welcomed as "saviors of peace." The Italians reserved an ecstatic welcome for Il Duce, and millions crowded along the railroad line from the Brenner Pass to Rome, shouting hurrahs as the train went by. The demonstrations in London were more restrained, and Winston Churchill and Anthony Eden (foreign minister until his resignation on February 20, 1939) distanced themselves from Chamberlain. As for Stalin, given the fact that Hitler had yielded to the West (which he had approached during the war in Spain), he understood that the British and French were not hostile to Hitler's objectives in the East. Stalin therefore began to think about a German-Soviet agreement.

The world had barely breathed a sigh of relief over its narrow brush with danger when the dismemberment of Czechoslovakia began. On September 30, 1938, the world press had announced that Czechoslovakia was safe: the country had had to give in to Hitler's pressure, but its territorial integrity was ensured. However, on October 2 Poland began its military occupation of the Teschen region and annexed its 230,000 inhabitants. On October 7, an independent government was set up in Slovakia, headed by a priest, Monsignor Josef Tiso. On October 11, the same thing happened in Ruthenia at the hands of another priest, Monsignor Volosin. Both priests were funded and guided by German "advisers." At this point, the president of the republic, Eduard Benes, submitted his resignation and was succeeded by Emil Hacha. Next Hungary made territorial claims. To preclude Czechoslovakia suffering military occupation (as it had at Polish hands), Hacha urged acceptance of the Vienna Award (November 2). In this award, the Italian and German foreign ministers, Ciano and Ribbentrop, had established that Czechoslovakia was to grant Hungary a border territory of 3861 square miles, with a population of 1 million. All that remained under Prague's governance were Bohemia and Moravia. But not for long. On March 14, 1939, Hitler summoned President Hacha to Berlin. While his guest waited to start talks, he ordered the Wehrmacht to occupy the two regions, which was done with lightning speed, to the outrage of the entire Czech population. Once everything had been completed, the Führer finally agreed to an audience with poor Hacha to inform him that he could retire, since Bohemia and Moravia had become German "protectorates" and Baron Konstantin von Neurath had been named "Reichsprotektor."

This act of international banditry against Czechoslovakia reawakened the conscience of the West. The British prime minister, Neville Chamberlain, finally took a stand and announced the end of the "appeasement" policy. France, which had been stung even more deeply, given its duties as an ally of Czechoslovakia, proclaimed the inviolability of Poland, its other partner in Eastern Europe. Belgium and Holland joined France in this declaration, while Great Britain also pledged to intervene on Poland's side in the event of new Nazi aggression. The press of Western Europe unanimously accused Hitler of wanting to rule the world by force and named him Public Enemy Number One. It was in this atmosphere that foreign ministers Molotov and Ribbentrop signed the non-aggression pact on August 23, with a secret agreement envisioning the division of Poland and central Europe between the USSR and Germany. During the signing ceremony, Stalin drained one glass of vodka after another. A young German official, overcome with doubt, grabbed the bottle from which the Soviet dictator's frequent shots were poured. He filled his own glass and brought it to his lips. It was water.

The year 1939 was the year of pacts. These were not gentlemen's agreements: they had secret terms and were signed without notice to partners who should have been informed. The Molotov-Ribbentrop Pact should not have been signed without prior consultation with Japan and Italy. These two nations were tied to Germany by the Anti-Comintern Pact, drawn up for anti-Communist purposes (to oppose the spread of Communist ideology.) Germany and Japan had signed this pact in November 1936, while Italy joined the next year. These three nations were also united by the mutual resolution to abandon the League of Nations (Italy was the last to leave Geneva, on December 11, 1937). With the three nations' defections, the League was a virtual failure. However, among Italy, Germany and Japan, political positions were not always unequivocal. At the beginning of 1939, Germany asked Italy and Japan to sign a tripartite pact that would link the three nations in the Pact of Steel, a full-fledged military alliance. Japan declined, while Italy's foreign minister Galeazzo Ciano was firmly opposed to siding with the Germans. However, Mussolini--who was Ciano's father-in-law, played a trick on him. While Ciano and Ribbentrop were meeting in Milan on May 6, 1939, from Rome Mussolini announced to the press that the Pact of Steel was about to be signed with Germany. Although Ciano disagreed with Mussolini, he was thus forced to go to Berlin on May 22 to sign the pact that thereafter irrevocably tied Italy to Germany. The Pact of Steel was the reason why Ciano never forgave Germany for the Molotov-Ribbentrop Pact (August 23, 1939). Germany signed this without reference to its Italian ally and in violation of the Anti-Comintern Pact in which the signatories (Germany, Italy, and Japan) had pledged to oppose the USSR--certainly not to reach agreements with it. The Japanese, they were so irritated that they denounced the Anti-Comintern Pact itself. During the Italian-German summit in Salzburg on August 11, 1939, the Germans dropped their disguise. Turning to Ribbentrop, Ciano asked, "So, you want the Danzig Corridor?", to which Hitler's minister responded, "Not anymore. We want war."

Japan could not expect much help from far-off Germany for its policy of Japanese expansion in the Far East, though it could expect trouble from Russia. This fear had driven Japan into signing the Anti-Comintern Pact; it would push it into denouncing the pact after learning of the secret agreement between Hitler and Stalin. During the 1920s and 30s, Japan had adopted strongly nationalistic positions with extensive rearming and the development of a powerful navy. On July 26, 1937, Japan began a war against China--without any formal declaration. Victory followed victory. The invading army occupied Peking, Shanghai, and Nanking, followed by Canton on October 21, 1938. The Chinese government, headed by General Chiang Kai-shek, had taken refuge in mountainous Chungking and, following a temporary truce with Mao Tse-tung's Communists, waged guerrilla warfare against the Japanese. During 1938 and 1939, there were continuous border incidents between Russia and Japan, which had occupied northern China. As a result, Tokyo did not trust Russia, which could attack the Japanese army from the rear.

During the Thirties, the United States of America was involved in New Deal programs to overcome unemployment--the legacy of the stock market collapse of 1929. Part of President Roosevelt's economic policy was the rearming of the nation. Boosting the military and armaments industries would absorb hundreds of thousands of jobless people and help relaunch the economy. The arsenals were filled with weapons that theoretically had no purpose, given the United States' increasingly stronger stance of political isolationism. In fact, no threats existed to the United States' integrity. But because of his "liberal" background, Roosevelt was unyieldingly hostile to Nazi Germany and to imperialist Japan. As for Italy, Roosevelt bore in mind the power of Italian immigration in the New World and knew full well the pro-Fascist inclinations of many Italian-Americans, but he never overestimated any actual threat. As a result of an economic policy focused on the military and armaments industries, the production of military aircraft doubled in just a few years, while the US fleet became the most powerful in the world.

It is possible that the Japanese-Chinese war in the Far East and the European war that broke out on September 1, 1939 with Germany's invasion of Poland, followed by the entry of Poland's allies France and Britain, could have remained two "regional" conflicts, although serious and painful ones. Yet these two initially regional wars developed into a world war destined to be "total." Before the Allied victory, World War II had involved practically every country in the world and had led to unthinkable atrocities: the Holocaust of six million Jews and the atom bombs dropped on Hiroshima and Nagasaki.

A few considerations may help us understand the war's horrific expansion. The English, French, and Dutch colonial empires, no longer as powerful as formerly, were unable to oppose Japan's maritime expansionism. Only the United States could do so. To prevent any such move, Japan decided on the preventive strike against the American Pacific fleet, anchored off Pearl Harbor. But the Japanese government underestimated the Americans: that cold-blooded attack triggered the United States' staunch decision to crush Japan forever. Hitler made a similar mistake when he invaded Russia on June 21, 1941: that fatal decision brought catastrophe for Germany, crushed in a war on two fronts, just as in World War I.

Germany and Japan were allies in name only. They never showed any true interest in coordinating an authentic strategic plan. The United States, Great Britain, and the USSR, on the other hand, coordinated plans at political and military summits. The United States and Great Britain created a unified supreme command, while the USSR received gigantic supplies of arms, aircraft, ships, provisions, and other products made by American industry. The world war became total war: it was fought in Europe and Asia, in Africa and the Middle East, in India and the South Pacific, in the Far East and in the Arctic seas. It involved the whole world from Britain in the northwest, to Canada, and to Australia in the far southeast. The human cost was horrendous. Among the military alone (excluding civilian casualties and mass extermination), a total of 8.5 million Russians, 3 million Germans, 1.2 million Japanese, 340,000 French, 325,000 Britons, 300,000 Italians, and 260,000 Americans died. As for civilians, accepted estimates should suffice: 100,000 in the fire-bombing of Dresden and 106,000 in the atomic bombing of Hiroshima. Horror of this scope, but above all the atom bomb--which the USSR soon came to possess--ensured that while World War I had laid the groundwork for World War II, this second world war was destined to act as a deterrent to a third world war.

On March 23, 1939, in a diplomatic note to Warsaw, Germany demanded the return of the Danzig (or Polish) Corridor, a strip of land uniting Poland with the Baltic Sea and dividing East Prussia from the rest of Germany. The Versailles Conference had assigned this corridor to Poland as a needed outlet to the sea. At the same time, Hitler asked for the re-annexation of Danzig, which the Conference had awarded to Poland and which was a free city protected by the League of Nations. The world immediately understood that Danzig and its corridor could become the *casus belli* of a new world war. In Europe a question--first posed by the editorialists of the leading French newspapers--began to raised: "Die for Danzig?"

From March 23, the pressure of events was relentless. On the 26th, Poland rejected the German request. The next day, Germany cut off diplomatic ties with Poland. On March 31, Poland obtained from France and Great Britain a commitment to guarantee its territorial integrity. On April 27, Great Britain took a step it had never taken in its thousand-year history: mandatory conscription during peacetime. In August the pressure became unbearable. Following days of tension and skirmishes along the Polish-German border and in Danzig (almost all of whose inhabitants wanted annexation to Germany), the eyes of the world turned again toward Italy, just like the year before during the Sudeten crisis. On August 21, Ciano convinced Mussolini to inform Hitler that Italy would back up the Germans if they were to attack Poland. On the 23rd, President Roosevelt sent a message to the king of Italy, Victor Emmanuel III, asking him to intervene to prevent war from breaking out. The next day, August 24, Pope Pius XII appealed to all the nations, exhorting them to use the power of reason.

It was useless. On the night of August 30, a Nazi SS force organized a fake assault on the German radio station in Gleiwitz, on the Polish border. Disguised as Polish soldiers, Hitler's troops raided the radio station and cold-bloodedly killed several employees--who were actually political prisoners transported to the station during the night to be sacrificed on the altar of provocation. The next day, Hitler screamed over the radio that Poland would pay dearly for this act. On September 1, the Wehrmacht invaded Poland. Italy immediately declared its "non-belligerence," asking that the Pact of Steel be suspended. On September 3, France and England declared war on Germany, followed by Australia and New Zealand. Great Britain, prepared for the worst, immediately sent a task force of 150,000 to France. On September 5, the United States declared its neutrality.

While the Polish army, led by General Sikorski, fought desperately against an enemy a thousand times stronger, the USSR attacked Poland behind its back. On September 17, the Red Army invaded the eastern regions, capturing 200,000 soldiers and 10,000 officers, massacring the latter after they had surrendered and then burying their bodies in a mass grave in Katyn Forest.

The war in the East ended in a matter of days. While the German air force bombarded Warsaw, the Polish army could only oppose the invaders with a few heroic and old-fashioned cavalry charges, like the ones launched on the River Bzura against two tank regiments, ending with the annihilation of the horses and cavalrymen. At the very beginning, the German Luftwaffe had destroyed the Polish air force on the ground at the airports. The few warships in the Baltic suffered a similar fate. German armored divisions broke through to the south and north and were already in sight of Warsaw by September 7. On September 18, the government and Marshal Rydz-Smigly, with the few army survivors, took refuge in Romania. Warsaw fell on the 27th. On September 30, General Sikorski formed a Polish government-in-exile in Paris.

France and England watched the annihilation of their ally from afar, without even enough time to plan an attack. In four weeks, Poland counted 70,000 dead, 133,000 wounded and 700,000 prisoners. Germany had 13,000 dead and 30,000 wounded. This marked the birth of the "Blitzkrieg" or "lightning war": Its symbol was the Junkers "Stuka," the plane that paralyzed the enemy with its terrifying whine, caused by the steel pipe fastened under the cockpit when it went into a dive to strafe and bomb.

Just as the USSR had done in the eastern Poland, Germany swiftly implemented a violent policy of domination and destruction.in its regions of vanquished Poland. Noblemen, priests, politicians, teachers, journalists, and professionals were interned in special lagers and silently done away with. Laborers were sent to work in Germany at half the salary earned by German workers. Factories were expropriated and given to German industrialists. In the cities, the Jewish ghettos were isolated by barbed wire. If lacking, ghettos were created. All the Jews from Germany, Austria, and the annexed regions were brought to the ghettos. A new governor, the sadistic Hans Frank, was brought in from Germany to apply the "new order." He would later use Jewish children who tried to flee the ghettos for target practice.

The French and English seemed paralyzed as they watched the lightning-fast collapse of Poland, as if their governments had not declared war on Germany on September 3, 1939. Nor did Germany undertake any action against the two nations. The three armies observed each other from afar: The English lined up in Flanders, the Germans ready to pounce at the foot of the Ardennes, and the French barricaded in the redoubts of the Maginot Line. It was the "*drôle de guerre*," the "strange war," and also the "*Sitzkrieg*," the "phony war." But at sea, the English and the Germans began to shoot and kill each other. On October 14, at Scapa Flow, the British base in the Orkney Islands (north of Scotland), a U-boat neutralized the defensive measures and torpedoed and sank the English battleship *HMS Royal Oak*. On December 16, in faraway Montevideo, at the mouth of the Rio de la Plata, the German battleship "*Graf Spee*" scuttled itself, unable to escape from the English cruisers with which it was battling. The ship was named after the German admiral who during World War I achieved fame in the South Atlantic.

At the end of 1937, an extensive barricade had been built in eastern France, under the supervision of the war minister, André Maginot. It was named after him, and the French felt safe behind it. This unbroken series of fortresses constructed of reinforced concrete, protected by armor with a invulnerable to any artillery attack or air bombing, with a ventilation system that included special filters to nullify the effects of gas. The fortresses, connected to each other by underground tunnels equipped with immense storehouses and arsenals to build bombs, ran along the entire border dividing France from Germany and Luxembourg. The Maginot line did not continue along the Belgian frontier, as France expected no threats from that quarter. But this was precisely the quarter through which Guderian's armored divisions would enter France.

For seven months, the world waited for something to happen. Something did but not on the much-watched Eastern Front. At the beginning of April 1940, Hitler decided to forestall the British intention of making a pre-emptive landing in Norway. Hitler proffered the reason of aiding Finland, which the USSR had attacked. Scandinavia, if controlled by the Allies, would have been a serious threat for Germany. General von Falkenhorst rapidly had prepared the invasion plans. On April 7, 1940, the Germans rushed into Norway's ports and airports. Some 200,000 Germans troops had been mobilized, together with 100 tanks, 1000 aircraft, and the entire fleet. The Norwegian army's defense was cut down mercilessly. By April 9--just two days after the onset of the attack--the Wehrmacht controlled the entire country from Oslo to Trondheim, Bergen, and Narvik.

For Great Britain this German success was a real insult. Norway's coast was just 310 miles from Scapa Flow, and careful reconnaissance work should have enabled the British to intercept the German fleet. Britain's reaction was swift: a seaborne attack was launched on the ports of Trondheim and Narvik. Ten German fighters were downed as opposed to only two English ones. But the attack--with numerous infantry landings on the coast--was repelled.

On June 9, 1940, Norway surrendered; the government and King Haakon VII fled to London, and the pro-Nazi deputy Vidkun Quisling formed a government that declared Norway to be Germany's ally. (This treason led to Quisling's execution at the end of the war.) Despite his victory, Hitler had to face a long season of attacks and sabotage from Norwegian army units that had retreated to the mountains and had remained loyal to the king. The second Blitzkrieg of World War II cost Germany 3692 dead, with 3734 dead among the British and Norwegians. But one-fourth of Hitler's fleet had been sunk, and holding Norway forced the Führer to keep numerous divisions immobilized over the nation's extensive territory.

On April 9, 1940, just two days after the attack on Norway, the third Blitzkrieg began: the attack on Denmark--"Operation Weserübung." This action was even swifter and encountered no resistance: indeed, by noon the Germans had entered Copenhagen. The radio then announced that King Christian X had declared Denmark's neutrality and placed the country "under Germany's protection."

Germany's Norwegian and Danish victories were certainly spectacular but bore challenging consequences. In America Roosevelt accelerated rearmament, intensifying the production of aircraft; in London the Chamberlain government fell and Winston Churchill moved into Downing Street on May 10.

136-137
Left: German soldiers advance in Norway after setting fire to a center of resistance faithful to the king, May 1940. Right: ships and wrecks in Narvik Bay, Norway, after the battle fought on April 10, 1940 between German and British forces.

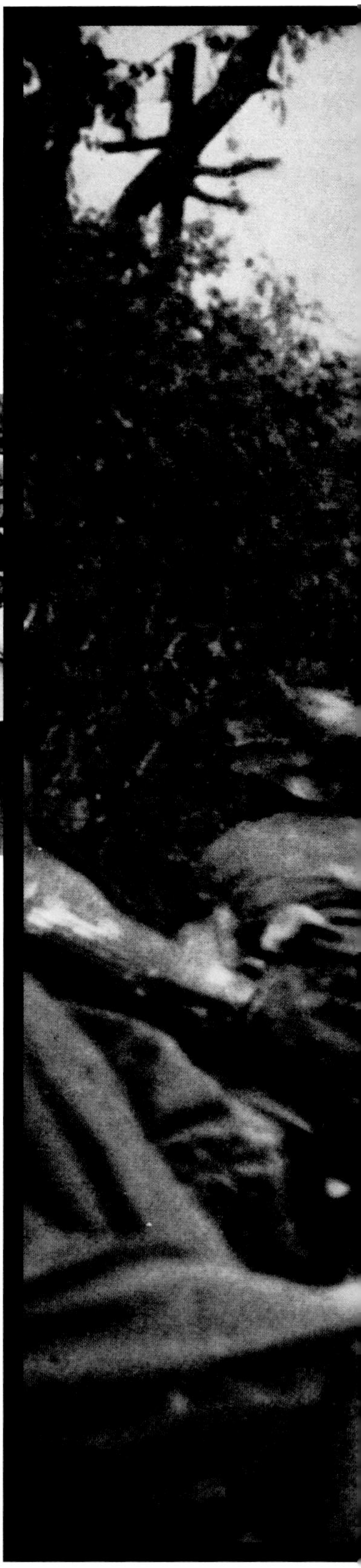

134-135
Top left: German infantry soldiers in the shelter of a trench on the outskirts of Warsaw, next to a tram yard, waiting to unleash the final attack against the capital; in the center, German troops remove the bar on the border with Poland on September 1, 1939, the day Poland was invaded and the day that began the Second World War. Bottom: a desperate Polish child cries next to the body of her sister, killed during a German air attack. Right: Troops of the Third Reich waiting on the outskirts of Warsaw to unleash their attack on the city.

141

Top left: the beach at Dunkirk, Nord-Pas-de Calais, June 22, 1940: the British soldiers are swimming to the boats that will carry them to safety across the Channel. Right: June 14, 1940, German Heinkel He-111s fly over Paris a few days before the French surrender. It wasn't necessary to bombard Paris to convince the French: all that was needed was the advance of General Guderian's tanks.
Bottom: Dunkirk's beach after the English retreat: the sand is covered with hundreds of Jeeps, trucks, armored cars and weapons.

140

German troops on horseback parade victoriously under the Arc de Triomphe in Paris after the conquest of the French capital at the end of June 1940, marking the end of the Blitzkrieg, the "Lighting War."

ITALY AT WAR

1940

On March 10, 1940, Hitler sent Ribbentrop to Rome to urge Italy to enter the war. But Mussolini hesitated: the army wasn't ready. The Führer and Il Duce met at the Brenner Pass on March 18. Hitler insisted: The von Manstein Plan was about to be carried out and an Italian attack against France by sea and from the Alpine passes would divert French troops from defensive measures against Guderian's armored troops. During that same period, Mussolini had received dramatic appeals from both Roosevelt and French premier Paul Reynaud (who had replaced the declared anti-Fascist Édouard Daladier), begging him to keep Italy out of the fray.

Churchill was the only great statesman with whom Mussolini had long cultivated a friendly rapport. Earlier, Churchill had publicly hailed the Italian dictator's work, defining him as "the defender of Europe against Bolshevism" and had become a regular and well-paid contributor to his newspaper, "*Il Popolo d'Italia.*" But Churchill began to play an odd game after moving to 10 Downing Street on May 10. This involved a mysterious correspondence between the two, never made public. In fact, after the execution of the Fascist leader at Lake Como on April 28, 1945, these letters were returned to Churchill and disappeared. Historians suspect that in them, Churchill may have exhorted Mussolini to enter the war to mitigate Hitler's demands and dissuade him from continuing hostilities against Great Britain as France was inexorably moving toward defeat. In light of this, Mussolini could urge Hitler turn against the USSR, the common enemy of both Churchill and Mussolini. A less likely theory about the letters suggests that in them, in exchange for Italian neutrality, Churchill promised Italy territory he could not legally deliver, such as Corsica and the French provinces of Nice and Savoy. This theory is implausible because France itself, in an extreme attempt to keep Italy out of the war, made it clear to Ciano that France would be willing to reward Italy for noninvolvement by ceding Corsica and Tunisia. The fact is that on May 30 Mussolini announced his decision to Hitler to enter the war on his side, and on June 10 he had a declaration of war delivered to the ambassadors of France and Great Britain.

The war fought on the Alpine front was a small one, draining and without glory, and sudden bad weather blocked the Italians' advance. On June 14, French and British warships bombarded Genoa, and on the 20th Italian soldiers attacked the Côte d'Azur and occupied Menton. But France was on its knees by this time, and on June 24 it signed an armistice with Rome. Mussolini settled for little: he requested and obtained access to the port of Djibouti in East Africa--a modest reward that seems to lend credence to the theory of a secret agreement with Churchill and Mussolini's desire to avoid raging against France. The short campaign cost Italy 1300 men dead and missing, 3000 wounded, 2000 frozen in the Alps. Precisely the "one thousand lives to be placed on the altar of peace" that Mussolini had cynically stated he needed, as Ciano noted in his diary. A thousand lives to play a role in the Führer's decisions: a terrible illusion.

142
Units of the Italian army's alpine artillery marching towards the Italo-French front in June 1940.

143
Benito Mussolini, Fascism's Duce and head of government, harangues the Italians from the historic balcony of the Palazzo Venezia in Rome.

144
A German raid on London, December 29, 1941: an apartment building just hit by German airplanes burns against the background of St. Paul's Cathedral. A dramatic scene from the legendary "Battle of Britain," fought in the skies over England with the carpet bombing of English cities and fierce aerial dogfights.

THE BATTLE OF BRITAIN
1940

After conquering France far too easily, Hitler directed his interest toward hated Britain, planning to invade the island presto. Operation Sea Lion envisioned a series of German landings from Bristol, in the west, above the Devon-Cornwall pensinsula, along the English Channel coast and northeast to the Thames estuary. As Army Corps A was landing on English soil with six divisions, the paratrooper corps were to be launched against the main airports.

The preparatory phase involved a general air offensive set for August 5, 1940, but postponed to August 15 due to bad weather. The lord of the imposing aerial campaign was Hermann Göring, the head of the Luftwaffe, who had promised his Führer he would deliver the "mortal blow" to Great Britain: for this purpose he put 1300 bombers and 900 fighters into the air. On August 15, as Churchill addressed Britain by radio, promising "blood, toil, tears, and sweat," the Adlertag (Eagle Day) initiative began. But a completely unexpected obstacle threatened the German bombers sent to destroy England's planes, to devastate the cities and, crush the population's morale. This was "Ultra." The information this top-secret decrypting machine provided helped Air Marshal Hugh Dowding, commander of the Royal Air Force, to identify the German bombers' routes. British fighters then flew into attack, significantly damaging the German raiders. Consequently, Göring increased the bomber escorts, sending along hordes of Messerschmitts. But British Spitfires and Hurricanes, not as fast but easier to maneuver, won most of the air battles. This was the season of airborne heroes, such as the Briton Peter Townsend and the German Adolf Galland. Nevertheless, victory in aerial battles was not decided purely by the pilots' skill and courage. There were also technological factors. The British had the Ultra device, and also radar, which could identify enemy aircraft still distant from their targets. Radar was effective even when clouds concealed planes from ground-based sighting. Often, the German aircrews never even reached their destinations. Targeted by anti-aircraft artillery, dozens of their planes were downed and their pilots were taken prisoner. British crews who were downed often made safe parachute landings and returned to battle. This factor was the core of the British victory in the Battle of Britain. Göring, who had performed his first "experiments" in Spain to evaluate the effect of bombardment on the psychological commitment of the population, had badly miscalculated: the heavy bombings from the air by the Luftwaffe planes multiplied the population's will to resist and fight to the end.

On September 6, according to Operation Sea Lion plans, 168 freighters, 419 tugboats, and 1910 barges laden with soldiers and tanks were concentrated in the French, Belgian, and Dutch ports controlled by the Germans, ready to sail for the coast of England. On September 7, the Luftwaffe began the most massive bombing of London since the war began. But Hitler hesitated to give orders to start. On September 17, he postponed Operation Sea Lion indefinitely. It was claimed that the 195 aircraft Germany lost during the Battle of Britain had made him pessimistic about the outcome of the invasion. But Hitler's full rationale for his decision remains one of history's great unanswered questions. It may be that espionage reports on the British population's stamina were the main factor in the Führer's decision. Incredibly, the German bombings had strengthened the British resolve to resist to the death. The Home Guard exemplifies this. Set up as a volunteer force, in just a few weeks it enrolled one million regulars, ranging in age from 17 to 65. As firearms were few, many trained with rifles and shotguns, pitchforks, and clubs. Firefighting squads were formed everywhere, and held field drills on how to capture German parachutists as they landed. The shells of old cars were left in fields to prevent German pilots from attempting crash landings. King George VI had himself photographed and filmed by newsreels as he practiced target shooting with his pistol in the gardens of Buckingham Palace. During the German bombing, the Queen and her daughters spent their days in London, an example for the people. Shops put up placards indicating "Business as usual." Nonetheless, the incendiary bombs killed thousands and London began to be choked with debris. The House of Commons was destroyed in a bombing raid; in a patriotic gesture, the House of Lords invited the members to use their chamber. Other bombing raids razed eight historic London churches to the ground.

Churchill directed operations from the basement of a Whitehall ministerial office block abutting St. James's Park (the Cabinet War Rooms). Despite the pressure of leading war operations, he hurried to every district in London and every city that had been bombed, ever unflappable with his cigar and bowler hat. He was the very image of Britain that no one would bring to its knees. Germany had given up on Operation Sea Lion but not on bombing Great Britain. The nation responded. On November 13, 1940, after waiting for Soviet Foreign Minister Molotov to arrive in Berlin on an official visit to the Führer, Churchill launched an unprecedented air attack on the enemy capital. Tens of thousands of homes were razed and thousands of people were killed. Molotov was forced to flee to an air-raid shelter: when he emerged, desolation, ruin, and death were all he could see around

him. Blinded with rage, the next day Hitler ordered an "exemplary retaliation." Coventry, a historic town in the English Midlands, some 120 miles north of London that supported a range of metal-working factories, was chosen. Nothing was to be left standing. Five hundred German planes swooped down on Coventry, dropping 590 tons of explosives. The historic town center, the cathedral, factories and housing were totally destroyed. On November 19, a similar attack was launched on Birmingham, a major industrial center, leaving 800 dead and 2000 wounded. On December 17 the RAF retaliated, destroying Bremen, Düsseldorf, and Mannheim. A horrendous war of annihilation had begun, and it targeted civilians. Bombings pounded the German cities. Every so often, but at increasing intervals, the Luftwaffe began to retaliate, as it did on December 29 when it launched 17220 tons of bombs on London, including 70,000 incendiaries. But Hitler failed to win the Battle of Britain. Since the beginning of the operation, he had lost 1733 airplanes, as opposed to 915 British aircraft. In one of his famous speeches, Churchill praised the Royal Air Force: "Never in the field of human conflict was so much owed by so many to so few."

146-147
Top left: the General Staff of the Luftwaffe, photographed on July 2, 1941, while planning attacks on the English capital; bottom, a German Heinkel flies over London waiting to discharge its load of death. Right: English children take refuge in a trench dug in the fields of Kent to escape the consequences of the German air attacks.

148-149
More scenes from the German bombardments of London in May 1941. The British capital was subjected to aerial attack for 76 consecutive nights, but the people's morale never wavered. In the picture on the top right, Winston Churchill inspects the House of Commons, destroyed by German bombardment.

LR

1940

THE WAR AT SEA
1939-1944

At the outbreak of hostilities, Great Britain immediately implemented a naval blockade of Germany, following the its First World War script. In reponse, Germany resumed the "Pirate War" with its submarines, the U-boats. The naval confrontation that began in late 1939 seemed to be a sequel to the battles of 1914-18.

On September 3, 1939, Admiral Dönitz's modern U-boats sank the English passenger ship *Athena* en route from Liverpool to New York with 1,300 persons on board. Of these, 112, including 28 Americans drowned--a tragic repeat of the sinking of the *Lusitania* in 1914. The aircraft carrier *HMS Courageous* was sunk on September 17, and on October 14 the U-47, commanded by the legendary Captain Prien, invaded the British base at Scapa Flow and sank the aircraft carrier *HMS Royal Oak*.

The Germans deployed more than one hundred U-boats in the Atlantic. Within a few months they had sunk 123 ships for a total gross weight of 3.8 million tons. In their attacks, the U-boat captains applied the so-called "wolf pack" technique: a U-boat would spot a convoy loaded with American supplies and heading for the English coast. The lone U-boat would follow the convoy for days, spreading the word and waiting for the "pack." When the other submarines had arrived, the attack was unleashed. This would be done at night, with the submarines submerged to achieve maximum torpedo speed and accuracy. The most successful and shocking example of this technique took place in mid-March 1943, when 23 U-boats attacked American convoy "HX229," sinking 138,744 tons of shipping. However, during the first years of the war, the widespread application of radar and depth- detection instruments (echo-sounders, sonar, and hydrophones) enabled the Allies to send many U-boats to the bottom. Admiral Dönitz began to feel increasingly responsible for the sacrifice of thousands of sailors condemned to a horrible death by asphyxiation on the ocean floor, and on May 24, 1943, he requested the Führer for permission to suspend attacks the Atlantic convoys. In another initiative, he planned an attack on New York with a submarine that would go up the Hudson River and land Italian commandos of the 10th MAS Flotilla (Motoscafo Anti Sommergibile; "Anti-Submarine Speedboat Unit"), but this enterprise never got off the drawing board.

A small mention is due to the Italian submarines in the Atlantic that operated out of the Betasom base near Bordeaux, in occupied France. The submarines *Barbarigo, Cappellini* and *Malaspina*, under the orders of commanders Grossi, Todaro and Leoni, earned praise for saving the survivors of the ships they sank. If it is legitimate to speak of "good" and "bad" submarines, there is no doubt that the Italians of Betasom deserved to be included in the former category. From May 1943 to May 9, 1945 (the date of the German surrender), the number of German submarines lost in operations on the British and American coasts alone was 151. The final accounting was tremendous: By the end of the war, Germany counted 630 submarines sunk and 215 scuttled. Of the 39,000 submariners, only 6000 survived. In the end, the three Axis powers would mourn 1038 submarines gone to the bottom of the sea, against a total of 263 for the Allies.

Along with the U-boats built for the "pirate war," the German Kriegsmarine launched another type of "pirate" boat in the Atlantic. It had to do with very heavily armed ships masquerading as harmless merchant ships flying the flags of various neutral countries, with crews dressed in fake uniforms to deceive enemy observers. In reality, these ships were equipped with cannons, mines, torpedoes and even motor torpedo boats hidden in their holds. The *Pinguin* and the *Atlantis*, for example, could be camouflaged, alternatively, as merchant ships, passenger ships or oil tankers. In total, these "pirate ships" sank 50 enemy vessels. Without being so sophisticated, many other armed merchant ships, belonging to all the belligerent countries, faced the risks of navigating through the seas of war. Another characteristic of the German Navy were the "pocket battleships": these were the fast and highly maneuverable. The most famous of which were the *Deutschland* and the *Admiral Graf Spee*. Spee was a First World War hero who on December 8, 1918, scuttled his ship off the Falkland Islands rather than surrender to the British. The *Admiral Graf Spee* had only a short fighting life. Its captain scuttled the ship off Montevideo Bay on December 17, 1939, trapped by the British fleet and having no ammunition left. The *Admiral Scheer* was launched in to the sea alongside the surviving *Deutschland*, now renamed *the Lützow*. Also in the Atlantic, the battle cruisers *Scharnhorst* and *Gneisenau* (named for generals who had won victories against Napoleon) sank 22 Allied ships in a series of naval encounters. Perhaps the most dramatic and spectacular episode was the hunt for the battleship *Bismarck*. Escorted by the heavy cruiser *Prinz Eugen*, the battleship had been sowing terror in the Atlantic. *The Bismarck*, which had been in service since August 24, 1939, was 813 feet long, had 104 cannon and a crew of 2,400 men, including cadets between 16 and 19 years old. The ship carried six reconnaissance aircraft, and could reach a speed of 29 knot. The only vessel capable of confronting the *Bismarck* was the British battleship *HMS King George V*, which was 744 feet in length, carried 74 cannon, and four aircraft, and had a maximum speed of 27 knots. On May 18, 1941, the *Bismarck*, commanded by Captain Ernst Lindemann, left Gdynia Poland, again escorted by the cruiser *Prinz Eugen* and other smaller ships. The flotilla was heading for the Atlantic. A powerful British fleet (the battleships *HMS King George V* and *HMS Prince of Wales*, the aircraft carrier *HMS Victorious*, four cruisers, and 17 smaller ships) left Scapa Flow, with the aim of confronting and sinking the *Bismarck*. First contact occurred on May 24 off Greenland, with the result that an English cruiser was sunk. Steaming at full speed, the *Bismarck* tried to throw off its pursuers, but the torpedo bombers put aloft by *HMS Victorious* gave her no respite. Seriously damaged, the Bismarck had to slow down, and soon all the pursuing ships were upon her. Subjected to a hail of fire, the great German battleship sank on May 27, 1941.

By the end of the battle of the Atlantic, a total of 1700 ships, including merchant and warships of all nationalities, had been sunk. As regards the chessboard of the Mediterranean, during the first phase of the conflict, the sea war against Great Britain was entrusted to Italy. Germany could not bother with it, since it was organizing operation Sea Lion. On the other hand, the Italian Navy in the Mediterranean was second to none. Its war fleet, greatly strengthened under Fascism, could count on two principal bases: La Spezia, in the north of the peninsula and Taranto, in the south. Great Britain, on the other hand, had the bases of Alexandria (Egypt), Gibraltar and Malta. Even an amateur, looking at a map of the Mediterranean, would have understood that, in order to win, Italy first had to eliminate Malta, in the center of the Mediterranean and only a 60 miles from the Italian coast: a permanent threat to the peninsula. Nevertheless, the conquest of the island--which the British admiralty had transformed into a well-armed fortress and the center for radar-assisted aerial attacks on the Italian convoys, carrying reinforcements for the troops engaged in North Africa, was not contemplated in Italian war plans. This error would soon turn out to be tragic for Italy's fortunes in North Africa.

The first clash between the two fleets occurred on July 9, 1940 at Stilo Point on the Calabrian coast and resulted in an Italian defeat: a cruiser and a battleship were put out of commission. But a worse setback awaited Mussolini on November 11, when British airplanes taking off from the aircraft carrier *HMS Illustrious*, attacked six Italian battleships anchored in Taranto, sinking the *Cavour* and seriously damaging the *Littorio*, the *Duilio* and two cruisers. Then, on November 27, there was yet another defeat during the battle of Cape Teulada; finally, on March 27, 1941, in the naval battle of Cape Matapan, the Royal Navy lost three cruisers and two destroyers. It should be noted that the two Italian navy squadrons were seriously limited by the lack of aircraft carriers, radar and, most of all, fuel; this was the reason why, rather than conduct a wide-ranging offensive against British bases in the Mediterranean, it had to limit itself simply to protecting merchant convoys that carried supplies to the Italo-German armies engaged in North Africa, continuously attacked by the Royal Navy.

Certainly, Italy's 10th MAS Flotilla (the Italian Navy's rapid-raid/guerilla unit) inflicted major damage on British battleships and cruisers that lacked support from carrier-borne aircraft. Among the unit's heroic feats were Commander Teseo Tesei's attack on Valletta (Malta's main port), in which Tesei lost his life; Cdr. Luigi Durand de la Penne's raid on the British naval base at Alexandria, Egypt, in which the battleships *HMS Valiant* and *HMS Queen Elizabeth* were sunk; and Cdrs. Birindelli and Ferraro's attacks against Suda and Haifa, respectively. Always in action, and a true nightmare for the British fleet, the submarine *Sciré*, captained by Prince Junio Valerio Borghese, transported the raiders to the attack point and retrieved them after the action, carrying them to safety. At the end of the war, the London Naval Museum dedicated an entire section to the feats of the 10th MAS Flotilla's men, whom Churchill called "the only Italians who won the Second World War."

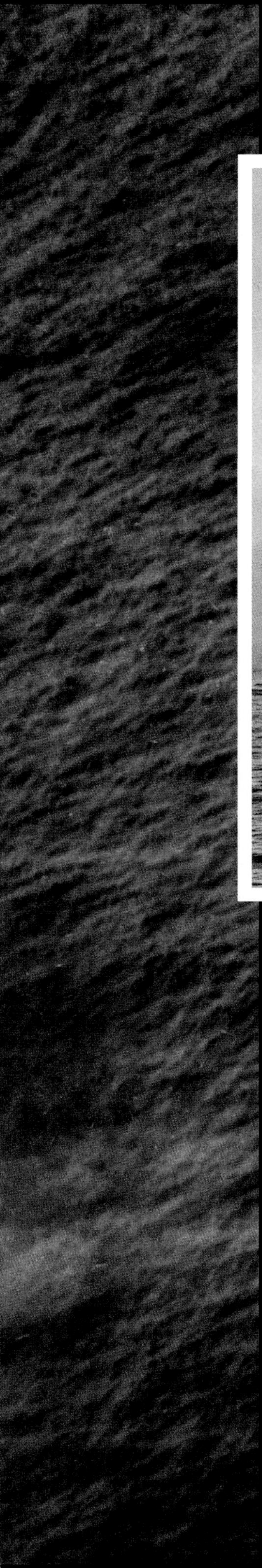

152-153
Pictures of the dramatic events of the sea war fought between the British and German navies. To the left: a German U-Boat hit by a British bomber.
Top right: the German pocket battleship Graf Spee *scuttling itself in the Atlantic Ocean; bottom, the German battleship* Bismark *responding to enemy fire. Although German submarines spread terror throughout the entire Second World War, British superiority was evident on the surface. Perhaps the most spectacular and dramatic episode was the hunt for the battleship* Bismark, *which had been spreading terror in the Atlantic. Confronted by the battleships* King George V *and* Prince of Wales, *the aircraft carrier* Victorious, *four cruisers and 17 smaller ships, it was sunk on May 27, 1941.*

EUROPE UNDER THE SWASTIKA
1940-1944

Germany's "new order" held sway over France, Norway, Denmark, Belgium, and the Netherlands. It called for hunting down Jews and "Aryanizing" national populations in order to create a Germanocentric Europe. Members of national pro-Nazi movements--"collaborationists"--worked with the invaders, sometimes out of self-interest but more often from ideological convictions. Many held posts in their countries' governments: Quisling in Norway, Léon Degrelle in Belgium, Van Thonningen in Holland. In Vichy France, alongside a resigned Pétain, Pierre Laval (shot after the war), and then Admiral Paul Darlan (assassinated in Algeria following the Allied invasion in 1942), took turns leading the government. Because local police obeyed the Gestapo, the French départments administered from Vichy provided no haven for anti-Nazi political refugees. The alternative for these exiles was to flee to England or to the French colonies in North Africa.

Living conditions in Western Europe under Nazi domination did not differ from those in Eastern Europe, governed by politicians who were Berlin's vassals: Admiral Horthy in Hungary, Monsignor Tiso in Slovakia, Ante Pavelic with his Ustashi (nationalistic Fascists) in Croatia. Persecution of the Jews raged everywhere except southern France. Here Ciano, the Italian foreign minister, had prohibited all actions against Jews.

In Holland, Anton Mussert's Nazi movement collaborated with Reich commissioner Seyss-Inquart, making it possible to deport 104,000 of the 140,000 nation's Jews to the lagers. Their number included Anne Frank and her family. However, a strong Resistance movement developed in the Netherlands. Members made bomb attacks on both the Germans and the local Nazis, and protected 300,000 workers from hard labor in Germany. A Resistance movement developed in Belgium; the Walloon region was more pro-German and formed an SS division that fought in Russia.

In Denmark, King Christian X was forced to confirm Erik Scavenius, a politician agreeable to Berlin, as premier. But here too the underground Resistance grew, conducting sabotage actions and managing to liberate groups of Jews destined to be deported. To protest Jewish persecution, the king had a Star of David stitched onto his coat. In Norway, the Resistance carried out undertakings of great strategic importance, including the destruction of the "heavy water" factory in Rjukan. This action took Germany out of the race to create the atom bomb.

France reflected the strongest contrasts and the most dramatic confrontations. There had been no response to De Gaulle's radio appeal of June 18, 1940, calling for an organized resistance. On the contrary, a number of people with openly pro-German tendencies emerged. They included pro-Nazi thinkers such as Pierre Drieu la Rochelle (later a suicide), critics such as Robert Brasillach (executed in 1945), and writers such as Céline (who survived). The Communists, who were collaborating with the Nazis out of obedience to Moscow, sided with the Resistance after June 21, 1941, and immediately sought to take over the movement. The leader of the French underground movement, the FFL (Free French Forces), was the former prefect of Chartres, Jean Moulin, who had created the CNR (National Council of the Resistance). Loyal to de Gaulle's instructions, he banned acts of terrorism because the Germans would retaliate against civilians. Which was precisely what the Communists wanted in order to carry out the Comintern's instructions. At a certain point, Jean Moulin was in the way: better to tip off the Gestapo, have him captured, and be rid of him. The Gaullist hero was captured and died under German torture. The coast was clear for the Communists. They set off bombs in theatres and restaurants frequented by the occupation force and bombed their vehicles. The Germans responded with terrible retaliations, such as the one at Oradour-sur-Glane, where 600--men, women and children--were led into the church and burned alive with flamethrowers.

Vichy soon lost even the semblance of independence represented by the régime. On November 11, 1942, the Germans stripped the government of its powers for its failure to react with military action to the Allied invasion of the Moroccan coast: From then on, the Germans occupied all French territory except the deep south and coastal region under Italian jurisdiction. In response, the Italians occupied Corsica and seaborne Italian-German troops took possession of Tunisia.

155
Episodes from the partisan war against the German occupiers and repression by troops of the Third Reich: top, the results of an attack on a German military train; center, French Maquis in action with fuses and explosives along a railway line; bottom, captured partisans guarded by Vichy troops, allies of the Third Reich.

1940
1944

WAR IN AFRICA
1940-1943

156
September 1940: having crossed the border between Libya and Egypt, Italian troops and vehicles advancing, preceded by intense artillery fire

Italian East Africa constituted a true *casus belli* between Italy and Great Britain ever since 1936, when the League of Nations voted sanctions and an economic blockade against Rome, with the aim of preventing Italy from increasing its colonial empire. It was thus predictable that, once Mussolini decided to enter the war against the Allies, he would turn his attention to the British colonial empire. For this reason, Italy's first major military attack in World War II was unleashed against British Somaliland, on August 16, 1940. Italian troops commanded by Viceroy Amedeo d'Aosta attacked along the British-Somali frontier, and advanced rapidly toward the interior. However, the British called in large numbers of troops from nearby Sudan, Egypt, and their other African colonies.

The British then reversed their defeat. By February 1941, they had driven the Italians beyond the border, occupied all of Italian Somalia and Eritrea, and had begun a march on Addis Ababa, the capital of Italy's Ethiopian empire. After an Italian resistance lasting two months and marked by the battle of Keren, Addis Ababa capitulated on April 5. On May 18, the last resistance ended at Amba Alagi, where the Duke of Aosta had retreated, still fighting. There he surrendered to the British, who deprived him of neither his rank nor dignity. He died several months later from a sudden illness. Several Italian detachments resisted at Gondar until November 28. On May 5, Haile Selassie, Emperor of Ethiopia, who on that very day five years before had had to abandon Addis Ababa to take refuge in England, made his return to the ancient capital of the Kingdom of Sheba.

If clashes in East Africa were bloody, the confrontation in North Africa was outright savage: here, for almost three years, the Italians and British confronted each other in a hard, but chivalrous war. Here also thousand of Germans commanded by the Third Reich's most popular commander, Erwin Rommel, lost their lives.

Italy made the first move in the North African chess game, with its advance in September 1940 from Libya toward Egypt, with the aim of capturing Alexandria and the Suez Canal. General Rodolfo Graziani's 10th Army reached Sidi-el-Barrani, but was forced to halt there and confront the British counterattack led by General Wavell. The battle, which began on December 9, was the first of a endless series of battles that saw incredible acts of heroism on both sides, but which ended with a defeat for the Italians. They left 38,000 prisoners in enemy hands at Sidi-el-Barrani, and another 25,000 at Bardia. It was a miserable winter for Graziani: at the end of February 1941, Cyrenaica was lost. The British advance halted at Sirte because German success in Greece forced Wavell to shift divisions from the desert to Piraeus. The advance resumed on November 18 with the onset of a new offensive by the British 8th Army, now commanded by General Sir Claude Auchinleck. The British took Tobruk and Benghazi after desert battles. The final toll was 17,700 British dead, 20,000 Italians, and 13,000 German. The Axis counteroffensive began on January 21, 1942. The armies retook Benghazi, El Gazala, and Tobruk, where the Germans took 25,000 prisoners. The Axis advance toward Egypt seemed unstoppable. On June 28 Mussolini arrived in Tobruk, ready to enter Alexandria on a white horse, bringing reality to the iconography with which the Fascist regime was already portraying him. But Auchinleck had set his line of last resistance at El Alamein, barely 63 miles from Alexandria. Here, the cruelest battle of all the African front campaigns raged throughout the entire month of August. Together with the British 8th Army's tenacity and Rommel's Afrika Korps' combativeness, the sacrifices of Italy's "Lightning" Division and the "Young Fascists" Battalion are fully worthy of remembrance. Almost all the soldiers were student volunteers;

they sacrificed their lives throwing themselves under tanks to blow them up with magnetic "bloodsucker" time bombs.

Led by General Sir Bernard Montgomery, the final British offensive advanced from El Alamein on October 23, 1942. Its military might was crushing: total domination of the skies and 1100 tanks against 500. The advance of the mechanized infantry was supported by landings at Tobruk and Marsa Matruk. On November 20, Italy lost Cyrenaica again, this time forever.

On November 7, 1942, Allied forces disembarked at Morocco and Algeria to attack Rommel's Italo-German army. This was "Operation Torch," commanded by General Dwight Eisenhower, the future supreme commander of the Allied forces. That day saw the redemption of the French army: it had been victorious in the World War I, but was now defeated and torn apart by internal feuding. Along with Eisenhower, General de Gaulle disembarked with French soldiers who had waited for over two years in Great Britain for the day in which to renew their honor and reputation. This landing of the three should have been an occasion for the French to rediscover national unity, but French troops, loyal to Vichy, resisted: at Casablanca, Algiers, and Oran, they opened fire on the landing craft. The French North African officials and troops had no quarrel with the Americans, but detested the British, unable to forget the fate of companions in arms at Mers-el-Kebir. This attack on the French fleet was designed prevent it being scuttled by its senior officers after the Franco-German Armistice signed at Compiègne following France's defeat in 1940. Naturally, the few French troops were unable to stop the landings. On November 8, Admiral François Darlan, representing Marshal Pétain, signed an armistice. With the approval of General Eisenhower, Darlan became head of state of Vichy France. However, he was mysteriously assassinated on December 24 (by Vichy loyalists, or more likely by British secret agents, in view of his intractability in dealing with the British). He was succeeded by Admiral Henri Honoré Giraud, with the title of High Commissioner for French Africa.

Hitler's revenge for the French "betrayal" in Africa was not long in coming. On November 10 a German army invaded the south of France, completely discrediting the Vichy government and forcing French officials to choose only between the Third Reich or the Resistance. Most chose the second path and tried to leave France via Spain to join the new French army in North Africa. Meanwhile, on November 26, the French fleet anchored at Toulon, under attack by the Germans, chose to scuttle itself rather than to surrender.

The unified Axis command in North Africa decided to land a fighting force in Tunisia. The challenge was to combat the Allied landings in Algeria and Morocco, to rush to aid the Afrika Korps (now facing defeat in Libya), halt the Anglo-Franco-American advance toward Cyrenaica, and block the British thrust from the southeast. Thus the incoming Axis troops (two Italian and three German divisions) would be fighting on two fronts. These troops were commanded by General Giovanni Messe, who had 250,000 men and had to confront the British 1st and 8th Armies (under Field Marshal Montgomery) as well as the American 5th Army (under General Omar Bradley). The American 5th Army, in addition to its "goumiers," (Moroccan volunteers), also could draw upon the French combat groups led by Generals Leclerc, Koeltz, and Magnan, and, above all, the diamond drill of General Patton's Tank Corps, later destined for triumps in Sicily, Normandy, and Central Europe. While Montgomery pressed on from Libya, the French and American force was ready to unleash its offensive from the west. The Allied armaments were unbeatable: the British 8th Army alone had 120,000 vehicles, ranging from 24-ton trailer trucks to Jeeps.

On March 16 Montgomery attacked along the entire Marenth Line with 620 Sherman tanks against the 94 Italian tanks that were left in the "Centaur" Division. The Italians resisted for 15 days. Between April 7 and 10, the Italo-German retreat began along the Chotts-Akarit Line, followed by the second retreat on the Enfidaville Line. On April 10 Montgomery occupied Sfax and Kairouan; Susa fell on the 12th. Fighting continued until May 6 when, at 3.00 a.m., General Alexander unleashed an attack driven by 800 tanks, 500 pieces of artillery, and 400 bombers. By May 7 all was lost for the Axis: the British conquered Tunis, the Americans Bizerta; Von Arnim (Rommel's successor) was captured at St. Marie du Zit by the 4th Indian division. The Afrika Korps then surrendered to the Americans, and the 5th Panzerarmée crumbled. The 1st Italian Army laid down its arms on May 13, after receiving orders from Rome.

The Allied "booty" was over 200,000 prisoners and 16 German and 10 Italian generals. In North Africa, the Axis had lost 827,000 men as opposed to 227,000 for the Allies.

158-159
Top right: Scottish troops with fixed bayonets, launch an attack against the Italo-German positions at El Alamein, July 24, 1942. The battle of El Alamein was one of the bloodiest and, at the same time, most determined of the World War II. Center: Italian volunteers from the Bir-el Gobi Battalion in action. Bottom: after surrendering on the Amba Alagi, Italian soldiers with their commander, Duke Amedeo d'Aosta, in the lead file past the British who are presenting arms and giving them a military salute. 1941 saw Italy's the honorable surrender of East African colony, won in the war of 1935-36. To the right: A German tank soldier surrenders to a British soldier, who faces him with rifle leveled.

THE BALKANS
1939-1945

In 1934 Mussolini had mobilized his army in support of Austrian independence. In 1938, he had to suffer Austria's incorporation into the Third Reich. He now thought to give the Führer, to whom he was indissolubly bound, tit for tat in an operation that was almost an exact copy of the Anschluss. Hitler had taken Austria: he, Mussolini, would take Albania. First he offered King Zog an Italian protectorate, and then, seeing the sovereign's hesitation, he sent him an ultimatum: Take it or leave it. King Zog decided to leave it and fled to Greece with his wife, Geraldina. Italian troops disembarked at Vlöre without firing a shot, and were received with jubilation by the population. Victor Emmanuel III added the title of King of Albania to those of King of Italy and Emperor of Ethiopia. Mussolini requested the king to name him supreme commander of the Italian Army, the title Hitler held in the Third Reich. The king granted his request only in part, assigning the Duce command only of troops operating on the war fronts. By now, Fascism was a dictatorship divided by the dyarchy of Mussolini and the King. The Führer had several times exhorted the Duce to liberate himself from the monarchy, but Mussolini had never dared. He knew the Italian people's feelings; for them the Savoyard was still and forever the "Soldier King" of the World War I. The Court harbored hostility toward Nazi Germany: the Italian monarchists considered the Nazis to be vulgar bullies. Hitler returned the compliment, in private conversations calling Victor Emmanuel "that imbecile." This was the framework of relationships within the Axis when Mussolini, fed up with Hitler presenting him a series of faits accomplis, decided to launch an attack on Greece from Italy's Albanian bases. The date set was October 28, the anniversary of Fascism's taking power in Italy in 1922. First, Italy sent Greece an ultimatum, demanding several bases on Greek territory from which to oppose the British fleet's incursions into the Mediterranean. Greece refused; Italy commenced military operations. The Italian Air Force bombed Patrasso and the Alpine divisions began to attack Macedonia. That day, Hitler was on an official visit to Florence. Personally informed by the Duce of the attack, he ratified it, offered his congratulations, and predicted its success, although with clenched teeth. Italy needed it. In fact, conducted with inexperience and tentativeness by a command that never believed in it, the operation failed almost immediately. The Greeks pushed the 100,000 Italian invaders back beyond the frontier, and in November and December occupied Koritza and then Gjirokastër, both in Italy's Albanian territory. Britain hastened to the defense of Greece, building naval bases and airports on the island of Crete, sending troops to Piraeus and airplanes to the Greco-Albanian front. On the night of November 11-12, British air-launched torpedoes sank three Italian battleships in Taranto: a real blow for Mussolini.

Hitler then decided to intervene and had his strategists develop Operation Marita to conquer Greece from Bulgaria. On March 2, 1941, the German 12th Army (Field Marshal List) entered Bulgaria, which had become a member of the Tripartite Alliance the day before. On March 27, a military coup in Belgrade deposed the Regent (Prince Paul) and entrusted the government to the very young Peter II. General Simovic assumed the duties of head of government in the name of the conspirators, and made a diplomatic approach to London. That was all Hitler needed: he modified Operation Marita

160
Italian soldiers parade through the streets of Ljubljana, capital of Slovenia, after the capitulation of Yugoslavia, which had attempted in vain to resist the Führer's ultimatum.

and sent an ultimatum to Yugoslavia: if German troops were not allowed transit through their territory to Greece, Belgrade would be razed to the ground. The ultimatum was dryly rejected. At dawn on April 6, 1941, 400 German bombers attacked Belgrade. Hundreds were killed. Simultaneously, German armored divisions entered Yugoslav territory. In a few days, King Peter's army was destroyed: 23 German divisions occupied the country, taking 344,000 prisoners. The King and the government fled to London.

Then it was Greece's turn. From Bulgaria, Field Marshal List, at the head of the 12th Army, broke through the Metaxas Line and took Salonika on April 9. From Yugoslavia, Italo-German troops flooded into Macedonia, aiming for Athens. Their advance was slowed on Mount Olympus by the unexpected resistance of English troops who had arrived by sea from Egypt. But the Axis troops overcame this obstacle. On April 20, Greece signed an armistice with Germany and, on the 23rd, with Italy. The British Expeditionary Corps (two infantry divisions and an armored brigade) managed to re-embark before German tanks began to rumbled through the streets of Athens and Piraeus on April 27. The occupation of the Peloponnesus and the Aegean Islands followed, and on June 1 came the occupation of Crete, achieved by General Model's spectacular paratroop assault--Crete was the first large territory conquered exclusively from the air. For the *Fallschirm* Germans, the operation was hard and cruel. After fierce fighting, 15,000 Britons managed to re-embark for Egypt, leaving 12,000 prisoners in German hands.

The Axis had virtually won the war in the Balkans, but had to reckon with a strong resistance movement in Greece and especially Yugoslavia. Here, in addition to the Chetniks (monarchist military bands under the command of General Draza Mihailovic), there was a strong underground Communist movement led by Josif Broz ("Tito"), a veteran of the Spanish Civil War. Tito did not get along with Mihailovic. Beyond ideology, the Chetniks were Serbs and the Communists were mostly Croats and Bosnians. In Croatia, an ephemeral kingdom had been established under Italian protection and entrusted to the Duke of Spoleto, a cousin of Victor Emmanuel III, but real power lay with the hated Fascist dictator Ante Pavelic and his Ustashi.

In Yugoslavia there developed first a savage civil war among Croats, Serbs, and Bosnians and, second, an insidious resistance against the Italian and German occupiers, who reacted to partisan attacks with terrible reprisals. Often, the hatred between Communists and Chetniks led to ambushes between the two "resistance" groups. Little by little, Tito gained the upper hand, and in 1945 he was able to gather 800,000 partisans around the red flag. Many were Italians who had turned their weapons on the Germans after September 8, 1943. Tito had Mihailovic tried and executed. Shamefully, the Chetniks the Allies took prisoner in Italy were returned to Tito and certain death. There was also a resistance movement in Greece, the ELAS (national liberation army) headed by Marcos, a Communist who earlier fought against the Germans; but after the King returned with British support, he turned his weapons against the legitimate government. At this point, Churchill intervened and ordered British troops to stifle mercilessly a resistance subservient to the Soviet Union. The inexorable Russian advance into the heart of Europe shaped the situation in the Balkans.

161
A column of German Panzer PzKw III *parades below the Acropolis: from Yugoslavia Italo-German troops flooded across Macedonia and turned towards Athens, which was reached on April 20, 1941.*

THE RUSSO-FINNISH WAR

1940

On November 30, 1939, the USSR invaded Finland, despite the fact that on the outbreak of war, Finland, together with Norway and Sweden, had declared neutrality in the war between the Germany and the western powers. What led to the USSR's criminal act? Stalin had presented an ultimatum to the Finnish government, peremptorily demanding a naval base and 2702 square miles of territory on the Isthmus of Karelia. The USSR sent this ultimatum under clauses of the Ribbentrop-Molotov Pact (an authentic *pactum sceleris* between two regimes devoid of scruples), in which each had assigned itself "areas of influence." The majority of Poland and all the Eastern European states would go to Germany; the remnant of Poland, the Baltic States, and Finland would go to Russia. Germany absorbed Poland immediately after defeating its army in Warsaw; the three Baltic States (Estonia, Latvia, and Lithuania) had preferred not to resist and submitted. But Finland did not.

Despite the fact that Marshal Karl Mannerheim, commander of the Finnish armed forces, was in favor of granting Stalin's request, the government decided to defy the Moscow despot. This decision was consistent with the government's political line that since 1930 had outlawed the Finnish Communist party, and also in keeping with a non-aggression pact the USSR had signed with Finland on January 21, 1932. But the illusion that Stalin could respect a promise did not survive long. That Thursday, November 30, 1939, the Russians crossed the Finnish border with a gigantic force: a total of 500,000 men, 1500 tanks, and 1000 airplanes. The Finnish army was clearly inferior in men and equipment: 200,000 men, no tanks, and about a 100 airplanes.

The League of Nations' condemnation of the Soviet Union for being "in violation of international law" was useless. The Finns resisted their aggressors. Marshal Mannerheim had led the White Army during the war fought against the Red Army. At that time, Mannerheim had routed the Reds with the help of a German division commanded by General von der Golz, on December 6, 1917 a unit that had hurried to the aid of Finland. This time, however, help from Germany did not arrive, even though repeated popular demonstrations were held in front of the offices of the Soviet embassies in Berlin and Rome. The criminal German-Russian non-aggression pact signed by Ribbentrop and Molotov prevented Hitler from sending his men into Finland; in turn, Hitler's move in occupying Norway prevented France and England from landing an expeditionary rescue force on Europe's northern edge.

So the Finns were forced to fight alone in a guerilla war to the death that was waged inside the Arctic Circle at temperatures of 40°C below zero. The Russians were defeated in the battles of Suomussalmi and Tolvajarvi. Here bottles filled with gasoline, with a fuse in the cork, were used against Russian tanks. The Finns named their weapons "Molotov cocktails" as a sign of derision for Stalin's foreign minister and right-hand man, and this weapon has kept that name ever since.

After more than two months of ferocious combat, Stalin sent a new contingent of 800,000 men to Finland and also doubled the number of armored units. It was time to put an end to Finland; the war was making a laughingstock out of the Red Army in front of the whole world. The Finns resisted on the Mannerheim Line until March 12, 1940, but then the day on which they signed a peace treaty with Moscow. Helsinki was forced to grant its neighbor the Isthmus of Karelia and part of eastern Karelia as well as transit rights through the Petsamo area. The Finns suffered 25,000 dead and 55,000 wounded. Compared to these losses, Soviet losses were enormous: 200,000 dead, 300,000 wounded, 1,600 tanks destroyed, and 630 airplanes shot down. Given these numbers, and reflecting on the apparent ease with which the lean, poorly armed Finnish army had inflicted such terrible blows on the Red Army, Hitler was convinced that the USSR was a giant with feet of clay. It would be incapable of sustaining a modern war brought by the German war machine.

With the German attack on the Soviet Union on June 21, 1941, Finland's day of revenge had arrived. Mannerheim accepted a significant degree of German help, including an Alpine Army dispatched to northern Finland. Then it declared war on Russia and on its ally, Great Britain, reoccupied the territory lost in 1940, and participated in support of the Reich's Army Group North in the long siege of Leningrad, preventing the city from receiving provisions from the west. The situation turned against Finland following the collapse of the German offensive in Russia. To avoid a second invasion of the country, the new Finnish government denounced the understanding with Germany and invited German troops to leave the country and withdraw to Norway. The invitation was accepted because, by now, Hitler no longer had the power to impose his will.

The Second World War

163
Top: a Helsinki neighborhood appears half-destroyed after bombardment by Soviet airplanes; center, Finnish soldiers lie in ambush in the snow; bottom: a Soviet baggage train surprised and destroyed at Suomussalmi by a partisan action.

The attack on Russia, begun on June 21, 1941, was distinguished by quick successes and an advance that, at first, seemed unstoppable. Top: several Waffen-SS display a war trophy, a battle flag captured from an enemy detachment.

Bottom left: a fleet of German Stuka Junker Ju-87s bombing a deserted heath covered with snow where identifying the enemy is extremely difficult; right, a detachment of German infantry attacking on the Russian front, November 1941.

THE EASTERN FRONT
1941-1944

On the night of June 21-22, 1941, with neither an ultimatum nor a declaration of war, Germany attacked the Soviet Union in the most criminal military action in recorded history. Three army groups flooded across Soviet territory. Army Group South crossed the Carpathians with the aim of capturing Kiev, Army Group Central crossed the Pripyet marshes with the aim of capturing Smolensk, and the Army Group North traversed East Prussia with the aim of seizing the Baltic regions and Leningrad. In what was to be the last Blitzkrieg of the World War II, 152 German divisions (of which 33 were mechanized) crushed the Red Army's every attempt at resistance. The German forces could have found 170 Soviet divisions blocking their way if Stalin had not deployed them in Siberia because of his never-abandoned fear of an attack by Japan--the same Japan from which the master spy Richard Sorge had sent detailed information about Hitler's planned aggression. But the Soviet dictator had given the reports no credence, believing Hitler to be incapable of the invasion.

During the first days of the invasion, this tragic error cost Stalin the destruction of 1800 planes on the ground and also Bialystok. A 40-division force of Army Group Central captured the city, with a booty of 330,000 prisoners. This 40-division force was the spearhead of the German invasion. It was also the first of the three Army groups to reach its objective, taking Smolensk and capturing another 310,000 Soviet soldiers in the city, only 250 miles from Moscow.

Since the beginning of Operation Barbarossa, Army Group Central had covered 497 miles in only 20 days. On par with Stalin's error of refusing to believe his secret service's reports, Hitler made the irreparable mistake of stopping Army Group Central's advance when Moscow was within reach. He delayed the capture of Moscow by ordering Army Group Central to advance to two distant objectives, Kharkov and the Ukraine. This amateur strategy was based on the belief that it was important to conquer the Donetsk industrial basin and interrupt the Soviet Army oil supply from the Caucasu. In executing the Führer's orders, Army Group South surrounded Kiev. The German troops captured another 660,000 prisoners, pursued the survivors beyond the Donetsk, and then occupied the factories. By the end of September, the Donetsk basin and the main Soviet factories were in German hands. As of that date, the Wehrmacht's loses, including dead, wounded, and prisoners, totaled 550,000 men, less than one fifth of Soviet losses.

Army Group North conquered the Baltic Republics after a series of battles and on September 15th began its siege of Leningrad, a city of more than 3 million inhabitants. An enormous number of soldiers were involved in the 900-days siege. Leningrad also sheltered the entire Russian Baltic fleet in its port. Hitler's ordered that the city was to be taken by famine, not force; it was to be hammered by artillery and airplanes every night. The siege reflected an ideological rather than a strategic value: the inhabitants must pay dearly for their city's hated name: Lenin. The siege was carried out by German troops to the southeast and by Finnish troops to the north; the unified command was in German hands and orders came directly from Berlin.

The attackers' cordon was impenetrable. Food reserves would feed the besieged for a month at most. Some provisions came across Lake Ladoga, but with the arrival of the ice season, even those were interrupted. Inhabitants starved to death by the thousands: dogs, cats, and horses were sacrificed, then the inhabitants ate surrogate foods developed by the University's Scientific Institute, such as flour made from wallpaper. But these were mere stopgaps. By Christmas Day, 1941, in the first year of the siege, 3,700 people had died of starvation in hospital corridors; during February 1942 alone 72,000 died. German aerial bombardments wreaked massive destruction, yet no one could leave the city without the risk of being machine-gunned by the besiegers. The "official" death tally for the siege totaled 632,000 dead, but there were certainly more, at least one million.

On two occasions (late winter 1942 and in January 1943), Russian offensives tried to break the siege. During the second offensive, the Russians managed to open a corridor to Lake Ladoga to resupply the famished city and evacuate the wounded and dying: in 17 days they built a highway and a railroad. But only in January 1944 did the Red Army succeeded in definitively breaking the encirclement. During that offensive, Andrei Vlasov, a Soviet general captured by the Germans, reacted with disgust to Stalin's insensitivity to the Leningrad population's sufferings. Vlasov raised an army of anti-Communist Russians, mostly Cossacks and Ukrainians, from among prisoners held in Germany. Later, the Vlasov army fought against the Anglo-American advance on the western front. Captured by the Allies at the end of the war, the soldiers were "returned" to Stalin and to certain death together with their commander.

THE EASTERN FRONT
1941-1944

After taking Kiev, and with Army Group North immobilized in the siege of Leningrad, Hitler ordered the attack on Moscow. On October 12, 1941, during the battle of Vyazma, the Germans captured 660,000 prisoners. On October 19th, Stalin and the government moved to Kuibyshev, some 550 miles southeast of Moscow. Anticipating a long siege as at Leningrad, Stalin appealed to the Muscovites, harking back to motherland, ancestors, and the glory of the Tsars-traditions that Communism had always used for fodder. The Muscovites responded. The civilian population cooperated with the "People's Commissars": one hundred trains a day, organized by volunteers, carried untested Siberian troops to the city.

On December 5th and 6th, a wave of bitter cold blocked the German advance: they had been struck by "General" Winter, the predictable Russian ally that had defeated Napoleon Bonaparte and Charles XII of Sweden before him. General Winter now threatened to erase Hitler's military success: 3 million prisoners, 20,000 tanks captured or put out of commission, and 15,000 airplanes destroyed. But Hitler, not satisfied with his strategic error at the onset of the invasion, replaced Field Marshal Walther von Brauchitsch with himself as supreme commander. He wanted to imitate Napoleon without having his experience.

At Germanys' side, Romania (June 22, 1941), Italy (June 23rd), Slovakia (the 24th) and Hungary (the 27th) had descended into the field against the USSR. In all, 41 divisions from four different countries were supporting the Wehrmacht. These troops were attacked by General Winter as well as the German comrades were. In short, the sea of mud, the *rasputitsa*, swallowed up tanks, trucks, and artillery: in a month theylost 150,000 vehicles. Only caterpillar-tracked vehicles could have advanced, but they had not been provided. At 40°C below zero, the panzers froze up and airplanes couldn't take off. Stalin took advantage of these difficulties and launched a series of counteroffensives. The Russian soldiers, properly equipped with shoes and clothing suitable for any temperature, and began to strike hard. In the south, Field Marshal von Rundstedt asked for authorization to make a strategic withdrawal: He was removed and replaced with von Reichenau, who nevertheless executed his predecessor's plan. Hitler also replaced Guderian and von Bock, two of the Wehrmacht's best generals, and put puppet generals in their place. All the prerequisites for Operation Barbarossa's failure were now in place.

In February 1942, Mussolini decided to make a deeper commitment to the Russian campaign and created the ARMIR (the Italian Army in Russia) formed from 3 Alpine and 1 infantry division. These 4 divisions went to join the 3 divisions of the CSIR (Italian Expeditionary Corps in Russia), at the front since July 1941. General Giovanni Messe, who did not get along well with his German colleagues, commanded the CSIR's 60,000 combatants. In all, there were now 300,000 Italians at the front, commanded by General Italo Gariboldi. The terrible winter of 1941-42 brought a near halt to military activities. Then, in early summer 1942, ably assisted by the Italians (and also by the Romanians and Hungarians), the Wehrmacht resumed a vast offensive. Successes included the taking of Sebastopol on July 2, 1942, after an eight-month siege, in which Italian assaults from the Black Sea had major effect. The German armies resumed their advance toward the Caucasus, winning a victory at Rostov-on-Don and occupying the Ukraine.

The ARMIR, though being well commanded and composed of extremely courageous troops, lacked the armaments and equipment required. Even so, the Isbuscenskj charge (in which the Savoy Cavalry Regiment hurled itself against Soviet tanks, breaking the encirclement) was to become legendary. The three Alpine divisions (the *Cuneense*, *Julia*, and *Tridentina*) had brought mules, expecting to be employed in the mountains of the Caucasus. Instead, the OKW strategic plans had them fighting in the plains, where mules were not needed. The ARMIR was deployed on the Don, between the Hungarian 2nd Army and Romanian 3rd. After the German rout at Stalingrad, the three Alpine divisions, trapped by the meandering Don, retreated on foot, pressed by the Russians and crossed hundreds of miles in bitter cold. Sapped by useless boots and frozen limbs, the Italians left behind 70,000 dead and missing and another 100,000 prisoners in Russian hands, 30,000 of whom never returned to their homeland.

At the resumption of the offensive in June 1942, the Axis contingent in Russia was 233 divisions strong, a total of 4 million men. The conquest of *Lebensraum*, that "vital living space" to the east, had turned out to be much more problematic than Hitler had ever imagined. Also in the 1920s, Hitler could not have foreseen two elements that were determining the German defeat. The first was the formidable flow of arms, trucks, food, and technology that continued to reach the Red Army by way of Alaska and

Siberia. The second factor was the shrewd performance of that faux-Bolshevik, Stalin, who was able to reanimate the Russian people, discouraged by twenty years of "dictatorship of the proletariat," by dusting off myths from the past. Now, the most heroic units were rewarded with a promotion to "Guards," aping the Tsars' lexicon. Next the hated "political commissars"(party spies placed in control of military commanders), were momentarily pushed aside by a simple decree, only to return once the German defeat was in sight.

On the other side of the front, Hitler the "strategist" continued to rack up mistakes, such as detaching numerous units marching with body of the Wehrmacht toward the oil fields south of the Caucasus. These units he sent to reinforce the attack on Stalingrad, which the Russians had no intention of surrendering. Stalingrad, like Leningrad, was an objective of scant strategic importance. Its name was the reason Hitler had to annihilate it. Before the final attack, set for September 10, 1942, the city was bombarded from the air, resulting in 40,000 civilian victims. Then the 6th Army was unleashed under General Friedrich von Paulus. The attacks continued until November 19th, with street-by-street and house-by-house fighting. Courageous workers defended the Red October factory foot by foot; they were promoted to the rank of "Guards." From the eastern bank of the Volga, 300 Katyusha rocket launchers hammered the German positions. From loudspeakers, Russian propaganda spread a mournful refrain, "Every minute that goes by, another German soldier dies." The Germans responded with portable megaphones, "Russ! Bul bul u Volga!"(Russians! You'll send up little bubbles from the bottom of the Volga!).

On November 19th, General Zhukov unleashed an offensive on the flanks of the 6th Army, with the objective of surrounding von Paulus. Some 250,000 Germans thus found themselves trapped in the rubble of Stalingrad. From Berlin Hitler ordered, "Fight to the death," and promoted von Paulus to field marshal, "because no German field marshal in history has ever surrendered to the enemy." But the German combatants were slaughtered by hunger, cold, and disease and the shells of 5000 cannon that fired without respite from the ring Zhukov had formed around the city: desertions began on improvised pontoons and tree trunks thrown into the Volga. During one week, 350 German soldiers were shot in the back as traitors. But by then no hope remained for the 6th Army. On February 1, 1942, Field Marshal von Paulus, Hitler's most faithful subject, surrendered. Imprisoned by the Russians, he was from that moment on Hitler's enemy (as Vlasov, on the opposing front, had become Stalin's enemy). However, at the end of the war, instead of going to the gallows like Vlasov, he was to receive a pension from Communist East Germany. Zhukov's prize consisted of 750 airplanes, 1500 tanks, 500 armored cars, and 8000 cannons. Some 140,000 German soldiers had died in the inferno of Stalingrad, 20,000 were missing, 70,000 were wounded, and 90,000 taken prisoner. Only 5000 returned home.

Having annihilated the German 6th Army, Zhukov broke through the lines held by the Italian and Romanian armies on the Don: during the first months of 1943, the Russians advanced along the entire front, from the North Sea to the Caucasus, without encountering any resistance. Hitler had prepared a maneuver to break through the Russian front in July, but at the last minute the he suspended the action because of the need to send German divisions into Italy, where the Anglo-Americans had landed and were advancing up the peninsula. Now the Russian advance was unstoppable. Kiev was liberated on November 6th. The Red Army entered Galicia and Romania between January and April 1944. At this point, the Russians had 12.5 million combatants in the field. For Army Group Central, the day of reckoning came in June 1944: 28 out of 40 German divisions were surrounded and forced to lay down their arms.

The Red Army then overran German-occupied Poland and reached the Vistula in time to watch the agony of Warsaw. Here, on August 1, General Bor-Komorowski, counting on the speedy Russian advance, had sparked a rebellion against the Nazis. Polish partisans, supplied with arms by Anglo-American ships, were fighting in the streets. They hoped the Russians would intervene to save them from being overwhelmed, but the Russians preferred to head off toward Czechoslovakia, taking Prague on September 1. The Warsaw Uprising lasted 63 days. Once they were certain the Russians would not intervene, the Germans released their fury on the martyred city, destroying it house by house. On October 2, the remains of the Polish Army capitulated. While General Stroop was sending Hitler a telegram stating "Order reigns in Warsaw." Inhabitants who had survived the massacre were deported to Germany.

171
A German tank soldier watches the oil field at Maikop, in the Caucasus, in flames, set on fire by their defenders to prevent their falling into enemy hands.

168-169
Death passed through here: after a Nazi reprisal on the Kerch peninsula, in the Crimea, the landscape appears covered with bodies: the victims' relatives have nothing left but grief and desperation.

170
A few weeks after launching the attack on the USSR, Hitler committed the unpardonable mistake of halting the advance of the Army Group Central when Moscow was already within reach, diverting it towards the oil wells in the Caucasus. In the photograph at the top, a German infantryman hurls a hand grenade during the advance towards Moscow in the summer of 1941; center, Russian soldiers surrender to the German invader near Minsk; bottom, two young partisans are hanged by the SS on the road to Moscow.

172-173

Left: Women wander amid the rubble of Leningrad in search of food; right, above, civilians struggling to retrieve water from under the ice. The siege of the city, begun September 15, 1941 and ended in 1944 after 900 days, was the longest in the history of World War II. The other two pictures refer to the battle of Stalingrad: center, Russian combatants in action amid the ruins; bottom, this smoking rubble made up the city's desolate landscape after the German surrender.

174-175

Left: Russian infantrymen seek shelter during a violent German cannon barrage; above right, the Russians launch a deadly Katyusha rocket attack against the fleeing Germans; center, the Führer's troops retreat across the steppes on horse-drawn sleds; bottom, Italian Alpine troops from the Tridentina Division retreat towards the west after the battle of Nikolayevka.

1941

CARPET BOMBING
1940-1945

From early 1942, it became Germany's turn to suffer "carpet" bombing. Churchill convinced Roosevelt that it was a necessity, though Roosevelt showed considerable reluctance, concerned about the inevitable deaths of women and children. Churchill also ordered nighttime raids on German and Italian cities, to weaken the population's morale. Roosevelt won the concession that the massacre of civilian populations would be at the hands of British pilots; American pilots were reserved for strategic and industrial targets. In this way, Roosevelt was able to lighten the burden on his conscience.

A Royal Air Force raid reduced much of Cologne to rubble: the British spared the cathedral, dropping leaflets to boast about their precision targeting. Hamburg and Berlin also suffered catastrophic bombing. During 1943 alone, the RAF dropped 49,000 tons of explosives on the German capital, leaving thousands of dead and a million homeless. On July 27, the bombing of Hamburg resulted in a firestorm that raised street temperatures to 1832°F, while the suction created uprooted trees and a 155-mph wind whipped people into the flames. In the air raid shelters, people died of suffocation and then were incinerated.

The most frightening bombing was that of Dresden on the night of February 13, 1945. Personally directed by Sir Arthur Harris, head Bomber Command (and nicknamed "the butcher"), the raids lasted for 14 hours and killed 100,000 people. A majority were wounded soldiers in improvised hospitals, Allied prisoners of war, and refugees from the eastern zones, who had wearily reached Dresden with their meager household goods, camping in the streets under the trees. These refugee civilians believed that a city of art like Dresden would never be bombed; indeed, the German spared Florence, Venice, and Ravenna. But in Dresden's case, 805 English bombers poured out 2,558 tons of fragmentation and incendiary bombs. The asphalt in the streets melted; people in the shelters were burned alive. Then reinforcements arrived: 450 American B-17 bombers: Roosevelt had overcome his troubled conscience.

The bombing of urban centers caused "mass evacuation," the wholesale flight of families to the countryside. The phenomenon was especially acute in Italy, where Rome, Milan, Turin, Genoa, and Naples where depopulated through their inhabitants' flight to their peasant grandparents' old country houses. There was almost no mass flight in France, where the Allies decided not to pursue bombing that would have been counterproductive. Nor was it very marked in Germany, where urbanization had not been as strong as in Italy. Germany had enjoyed sufficient time to build adequate air raid shelters for its cities' inhabitants, even if these refuges failed to serve the population from the Hamburg and Dresden firestorms.

But up to what point is it justifiable to bomb cities? During World War I, the Germans had practiced bombing from dirigibles over Great Britain; the Austrians had done so from aircraft over Milan and the cities of the Veneto. Then in the 1930s, the Italian General Giulio Douhet had written theoretical works on aerial bombardment as a means of weakening the enemy's spirit of resistance. Hitler's Condor Legion was to apply Douhet's theories to Guernica during the Spanish Civil War. Göring, in particular, was convinced that Douhet had hit the target: in 1940, he ordered the bombing of Rotterdam (which prompted the Dutch surrender), followed by massive bombing during the Battle of Britain. London suffered aerial attacks for 76 consecutive nights, but the people's morale never wavered. Night after night, over 200,000 Londoners slept in the Underground (London's subterranean transportation system), while the grottoes of Chislehurst (southeast of London) were equipped for tens of thousands of Londoners who went there by train every night. Douhet's theory began to totter. But at the end of the Battle of Britain another scholar, Frederick Lindemann, who had Churchill's ear, declared himself convinced that nighttime bombing raids would weaken the German people's morale and bring them to rebel against Hitler. Thus began the systematic destruction of German cities, but it was not this that brought about Germany's collapse.

177

A squadron of American B-17 Flying Fortresses crosses the skies of Germany at high altitudes amid the wake of condensation produced by their engines. This is the famous "box formation" that caused so much destruction to the cities of the Third Reich. Defended by thirteen machine guns, these four-engined aircraft were a hard nut for German fighters to crack.

178-179

Left, American bombs fall on strategic German installations. Top right: a fleet of US B-17s in action over a German city in 1943; center, a desolate image of Dresden, the hardest hit with 200,000 dead during a single night of attacks; bottom, an emblematic image of Cologne, where only the cathedral remains intact because of a challenge thrown down by British bombsighters who had announced to the population that the historic church would not be touched while the surrounding homes were razed to the ground. In total, 1,350,000 tons of bombs were dropped on Germany, compared to the 65,000 that fell on Great Britain.

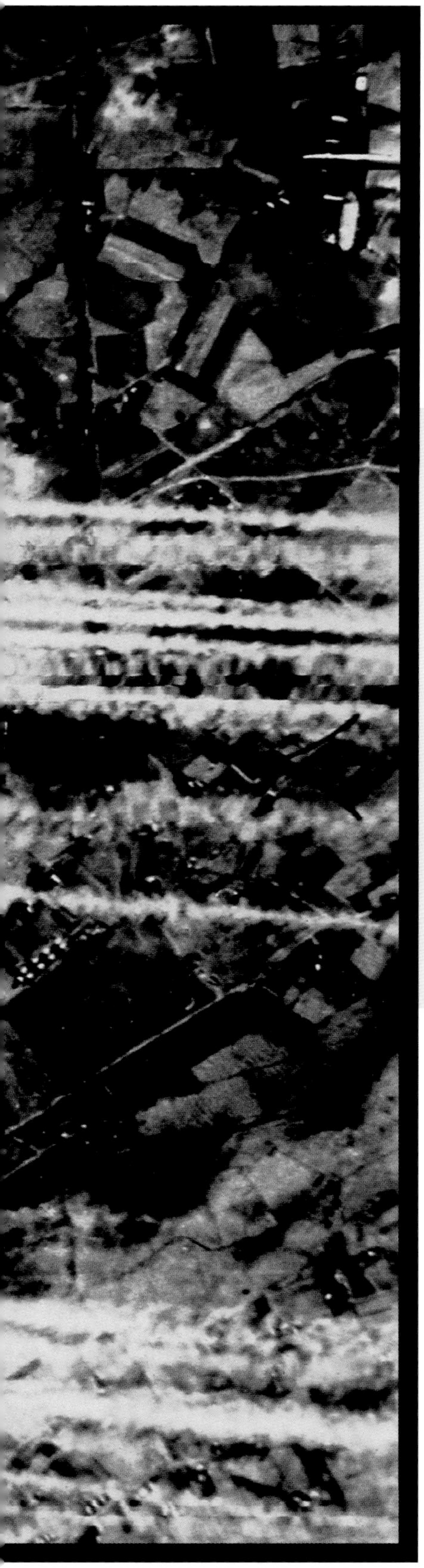

1940
1945

THE ITALIAN FRONT AND THE END OF FASCISM

1943-1945

During the Casablanca Conference (January 14-26, 1943), the Allies made the decision to attack Fortress Europe with a landing in Italy--Operation Husky. But first the battle for Tunisia had to be won and Axis resistance in North Africa stamped out. After these aims were achieved, Operation Husky was given the go-ahead. On July 10 and 12, 1943, after two murderous aerial bombardments, the islands of Pantelleria and Lampedusa were occupied, with the capture of 11,000 Italians. Also on July 10, an expeditionary corps was formed from the American 7th Army (General George S. Patton) and the British 8th Army (General Sir Bernard Montgomery). Sir Harold Alexander, this new force came ashore on the Sicilian beaches of Agrigento and Siracusa: 2800 boats landed 160,000 men, 14,000 vehicles, 1800 cannon and 600 tanks. The island was defended by 100,000 Italians and Germans. They had 500 cannons, 255 tanks, but no aircraft. In 38 days, from July 10 to August 17, 1943, all of Sicily fell to the Allies.

On July 19, the Americans struck Rome: 500 bombers dropped a thousand tons of bombs on the capital, causing the deaths of 2000 civilians. Pius XII who had never left the Vatican, hurried among the dead and wounded on the bomb sites, raising his arms to heaven in a dramatic invocation to God. From his plane Mussolini, who was returning from his meeting with the Führer and still smarting from his criticism, saw smoke rising from the capital. On the evening of July 24, with Sicily lost, the Grand Council of Fascism--the regime's supreme body that had not met since 1939 because Mussolini, as a dictator, no longer wanted anyone's advice--convened at the Duce's request. It gave the dictator a vote of no confidence, returning all powers of supreme decision-making to the King. Since Mussolini did not react (and even his son-in-law, Galeazzo Ciano, had decided against the dictator); it was a death knell for Fascism.

In the afternoon of the next day (July 25), Mussolini was arrested by order of the King and taken to the island of Ponza. In his place, Marshal Pietro Badoglio was named the head of government. He hurried to make a radio broadcast to the Italian people, stating "The war continues." In short, no one should be deceived that the fall of Fascism necessarily meant peace; Italy would have to continue fighting alongside its German ally. But Hitler, distrusting Badoglio, began to send armed forces into Italy: 6 infantry divisions, 2 armored divisions 1 paratrooper division, an Alpine Brigade, a detachment of SS, and airplanes, which were added to the 4 divisions fighting in the south, trying to stem the Allied advance.

While Hitler was taking precautions against the probable Italian surrender, the Allies were pressuring the King to give in. In August, a series of terrible bombardments brought destruction and death to Rome, Turin, Genoa, and Milan. The Badoglio government, already in negotiations with the Allies through its emissary in Lisbon, picked up the pace. On September 3, Badoglio's plenipotentiary, General Cassibile, signed the so-called "short armistice" in Sicily. It consisted of only 12 clauses, to be followed by others. The main ones required Italy to turn over its fleet and air force. During the negotiations, it was agreed that the armistice would be announced five days later to allow for two landings, one south of Rome, the other north, and the simultaneous descent of a paratroop division in the capital. This commitment was honored only in part. No airborne division arrived in Rome and no landing was attempted north of the capital. The American 5th Army (General Mark Clark) landed at Salerno at dawn on September 9. Operation Avalanche (the operation's code name) in no way corresponded with the reality: General Clark's Americans managed to reach land with difficulty, with losses caused by German fire.

On September 8, in the late afternoon, Eisenhower unilaterally announced Italy's surrender, broadcasting it via the Italian radio system. Rome was still surrounded by German troops: this forced the King and government into the so-called "flight to Pescara." In this Adriatic port a warship was waiting to carry them to Apulia, a region of southern Italy that was free: no longer occupied by the Germans and not yet invaded by the Allies. In reality it was not a flight but a necessary precaution to avoid capture of the King and government by the Germans, with the probable result of forcing them to reject the armistice. Capture would have resulted in a power vacuum, leaving Italy in the hands of two occupying armies with consequences certain to be tragic for the civilian population. Moreover, during the entire Second World War, the enemy's final unstoppable approach triggered the same preoccupation: save the representatives of the state. This had been so in Poland, Yugoslavia, Norway, the Netherlands, Bulgaria, and even in Great Britain where, in view of Operation Sea Lion, preparations had been made for the flight of the Royal Family and the government to Canada. Only the self-mutilation of certain Italian historians has spread the "Gospel of the King's Flight," ignoring the Allies' own less-than-proud judgments of the September 8 events. "A dirty business" (Eisenhower), and "The biggest bluff in history: we got our hands on an entire fleet in exchange for nothing" (Harold Macmillan, representing the English government, echoing the sentiments of the Allied General Staff).

Churchill sought a rapid conclusion to the Italian campaign in order to be able to advance toward Austria and southern Germany and to save as many as people in Eastern Europe as possible from the Red Army. Roosevelt, on the other hand, wanted to conquer Germany starting from Northern Europe, in order not to compete directly with the USSR. The American view prevailed, and at the Quebec Conference (August 1943) Churchill grudgingly accepted it. The Italian front thus became secondary, only good for keeping the greatest possible number of German divisions occupied. This decision sealed the fate of Rome and the government of King Victor Emmanuel III. As was feared, the German reaction to the Italian surrender was brutal, due to the tragically mistaken communiqué in which the Badoglio government suddenly ordered its troops to cease all belligerent activities against the Allies, but to react "to attacks from any other source." If the precise order had been to oppose any abuses of power by the Germans, the Italian army units would probably have reacted differently. As it was, the divisions commanded by Kesselring and Rommel disarmed the Italian army and captured 400,000 men. In addition, those who fell into German hands in Greece, the Balkans, and the south of France, were in total another 200,000.

Few were the episodes of resistance. Around Rome, the armored *Ram* division, commanded by General Raffaele Cadorna, destroyed dozens of German tanks. In Orte, General Caracciolo di Feroleto, faced by a German platoon ordering him to surrender, grabbed a rifle and personally fired at the German officer. At La Spezia, the Alpine division, *Alpi Graie*, fought until September 11. At Salerno, there was a splendid episode of resistance by General Ferrante Gonzaga, killed by the Germans in a cowardly manner. At Bari, General Bellomo defended the port to the end. At Piombino, a popular insurrection broke out on September 10, during which 600 German soldiers and sailors fleeing from Corsica were killed when they attempted a landing. However, on the Greek island of Cephalonia, the Germans took a pitiless German reprisal against the *Acqui* division. In Yugoslavia, 2 Italian divisions fell apart: half surrendered to the Wehrmacht, but half, fleeing into the mountains, gave life to the *Garibaldi* division that fought the Germans until the end of hostilities. In the Dodecanese, resistance by Italian soldiers was quashed: 40,000 Italians fell into German hands along with several thousand British soldiers.

The fleet took to sea to deliver itself to the Allies in Malta and in the ports of Algeria. Five battleships, 8 cruisers, 38 submarines, and several dozen minor ships together with 250 aircraft reached their destinations. The battleship *Roma*, the fleet's flagship, did not make it to safety: en route to Malta was hit by radio-controlled bombs dropped by German. The ship sank, and all 1500 sailors and the fleet's commander, Admiral Bergamini, lost their lives. The remaining ship, under the command of Admiral De Courten, soon took to sea again to fight alongside the Allies in the Atlantic, the Red Sea, and the Indian Ocean. The only exception was the 10th MAS Flotilla, known for daring hit-and-run attacks on Allied shipping and bases in the Mediterranean. Its commander, Prince Borghese, refused to surrender to the Allies, and positioned his unit to defend the La Spezia naval base. He rejected the German ultimatum to surrender, and ordered his men to prepare to open fire. The arm-wrestling ended with Cdr. Borghese and the German commandant of La Spezia signing a singular "pact of alliance" that recognized their equality. Excited by the Prince's initiative, thousands of young Italians signed up as volunteers in the Flotilla.

During Italy's tragic September, events moved forward relentlessly. On the 10th General Calvi di Bergolo, the King's son-in-law, who had remained in Rome in command of the Army Corps stationed there, made a formal surrender to General Kesselring in the German HQ in Frascati. On September 12, German paratroopers liberated Mussolini and took him to Germany. To save Italy from the scorched-earth policy implemented by the Germans in Poland, Hungary, and Bulgaria, he agreed to form a new republican state in German-occupied Italy. During his meeting with the Furher, in the Wolf's Lair, at Rastenburg, East Prussia, Il Duce, was forced to accept a request to return as head of state. His conscience obliged him to accept, but his most fervent desire would have been to retire from politics, as he had written to Marshal Badoglio immediately after his arrest by the carabinieri on July 25, 1943, in Rome. A Northern Italian state was established in opposition to the King's government in Brindisi. It was to be called the RSI, the Repubblica Sociale Italiana. In fact, the RSI entered history as the "Republic of Salò," that being the Lombard city where the RSI's official press agency was located. The agency sent dispatches to the newspapers by teletype, captioned, literally, from Salò. This was the beginning of the Italian civil war.

To the first call to arms (for those born in the years 1924-25, decreed on November 9, 1943), 51,000 young men responded, 45,000 recruits and 6000 volunteers--only 40 percent of the expected total. No one showed up for the call of May 1944, despite institution of the death penalty for resisters. Draft-age men fled to the mountains, joining the partisan bands (or fleeing to neutral Switzerland if they had the means). Government missions sent to concentration camps in Germany to convince the Italian prisoners to enlist in the armed forces of the RSI also failed: out of 600,000 prisoners, no more than 50,000 responded. In spite of everything, Marshal Rodolfo Graziani, the RSI's defense minister, managed to organize four divisions: the *Italia*, *Littorio*, *San Marco*, and *Monterosa*. These he sent to be trained in Germany. On the other hand, many volunteers flocked to join the Germans fighting against the Allies. Over 100,000 joined the National Republican Guard commanded by Renato Ricci. The 10th MAS Flotilla gathered over 30,000 volunteers, the majority of whom sacrificed themselves the fighting aganst the Allies at Anzio and Nettuno and against the Slav partisans in Friuli and Venezia Giulia. Finally, in July 1944, the Fascist Party was militarized, it's 300,000 members armed and incorporated in the Black Brigades to work in the cities now under constant bombardment by the Allies and to meet attacks from the Resistance.

The first Resistance groups were formed in Piedmont made up of officers and soldiers of the 4th Army who had escaped the German roundups. These groups defined themselves as "autonomous," independent of any party, faithful only to the King and the Brindisi government, whose orders were to sabotage German military activities on Italian soil. Among the units the Germans feared most were those of the Di Dio brothers in Val d'Ossola and Major Enrico Martini Mauri in the Monferrato (Piedmont), as well as the *Osoppo* in Friuli. This last was opposed and attacked from behind by the Communists because its members fought simultaneously against the Germans and against Tito's Communist Slavs, who were seeking to take control of Italian territory in the Friuli region. Edgardo Sogno ("Commander Franchi") deserves a separate mention. Born a nobleman and linked to the royal family, he was the Italian Resistance's most audacious hero, a Scarlet Pimpernel, perpetrator of legendary escapades. Sogno was a modern D'Artagnan, he even entered an SS barracks dressed as a German officer. His personal prestige with the British was such that it convinced them not to cut off aid and supplies to the partisans.

The Socialists founded the Matteotti Brigades, named after the politician assassinated by the Fascists in 1924. The Liberals formed the Justice and Liberty Brigades commanded by Ferruccio Parri. Finally, the Communists, with the Garibaldi Brigades commanded by Luigi Longo, were without doubt the most battle-hardened Resistance units, representing at least 40 percent of its total.

There were also GAPs (Patriotic Action Groups), which were subordinate to the Communist party and thus to Moscow. Their specialty was political assassination, not of the worst Fascist tyrants, but of Fascism's more moderate supporters. The GAPs believed that moderates had to eliminated in order to avoid the risk that their conciliatory spirit might cool the partisans' more violent impulses. A series of impressive crimes was perpetrated: the victims included the great philosopher Giovanni Gentile, the scientist Pericle Ducati, pro-peace journalists, and even several members of the monarchist Resistance.

In Malta, on September 29, Marshal Badoglio (heading the government), was forced to sign the "long armistice" (44 clauses rather than the 12 signed by Cassibile). Italy had to renounce its sovereignty and accept rule by AMGOT (Allied Military Government Occupied Territories.) Article 16 made gallant men out of Italians who had betrayed their country, aiding the Allies while their fellow soldiers were fighting and dying in Greece, Africa, and Russia. Based on the laws in force, these men would have been subject to the death penalty. The "long armistice" also prohibited Italy from taking part in any military action, a prohibition dropped after Badoglio's government declared war on Germany on October 13. Now the Italians were "co-belligerents." The new units (the 1st Motorized Group under

General Dapino, and the CIL, Corpo Italiano di Liberazione, under Marshal Messe) fought alongside the Anglo-Americans to regain Italy, rendering service fully on par with that of de Gaulle's Frenchmen, who fought to regain their homeland. But at the end of the war, the two nations received very different treatment: France among the "Big Four," Italy among the defeated.

The German armies in Italy had anticipated two lines of resistance: the Gustav Line (from the Garigliano River to Pescara) and, farther north, the Gothic Line (from Pisa to Rimini). For the Allies, the advance up the peninsula was hard and bloody, as the British and American war cemeteries spread throughout the peninsula amply attest. The British advanced along the Adriatic coast and the Americans along the Tyrrhenian. On September 20 the Germans vacated Sardinia. They occupied Naples on September 30, and left Corsica on October 5. But the Gustav Line, which hinged on Cassino, blocked the Allies' advance farther north. On January 22, 1944, General Clark landed with his men at Anzio and Nettuno, north of the Gustav Line, attempting to take Rome and thus thwart German resistance. The enterprise turned out to be harder than anticipated. The German 14th Army (General von Mackensen) and Italian units from the new Repubblica Sociale and the independent 10th MAS Flotilla blocked 150,000 Americans at the bridgehead formed near the two landing points. The Americans were unable to advance and the Axis forces were unable to push them back into the sea: bloody clashes ensued for four months.

Farther south, the Americans had been blocked at Cassino since October 1943. The city was a linchpin in the march on Rome. But the German 10th Army, with its spearhead paratrooper division, proved to be an insurmountable obstacle. During the winter, the Allied ranks were reinforced. In the two armies placed under Alexander, not only Americans and Britons were fighting, but also Frenchmen, Moroccans, Poles from General Anders' Armed Corps, Australians, New Zealanders, Brazilians, and even a brigade formed by Jews who had escaped the German raids in the Polish ghettos. During the siege of Cassino, the American Army Air Corps criminally disgraced itself: the destruction of the historic Benedictine abbey of Monte Cassino. The abbey, one of the most famous in the world, dated from the 6th century and possessed works of art of inestimable value. A series of savage raids in February 1944 reduced the abbey to rubble. The raids were based on the belief that a unit of German paratroopers may have been holed up inside. The information was false. However, three hundred women and children had found refuge there, and all died along with the abbot and the monks.

Cassino fell on May 18, 1944. The road to Rome was now clear. The advance was coordinated with the bridgehead at Anzio, and from there on May 22, four months after the landing, the Allied breakthrough was launched. The Germans gave up the defense of Rome so as not to destroy the city, which is part of the world's historical and cultural patrimony. They didn't even blow up the Tiber bridges, and General Clark entered Rome on June 4 without firing a shot. Just before evacuating Florence on August 4, the German 14th and 10th Armies destroyed the Arno bridges, with the exception of the most famous, Ponte Vecchio. They dug in behind the barracks and forts of the Gothic Line, which crossed the Apennines for almost 186 miles, from Pisa to Rimini. Here, during the winter of 1944-45, one of the longest, most exhausting, and bloodiest campaigns of the entire Second World War was fought. It was series of battles that marked the difficult advance of the American 5th Army (General Mark Clark) along the western salient and the speedier climb of the British 5th Army (General Oliver Leese), which included the I.I.LO.'s (the Italian Intelligence Liaison Officers.

The British and American advance and the winter battle were marked by ferocity in which the German SS disgraced itself. In reprisal for attacks carried out by partisan forces, the SS destroyed entire villages and exterminated their inhabitants, as in the case of Marzabotto (1800 dead), Sant'Anna di Stazzema (600 dead), and dozens of other Apennine villages.

These massacres tore open a vein of hatred toward the Germans, and by implication toward their allies, the Fascists, even if they were innocent of the cruel reprisals. Fighting alongside the Allies were four Italian divisions (called "combat groups" to deny them the honourable title they fully deserved), and another eight divisions were held in reserve behind the lines. In total, 250,000 Italian soldiers had returned to put on the gray-green uniform and fight under the Tricolor flag bearing the Cross of Savoy. The partisan forces made their contribution, modest along the Gothic Line, when not actually counterproductive because of German reprisals, and more effective in the north, with attacks and sabotage damaging the Fascist formations.

185
Immediately following the Allied landing in Sicily: the 7th Royal Marine Battalion, advances along the perimeter wall of Catania cathedral . The landing was the first Allied land attack on "Fortress Europe"

184
Top: Anglo-American troops land in Sicily, initiating an extremely rapid campaign that encountered little resistance from the Italians: from July 10 to August 17, 1943, in just 38 days, all of Sicily fell into Allied hands. Center: US tanks, after taking Palermo, advance towards the Straits of Messina, August 13, 1943. Bottom: an American Sherman tank enters Messina on July 26, 1943, greeted by a population waving white flags as a sign of peace and surrender.

383

188-189

Left: German troops in the Alpine foothills shelling a partisan position during the winter of 1943-44. Top right: a dramatic picture of German anti-partisan reprisals in Northern Italy, occupied by Wehrmacht troops; bottom, the effect of the bombardment of Milan on August 13, 1943 inside the Galleria Vittorio Emanuele II; in addition to Milan, Rome, Turin and Genoa, were heavily bombed.

186-187

Left: Allied troops land at Salerno, September 9, 1943. That landing, bitterly opposed by the Germans, was the only Allied military action in support of the Italian Monarchy, which had signed the surrender the day before.
Top right: American ships unload supplies of food and war materials at the port of Anzio; center, Allied tanks parade triumphantly before the Coliseum in Rome; bottom, against the desolate background of the ruins of Cassino, English stretcher bearers help one of the wounded.

1943
1945

1943
1945

THE NORMANDY INVASION
1944

The Atlantic Wall, the line of fortifications the Germans set up to defend Nazi Europe from a British-American invasion, was not easy to breach. The British had tried a test invasion of Dieppe on August 19, 1942. The landings ended in a massacre. And yet it was on the French north coast that the mortal blow was struck against the Third Reich. Dwight D. Eisenhower, Supreme Commander of the Allied Expeditionary Forces, made the decision. Churchill would have preferred Italy or perhaps the Balkans, in order to charge faster toward the east and check the Soviet advance into the heart of Europe. But by this time the Americans were making the major strategic decisions. The decision to invade France and to land on the Normandy beaches was made during the Teheran Conference, held in late 1943. The invasion was to commence no later than late spring 1944, a deadline fixed upon to mollify the USSR, which had long been asking the Allies to open a second front. Understandably, Russia was weary of bearing nearly the entire burden of the war. Germany had concentrated nearly 200 of the Wehrmacht's 300 divisions in Russia; of the remainder, only 50 were sent to France. The rest were divided among Italy, the Balkans, and Scandinavia. Stalin's goal was to compel the Germans to pull their forces from the eastern front and send them to France to block the breach caused by the invasion. Thus the breach had to be more than a simple bridgehead: it had to be a gigantic thrust into the heart of the Third Reich.

In fact, what swooped down on the coast of Normandy at 6:30 on the morning of June 6, 1944 (D-Day), was an avalanche of men and equipment. In the first five days alone, 5000 ships (of which 800 were warships) backed by 11,600 aircraft, poured 620,000 men and 220,000 tons of matériel onto the five chosen beaches. In just a few hours, using gigantic floating jetties, the Allies created artificial ports for the flow of ships that was constantly sailing between Normandy and the British coast. In record time, a pipeline was laid across the English Channel; to refuel the 95,000 vehicles (tanks, armored cars, trucks, jeeps, and motorcycles) that had rolled off the giant pontoons. Of course, the invaders suffered horrendous losses at Omaha Beach, on the first day, 10,000 Americans lost their lives and more than 20,000 were wounded. The D-Day beaches had code names: Omaha and Utah (American landings); Sword, Juno, and Gold (British-Canadian landings). At Omaha Beach, the Ranger units fell into a trap: the area was backed by hills dominated by numerous defense posts that enabled German fire to confine the attackers on the beach. The situation calls to mind the fate of the British who landed at Gallipoli during World War I.

An equally great number of Allied soldiers died on other beaches, at least in the early hours before the Atlantic Wall defense posts could be neutralized. The American paratroopers who had landed during the night behind the German front line defenses were unable to capture either Bayeux or Caen, their two main inland targets. The armies' advance from the coastal bridgeheads was slow and bloody. After days of fierce battles, Cherbourg and the Cotentin peninsula fell, while armored units tried to penetrate Brittany. Unfortunately, during this operation, American planes accidentally bombed their own troops, with hundreds of casualties. On August 17 (more than two months after D-Day), Saint-Malo was taken, followed by Brest on September 19, but Lorient and Saint Nazaire held out until the end of the war.

In reality, for two reasons Germany's reaction to the invasion was slow and inadequate. First, the Wehrmacht's upper command echelons, including that headed by Rommel, were in turmoil. Many senior officers were directly involved in plotting the July 20 attempt on Hitler's life, which took place on in the "Wolf's Lair" command post at Rastenburg, East Prussia. Second, the Führer was convinced that the real invasion would take place at Calais. On June 6, informed that the invasion was under way, he thought it was a ruse and avoided using his reserves in Normandy. Had he done this, the German divisions could probably have driven the troops back into the sea. By the time Hitler realized that he had miscalculated and that the Normandy landings marked the real attack against Fortress Europe, it was too late. By then, the Americans had penetrated deep into vital territory: General Patton's vanguard had broken through southeast Normandy, opening up the way to Paris.

On the southern front, an Allied force landed in Provence on August 15 (Operation Dragoon). Churchill had interrupted his visit to the Italian front to observe the invasion from the deck of a warship. The British-American forces advanced very rapidly: within a few days, they reached and captured Lyons. Resistance activities increased, and Paris rose in rebellion on August 19. In contravention of Hitler's orders, the German commander refused to destroy the city and ordered his forces to retreat. On August 25, General Charles de Gaulle entered Paris, welcomed by the delirious crowd.

1944

191
These photographs, taken by Robert Capa, relive the frantic moments of the Allied landing on Omaha Beach in Normandy, June 6, 1944. It was payback time.

192-193
More scenes from the Normandy invasion: amphibious vehicles and British and American half-tracks spread across the beach, protected by barrage balloons from enemy fighters, by now reduced to a minimum. During the first five days of Operation Overlord, 5000 ships, of which 800 were warships, supported by 11,600 aircraft, carried 620,000 men and 220,000 tons of matériel across the five chosen beaches. The attackers suffered huge losses: during the first day of the invasion alone, 10,000 men died and more than twice as many were wounded.

The Normandy Invasion

1944

194
The face of this German officer, captured by Allied forces during their victorious advance, reveals the suffering and exhaustion caused by this debilitating war and its dramatic epilogue.

195
American tanks entering the French village of Flere in an apocalyptic scene that illustrates the ferocity of the clashes that were a prelude to the definitive destruction of the Führer's dreams of grandeur.

196-197

Left: the festive people of Paris pass before the Arc de Triomphe: it's August 25, 1944 and the nightmare is over. Top right: Partisans build barricades in the streets of the French capital: the Resistance is now close to victory; center, German prisoners forced to parade through the streets of Paris, flanked by a hostile crowd. Bottom: the Allies liberated the cities of Northern France one after another and everywhere vendettas and reprisals were unleashed against those who collaborated with the Germans: in the picture, a "collabò" with shaved head clutches her baby to her breast amid the scorn of the population.

THE FUHRER MUST DIE

1944

198
Rastenburg, East Prussia, July 20, 1944: Adolf Hitler and Benito Mussolini view the Wolf's Lair, devastated by the bomb planted by Colonel Klaus Von Stauffenberg in an attempt to assassinate the Führer.

Ernst Otto Remer, commander of the Grossdeutschland Infantry Regiment, headquartered in Berlin, is the man who, on July 20, 1944, caused the failure of the German military officers' plot to kill Hitler and defeat Nazism. It was he who arrested the conspirators in Berlin. All were sentenced to death and hanged. From that day on, Otto Remer, then barely 33 and whom the Führer promoted to general, has remained indirectly responsible for the death of 7000 of the finest representatives of Germany's aristocracy and culture--men far removed from the average Nazi. "I only did my duty," Remer continued to insist, even after the war, "I am completely at peace with my conscience. Like all German soldiers, I had sworn fidelity to the Führer. If he had been killed in the attack, I would not have hesitated to obey the orders of my superiors, asking me to arrest all the Nazis in Berlin. But, since he survived, I could do nothing but place myself at his disposal."

Diametrically opposed is the famous declaration of another German general, Ludwig Beck, who, had he succeeded in the Putsch against Hitler, would have become the new head of state. He said: "There are limits to fidelity to the supreme command, in the event that one's conscience and responsibility prohibit executing an order." The armies of the world's democratic nations have officially adopted this tenet, even if unaware of the aims and fate of General Beck and his generous and unfortunate companions. Yet in Germany, the story of July 20, 1944 is practically unknown; in fact, it is wrongly believed that there was no resistance to Nazism in Germany. Nothing could be more false. The birth of the anti-Nazi resistance movement occurred long before July 1940. In May 1938, it became obvious that Hitler intended to invade Czechoslovakia. General Ludwig Beck (then the Army's chief of staff) was aware that a German invasion of Czechoslovakia could result in a world war since Czechoslovakia had defensive alliances with France and Great Britain. He took the unprecedented initiative of declaring a "strike of the generals." He let Hitler know that, if he did not renounce his aggressive proposition, the commanders would no longer attend his military conferences, but would send their chiefs of staff. The Führer took their threat literally: "The Generals don't want to work? Fine, I'll replace them with their underlings." And so he did, relieving dozens of commanders en masse. Beck resigned and threw himself headlong into preparing a coup d'état to be triggered the moment that France and Britain solemnly declared their intention to honor their treaties, which he had no doubt that they would do. Beck then consulted with other supporters of the Resistance, among them Carl Gördeler (mayor of Leipzig), Ulrich von Hassell (former ambassador to Rome), Field Marshal Erwin von Witzleben (commander of the Panzerdivisione), General Erich Höpner, and supporters from the Catholic and Protestant churches. Together they nominated a new government, made plans for the return to democracy, and drafted a military plan to neutralize the Nazi forces and arrest Hitler and his ministers.

Unfortunately, when all was ready, the about-face by Neville Chamberlain, the British prime minister, and Édouard Daladier the French premier, threw everything up in the air. Timid and cowardly before Hitler, the two statesmen accepted Mussolini's offer of a "an urgent meeting " in Munich "to avert a war." They then accepted all of the Führer's conditions. Czechoslovakia was abandoned to its fate, the Duce came out wearing the halo of "the savior of the peace," and the German Resistance had to renounce its plans, as no soldier would take up arms against a Führer who was conquering Europe without firing a shot.

From that moment, Beck and his friends began to think seriously about killing the Führer. Hitler was, as Beck said, "the capital enemy of the entire world," and in this definition he included the unacceptability of the persecution of the Jews. In addition, Hitler's death would be necessary to release all the German armed forces from their oath of loyalty, taken not to the State, but to the person of the Führer. In fact, since 1935, Hitler had restored the ancient oath made to the reigning Kaiser, replacing the latter's name with his own. For a German soldier the oath was terribly serious, as demonstrated by Major Ernst Otto Remer.

There were dozens attempts to kill Hitler, but, all failed: none of the aspiring attackers managed to get near the Führer. A living cordon of his faithful SS was always on protective duty; in addition, Hitler adopted incredible security measures to protect himself. He wore a special protective vest under his uniform; his cap was lined with steel plates (and hence weighed 5.5 pounds), and his armored Mercedes had powerful reflectors on the sides and rear to blind any snipers.

More than anything, the Resistance lacked young, energetic, and decisive leadership. Such a man emerged, almost naturally, toward the end of 1943. Colonel Claus Philip von Stauffenberg, a count by descent of title, came of an old, noble Swabian family. He was a fervent Catholic and had participated in the anti-Nazi opposition since his high school days. Disgusted by the persecution of the Jews, he preferred to be at the front, where he had risked his life thousands of times. In North Africa, he had lost an eye, his right hand, and two fingers from the left. He had then been recalled to Berlin with the post of chief of staff of the Hersatzheer, the Territorial Army. He could now put his plan, Operation Valkyrie, into place. Hour "X" arrived on July 20, 1944. On that day, Stauffenberg was called to Rastenburg, Hitler's military HQ in East Prussia. Before leaving Berlin, von Stauffenberg he made his confession to the Bishop of Berlin, Cardinal von Preysing, communicating his intention and receiving absolution. He carried a corrosive acid bomb in his briefcase, timed to explode exactly ten minutes after he broke the vial. Before entering the bunker, he warned the operator, "I'm expecting a telephone call from Berlin." It was the excuse that allowed him to leave. But an officer who could not reach the military map spread out under Hitler's eyes because of the briefcase von Stauffenberg had left between his feet, moved it almost inadvertently. The heavy table base now stood between the brief case and the Führer. The officer's action killed him and two other generals, but saved Hitler. Hearing the explosion, Stauffenberg telephoned the password to Berlin and hurried to the airport. Two hours later he was in the capital, in the Bendlerstrasse, location of the Territorial Army HQ. Here there was conflicting news. It appeared the Führer was not dead. "It's not true!" von Stauffenberg shouted, "he's dead, I killed him with my own hands!" He gave the go-ahead for the operation. Orders went out in Europe: The Führer is dead; you must maintain public order, disarm the SS, occupy the Nazi Party HQ, and arrest Hitler's ministers and officials.

At the headquarters of the Grossdeutschland Regiment, young Major Ernst Otto Remer received the order to occupy all the government ministries. He hurriedly gathered 300 soldiers and executed the order within just a few hours. Then, he reported to his superior officer, General Paul von Hase, military governor of Berlin. "Further orders?" "Yes, go the Ministry of Propaganda, arrest Goebbels and bring him to me, here." A few minutes later, Remer burst into the minister's office with a pistol in his hand, "You're under arrest!" "Major, are you crazy?" Goebbels replied, "have you forgotten your oath of loyalty to the Führer?" "The Führer is dead, I am released from my oath." "It's not true, the Führer is alive, I can prove it to you." And Goebbels put him on the telephone to Rastenburg. A few seconds later, Remer heard Hitler's raucous voice through the receiver, "This is the Führer, don't you recognize my voice, Major? A group of traitors has tried to kill me. Obey only Goebbels' orders, do you understand? I will give you the Iron Cross, first class, with swords and diamonds. As of this moment, you are a general." From that moment, Remer became the nemesis of the putsch. Within two hours he had unblocked the ministries, occupied the Kommandantur, arrested von Hase, surrounded the Bendlerstrasse, placing machine guns all around it, and rushed inside to capture von Stauffenberg, Beck, and all the rest. That same evening, Beck killed himself with a pistol, while von Stauffenberg and his closest collaborators were killed by a firing squad in the courtyard of the building. This was only the beginning. By the end of the repression, there were 7,000 victims, among which were the finest names of the army, the secret services, the nobility, the clergy, the professions, culture, and diplomacy. Hitler reserved a special end for these heroes: They were hung up on butchers' hooks, suspended by piano wire. The SS filmed their agony, and the film was shown in Hitler's reception rooms for the sadistic pleasure of the dictator and his intimates, among them Ernst Otto Remer, proud and puffed up in his new general's uniform.

THE FÜHRER'S FINAL OFFENSIVE AND HIS SECRET WEAPON

1944

Following the liberation of Paris, the Allied advance moved ahead at a breathless pace. On August 21, Marseilles was liberated, then Rouen on the 30th. On September 3, British columns liberated Brussels, while on September 11 the Allies reached the German border, but were forced to stop. The Wall fortifications and Germany's strenuous resistance now nullified every Allied effort. The only breach occurred on October 21, 1944, with the capture of Aachen, but with serious losses.

The advance had stopped. The OKW strategists had perfected plans for "Operation Greif" in the hopes of repeating the German army's 1940 successes in the northwest. Operation Greif was a return to the 1940 starting positions, when the German army, using the Manstein Plan, had broken through the enemy's front lines, penetrating the Ardennes and closing around the British task force in a vise in Belgian territory. Conditions had changed since then. With the arrival of the American troops, the Allies' forces had nearly doubled in size; and following its post-D-Day humiliation and defeats, the German army had lost its former cockiness.

Operation Greif, ("Hitler's final offensive") was prepared down to the last detail. German soldiers who were perfectly fluent in English infiltrated behind the enemy lines to wreak havoc among the Allies. These "werewolves." spread panic. The Germans launched their counter-offensive on December 16. For over a month, a savage war was fought in the snow, with the Allies retreating along the entire front before a German advance of over 63 miles. The Allied high command began to panic. It was probably during those weeks that Churchill secretly solicited Mussolini's help to convince Hitler to give up his counteroffensive in the west and concentrate on the advance of the Red Army. Recordings made of the mournful telephone calls-- which yielded no results--from Il Duce to the Führer prove this hypothesis.

The Ardennes offensive could well have ended in a catastrophic defeat for the Allies had the Americans at Bastogne, surrounded by German armored divisions, failed in their tenacious resistance. The battle marked the end of Operation Greif. On January 20, 1945, General Patton, leading three armored divisions, began to drive the Germans back from the positions they had gained.

Shortly before the surprising German counterattack in the Ardennes, the Allies who had reached Belgium had to confront another unexpected danger: during October and November, Antwerp was subjected to a terrifying missile attack that killed 4000 civilians and some 700 Allied soldiers. The cause of such destruction was the V2 rocket, one of the Führer's "secret weapons." The advent of the rocket engine, built in Germany since 1939, had opened a new era in aerial war. Germany was the first country to deploy fighters and bombers equipped with this revolutionary method of propulsion. Nevertheless, the *Arado Ar234* and the *Messerschmitt Me262* and *Me163*, arrived too late to change the outcome of the conflict. The same can be said for the means of destruction created at Peenemünde, in northern Germany, where there was a young scientist working alongside General Dornberger named Wernher von Braun, the father of the Saturn rocket that carried man to the moon in 1969. At Peenemünde the V1 and V2 rockets were developed (the V from Vergeltungswaffe ("vengeance weapon"). The V1's were essentially small pilotless airplanes, with a reaction engine in place of the propeller and a bomb where the engine would normally be. However, fighter planes or anti-aircraft guns could shoot them down with relative ease. The V2's were true rockets that could not be intercepted--and, in fact, never were--because they traveled about 31 miles above the surface of the earth, at a speed of 3100 mph, and at that time there were no supersonic aircraft.

The first V1 fell on London on June 12, 1944. Three months later came the much more deadly V2s. But Allied bombardment of Peenemünde slowed the production of these weapons around which expectations of victory had developed. In total, 9000 V1's and 1,115 V2's were launched against London, and the number of victims was 5000 and 3000, respectively: a tragic "booty" in human lives. The Allies also achieved important advances thanks to radar: it allowed planes to identify enemy submarines at night and to sink them with bomber-borne torpedoes. As a result of radar, the U-boats suffered enormous losses in the North Sea and the Atlantic. Finally, the Allies were also helped by the mass production of the American B-17 and B-29 "Flying Superfortress" aircraft. By the end of the conflict, Germany had lost 72,000 planes; Britain had dropped 1,328,400 tons of bombs on Germany (vs Germany's 63,960 tons dropped on Britain).The United States manufactured 293,000 aircraft; Great Britain, 145,000; and Germany, 91,000. These numbers, not more abstruse theories of war psychology, identify the real reasons for victory and defeat.

202-203
Top left: more pictures of the operations the Führer ordered in the Ardennes; center, the torn remains of an American soldier lie beside a small truck hit during a German V2 attack against Antwerp, just liberated by the Allies. Bottom, an English fighter attacks a V1 in flight; right, German soldiers advance in the Ardennes after having destroyed an American half-track: it's January 2, 1945 and Hitler's "flick of the tail" is by now nearing its conclusion.

204-205
Top left: American tank troops have just captured an entire German detachment south of Bastogne; bottom, US troops patrol the streets of the Belgian city, reduced to a pile of rubble, but now liberated.
Right: American infantry from the 290th Regiment positioned in a snowy wood near the village of Amonines, in Belgium.

200
A German soldier in action during the Ardennes offensive, launched by the Führer in Southern Belgium in late fall 1944, with the delusion that it could stop the Allied advance. The operation, which has become known as the "flick of Hitler's tail," was carefully prepared in detail.

1944

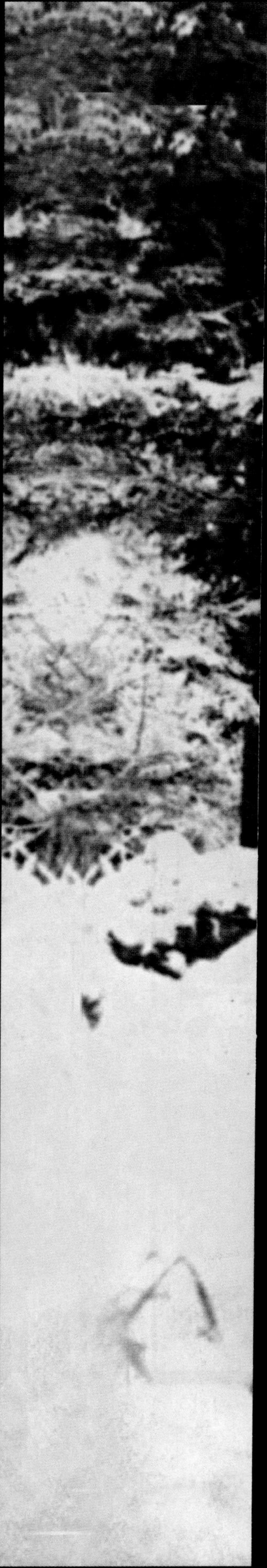

206
Left: The hanging of a partisan, executed by the 10th Mas in Ivrea in 1944; right, Mussolini has the battalions of the Republican National Guard pass in review at Brescia in March 1944.

207
Milan, Piazzale Loreto, April 29, 1945: the martyred bodies of Benito Mussolini and Claretta Petacci hang from the roof of a gas station where they where hung by the two partisans who collected the two cadavers from Lake Como.

Mussolini's Death
1945

On April 9, 1945, the Allied general offensive broke out along the Gothic Line. The line collapsed on April 21 and the Allies and the Italians of the CIL spread over the Lombardy plain and crossed the Po. The German general, Karl Wolff, who was secretly negotiating in Bern with Allen Dulles, the United States' special envoy, surrendered in the name of all the 800,000 men under the command of General von Vietinghoff, who had succeeded Field Marshal Kesselring in March. This number included the armed forces of the Repubblica Sociale Italiana (RSI) under Marshal Graziani. Benito Mussolini and most members of the RSI's government left Milan on the evening of April 25, 1945, after refusing an order to surrender presented by the CLNAI (Committee for the National Liberation of Upper Italy). The CLNAI, which acted under a mandate from King Victor Emmanuel's Rome based government, were charged to direct and coordinate the anti-Fascist war in the north. But Mussolini's column was taken prisoner by a partisan unit while heading toward the Valtellina, an Alpine valley, where Mussolini planned on waiting for the arrival of the Americans to hand himself over. The CLNAI then violated an obligation that the King and the Rome government had undertaken under the terms of the September 8, 1943 armistice with the Allies. This obligation required the surrender of Mussolini to the Allies. But the CLNAI decided to shoot the Duce and his ministers immediately and hurriedly assembled an execution squad in Dongo, the village on Lake Como where Mussolini and his ministers had been taken prisoner.

When the "executioners" arrived on the afternoon of April 28, 1945, they found someone had already done their work. Mussolini and his lover had been assassinated in the early hours of the morning by partisans acting on orders from British agents. This fact was revealed by expert examination of their bodies. It was vital for Churchill, as British prime minister, to prevent Mussolini from revealing the secret contacts they had continued, to the disadvantage of the Soviet Union, right up until the collapse of the Axis. The Italian government later gave Churchill some of the Duce's personal records; they proved that the contacts had occurred. (Copies of these records that the Communists obtained during the dramatic hours in Dongo were in turn sold to Churchill's agents, who several times returned to Dongo to make sure that the operation had been successfully concluded.)

The German plenipotentiaries signed the surrender in the Royal Palace of Caserta, near Naples, on April 29, 1945. The cease-fire was set for 12:00 GMT on May 2. After May 2, in keeping with provisions of the articles of surrender, the Allies disarmed the partisan bands. But after this date, and even after the fall of the monarchy following the national referendum of June 2, 1946, the Communists continued to assassinate Fascists or, at any rate, their own most unyielding adversaries. No fewer than 40,000 Italians, including a hundred priests, were to die in this fratricidal bloodshed before legality and civil peace were definitively restored in 1948.

THE END OF GERMANY AND HITLER'S DEATH

1944-1945

Under pressure from the Red Army, now at Romania's frontier, King Michael followed the same script that King Victor Emmanuel had done a year earlier. With a coup d'etat, he deposed his fascist premier, Marshal Antonescu, on August 23, 1944, and had him arrested, exactly as Victor Emmanuel had done with Mussolini. He then ordered the suspension of hostilities against the Russians. The Germans reacted by bombarding Bucharest, so King Michael declared war on Germany. On August 30 the Red Army entered Bucharest and from there reached the Ploesti oil fields, delivering a terrible blow to the Germans because these were the Reich's only source of energy.

On November 2, 1944, Athens was declared an "open city" and German troops left Greece. Where they had committed war crimes, it was a bloody retreat, marked by attacks from the Greek resistance. Bulgaria had declared war on Great Britain and the United States, but had maintained neutrality toward the USSR. When on September 1, 1944, the Red Army arrived on its borders, the government let Stalin's soldiers occupy the country. From then on, Bulgaria was a satellite of the USSR. On October 28, a new Communist government was formed, headed by Kimon Georgiev, whose first measure was to declare war on Germany. From Bulgaria, the Red Army penetrated Yugoslavia to defeat German resistance and, on October 20, 1944, entered Belgrade alongside Tito's partisan formations.

On October 15, 1944, Admiral Horthy, head of the Hungarian state and a loyal ally of Hitler, addressed an appeal to the USSR, requesting an armistice. Hungary had lost thousands of soldiers in the disastrous Russian campaign and Horthy now felt the breath of the Red Army on his neck. In response, the Germans arrested him and deported him to Germany. This would surely have been Mussolini's fate had he sued the Anglo-Americans for peace in July 1943, as those close to the monarchy wanted him to do. Power passed to Ferenc Szalasi, the last pro-German premier. On December 29, 1944, Budapest too fell into the hands of the Red Army. By now the picture was clear: Eastern Europe, "liberated" by the Red Army, would become Communist and suffer the loss of its liberty for 44 years, until the fall of the Berlin Wall.

In January, with the failure of its Ardennes offensive, Nazi Germany had lost all hope of resisting the Allied offensives from the east and the west. The Reich's cities had been devastated by incessant aerial bombing. Its war industries were no longer able to produce munitions, planes, or ships: of the 126 new electric submarines with rechargeable batteries (and thus exempt from needing oil fuel supplies) laid down in the shipyards at the end of 1944, only two were built. Hitler was devastated by Parkinson's disease, his right arm was ankylosed after the explosion of von Stauffenberg's bomb in his Rastenburg HQ on July 20. In January 1945, he left the "Eagle's Nest" in the Berchtesgaden complex in the Bavarian Alps, and returned to Berlin to shut himself up in Chancellery bunker (the Führerbunker), 65,5 feet underground. On March 7, Cologne fell, and the Americans seized the Rhine bridge at Remagen, undamaged and passable. This marked the end: within in ten days, the bridgehead over the great river was 31 miles deep. Other Allied columns advanced down the Moselle valley and crossed the Rhine at Oppenheim. In the Ruhr, the German industrial heartland, 21 trapped German divisions surrendered on April 18. Frankfurt

208
Germany, March 8, 1945: American troops advance through the ruins of the city of Cologne; in the background rise the twin spires of the gothic cathedral.

fell on March 29, Stuttgart on April 22, Munich on April 30, and Salzburg on May 3.

The Italian armed forces had surrendered on April 29. The advance no longer encountered any obstacles from the Germans, but the American and British commands had to consider the advance of the Red Army. By April 19, Leipzig was in the hands of the Americans, and from there it would be easy to push east to deny the Russians as much territory as possible. In effect, several Allied commanders acted on this goal, including Patton, the true mastermind of victory. However, the Yalta agreements had to be respected. Because of this, Eisenhower ordered his troops to stop at the River Elbe, where in Torgau, on April 25, the first contact occurred between the Russian and American troops. In the north, on May 3 the British columns occupied Hamburg. For political and diplomatic reasons, the satisfaction of capturing Berlin was left to the Russians. Having occupied Czechoslovakia, the Red offensive pointed north to Berlin and south to Vienna. Stalin wanted his troops to be the first to enter the Third Reich's two most important cities, and had demanded this privilege from the Allies at the Yalta Conference. On April 13 the Russians took Vienna and three days later the battle of Berlin began. On April 23, Hitler's control of events was threatened. Göring asked for supreme command, and Himmler contacted the Swedish diplomat Count Bernadotte, asking him to forward to General Eisenhower an offer for Germany's surrender in the west. The two Nazi leaders, wrongly convinced that Hitler had thrown in the towel, hoped at least to resist the Red avalanche. (Among some Nazis, a wild and totally unrealized hope existed that the Allies might join the Germans in opposing the Soviet advance into Europe.) But Hitler was far from ready to let go of power: He discharged Göring and Himmler and also had General Fegelein (married to one of Eva Braun's sisters) shot because he had not mounted sufficient resistance to the American advance. On April 29, after hearing the news of the Duce's execution on the radio, Hitler married Eva Braun and wrote his will. He named Admiral Dönitz his successor as President of the Reich and as Supreme Commander of the Wehrmacht; Goebbels he named as Reich Chancellor; Bormann as secretary of the National Socialist Party, and Seyss-Inquart as Foreign Minister. The following day, in the early afternoon, he killed himself along with his wife, she ingesting a cyanide pill and he firing a revolver in his mouth. In a room a few feet away, Joseph Goebbels also took his own life after killing his wife and six children, all of whose names began with the letter "H" in honor of Hitler.

Receiving notice of the Führer's death, General Weidling, the commander of Berlin's 70,000 defenders, surrendered to Soviet Marshal Zhukov on May 1. After signing the surrender, Dönitz and his ministers retired to their homes, but on May 23 American army personnel arrested them and imprisoned them pending trial. On May 2 the Russian entered Berlin, raising the hammer and sickle flag over the Brandenburg Gate. During their advance into German territory, the Russians left behind scorched earth, raped women and slaughtered civilians. Some 2 million Germans in the north (women, children, and the elderly) were saved by ships that for months had shuttled between the Baltic and North Sea ports. For other citizens of the Third Reich, a more bitter fate awaited. The Russian poet Ilya Ehrenburg had predicted, "They will curse the day they were born."

209
Berlin, April 30, 1945: Soviet soldiers unfurl the red flag with the hammer and sickle over the ruins of the Reichstag, the German parliament. Germany surrendered.

The End of Germany
AND HITLER'S DEATH

210

Top: German soldiers who have just surrendered march to Berlin under the threat of a Russian Army T-34 tank, in front of the Brandenburg Gate, the site of proud parades by the Wehrmacht and the Waffen-SS. Bottom: Soviet soldiers advance down a Berlin street, under the fire of the last defenders; in the foreground is a German solider who has just been killed.

211
The remains of the Reichstag, the austere palace from which Adolf Hitler used to give his most important speeches and announce the Wehrmacht's thunderous victories. On April 30, while the Russians advanced on the capital of the Reich, Hitler committed suicide in the bunker of the Chancellery, together with Eva Braun, the woman he had just married.

212
No Auschwitz photograph ever needs comment: the desperation etched into the prisoners' faces is worth more than a thousand words.

THE HOLOCAUST
1942-1945

On an inspection visit to the Gestapo headquarters in Budapest in 1944, SS Colonel Adolf Eichmann, said, "A hundred dead are a catastrophe, 5 million are a statistic." At Nuremberg in 1946, the world learned for the first time that 6 million Jews had been gassed in the Third Reich's extermination camps. Hostile intentions toward Germany's Jews predate the advent of Nazism. The hostility reflected an almost Wagnerian crescendo. Hitler's anti-Semitism shows the influence of Karl Lüger, the Christian Socialist mayor of Vienna. For Lüger, as for Hitler, mixing the races was the greatest sin, and worst when involving the Jews. He believed that miscegenation had led to the fall of the Austro-Hungarian Empire. What difference did it make if 100,000 Austrian and German soldiers of the Jewish "race" had fought during the First World War and that 12,000 had died?

Both Lüger and Hitler claimed that the Jews would always be parasites, growing fat on the genius of others, never creating, only destroying. Moreover, Jews deceive the world by pretending to have a religion. But Judaism is not a religion but a people, a race. It is a mistake to think that there is such a thing as a German Jew in the same way that there are German Protestants or Catholics, that there is an Italian Jew in the same way as there are Italian Waldensians. There are just Jews, period. In *Mein Kampf*, the summa of his thought Hitler stated: "Once again the National Socialist movement must discharge its formidable task. It must ceaselessly call to memory the true enemy of today's world. In the place of hatred against other Aryans, from whom everything can separate us, but to whom we are all united by common blood and civilization, we must turn our general fury against the enemy of mankind, the Jew, the real source of all our suffering. National Socialism must act so that, at least in our country, the mortal enemy is recognized so that the fight against the Jews will show other peoples the way to salvation for Aryan humanity."

Hitler wrote *Mein Kampf* (or rather dictated it to his devoted follower Rudolf Hess) in 1925, after the failed Beer Hall Putsch which resulted in the future Führer and his collaborator and secretary were being held in the fortress-prison of Landsberg in Bavaria. The volume is laced with incitements to anti-Jewish hatred like those cited above. From at least the 1930s, a copy of *Mein Kampf* was on display in almost every German home. Its main themes are few and clear: the German-speaking peoples must reunite in a single Reich; the living space of the Germans is to the east, as far as the Urals; the Jews must be swept away. While waiting to implement the first two aims, Hitler passed right on the third. On March 23, 1933, he obtained plenary powers from the Reichstag, the German parliament. On April 1, 1933, the government declared a "mass boycott" of Jewish stores as a "response to the anti-government campaign of both domestic and foreign Jews."

On April 17, 1933, the Hitler government passed "the law for the recovery of the bureaucracy," the first of more than 400 decrees that little by little excluded the Jews from military service, deprived them of citizenship, of the option to practice medicine, teaching, or journalism, of the right to receive unemployment benefits, and on and on. "Recovering the bureaucracy" meant chasing the Jews out of every public job. On March 20, 1933, Hitler's minister of the interior, by his own decree, opened the Third Reich's first concentration camp (Lager) in Dachau, a suburb of Munich. He ordered that 5000 detainees held in jails all over the country be transferred there. The Dachau prisoners were "politicals," for the most part Communsts. Shaved bald, they had to wear a uniform with vertical stripes and follow military-type discipline. They were required to attend "reeducation classes" every morning. In the afternoon they performed manual labor. The régime was not apologetic about Dachau, but boasted of it, to the point that interior ministry officials organized visits to it for journalists. But soon Hitler's government played another tune. In 1935, the Lager was turned over to the Gestapo, which shortly thereafter opened new camps at Oranienburg, Sachsenhausen, and Buchenwald. Flossenburg was established in 1938, Mauthausen-Gusen, Ravensbrück, and Stutthof in 1939, Bergen-Belsen in 1940, and Gross-Rosen in 1941. In the meantime, the population of the Lager had changed: to the politicals, who wore a red triangle on their jackets, were added common criminals (green triangle), homosexuals (pink triangle), Jehovah's Witnesses (violet triangle), and the "asocials" (black triangle). The majority were Jews. Their triangle was yellow, the color adopted in the Middle Ages for plague victims. In March 1938, with the annexation of Austria, another 185,000 Jews became part of the Third Reich. Then, within a few months, it was the turn of the Jews of the Sudetenland, then those of Prague, and finally those of Poland, a good 2 million Jews in all.

THE HOLOCAUST
1942-1945

In 1938, the Nazis began launching pogroms, manhunts for the purpose of killing Jews, and reopening ghettos. During the night of November 9, the Reichskristallnacht, the "night of broken glass," took place. Thousands of Nazis, aroused by the news that a young Jew had assassinated the secretary of a German embassy, devastated synagogues, set fire to Jewish stores and homes throughout the country, killing and wounding Jews. Official figures stated that 815 stores destroyed, 171 residences burned down, 195 synagogues devastated or burned, 36 Jews killed and 36 seriously wounded. In reality, the consequences of the Kristallnacht were much more terrifying: more than 7500 stores were destroyed, while the number of dead is unknown. At least 20,000 illegal arrests made by the SA and SS. Some 10,000 of the arrested Jews were sent to Buchenwald, where there was already a lager in operation dedicated to "enemies of the Reich."

On August 25, 1939, the German and Soviet foreign ministers, Ribbentrop and Molotov, signed a "non-aggression pact," an understanding between their two brigand nations to divide up Poland and the Baltic states and give themselves a free hand in their policies of imperialist expansion. A shared anti-Semitism cemented this wicked pact. Stalin hated the Jews no less than Hitler: all the founding fathers of Soviet Russia that were of Jewish origin (Zinoviev, Kamenev, Bukharin, Trotsky, etc.) had been, or were about to be, liquidated. This pact was the preface to the World War II. On September 1, 1939, Wehrmacht troops flooded into Poland. Following were SS units dispatched by Heinrich Himmler, leader of the dreaded organization now charged with "taking care" of the Jews. The SS immediately applied the measures they had already adopted in Germany against the Jews. In Austria, the anti-Jewish laws had been in force from 1938, and in Czechoslovakia since the 1938 occupation that followed the failed Munich summit.

In Italy, the Fascist regime, aping its German ally, passed racial legislation in 1938 that excluded Jews from teaching, the professions, and public functions, but never applied the legislation with the fanatical zeal that Germany did. However, following the armistice signed by the Allies and Italy on September 8, 1943, the situation deteriorated badly. The Germans treated the Rome ghetto with particular ferocity: a few minutes after midnight on October 16, dozens of Nazi platoons erupted in the ghetto, sending women, children and elderly to Auschwitz.

Those who wanted to escape had until March 15, 1939. On that day, the Nazis prohibited Jewish emigration. The poor (the overwhelming majority of the 375,000 Jews still living in Germany) had no choice but to remain. The transfers to the East began on October 16, 1939, when 20 railroad convoys departed simultaneously from Berlin, Vienna, Prague, and Cologne, all bound for Lódz. Each train carried 1000 Jews. They were German families who had voluntarily accepted an offer to move to the Lódz ghetto where, they had been told, the cost of living was lower, it was easy to find a house and work, and there were fewer restrictions. It was a trap. Once at their destination, they were forced to live 7 to a room. During the first 18 months after arrival, 14,000 died. Not all the Jews believed the fable of moving "for work in the East." On April 3, 1942, 57 of a "transport" of 523 Berlin Jews, 57 did not show up for the departure: they had taken their own lives. Every *Transportliste* arrived at its destination with crosses penciled next to dozens of names: these marked not only those who died during the trip, but also suicides. On October 3 of the same year, a terrible record was set: 208 out of 717 Jews (almost always entire families) destined for Auschwitz, had preferred to take their own lives.

One of the saddest and best known episodes of anti-Semitic persecution took place in the famous Warsaw ghetto, for centuries the largest Jewish enclave in the world. In September 1939, when the Polish capital fell into German hands, its population was 360,000 Jews and 80,000 Catholics, a total of 440,000 people. There were businesspeople and craftsmen, there were banks and synagogues. The occupiers' first act was to require the Judenrat, the ghetto's Jewish council," to take charge of finding lodgings for Jewish families from Germany that had "requested" to be transferred to the East. In less than one year, 60,000 German Jews took up residence in the ghetto. By August 1940, the fence was begun. Initially, wooden poles and barbed wire, then a brick wall. For the time being Jews could still exit and enter the walled-in area, as long as they wore a yellow star sewn on their chest. On October 16, 1940, the German Governor, Dr. Hans Frank, promulgated a decree: the ghetto was declared an "infected area." The "Aryans" had 15 days to leave. Jews residing in other Warsaw neighborhoods (180,000) were required to move in. Private negotiations for the sale or exchange of furniture were allowed: this allowed the "Aryan" residents of the ghetto to pocket at least doubled the market value of their houses in just a few days. By the end of the operation, the population density of the ghetto had risen to 5.5 people per room. A month later, at dawn on November 15, 1940, Friesian horses pulling machine guns appeared opposite the 14 entrance points to the ghetto: about 100,000 workers, employees, artisans, and professionals who went to work in the city every day could no longer leave. Let them fend for themselves, or let the Judenrat take on the problem. Let the Jewish Council provide work inside the ghetto so that hatred, envy, and rancor can well up among the Jews. Let the *Ordnungsdienst*, the Jewish police, maintain order inside the "infected zone" and calm their hotheads. Let the *Hausbesorger* (building manager or apartment-house administrator) regulate the unfortunates who, beginning in October 1941, were crammed 14 to a room. Dr. Frank, who issued these pitiless ordinances from the Brühl Palace (the Governor's residence), was personally a sadist. Overcrowded housing in the Warsaw Ghetto resulted in frighteningly unhygienic conditions and recurring epidemics. During the summer of 1941, typhus killed 15,700 people. July 22, 1942 saw the beginning of the "reduction" of the ghetto--the transfer of the Jews to the extermination camps at Auschwitz, Treblinka, Majdanek, and Chelmno.

The operations were carried out in a climate of incredible ferocity; those who reacted with even the slightest gesture toward the SS were killed on the spot. Perhaps this accentuation of hate and violence or the progressive emptying of the ghetto allowed those who remained to catch a breath of air and to consider resistance. But surely knowledge of the extermination that awaited the departing was at the root of the rebellion. The armed resistance movement began in April 1943, when the "Jewish Combat Organization *Hechalutz*" was formed. They succeeded in getting deliveries of arms, especially pistols and hand grenades, from the Polish Resistance, the Armja Krajowa, even though they always had to pay through the nose with money subtracted from their requisitions. But they used those pistols to sow death among the Germans and their few Jewish servants. The Germans began to be afraid. They interrupted the deportations. The rumor that the Jews were fighting in the Warsaw ghetto spread throughout Poland. There were cases of deportees who broke through the walls of the cattle cars to jump from the moving trains. Finally, the Jews had found the energy to react. At the end of June the "combat groups" numbered 22. The Germans exterminated the Jewish resistance fighters down to the last man in an inferno of fire, hunting them down with flame throwers in the underground passages that they had dug, often with their bare hands. By the middle of July it was all over. General Stroop, having blown up the last ghetto building with dynamite, telegraphed the Führer, "Order reigns in Warsaw." But in those weeks between the spring and summer of 1943, Israel was resurrected. The harm that Nazi Germany did to the Jewish people remains an "enterprise" unequaled for cruelty, brutality and numbers.

When American soldiers entered Buchenwald on April 11, 1945, they were unable to face the tidal wave of horror and indignation that overcame them: they found before their eyes a suffering people, devastated in mind and body, destroyed by torture--physical no less than psychological--humiliated and abused. The reaction of the British soldiers who reached Bergen-Belsen on April 15 was no different: there were 30,000 survivors, reduced to living skeletons, devoured by fever and typhus; following their liberation, they were dying at a rate of more than 300 per day. The number of corpses was even higher: 35,000 bodies lay piled one on top of the other, thrown away without pity, marked by privation and suffering. The atrocious events were soon revealed, causing remorse in those who had preferred not to see and not to know; moreover, Hitler's madness was facilitated by the tacit cooperation of people with no courage to oppose him. The extermination camps were run with methodical precision: upon their arrival, the prisoners were divided into the healthy and sick: the former were sent to forced labor, the latter to die. The same fate awaited the weak, the old, women and children who were sent to the gas chambers and eliminated. For those whose lives were spared, it was the beginning of an endless nightmare: in addition to the back-breaking labor they performed, they were forced to submit to every kind of humiliation and often torture so atrocious that only a deviant mind could have conceived it. Very few were able to survive more than 6 months before privation, exhaustion and disease had the better of them. The "final solution," the systematic extermination of the Jewish people planned by Himmler in 1942, was implemented with scientific precision and determination. Six million Jews murdered, in addition to thousands of political dissidents, gypsies and homosexuals - should have resulted in an absolute imperative that genocide on such a scale should never happen again: unfortunately, history has shown us that mankind is a very slow student indeed.

216

Top: during the Warsaw Ghetto uprising, the rebels fire from the rubble with a hodge-podge of pistols and rifles: they were exterminated to the last man in an inferno of fire, hunted down with flame throwers in the underground passages they had dug, often with their bare hands. Bottom: this photograph was taken in Warsaw in the summer of 1945: the war is Europe is over and where the Jewish ghetto once stood there are only piles of rubble. Not one building was left standing after the suppression of the insurrection, carried out under the orders of General Stroop. After destroying all the houses and killing all the inhabitants, Stroop telegraphed Hitler, "Order reigns in Warsaw."

1942
1945

217
A world-famous photograph: Jews rounded up by the SS during the destruction of Warsaw begin their journey to the death camps. The small boy (first row, next to his mother) survived and was located in America 50 years later.

218
Left: Jewish prisoners in Buchenwald, after a back breaking day at forced labor "rest" in their wooden bunks where they sleep heaped together like animals. Liberated by the Americans of the 80th Infantry, many died during the days that followed, a result of their seriously deteriorated physical condition.

219
Top left: Exhausted Jewish prisoners are transferred to hospitals in the Wobbelin concentration camp, May 1945; right, German officers move the bodies of hundreds of Jews in Bergen-Belsen. Bottom: April 13, 1945, American soldiers look at the remains of over 500 victims, burned by the SS in Gardelegen to prevent their liberation.

1945

THE WAR IN THE FAR EAST
1941-1945

Japanese expansionism and the Pearl Harbor attack

In the second half of the 1930s, the enormous increase in Japan's population (from 50 million to 90 million in 20 years) led the hungry island nation to seek "living space" in the vast expanse of neighboring China. Even if it was not openly apparent, Emperor Hirohito (who had reigned over the Japanese Empire since 1926), supported the expansionist aims of the minister of war, Hideki Tojo. A Japanese military contingent had been stationed in Peking since the Boxer Rebellion of 1900. Japan's pretext for attacking China was an "incident" that took place on July 7, 1937, at the Marco Polo Bridge in Peking, where Chinese Nationalists attacked a Japanese military squad and killed the soldiers. The Japanese Diet and the national press blew up the "Chinese provocation" out of all proportion. The government then urged an invasion according to a plan that had been prepared in minute detail for some time. Success was assured: all Chinese ports, major cities, and immense territories fell into the hands of the invading army. The USSR offered assistance to Chiang Kai-shek's government and the League of Nations condemned the war which, even if undeclared, was fierce and bloody. These two political actions convinced Tokyo to abandon Geneva and, together with Italy and Germany, sign the Anti-Comintern Pact, which was also anti-Bolshevik.

The situation became very tense along the Sino-Soviet border. Soviet and Japanese soldiers constantly skirmished, with the risk of a full-scale war. Following the outbreak of the Second World War in Europe and the fall of France, Japan set its sights on French colonial possessions in Southeast Asia. It occupied northern Indochina, while sizing up the British colonies. However, Japan's toughest enemy was not Great Britain but the United States, since Japanese military activities prevented the US from exerting control over the enormous Chinese market or promoting its expansion. The United States then imposed a series of economic sanctions against Japan, including the freezing of Japanese credit in America. Tokyo took this as a serious affront, tantamount to an act of war, albeit undeclared. It therefore took protective measures against the risk of a war on two fronts by signing a non-aggression pact with the USSR on April 13, 1941. The Japanese did this behind Hitler's back (repaying him in kind for the Molotov-Ribbentrop agreement of August 1939), signing the pact almost on the eve of Germany's aggression against Russia. As a result, at a crucial moment in the Second World War, Germany was to find itself without the Japanese support on which it had counted.

In October 1941 a government crisis occurred in Tokyo. The hesitant and compliant Prince Fumimaro Konoye was replaced as prime minister by the hard-line nationalist Tojo. He formed a government of military men--and Japan's entry into the Second World War was only a matter of weeks away.

On November 5, 1941, Tojo ordered the commander-in-chief of the fleet, Admiral Osoroku Yamamoto, to prepare to attack the American naval base at Pearl Harbor, Hawaii. Yamamoto, who had been in charge of the fleet since 1939, was personally opposed to the plan, but carried out Tojo's orders: they had the emperor's approval.

The assault on Pearl Harbor was launched at 7:55 local time on Sunday, December 7, 1941,with a combined air and sea attack by aircraft carriers, submarines, and warships. A total of 19 American ships were sunk, including eight battleships; thousands of officers and sailors died. Much speculation has occurred as to whether President Roosevelt had in fact been alerted to Japan's intention through information received from the secret services. Right from the start he had favored intervening in the Second World War, but was held back by the isolationist tendencies prevalent in American public opinion. The attack on Pearl Harbor provoked great indignation throughout the country. Overnight those who had been in favor of neutrality dropped from sight. Roosevelt declared war with the pressure of public opinion almost palpable. Concurrently with the United States' declaration on December 8, Japan also received a declaration of war from Great Britain. Shortly thereafter, on December 11, Italy and Germany declared war on the United States, thus sealing their ultimate fate.

The Japanese offensive was swift and brutal--an authentic Japanese-style "Blitzkrieg." On December 11 (the day of Italy and Germany's declaration of war against the United States), Japan achieved a series of successful strikes in the eastern theatre. These included the attack on northern Malaya and the Philippines, the occupation of Bangkok, the siege of Hong Kong, and landings on many Pacific islands, including Guam.

The British garrisons were taken by surprise, partly because their commanders underestimated the Japanese threat.

THE WAR IN THE FAR EAST 1941-1945

David Boyle, in his book, *The Second World War*, mentions Sir Robert Brooke-Popham, commander of the British forces in Malaya, saying that he considered the Japanese "subhumans wearing dirty gray uniforms": a form of "presumptuous racism," Boyle comments.

A closer look at the circumstances in which the Japanese obtained their greatest victories provides insight into their attack tactics. On December 8 (one day after the Pearl Harbor attack), Japan landed two infantry divisions of marines on the beaches of southern Thailand and in Kota Baharu, south of the Malayan border. The British admiral defending the area, Tom Philips, made a grave mistake in sending two battleships (*HMS Prince of Wales* and *HMS Repulse*) to intercept the landings, without providing any air cover. Japanese bombers equipped with long-range guns trapped the two ships. They were sunk, taking hundreds of sailors with them to the bottom of the sea.

Airplanes played a vital role in the days that followed. All the British colonies were subjected to heavy bombing. On December 12600 civilians were killed in the bombing of Penang, an island off northwest Malaya. Churchill was to write in his memoirs: "Japan held absolute sway, while we were everywhere weak and defenseless."

Hong Kong resisted well beyond the limits of its defensive capabilities. Although he only had two Canadian infantry battalions, the governor, Sir Mark Young, refused to accept unconditional surrender. The Japanese landed in force on December 18, but did not manage to achieve victory until Christmas Day, after taking 11,000 civilians prisoner (almost all the Canadians had been killed), many of whom were then run through with bayonets. This was the first example of the dreadful fate that awaited hundreds of thousands of Japanese prisoners.

In an effort to counter the Japanese "Blitzkrieg" both on land in Chinese territory and at sea--Yamamoto's constant attack--the Allies set up a multi-force commando unit. Called ABDA (after its American, British, Dutch and Australian components), the force was commanded by General Sir Archibald Wavell. He quickly put together a small fleet of cruisers, destroyers, and submarines with the aim of transferring at least 45,000 soldiers to Malaya. These included British and Dutch troops from India and Australians and Americans coming directly from their homelands.

The commander of the Japanese troops in Malaya was General Tomoyuki Yamashita. In 1939-40, he had studied "Blitzkrieg" techniques in Germany. He provided his men with bicycles so that they could move rapidly through the jungle, keeping away from the roads. In this way he managed to occupy swiftly the entire Malayan west coast, taking 40,000 British and Indian soldiers prisoner. On January 31, 1942, the British commander, General Arthur Percival, retreated to the island of Singapore. This British bastion therefore became Japan's next target.

Yamashita launched an attack on the night of February 7. The Japanese troops, numbering 13,000, crossed the strait separating the island city from the mainland in rubber dinghies, while the air force bombed the center of Singapore. As Hitler was to do later with the defenders of Stalingrad, Churchill ordered, "No surrender." But after a week of very heavy fighting, often hand-to-hand and with bayonets, Percival appeared with a white flag in front of Yamashita's bunker.

The Japanese carried out savage reprisals: 5,000 Chinese civilians--mostly from the educated middle class (government officials, industrialists, company directors, and other professionals)--were killed for having chosen to serve British interests rather than Tokyo's. Large numbers of prisoners were also taken: 32,000 Indians, 16,000 British, 14,000 Australians. Half of them died in concentration camps. The capture of Singapore was celebrated in the streets of Tokyo, and Japanese flags waved from every house.

On January 10, General Yamamura landed on the islands of Borneo and Celebes on He wiped out the Dutch defense and gained possession of the Dutch East Indies' true wealth, the oil wells. Less than a month later, on February 4, Japanese planes attacked the ABDA naval squadron. During the attack, the Dutch commander in chief, Admiral Karel Doorman, was killed in action on the flagship *De Ruyter*, which was sunk. ABDA suffered irreparable damage, and on March 1, it ceased to exist as a fighting unit. Five days after the ABDA attack (on February 9), the Americans sustained a similar defeat in the naval battle of the Java Sea. Immediately afterwards, Timor, Sumatra, and Java capitulated. Java's civilian population rebelled against the 25,000 Dutch soldiers of the garrison, applauding the Japanese "liberators." Japanese imperialist ideas were beginning to find some purchase. By the end of these victorious operations the Japanese army had taken 100,000 Dutch, British, Indian, and Australian prisoners.

222-223
Pearl Harbor, December 7, 1941: the surprise attack by Japanese bombers transformed the American naval base and air station into an inferno. Top left: dense spirals of smoke rise from the battleships Tennessee *and* Arizona*, hit dead on; bottom, the picture shows the devastating effects of the attack on the airport hangars on Ford Island; center, stunned American sailors watch the terrifying explosions that signal the end of the destroyer* Shaw*; top right, Japanese* A6M2 Zero *fighter planes hurry to take off from the deck of the aircraft carrier* Shokaku*, sailing in the waters off of Hawaii. These very agile fighters escorted the two waves of* D3A *and* B5N *bombers that sank the pride of the US Navy in just a few minutes.*

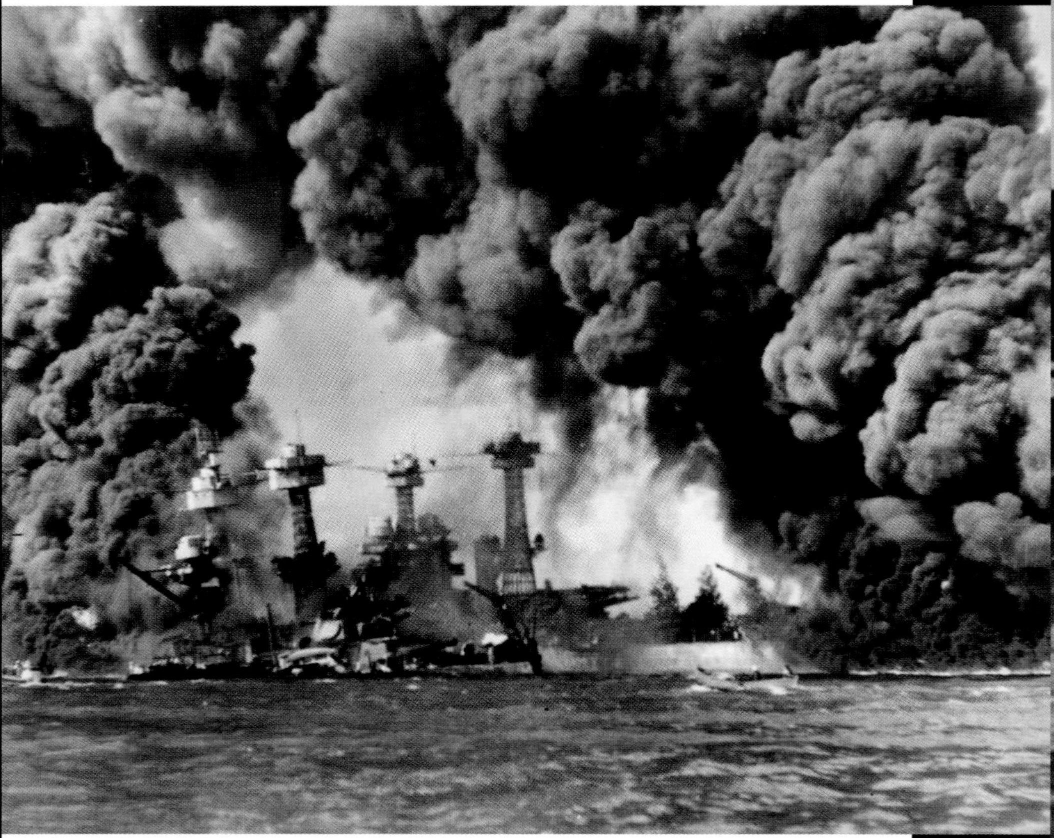

The Pearl Harbor ATTACK

224
Bottom, a few hours after the treacherous attack, several American soldiers look on in dismay at the contorted and flame-devastated remains of the two destroyers, the Cassin *and the* Downes, *surprised by diving* D3A VAL *bombers in dry dock; the background the mass of the battleship* Pennsylvania *stands out, also damaged. Right, the battleship* Arizona *is sinking, devoured by flames; in a few seconds over 950 sailors perished on this great ship, while another 250 were mortally wounded: there were only 337 survivors.The wreck of the* Arizona, *which still lies where it sank, is today a shrine dedicated to all who fell at Pearl Harbor.*

THE RISING SUN ADVANCES
1941-1942

In America, the Pearl Harbor attack had given rise to hostile feelings toward the large Japanese-American community. In March 1942, 110,000 Japanese-Americans were ordered to leave their places of residence and work and to gather at assembly points prior to being sent to internment camps. A few days later the measure was extended to include the west coast's Italian-American community, which was much more numerous than the Japanese one.

Having no more incentive to remain neutral, the American people rallied wholeheartedly behind President Roosevelt and the Congress in wanting to retaliate. All economic activities were immediately channeled into the war effort. Resources were mobilized to produce arms, ships, and planes, and in just six months, the factories turned out war equipment to the value of $100 million (a sum then in excess of the US gross domestic product). The main objective was to rebuild the American fleet to match the size of the expanded Japanese fleet, which had recently added its first three super-battleships, armed with 450mm guns.

With the help of these powerful vessels Yamamoto had no trouble getting the better of the British fleet, which, commanded by Admiral Sir James Somerville, had five battleships and three aircraft carriers. By the end of the battle, in which the lethal Japanese "VAL" Aichi D3As aircraft played a decisive role, the aircraft carrier *HMS Hermes* and the cruisers *HMS Cornwall* and *HMS Dorsetshire* had all been sunk (this last had sunk the *Bismarck*).

The Japanese launched their attack on Burma in the last days of 1941. Gaining control of the Burma Road was a strategic necessity: it would close the long route traversing Burma through which the Allies supplied and provisioned the Chinese resistance led by Chiang Kai-shek and Mao Tse-tung. The supreme Allied commander, Sir Harold Alexander, decided that priority should be given to defending the Indian border against possible Japanese aggression. Burma was abandoned to its fate, and on March 8, 35,000 Japanese troops entered Rangoon, assisted by a local "fifth column."

But before the Japanese could definitively take over the Burma Road, Chiang managed to send down from China two Chinese nationalist armies of 100,000 men, to be commanded by the General Stilwell, an American. Through their fierce fighting, the Chinese soldiers managed to slow down the Japanese advance toward India. But there was a heavy price to pay as the Sino-British troops made a painfully slow and exhausting retreat. As it withdrew toward the Indian border, this enormous army of 160,000 ragged, shoeless men, their uniforms in tatters, with no provisions and very little ammunition, formed a human wall between the Japanese and their objective.

228
Top left: soldiers of the Rising Sun reach their quarters in Pandu Ghat, Burma; right, assault troops in action in the Burmese jungle near Kohima. Bottom: Chiang Kai-shek's Nationalist Chinese soldiers attempt a desperate resistance against the overwhelming Japanese forces along the Salween River near the Burmese border.

229
Aerial view of the legendary Burma Road, the long, impassable artery that crossed Burma and represented the only supply road for the Chinese resistance and the only escape route towards China for British troops, pressed by the unstoppable Japanese advance hot on their heels.

AMERICA DEFEATED IN THE PHILIPPINES
1942

If Japan's Burma campaign was a blistering defeat for the British army, then Japan's Philippines campaign was even more so for the Americans. General Douglas MacArthur was sent to the Philippines (an American protectorate) in the summer of 1941 because the United States feared a Japanese attack on the islands. On December 8, just 24 hours after the attack on Pearl Harbor, the Japanese air force carried out a series of air raids, destroying American aircraft on the ground at the airports of Luzon. On December 10, General Masaharu Homa's marine corps started its landing on the island of Luzon. About 57,000 arrived-- half the number of MacArthur's contingent. The Japanese carried out the saturation bombing of Manila, forcing MacArthur to leave the capital undefended and an easy target for the Japanese. They occupied it on January 2, 1942, a mere four weeks after Pearl Harbor. The Americans had entrenched themselves on the Bataan peninsula, to the south of which stood Corregidor fort, at the entrance to Manila Bay. The Philippine president, Manuel Quezon, had also taken refuge here. In Bataan, climatic conditions and tropical diseases hindered military operations, taking thousands of lives among the Americans and Japanese. MacArthur hoped in vain for reinforcements to arrive from across the sea, but the Japanese fleet controlled the shipping routes. Thus on March 11, 1942, MacArthur obeyed Roosevelt's order to pull out of Corregidor and go to Australia. Before he left, he swore: "I shall return."

General Jonathan Wainwright, to whom MacArthur had passed the command of Corregidor, decided to resist to the end. After pounding the fort with artillery, the Japanese landed and engaged in hand-to-hand fighting in the rubble created by the explosion of the magazine. On May 6 the Americans surrendered, but for more than a month soldiers who had refused to give up their weapons continued to fight as guerrillas in the jungle. The battle of the Philippines was marked by a tragic loss of life: 30,000 Americans and 110,000 Filipinos killed or taken prisoner, 12,000 Japanese killed.

In barely six months Japan had taken possession of lands rich in agricultural products, oil, and mineral deposits, and ruled over 450 million people. Its policy with regard to the conquered peoples was to encourage anti-European movements and pro-Japanese governments. In Indonesia an "Indonesian Central Council" was created to foster Indonesia's friendship with Japan. Burma declared itself independent, as did Thailand and the Philippines. The emperor of Annam, Bao Dai, also had Japanese support in bringing Tonkin and Cambodia into his kingdom, which he now called Vietnam. Like their German allies, the victorious Japanese appeared unbeatable. However, these two allies could not jointly agree on a single move. Until then, these victors, or rather these perceived victors, had each been waging an individual war--and making the same mistakes. The Japanese were acting in newly conquered Southeast Asia exactly as the Germans had acted in the Ukraine and Georgia: applying a policy of oppression of the people and extermination of opponents. The Germans did this in Georgia and the Ukraine; the Japanese did it in Southeast Asia. They effectively quashed the enthusiasm of much of the local population. For a moment the "liberated" populations had felt freed from the exploitative yoke of the British, Dutch, and French. Indeed, a number of Indian nationalists went to the Japanese commands to sign up as volunteers in the Emperor's army in order to free their country from the British.

Unfortunately for them, the Japanese did not recognize their opportunity and alienated all the subjugated peoples. As for the prisoners of war, half of them died in concentration camps their rights denied in clear violation of the Geneva Convention. They were starved (receiving only 400 grams of rice a day), often beaten, and used in medical experiments that at times proved lethal. The guards often urinated in the water before distributing it to the prisoners. During the forced marches, those who fell down from exhaustion and dysentery were finished off with bayonets. The most famous was the Bataan Death March in the Philippines, which occurred after the surrender of Corregidor: 10,000 American and Philippine prisoners lost their lives during the hellish trek.

The British and Australian prisoners met with the same cruelty in Burma. They were forced to work in inhuman conditions to build the railway connecting Bangkok, Thailand with Rangoon, Burma. A cholera epidemic broke out among the prisoners and 13,000 died. Those who came down with cholera were shot at once to limit the spread of the disease. By the time the railway was finished on October 25, 1943, 50,000 Allied prisoners and 250,000 slave laborers taken from Burma, Java, Malaya, and China had lost their lives. To cover up these crimes, the survivors were exterminated during the Allied advance so that there would be no witnesses left. On Luzon, at the last minute, American paratroopers descended from the sky managed to save 500 prisoners who were about to be "executed," or rather mown down, by machine-gun fire. Many have questioned why the Japanese treated their prisoners so badly. The conventional answer has been that, according to the *bushido*, the traditional Japanese military code of war, those who surrender lose their honor and every right to respect.

232-233
Top left: Japanese soldiers rejoice over the victory at Corregidor; center, a Japanese landing craft approaches Manila, by now in flames; bottom: Japanese infantrymen land at Singora, Malaysia. Right, the last American defenders leave the bunkers on Corregidor, after a strenuous but vain resistance: for them, the victors were to have no pity.

231
During the initial phases of the conflict, the unmistakable battle flag of the Japanese army became the feared symbol of the Japanese war machine. Incredibly dedicated, the combatants of the Rising Sun knew only one rule: victory or death.

234-235
Several tragic images from the "Bataan Death March," following the surrender of the American garrison in the Philippines. On that occasion, over 10,000 prisoners perished from hardships and starvation during their transfer to the Japanese concentration camps.

1941

THE BATTLE OF MIDWAY: THE COUNTERATTACK BEGINS
1942

The first battle between American and Japanese aircraft carriers was fought in the Coral Sea from May 4-8, 1942. The Japanese fleet suffered serious losses, nothing, however, compared to the losses the Japanese incurred in the air and sea battle of the Midway Islands, fought in June 1942). This battle was to fill Americans with admiration for Admiral Chester W. Nimitz. In the middle of the Pacific Ocean north of the Hawaiian Islands, where the blistering offensive of Pearl Harbor had taken place, the American fleet sank four Japanese aircraft carriers in a single day. Perhaps the winds of fortune were beginning to change. But it is necessary to examine what events in Southeast Asia led to this change.

Japan was under the illusion that Hitler's invasion of the USSR would bring Stalin's defeat and force the United States to negotiate a peace and forgo all hope of a counteroffensive in Southeast Asia. But the Americans, had sought revenge on Japan ever since the Pearl Harbor. The Roosevelt administration had employed all the country's resources in preparation for the war with Japan and its allies. America had developed and built 60,000 military aircraft, 75,000 armored tanks, and 1 million tons of merchant shipping. As the men poured into training camps for recruits, women took their place in the factories, giving rise to the legend of "Rosie the Riveter." When the ABDA commando force was disbanded (March 1, 1942), operational responsibilities were distributed as follows: supreme command for naval operations to Admiral Chester Nimitz; the Southwestern Pacific to General Douglas MacArthur; and Sumatra and the Indian Ocean to the British. At Midway, Nimitz was to score the first historic defeat of Japan. But first he wanted to leave a unique calling card: an air attack on Tokyo.

On April 18, 1942, the inhabitants of the capital watched almost incredulously as a squadron of bombers approached the city. Sixteen Mitchell B25s had taken off from the aircraft carrier *USS Hornet* and were now approaching the Japanese coast, escorted by the aircraft carrier *USS Enterprise*, with fighters on board to protect the bombers. Colonel James Doolittle, a famous airplane racing pilot in the 1920s and 30s, led the attack. Before the Japanese anti-aircraft guns could counterattack, the bombers dropped their lethal cargo on the buildings in the center of Tokyo. The crews of the three aircraft that were forced to land in Japanese territory were surrounded and lynched by the crowd. The incursion led the Tojo government to order the attack and sinking of all enemy aircraft carriers at sea. To attain this objective, it was necessary to attack the Midway Islands. Located northwest of the Hawaiian and equidistant from Japan and the United States, the two small island were a strategic point from which to control all ships arriving from the United States to support operations in the eastern Pacific war zone.

While Yamamoto was planning the operation, on May 7, 1942, the battle of the Coral Sea took place. The Japanese fleet on its way to attack Port Moresby (the capital of New Guinea) in the first step in the planned conquest of Australia encountered two American aircraft carriers under the command of Admiral Frank Fletcher. These were the *USS Yorktown* and *USS Lexington*, escorted by seven cruisers. The Americans sank the Japanese aircraft carrier *Shoho* and badly damaged the *Shokaku*, but lost the *Lexington*. The outcome of the Coral Sea battle was decisive in dissuading Japan from invading Australia, and certainly reinforced Yamamoto's resolve to conquer the Midway Islands and build a vast airport to act as a barrier against all the ships arriving from America. Yamamoto examined his strategy and tactics from every angle. First he launched a diversionary attack on the American-held Aleutian Islands off Alaska, hoping to lure the entire US fleet there away from the Midway Islands. But the Americans managed to intercept the Japanese high command's communications and discovered Yamamoto's plan. Nimitz therefore gave orders to do nothing about the Aleutian Islands and sent three aircraft carriers and eight cruisers to the Midway Islands.

The Japanese, however, were arriving with seven battleships, six aircraft carriers, 14 cruisers, and a great number of destroyers and submarines. The battle started on June 4, 1942: 108 Japanese bombers pounded the two islands, destroying American aircraft in the air and on the ground. At this stage Nimitz ordered the bombers on the carriers *Hornet*, *Enterprise*, and *Yorktown* to go into battle. Fifty Dauntless bombers descended on the Japanese fleet; the aircraft carriers *Kaga*, *Akagi*, and *Soryu* were sunk. The ammunition magazines on all three exploded and terrible fires ripped through the vessels as they went down, killing many of their crew. Shortly after the aircraft carrier *Hiryu* sank. The flagship of the American fleet, the *USS Yorktown*, was hit; Fletcher had to abandon it after handing the command over to Admiral Raymond Spruance. The battle ended with the sinking of the Japanese cruiser *Mikuma*. "We have lost the habit of winning," Admiral Nagumo commented bitterly.

1942

237
Several phases of the Battle of the Coral Sea, fought on May 8, 1942. Top: the Japanese aircraft carrier Shoho *is hit dead on by American bombers; center, the aircraft carrier* Shokaku *tries to flee US airplanes; bottom: the American aircraft carrier* Lexington, *mortally wounded, is wrapped in flames.*

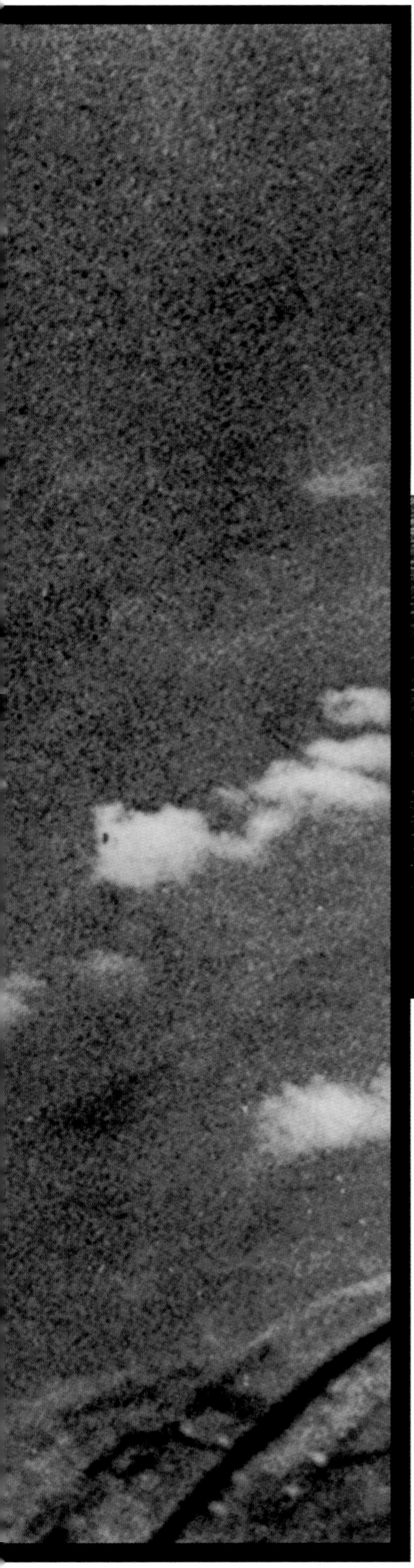

238
Douglas SBD Dauntless *bombers over-fly a burning Japanese navy ship off Midway Island. During the course of the extremely violent battle fought on June 4, 1942, the bombers that took off from American aircraft carriers played a decisive role, sinking four enemy aircraft carriers. It was a tremendous blow for the Japanese fleet.*

239
Another three moments from the Battle of Midway, the air sea battle that marked counter-attack that stopped the Japanese advance in the Pacific. Top: the aircraft carrier Yorktown, *hit several times, tries a desperate evasive maneuver; center, the Japanese aircraft carrier* Hiryu *is photographed already prey to the fires that will cause it to sink; bottom: the crew of the* Yorktown *hurry to abandon ship, mortally hit by bombs dropped by Japanese bombers.*

GUADALCANAL, NEW GUINEA, BURMA: THE ALLIES STRIKE BACK

1942

The American victory at Midway was auspicious for Admiral Nimitz, whose plan was to take back from Japan all the territory it had gained so far. American counteroffensive operations started on August 7, 1942, when Nimitz's ships landed a division of Marines on Guadalcanal (the southernmost of the Solomon Islands), to capture the island and put America back on the map in Southeast Asia. It was not easy: the Americans were forced to fight for a good six months against Japanese forces who had orders to resist to the death.

Guadalcanal is an island about 93,5 miles long. In mid-1942 the Japanese started building a military airbase on the island. They had to be stopped. On August 7, 11,000 Marines landed on Guadalcanal and 6000 on nearby Tulagi. The Japanese sent up carrier-based planes to bomb the Marines' bridgeheads, and ships under Admiral Mikawa's command effected a naval blockade of Guadalcanal to prevent the arrival of reinforcements. An American squadron commanded by Admiral Robert Gormley attacked the Japanese squadron. The sinking of the aircraft carrier *Ryuio* was the first American success. Then came the land battle between US and Japanese marines, fought on the hills known as "Bloody Ridge." It was a bitter and prolonged battle, since neither side had the slightest intention of surrendering. There was also heavy fighting at sea. The United States lost the aircraft carriers *USS Wasp* and *USS Hornet*, while the *USS Enterprise* and the *USS Saratoga* were badly damaged. Japan lost 200 aircraft, and two of its aircraft carriers were put out of action. The fighting on land and sea lasted four months. The wounded Japanese lay on the hillsides and beaches pretending to be dead, only to lob hand grenades at advancing US soldiers. In January 1943 the ratio was 25,000 Japanese without supplies to 50,000 well-armed Americans. The Japanese were close to being annihilated when the high command in Tokyo decided to evacuate the survivors. Guadalcanal thus went down in the annals of American history as a military victory. A total of 25,000 Japanese died; the last Japanese soldier surrendered in the jungle in October 1947, unaware that the war had been over for more than two years.

The second major campaign in the American counteroffensive took place in New Guinea. General MacArthur was the principal actor. In the eyes of the Australians he was already a military leader of the highest caliber; he had calmed the waves of panic that had swept through the population at the news of Japanese landings in New Guinea. MacArthur had exhorted the inhabitants of Sydney not to abandon the capital but to hold firm and follow the example of the heroic defenders of Port Moresby, the capital of New Guinea. Throughout 1942 the Japanese made repeated but unsuccessful attacks to capture Port Moresby. On September 15, American reinforcements arrived in the town. They drove the Japanese back beyond the mountains. There swamps, crocodiles, and epidemics killed thousands of combatants, 12,000 alone among the Japanese. The survivors, driven into the sea by the joint Australian and American offensive, chose to drown rather than surrender.

The third chapter of the Allied reconquest was the Burma campaign, in which soldiers drawn from British Commonwealth nations stopped the Japanese invasion of India. After conquering Singapore, Japan thought itself invincible, able to occupy (or "free from the British yoke," as Tokyo's propaganda put it) the vast country of India. In Burma an "Indian liberation army" had been formed under the leadership of the anti-British Indian nationalist, Subhas Chandra Bose. Some 25,000 Indians taken prisoner by the Japanese during the advance into Burma had also enrolled as volunteers to fight against their former British officers. The Sikhs and Gurkhas, however, remained staunchly loyal to the British.

With the aim of thwarting the Japanese plans, Churchill appointed Admiral Lord Louis Mountbatten as supreme commander of the Burmese front. He was a witty officer, 42 years old, and very popular among the troops. Second in command was General Joseph Stilwell, a sprightly 60-year-old American, who was equally popular. Mountbatten and Stilwell were an extraordinary pair; both possessed the rare skill of being able to unite and instill with enthusiasm soldiers of different backgrounds and nationalities. The way General Wingate's 3,000 "chindits" (specialists in guerrilla operations) worked in perfect harmony with the American air formations commanded by the daring Philip Cochran, assigned to support chindit operations, is just one example. At the end of 1943 the Japanese launched their attack on India, focusing on the border cities of Imphal and Kohima, which they besieged. An airlift was organized to send in supplies and evacuate the wounded in both cities. In addition, the Japanese were pounded for months by Allied bombers, clearly superior to the Japanese air force. In July 1944 the siege ended in total defeat for the Japanese, who lost 65,000 men in the disastrous operation. This marked the beginning of the reconquest of Burma, which ended victoriously thanks to an army commanded by Mountbatten. In it American, British, Australian, Indian, French, and Dutch soldiers fought heroically.

124457

241

Top: an American Boeing B-17E *over-flies one of the Solomon Islands after attacking Japanese positions; bottom: a column of marines advances in the jungle of Guadalcanal shortly before an assault on Japanese forces barricaded on the other side of the Matanikou river, October 1942.*

242

Left: a an M3 Stuart *light tank, just landed at Guadalcanal, hurries to return cover fire for a platoon of Marines; Right: the Marines gain ground on the island of Guadalcanal during the first phase of the offensive in the Solomons in August 1942.*

1942
1944

Top right: a dense cloud of black smoke rises from a Japanese navy ship hit by US bombers off Guadalcanal, summer 1942.Bottom: the last dramatic moments of the American aircraft carrier Wasp, *sunk by a Japanese submarine in the waters of Guadalcanal during the first days of the September of the same year: all it took were two well-placed torpedoes to annihilate this colossus.*

1942
1944

244
The last quiet moments before the inferno: these Marines hurry to disembark on the beach at Aitape, in New Guinea, under a deadly Japanese barrage. Forty percent of them did not make it. During the landing operations, the greatest number of losses were recorded during the first minutes of action, when the attackers found themselves in the open.

245
Top: Marines just landed at Rendova, in the Solomon Islands, June 30, 1943. Bottom: a Sherman tank opens the way for US infantry engaged in close combat on the island of Bougainville; the arrival of this tank, heavily armed and defended, signaled a decisive turn in the conduct of American war operations.

1942
1944

246
The bodies of these Japanese soldiers testify to the violence of the fighting following the American landings in Burma and New Guinea. During these clashes the Americans lost almost 90 percent of their troops.

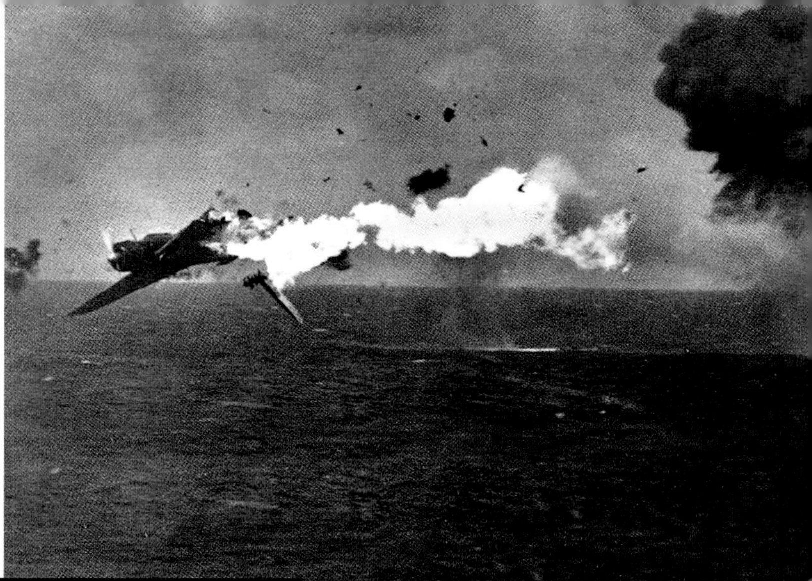

247
Top: a Japanese torpedo boat is hit by anti-aircraft artillery from an American aircraft carrier, off of Kwajalein; center, these Japanese soldiers stationed at Tarawa, killed themselves rather than be taken prisoner; bottom: a group of Marines finds shelter in the craters made by artillery fire, on Tarawa.

248-249
These three images capture the Allied counteroffensive in Burma, occupied by the Japanese in May 1942. Left, British soldiers unleash heavy mortar fire against Japanese positions during the fighting to conquer Meiktila. Top right: an Indian soldier in the British contingent has just launched a phosphorous grenade during the violent clashes in the Arakan region; bottom: American medics provide first aid to the wounded of the 36th Division engaged in the attack on Pinwe.

1942
1944

THE RISING SUN SETS
1943-1945

The targeting and killing in early 1943 of Admiral Yamamoto, who had masterminded the "Blitzkrieg" of the East, badly damaged Japanese morale. America's role in the event only came to light at the end of the war. Military intelligence had managed to get hold of a timetable detailing the schedule of Yamamoto, the supreme commander of the Japanese navy. He was about to inspect Bougainville, in the Solomon Islands, in a morale-boosting exercise for the troops. The Americans prepared an aerial ambush, and on April 8, 1943 fighter plane intercepted Yamamoto's plane and shot it down. In March, after attacking the Solomon Islands, Nimitz established the second aim of the counteroffensive: to reconquer the Aleutian Islands, an ocean away to the north. As part of Alaska (and therefore American territory), the Aleutians were of great patriotic significance. The Marines put up stiff resistance to the Japanese; fighting went on for three months until, at the end of May 1943, the Japanese garrison had been exterminated.

In June 1943 the biggest American offensive was launched with spectacular naval battles in the gulfs of Kula, Kolombangara and Vella Lavella, in the Solomon Islands. The Americans scored victory after victory, taking the Gilbert Islands, the Marshall Islands, and the Admiralty Islands. This maneuver went down in military history as the "leap-frog tactic." The idea, developed by Nimitz , consisted of giving the opponent no respite: Having landed on one island, the Marines would then start new landings on anther island a few days later, while the first battle was still being fought.

The colossal operation culminated in the summer of 1944 when the Mariana Islands were recaptured. The first landings took place on June 15 on the island of Saipan. Altogether 130,000 US soldiers were involved. On June 19 an impressive air and sea battle was fought between the American fleet, commanded by Admiral Mark Mitscher, with 1000 fighter planes, and the Japanese fleet, commanded by Admiral Jizaburo Ozawa, with 300 aircraft. It was a massacre. The Japanese lost 218 planes and two aircraft carriers, including Ozawa's flagship, the *Taiho*, sunk by a submarine. The Americans lost 29 aircraft. The following day, June 20, the Japanese received the coup de grâce, when the aircraft carrier *Hiyo* and the battleship *Haruna* were sunk. On July 6, as the Japanese situation went from bad to worse, Admiral Nagumo and General Saito committed suicide to encourage their men to make the supreme sacrifice and defend the island of Saipan to the death. It was the start of a dreadful bloodbath. Entire Japanese units, pursued into the jungle, committed hara-kiri. Officers decapitated their soldiers one by one on the coral reef before taking their own lives. Some 22,000 civilians committed suicide in the underground caves where they were sheltering: they could not live with the shame of defeat. The fall of Saipan had dramatic political repercussions in Tokyo. General Tojo resigned as prime minister; all other government members resigned with him. A few days later the other islands, Mariana, Tinian, and Guam also fell. The Japanese troops on Tinian committed mass suicide by jumping off the cliffs.

Next came the Philippines. When Douglas MacArthur transferred to Australia after the heroic but unsuccessful defense of the Bataan peninsula, he stated "I shall return." And in October 1944 he did, and set out to reconquer the Philippines at the head of assault forces made up of the 6th Army plus four divisions. Roosevelt willingly consented to MacArthur's legitimate request for command; in this way he could keep a powerful rival well away from the presidential election campaign, due to take place at the end of 1944. MacArthur wanted a D-Day like the one that had shaken Europe. He chose the island of Leyte for the first landings since its wide gulf enabled the 3rd Fleet, commanded by Admiral Halsey, to afford protection to the assault troops (700 combat and transport units, with 200,000 soldiers). The operation started at dawn on October 20, 1944. Japan had organized a naval force under Admiral Kurita that should have been able to annihilate the American attackers and show the world that Japan was by no means beaten. But two American submarines, the *USS Dace* and the *USS Darter*, identified the fleet heading full steam ahead toward the gulf of Leyte and opened fire with torpedoes, sinking the flagship. Kurita was forced to transfer to the carrier *Yamamoto*, considered unsinkable. Meanwhile the marines, having gained ground in Leyte, advanced into the jungle, massacring the Japanese. In the sea off the islands, a series of naval battles was being waged. Though generally uncoordinated on both sides, they were to end disastrously for the Japanese units: three battleships, four aircraft carriers, and nine cruisers were sunk. The Japanese navy did not recover from this defeat.

At this point the "kamikaze" attacks began (kamikaze means "divine wind" in Japanese). During the battle of the Philippines, Admiral Amura, devastated by the loss of his own vessel, flew his plane, with a full load of bombs, in a suicidal crash into the carrier *USS Franklin*, destroying it. Admiral Onishi, commander of the 1st Air Fleet, then invited volunteers to imitate

Amura's heroic gesture. Thousands accepted his invitation. The first "kamikaze" attack came at the end of October 1944 in the Philippines, when four "Zero" fighter planes carrying 155 lb bombs attacked three enemy aircraft carriers, causing death and destruction. Later, in the battle of Okinawa, 1,800 "kamikaze" pilots took off, flew, dived, and died. Soon the volunteers moved on from flying fighters to a piloting a new type of missile, an 800-lb rocket-propelled unit launched by a bomber and piloted by a suicide volunteer until it reached its target. The name given to these pilots was "jinrai butai" ("divine sect"). From the onset of the kamikaze operation until the end of the conflict, 2,159 men gave their lives. On August 14, 1945, when Admiral Onishi heard that Japan had capitulated, he committed hara-kiri. The battle of the Philippines culminated in the attack on the island of Luzon on January 9, 1945. Admiral Iwabuchi decided to defend the capital, Manila, to the death and had no qualms about razing half the city, burying 100,000 Filipino civilians under the rubble. The savage cruelty included in the extermination of the patients in a hospital, who were tied to their beds and set on fire. In the end, the remaining Japanese took 5000 civilians hostage, hoping by this act to stop the American advance. When on February 27, 1945, MacArthur entered what was left of Manila he found everyone dead: the Filipinos assassinated, the Japanese having chosen suicide.

251

Top: faithful to the promise he made two years before, General MacArthur lands on the island of Leyte, in the Philippines, October 1944; bottom: amphibious craft from the 1st Marine Division gain ground on the island of Peleliu, in Palau, September 20, 1944.

252
US Marines engaged in a violent clash on the island of Saipan, June 1944: the fighting lasted 25 days and cost the Americans 15000 men, counting dead and wounded.

The Second
WORLD WAR

253
*Three more raw images of the battle for Saipan, in the Mariana Islands.
Top: a Marine tries to reassure a Japanese family that took refuge in a grotto in an attempt to escape the violence of the fighting; center, the mangled bodies of Japanese soldiers scattered along the beaches of Saipan; bottom: an American soldier delicately holds the tiny body of a Japanese child found seriously wounded in the island's mountains during the fierce battle of June 1944.*

254-255
Top left: an American landing craft approaches Leyte Island in the Philippines, the object of a furious naval bombardment on October 20, 1944; bottom: an impressive column of smoke rises from a Japanese bunker that served as a torpedo storehouse, destroyed by Marines on the island of Namur during the course of the invasion of Kwajalein, February 1944. Right, American soldiers building ramps out of sand bags, necessary to land tanks from the navy ships reaching the beaches on Leyte. It is November 11, 1944 and US forces are assembling a huge tactical and logistical force for the final conquest of the Philippines.

202

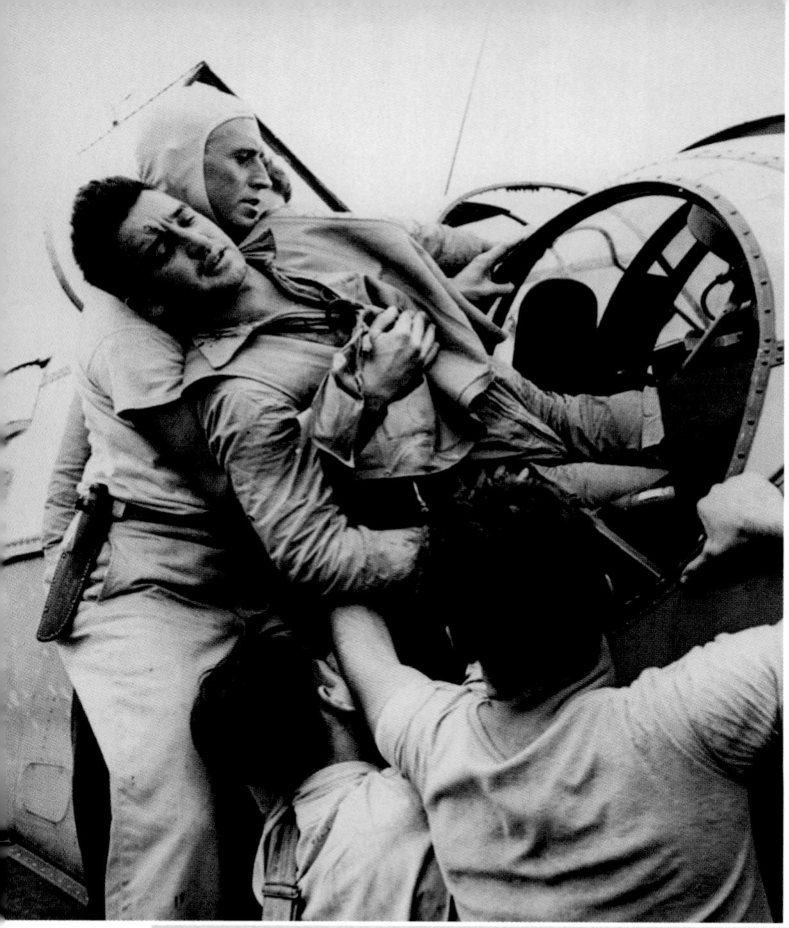

256-257

Top left: the machine-gunner of a TBF-1 Avenger bomber is aided on carrier Saratoga *after a raid on Rabaul; bottom: the impressive fleet plows the waters off the Philippines: two aircraft carriers in the foreground and three battleships behind them. Right, an F6F Hellcat fighter takes off from the deck of the* USS Yorktown II.

1943
1945

258-259

Top left: the American aircraft carrier Bunker Hill *in flames off Okinawa, May 1945, after being the target of a kamikaze attack; center, US sailors watch the evacuation of the aircraft carrier* Santa Fe, *mortally hit by a suicide pilot in March 1945; bottom: more effects of the double kamikaze attack on the* Bunker Hill, *that caused 372 deaths and 264 wounded in just 30 seconds. Right, this extraordinary picture freezes the last moment of a kamikaze pilot: an A6M Zero fighter-bomber about to crash with its deadly load into the battleship* Missouri, *May 1945. His sacrifice was in vain: barely three months later, on this very ship, representatives of the Tokyo government signed the unconditional surrender of the Japanese empire.*

1943

1945

Iwo Jima and Okinawa

1945

By 1945 only 600 miles of sea separated the spearheads of the American army from the Japanese coast. The first two assaults on Japanese territory bear the names of hard-won islands that have become legendary in the history of the United States: Iwo Jima and Okinawa. The assault on Iwo Jima started on February 19, 1945, after the island had been bombarded from the air and from the sea for two months. A total of 30,000 marines landed on this small island of only 8 square miles, reduced by the bombardment to an expanse of craters and blackened tree stumps. The scarred landscape, however, still harbored 21,000 Japanese, every last one ready to fight to death and defend every inch of this tiny patch of their homeland from being conquered. All 21,000 died, while American losses at the end of the four weeks of fighting were 6,800 dead and 10,000 wounded. This charnel field was rapidly "cleaned up," and massive trenches were dug to bury the dead. Being so close to Japan, Iwo Jima became a valuable base for the air raids destined to bring death and destruction to what remained of the Japanese cities.

The assault on Okinawa started on April 1, 1945. In terms of the number of troops involved and weapons capacity, it was an even bigger operation than the first phase of the D-Day landings in Normandy on June 6, 1944. A total of 1300 ships, supported by an impressive air force, landed 183,000 men of the US 10th Army on the island. Their orders were to drive into the sea or kill the 100,000 men of the Japanese garrison. After 80 days of furious battles, the victorious Americans had suffered losses to the tune of 12,600 dead and 6000 wounded; 130,000 Japanese had been killed, 42,000 of whom were civilians. In other words, almost the entire military garrison had given their lives. On June 21 the few survivors capitulated. The commander of the island, General Ushijima and his chief of staff, General Cho, had surrendered to save the lives of the last indomitable combatants. Immediately after signing the surrender they each asked for a dagger, went into a tent, and committed hara-kiri. It was in Okinawa, after observing the enemy's extraordinary display of self-sacrifice (and witnessing the deaths of 12,000 of his own men), that MacArthur's doubts about use of the atomic bomb finally ended. He came out on the side of the American scientists who were pushing for a "live" test. Another factor that influenced MacArthur's decision was that the Emperor still had at least 4 million soldiers capable of inflicting immense losses on the US Army.

260-261
This legendary picture is the very symbol of the American victory in the Pacific: the Marines planted the stars and stripes on the summit of Mount Suribachi, on Iwo Jima, in March 1945.

262
Faithful to the ancient Bushido code of valor, the Japanese defenders of Iwo Jima fought to the death, not able to conceive the idea of surrender. The Marines often had to use flame-throwers to flush them from their positions, with terrifying results. Of the 23,000 troops in the local garrison, none was captured alive. The Americans paid a toll of 6,800 dead and 10,000 wounded.

263

Top right, having just landed on the black beaches of Iwo Jima, the Marines, commanded by "Howlin' Mad" Smith, are greeted with a terrifying barrage of fire; bottom: American soldiers consolidate their positions on the shore, while the wounded are evacuated. The first line has advanced several hundred feet.

264-265
Episodes in the ferocious fighting on Okinawa between April and May 1945. Top left: a Marine destroys a Japanese position with a flame-thrower; center: several sappers view the devastating effects of an explosive charge set off in an enemy bunker; bottom: armored flame-throwers target a Japanese stronghold. Right, a Marine aids his friend, seriously wounded in the face, during one of the endless battles for Okinawa. American losses in three months of fighting amounted to 12,600 dead and 36,000 wounded, compared to 130,000 Japanese casualties.

1945

266-267

Left: the US fleet off Okinawa defends itself from Japanese air attacks with a violent barrage. On the facing page, top left: an American artillery position opens fire on the enemy lines in the southern part of the island; top right: an F4U Corsair launches a volley of rockets against strategic enemy positions; bottom: US navy ships unleash an inferno on the hinterlands of Okinawa.

ATOMIC DEATH AND THE DEFEAT OF JAPAN

1945

To break Japanese resistance, beginning in 1943 the US High Command had begun a deadly bombing campaign over Japanese urban centers: it was the most terrible air offensive in history, even greater than that suffered by Nazi Germany. However, Japan suffered not only because atomic bombs devastated Hiroshima and Nagasaki but also because B-29s "Flying superfortresses" pulverized Tokyo and Osaka, Yokohama and Kobe. They flew at fighter speeds for 4,000 miles at 32,800 feet, carrying 7.5 tons of bombs. On November 24, 1944, the first massive air raid was unleashed on Tokyo; on March 10, 1945, the first low-altitude carpet-bombing was carried out with incendiary bombs. Some 12 square miles of Tokyo were literally incinerated and about 100,000 inhabitants killed. A series of devastating raids over the country's major industrial cities followed. To escape the daily firestorms, tens of millions of Japanese left the cities to take refuge in the countryside, only to meet a shortage of food. As had already happened in 1940 when Britain was subjected to German air attacks, in Japan too the population's will to resist never flagged. On March 25, 1945, Japan enrolled in the "People's Volunteers," a force made up of all men and women between 13 and 60 years old. In the event of an invasion, they were to confront the enemy with whatever weapons they had, including canes of sharpened bamboo.

After hearing this news, Truman decided to use the atomic bomb, on which $2 billion had been spent. Truman had become president of the United States on April 12, 1945, the day Roosevelt died. He authorized the first experimental atomic bomb, explosion carried out on July 16 in the desert near Alamogordo, New Mexico. The explosion caused total devastation within a radius of 1 mile. Among those who thought the new weapon should be used in a "surprise" attack --without any warning to the enemy--were the bomb's two main developers, Fermi, Italian and Oppenheimer, German who had fled to the United States of America before the beginning of the WWII. The plane chosen to drop the atomic bomb on Hiroshima was a B-29, the "Enola Gay," named after the mother of its pilot, Colonel Tibbets. The uranium bomb was the equivalent of 20,000 tons of ordinary explosive. It pulverized 80 percent of Hiroshima's building and incinerated 70,000 people, a further 180,000 were left with wounds and terrible sores; they would later die of leukemia. The explosion created a temperature of 6000°C, three times higher than the melting point of iron. Hiroshima's 76,000 houses, 70,000 were completely destroyed.

In the West, the press reported the dropping of the bomb very much in terms of the US government's official news releases. It was not until August 13 that the *New Yorker* magazine broke the official wall of silence about the human cost of the horrific new weapon, publishing a special edition featuring John Hersey's article containing testimony from survivors. The account told of parents dying with their children in their arms, singing, *Tenno-heika, banzai, banzai*! ("We gave our lives for the Emperor").

Three days later on August 9, 1945, the second atomic bomb was dropped on Nagasaki: 40,000 citizens were incinerated and 60,000 wounded. In the years that followed, ten of thousands of unfortunates, contaminated by the two explosions, were to die from atomic cancer. On August 8, after being informed of the horrendous consequences of the bombing of Hiroshima and calculating that the nation had been brought to its knees, Stalin declared war on Japan. The USSR invaded Manchuria and Korea, thus preparing the terrain for a future bloody war.

As expected, Emperor Hirohito, appalled by the massacres of Hiroshima and Nagasaki, agreed to unconditional surrender "with exception of our sovereignty," a formula with which he sacrificed all his most loyal supporters but saved the crown and the very existence of the Empire of the Rising Sun. The surrender was signed on September 2, 1945, on board the battleship *USS Missouri*, anchored in Tokyo Bay, in the presence of General MacArthur. Ten days later, in Singapore, Admiral Mountbatten accepted the surrender of the Japanese forces in South-East Asia. The Second World War was over.

269
12:01 PM on August 9, 1945: the unmistakable mushroom cloud rises over the Japanese city of Nagasaki. Forty thousand inhabitants were vaporized in an instant and, at the epicenter, the crater was six miles in diameter. To break the Rising Sun's valiant will to resist, America was forced to use the terrible new weapon. This was the beginning of the atomic age.

270-271
Left, a survivor looks with incredulity at the remains of the Ministry of Agriculture building in Hiroshima. The explosion on August 6th killed 78,000 people with one blow, but in the years that followed practically none of the survivors of the disaster escaped death from the atomic plague. The images on the right feature Nagasaki and the tragic days following the dropping of the atomic bomb.

Summing Up the conflict
1945-1948

World War II cost humanity 55 million dead. Half were civilians, prisoners of war, concentration camps inmates. The Soviet Union bore the greatest toll: 20 to 30 million dead, about 20 percent of it's population. Next the Reich; 7 million dead (4 million civilians, 3 million soldiers). Third come China and the Jewish people, each with 6 million victims. Japan mourned 3 three million dead. Of other nations involved in the conflict, Yugoslavia lost 1.3 million (most were civilians); France, 600,000; Italy 600,000 (half were civilians); Great Britain, 320,000 soldiers and 62,000 civilians killed, and finally, the United States lost 300,000 soldiers. The remaining 17 million of the 55 million represent the human losses sustained by nations that fought in secondary conflicts, for or against the Axis powers. To the horrific total must be added the uncounted: the wounded and the mutilated, those who lost their minds, or who war reduced to poverty. Victory also marked the settling of accounts. During the Potsdam Conference, (July 1945) between Churchill, Stalin and Truman, the punishment of the defeated was addressed. It was decided to institute an international court of military justice; the judicial criteria were set at a meeting in London in August 8, 1945.

Nuremberg was chosen as the seat of the Court; there the great Nazi party gatherings had taken place. The trial of the Third Reich's leaders (the first of a series that continued until 1948) lasted from November 20, 1945 to October 10, 1946, and concluded with 12 death sentences, seven sentences of 20 years to life, and three acquittals. The death sentence against Martin Bormann was issued in absentia. Hermann Göring cheated the hangman, swallowing poison shortly before his execution. Joachim von Ribbentrop (Reich Foreign Minister); Alfred Rosenberg (Nazi Party theoretician); Arthur Seyss-Inquart (Reich Commissioner, the Netherlands); Wilhelm Frick (Reichsprotektor, Bohemia and Moravia); Hans Frank (Governor of Poland); Ernst Kaltenbrunner (Reich Security); Fritz Sauckel (Reich Labor Organization); Julius Streicher (virulent anti-Semitic propagandist) and generals, Wilhelm Keitel (head of the OKW); and Alfred Jodl (Army Chief of Staff) were hanged, then cremated, and their ashes were scattered in the Isar, the river that runs through Munich, the birthplace of Nazism.

In Japan, the International Military Court of Justice was installed in Tokyo. The principal defendant was Hideki Tojo, premier from 1941 to January 1945. Tojo shot himself upon arrest. He was given blood transfusions (American blood), survived, was imprisoned, tried, and found guilty. Many other politicians, including Prince Konoye (premier before Tojo), did succeed in killing themselves. The trials took place in 1948. Tojo was hanged as were generals Koiso, Matsui, Sato, Doihara, Araki, and Muto and the admirals Nagano and Shimada. American justice extended to the notorious American-born radio journalist, Iva Toguri ("Tokyo Rose"), sentenced to 10 years imprisonment. Some politicians (including ex-foreign minister Mamoru Shigemitsu) escaped a death sentence and later re-entered politics.

Protective clauses in treaties dictated by the Allies absolved many Axis collaborators of high treason against their nations. These clauses protected the many Italians, the few Germans, and the very few Japanese who had collaborated with the Allies. But the Allies showed no mercy toward the French, Americans, and Britons who had sided with the Axis. In France, firing squads executed hundreds of politicians, combatants, and even pro-German writers. Notorious among them were Pierre Laval, premier of the Vichy Government, and the columnist-critic Robert Brasillach. The writer Pierre Drieu La Rochelle took his own life. Even the elderly Marshal Pétain, hero of the First World War, was condemned to death, the sentence then commuted to life in prison. He died a year later. Ezra Pound, the famous American poet, ended up in a mental hospital in Washington, D.C. Released ten years later, he went to die in Italy, cradle of the Fascist creed he supported. John Amery (son of Lord Amery, former British colonial minister), who had broadcast from Radio Tevere in support of Fascism and Nazism, was hanged, as was William Joyce, ("Lord Haw Haw"), who broadcast from Radio Berlin. British severity did not even spare their own Major Boon, who had collaborated with the Japanese to mitigate the suffering of his men. The most unjust fate of all befell General Vlasov's Cossacks (who had defected to the Axis) and General Mihailovic's Chetniks (who had opposed Tito). The Allies captured members of these military groups in Austria and in Italy. These anti-Communist Russian and Yugoslav combatants (officers and men) were "returned" under various inter-Allied agreements, the former to Stalin and the latter to Tito. Once in their homelands, these men dangled from the gallows in their tens of thousands.

273
Top: the German General Kinzel signed the unconditional surrender of the German Army of North under the eyes of Marshall Montgomery on May 4, 1945. Center, World War II was over and the time came for settling accounts. Portrayed at Nuremberg are General Wilhelm Keitel and Hitler's former heir apparent, Rudolf Hess. Bottom: on board the USS Missouri, *anchored in Tokyo Bay, General Yoshijiro Umezu signed the unconditional surrender of Japan, in the presence of General Douglas MacArthur on September 2, 1945. Ten days later, in Singapore, Admiral Mountbatten accepted the surrender of the Japanese forces in Southeast Asia.*

1683

THE INDOCHINA WAR

FRENCH ACTIVITY IN SOUTHEAST ASIA: A LONG HISTORY.

In the 1700s, French missionaries established a moderately successful presence in Cochin China. Louis XVI (guillotined 1793) supported the missionary and trading endeavors and France obtained substantial concessions of land from the region's rulers. Under Napoleon III (1808-73), France began sending armies to Cochin-China, and military conquests were made. Even after Napoleon III's defeat in the Franco-Prussian War (1870) and the establishment of the Third Republic, imperialist expansion continued, reaching its peak (not only in France) toward the end of the 19th century.

By 1893 Cochin-China, Cambodia, Laos, Annam, and Tonkin were all part of what was then termed French Indochina. This region covered an area of 285,714 square miles and had a population of over 23 million. Rice was extensively cultivated and there was much rubber, wood, and coal. France, that since the 18th century had claimed an enlightened policy of "emancipating the masses," repaid the Indochinese peasants, timber workers, and miners for their labor by allowing their children to attend the many schools that had been built in the country. For the brightest and most deserving there were opportunities to attend the University of Hanoi, or even the Sorbonne in Paris, with all costs subsidized by the French government.

However, in the 1930s, France was to find that the best and the brightest of the Indochinese could become relentless enemies. Nguyen Ai Quoc, known to history as Ho Chi Minh, became a nationalist military commander and politician who first undermined French power and prestige, and then that of the United States. His name (along with Lenin and Stalin's) would be on the lips of thousands of left-wing students in demonstrations throughout Europe. These demonstrations started in Paris in 1968; they spread and continued for most of the 1970s.

In 1930 Ho Chi Minh was a promising young lawyer who had graduated in France with an excellent degree. He had not the slightest intention of serving French interests. Instead, he founded the Indochinese Communist party, financed by Moscow, as were Soviet-based Communist parties throughout the world. Like its counterparts in other countries, the Indochinese CP had only one aim: to convert the country to Communism one way or another.

The socialist-leaning France of the 1930s saw the rise of the Popular Front. In its domestic policies, the Front generously aided the Spanish Communist party; in its colonial policies it considered giving the colonies their independence. France therefore installed the puppet-emperor Bao Dai on the throne in Hanoi and created a Reform Commission chaired by Ngo Din Diem, a liberal and a Catholic. Highly unpopular among the conservatives, he had to seek exile in the United States. But in 1954 however, he returned to South Vietnam to be installed as president.

In 1941 Japan invaded Indochina. Local political tensions faded into the background until 1945. After the Japanese surrender in August 1945, General de Gaulle laid claim to Indochina on

274
Nam Dinh, south of Hanoi, Vietnam, May 25, 1945. While the Geneva Conference (commenced May 8) put an end to the conflict, a young Vietnamese mother and her child weep in a war cemetery for their husband and father who, with many others, died fighting with the French against the Vietminh communists.

1946
1956

THE INDOCHINA WAR
1946-1956

France's behalf and sent in an expeditionary force commanded by General Leclerc. By now nationalist pan-Asiatic, anti-European feelings were rife, having been in part fanned by Japanese propaganda during the war years. All regions of Southeast Asia wanted to be rid of the burden of 19th-century European colonialism.

The heart of the Indochinese (more strictly, the Vietnamese) independence movement was in the north. Ho Chi Minh therefore decided to establish his strictly Communist Viet Minh government in Hanoi (the old capital of Indochina), proclaim the deposition of Emperor Bao Dai, and ask the USSR for protection. The French reacted. First the French troops and the Communist militia merely skirmished near the port of Haiphong, the second most important city in the north. Then the French heavily bombed Haiphong on November 23, 1946, causing the deaths of 6,000 people.

The Viet Minh took their revenge. General Giap, the Communists' military leader, surrounded Hanoi with three groups of volunteers. On December 19, 1946, he gave the order to attack. The French garrison was overwhelmed and the Communist militia massacred hundreds of French civilians. During this same period the Communist movement gained other victories: Mao Tse-tung inflicted a bitter defeat on Chiang Kai-shek, forcing him to retreat, and Stalin declared his complete support for Ho Chi Minh.

General de Gaulle, whose term as president of France e was about to end, made one last attempt at appeasement. He met Ho Chi Minh in Paris and signed an agreement in which France officially recognized the Viet Minh government. But it was a fragile agreement. The Bidault government that succeeded de Gaulle's won a parliamentary vote to organize a military expedition to "re-establish order" in Indochina. The troops prepared to depart, first the Foreign Legion, then the young conscripts. A total of 560,000 men were mobilized in Indochina. For his part, Mao also sent men and weapons. After 1949, when the civil war ended in China, he greatly increased aid to Ho Chi Minh.

The French-Indochinese war lasted seven and a half years, until the final French defeat on May 7, 1954 at Dien Bien Phu (186.5 miles northeast of Hanoi). Operations at Dien Bien Phu had started on November 20, 1953, when French paratroopers were brought in to form the bridgehead from which a decisive attack would be launched to rout the Communist forces in the north. General Henry Navarre, appointed commander in chief in May 1953, devised a comprehensive plan. Two landing strips were built for the C-47s, a fortified camp set up, mine fields laid, and barbed wire fencing put up. In January 1954 there were 12,000 French soldiers in Dien Bien Phu equipped with tanks, artillery and fighter-bombers. But Giap had massed 50,000 men on the slopes of the valley. They were armed to the hilt and could communicate with each other via tunnels and trenches, thus deceiving the enemy as to their real numbers and movements. The attack on the French positions was launched on March 13, 1954. The two runways were destroyed by heavy artillery fire. In vain the French appealed to the Americans to bomb the Viet Minh positions in the hills. The United States did nothing: they feared the start of another Korea. At the end of April the Communists launched the final attack, and in the afternoon of May 7 red flags waved over the bunkers of the fortified camp. The French had lost 7,000 men, the Viet Minh 20,000. The total cost to France in lives lost during the Indochina war was 94,000. On May 8, 1954 the Geneva Conference was convened, with the goal of bringing peace to Indochina. France, Great Britain, the United States, China and the USSR all participated as well as the representatives (some more legitimate than others) of the former Indochinese states: Cambodia, Laos, North Vietnam (with Ho Chi Minh as its leader) and South Vietnam (Emperor Bao Dai). France was represented by its new premier, Pierre Mendès-France.

The Conference recognized the independence of Laos and Cambodia, the status quo Vietnam (divided into two parts along the 17th parallel), and required the French and North Vietnamese to evacuate within thirty days North Vietnam and South Vietnam respectively. India, Canada and Poland staffed an international supervisory commission created to see that the terms were carried out.

277
March 1954: French soldiers parachute into Dien Bien Phu to assist their comrades under attack by Communist General Giap's forces. The attack, initiated on March 13, cost the French defenders 7000 lives before May 7, when the Viet Minh victory was acknowledged.

278-279
Top left: the men of a Viet Minh anti-aircraft post, ready to respond to air attack. Center: various stages of the disembarkment of airborne troops conducted by the French in the area of Langson in July,1953, with the purpose of destroying important weapon and ammunition deposits of the Viet Minh army.

280-281
Top left: French fantrymen march toward the Mekong river; bottom: Viet Minh troops respond to a French air attack with a machine-gun. Right: French paratroopers in the April 1953 advance into Laotian territory.

282-283
Scenes from the battle of Dien Bien Phu, which marked France's final defeat. The Dien Bien Phu enclave, 190 miles northwest of Hanoi, was considered impregnable. It boasted numerous air strips, fences, and mine fields and had a defense force of 12,000 French soldiers with tanks, heavy artillery and fighter planes. General Giap threw 50,000 win-or-die men against the base. At the end of the battle, 7,000 French and 20,000 communist Vietnamese soldiers were dead. Bottom right: this picture shows the Viet Minh flag flying over the last French bunker to surrender.

1946
1954

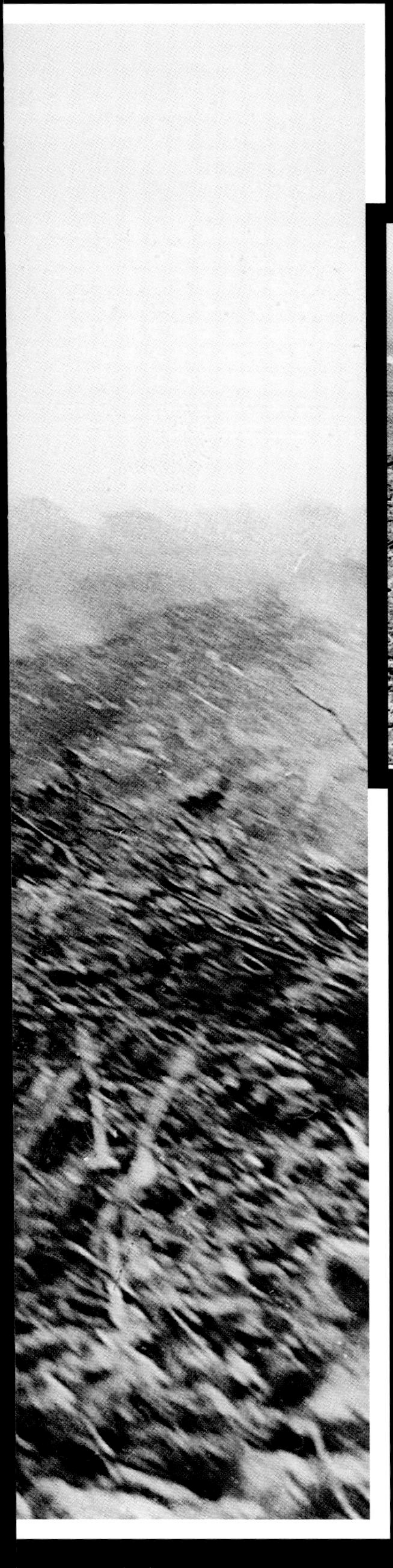

1946

1954

THE

ARAB-ISRAELI WARS

TWO FACTORS GOVERN EVENTS IN THE MIDDLE EAST. ONE IS THE CENTURIES-OLD CONFLICT BETWEEN THE ARABS AND THE JEW; THE OTHER IS OIL. DEPOSITS IN THE PERSIAN GULF ALONE COMPRISE 45 PERCENT OF GLOBAL RESERVES.

Whoever controls the oil of the Middle East controls the economy of the West, as the 1973 supply crisis proved. In November of that year, the oil-producing countries decided to increase radically the price of crude oil, giving rise to the 20th century's most devastating economic and industrial crisis. Hence the necessity for the major industrialized nations to ensure no single power bloc (including the Arab nations) controls the Middle East region. In the past, western European nations maintained a presence in the region through colonial mandates; today they seek access through Israel, which they attempt to ensure remains a reliable military power.

The history of the relatively recent creation of the state of Israel is also important to an understanding of the geopolitical background. The idea of re-uniting the Jews scattered throughout the world in a single state first arose in Germany at the end of the 19th century. Germany, together with France, was a nation with a highly developed anti-Semitic "culture," fully apparent in some social and political strata. This anti-Semitism was fueled by "thinkers" such as Count Joseph de Gobineau (1816-82) and Houston Chamberlain (1855-1927).

In 1897 Theodor Herzi, popular journalist of Neue Freie Press, founded the Zionist Movement (from Sion, the hill in Jerusalem on which the most ancient part of the city stands). The Movement's short-term aim was to buy land in Palestinian territory and its long-term aim was to establish an independent nation on the land purchased.

At the end of World War I, Great Britain, which had fought long and hard against the Ottoman Empire (a German ally), needed no persuasion to support Zionism, since such a movement would obviously be opposed to Arab expansionism. On November 2, 1917, the British foreign minister, Lord Balfour, declared Britain's support for "a national home for the Jewish people" in Palestine (the Balfour Declaration). Palestine, this land so sought after by Jews throughout the world, deserves a brief descriptive note. It was basically a southern province of Syria, a narrow strip of land, whose shores were lapped by the Mediterranean, inhabited by Arabic peoples who had lived by fishing and sheep farming from time immemorial--from before Mohammed (570-632 AD). British troops occupied it towards the end of 1918, as the World War I was drawing to a close. Not long after, at the Versailles Peace Conference, Britain obtained the "mandate" to govern Palestine. In reality, it became a British colony, although this term was no longer in use.

In 1920 the British started to implement the Balfour Declaration, encouraging Jewish immigration to Palestine and firmly repressing the protests of the indigenous Palestinians, who were apprehensive about the arrival of so many Jews. By 1939, 20 percent of Palestine's population was made up of Jewish families.

284-285

Bottom: a ship full of refugees is attacked near the Tel Aviv coast; right: a young Eastern European Jewish woman and her son arriving at the St. Luke refugee collection camp, near Haifa. The year is 1948, marked by the great exodus of Holocaust survivors to Palestine.

1948

THE FIRST ARAB-ISRAELI WAR
1948

At the end of World War II, a large number of Jews, survivors of the Nazi concentration camps, arrived in Palestine. They were a ragged persecuted people that had been the innocent victims of the Shoah--the Holocaust--one of the greatest horrors in the history of humanity. Yet, just when they had seized upon a new hope, terrible events such as the *Exodus* affair occurred. In July 1947 the *Exodus* reached Haifa, carrying 4500 Auschwitz survivors. The British refused them admission to Palestine, and was sent them back to Europe. The British were no longer as pro-Zionist as they had been after the First World War; they now had to deal with the Palestinians' anger and the terrorist attacks of the Israeli secret organizations such as the Haganah. The British desire to wash their hands of the whole Jewish resettlement problem grew stronger as the days passed.

By the end of 1947, more than 400,000 Jews had emigrated to Palestine. At this point the United Nations had to intervene to end the constant fighting between the Arab and Jewish populations. On 29 November 1947, the UN General Assembly approved Resolution 181, establishing the partition of Palestine into separate Jewish and Arab states and the termination of the British mandate on May 15, 1948.

The Resolution, under which only Jerusalem alone would remain under international sovereignty, had many obvious defects. For example, the borders between the two states had been drawn up in a rather haphazard way: the Arab state was divided into four separate areas and 500,000 Palestinians now found themselves resident in areas that had been assigned to the Jewish state. Tensions ran high.

On May 15 1948, the very day the British left Palestine for good, the Jews proclaimed the sovereign independent state of Israel, with Chaim Weizmann as president of the republic and David Ben Gurion as prime minister. The Palestinians, on the other hand, were neither as united nor as quick to create their state. They expressed their resentment in a series of attacks (the massacre of the Kfar Etzion Kibbutz), to which the Israelis responded eye for eye and tooth for tooth with the massacre of Deir Yassin, a Palestinian village. By this stage war was inevitable. With minimum delay, Lebanon, Syria, Iraq, Egypt and Jordan formed a political and military league, which declared war on Israel. The Israeli army (the Tsahal) immediately demonstrated its superiority in terms not only of the fighting capacity of its men, but also in its weaponry and military tactics. Israeli soldiers penetrated deep into Palestinian territory and forced their aggressors to seek a humiliating armistice in March 1949. This ended with the fixing of new frontiers that heavily favored Israel, which at this time occupied three-quarters of Palestine's pre-war territory. The Gaza Strip (a 6-mile wide coastal area in southern Syria) was ceded to Egypt and 250,000 Palestinian refugees immediately sought shelter there. Transjordan was annexed to Jordan. Jerusalem was divided into an Arab and an Israeli sector. The state of Palestine disappeared before it had even been created. Some 750,000 Palestinians (half the indigenous population) were forced to abandon their land and houses and seek hospitality in the neighboring Arab countries, which often only grudgingly accepted them. In addition to the 250,000 Palestinians housed in enormous camps in the Gaza Strip, hundreds of thousands took refuge in Transjordan, Lebanon and Syria. They have not become integrated but have remained fiercely attached to their own national identity; they continue to dream of liberation and of ousting the Jewish people. Such were the main events of the dramatic and painful Palestinian diaspora. In its complex totality, this event continues to be the cause of Palestinian acts of terrorism against Israelis and their allies.

Top left: an Israeli barricade blocks the road to Jerusalem; right: Arab troops ready to fight during the first Arab-Israeli war that broke out in 1948. Bottom: an Israeli phisician assists a young soldier wounded during fighting in the Holy City. The Tsahal, the newborn Israeli military, won the war and an armistice was signed in March 1949.

THE SUEZ WAR
1956

The armistice with Egypt, signed on February 24 1949, ended the First Arab-Israeli War, though Israel continued to fight against Jordan until its surrender on April 3. In the period between February and April, Israeli soldiers occupied the Oum-Rasrash area, thus ensuring them a route to the Gulf of Aqaba. This area was later to become the port of Eilat, Israel's "pearl of the Red Sea." It was at Eilat, in 1956, that Gamal Abdel Nasser, the Egyptian dictator, challenged Israel. Nasser was driven by historical events that require brief discussion. In 1882 Egypt had lost its independence because Great Britain wanted full control over the Suez Canal, the great new route to the East that was opened in 1869. From 1882, the ancient land of the Pharaohs had more or less become a British colony. It regained its independence in 1922, although this was only on paper as the British continued to maintain military bases along the Canal's eastern bank. Throughout World War II, Egypt had been a formidable base in the early defensive phase and later during the victorious British counter-offensive against the Axis troops. In 1952 a coup d'état led by two army officers (Colonels Neguib and Nasser) overthrew the monarchy of King Farouk and brought in a republic. The real strategist was Gamal Abdel Nasser: he wanted full independence for his country, its modernization and a position equidistant between the United States and USSR, the two blocs that had carved up the world. Great Britain's power was waning. Its bases along the Suez Canal were subject to constant guerrilla attacks. Britain then decided to abandon the positions and evacuated the last of them in June 1956. Nasser, in the first flush of success, sought further confirmation of his position by supporting the Algerian rebellion against the French and favoring Palestinian incursions from the Gaza Strip against the Israeli settlers. He negotiated a military agreement with Syria and Iraq to create a united command of the three nations' armies. Most importantly, in September 1955, he signed an agreement with the USSR. In this, Moscow undertook to send economic and military aid to Cairo, strengthening its hand against Israel. These events cannot, of course, be divorced from the factor of Middle-Eastern oil and its actual and potential weight in political strategizing. It should have been clear to all that Nasser's aim was to free his country from Western control and thereby to be able to play an ever more important role on the international stage. On July 26 1956, reassured by the Soviet Union's support, Nasser announced the nationalization of the Suez Canal. From now on the tolls paid by the world's shipping would go toward paying for the building of the new Aswan Dam, which western banks had refused to finance. Nasser also ordered that Israeli vessels or vessels chartered by Israelis were to be refused use of the Canal. Nationalization of the Canal was a serious blow to Britain, which had promoted the original Suez Canal Company and had remained its major shareholder. France too was aggrieved: it had had enough of watching Egypt finance the Algerian rebellion, and was also keen to vindicate its recent defeat of Dien Bien Phu in Indochina through a coup or an advance in some other region. All needed elements were in place for another war. Nasser made matters worse by suddenly closing the Gulf of Aqaba to Israeli shipping, declaring that the Gulf was an Egyptian zone and whoever wanted to enter it had to have permission from Cairo. Israel responded by mobilizing its army in preparation for an attack on Egypt. During this same tense period, students took to the streets in Budapest in rebellion against the Communist government. In a matter of days the explosive situation degenerated into a bloody conflict between the Hungarian insurgents and Soviet soldiers. It ended with 82,000 dead, 200,000 Hungarians deported to the USSR, and much of Budapest destroyed by Soviet T34 tanks. On October 29 Israel launched an attack on Sinai and quickly routed the Egyptian army, although 8,000 Israeli soldiers were either killed or wounded. Israeli tanks spread out toward the Red Sea. On the 31st, France and Britain, safe in the knowledge that Soviet Union was too fully occupied with the dramatic events in Hungary to come to the aid of its ally Nasser, landed 90,000 men at Port Said. This followed the bombing of Egyptian airports and parachute unit landings to seize military objectives. Egypt was crippled. Needing to react forcefully, Nasser put the Suez Canal out of action by sinking some merchant ships. The UN Security Council met, but the British and French representatives used their veto power to prevent it from reaching any decisions. On November 5 Anglo-French troops occupied Suez. President Eisenhower (who had maintained a prudent silence in face of the massacre of the Hungarian people at the hands of 400,000 Soviet invaders), now spoke out. The United States demanded the immediate convocation of the United Nation's plenary assembly (where the major powers had no right of veto). The assembly voted sanctions against Great Britain and France, which were characterized as aggressors and ordered to cease hostilities at once. At almost the same time (on November 6), the USSR (in process of extinguishing Hungary's independence) entered the Suez scene. Moscow sent a veiled threat to Anthony Eden and Guy Mollet, the respective leaders of the British and French governments: if they did not order their troops to leave Suez immediately they ran the risk of an atomic war. Britain and France recognized reality. Iso-

lated and condemned by the UN vote (64 in favor of Eisenhower's motion, 5 against), they immediately announced their withdrawal from the Canal zone and preparing to hand it over to the United Nations' troops. The Suez Canal incident was last occasion when two European powers were involved in a military face-off at an international level. European aspirations on the global chessboard were now limited. Although Nasser had earlier suffered military defeat at Israeli hands, he came out of the Suez War as victor. He took his revenge on his enemies and Israel's allies by nationalizing British and French banks, businesses, and companies, and by expelling thousands of Europeans from Egypt.

289
The photos on this page show the Second Arab-Israeli war which broke out on November 29, 1956, with Israel's surprise attack on Egyptian positions in the Sinai. Top: an Egyptian fuel depot in Port Said hit by Israeli fire is burning with heavy and black smoke. Bottom left: Israeli Sherman *tanks proceeding toward jordanian border; right: French and English troops landing near Port Said, Egypt, to free the Suez Canal region.*

THE SIX DAY WAR
1967

In 1958 Syria joined Egypt to form the United Arab Republic (UAR). Israel, caught between two enemy powers, took counter-measures. It built up its armed forces and developed its own atomic bomb. The Palestinians, who were still on a war footing with Israel, persuaded the United Nations to set up an office to provide assistance to their refugees. They also founded Al Fatah ('Victory'), a resistance movement that used the Algerian National Liberation Front's successful guerrilla tactics. Al Fatah quickly found a leader in Yasser Arafat. Alongside Al Fatah, George Habbash and Wadi Haddad founded the more violent Popular Front for the Liberation of Palestine (PFLP). Later, in 1964, the two organizations united to become the Palestine Liberation Organization (PLO), financed by Nasser.

Years of constant tension, attacks, massacres and deaths followed. Grenades devastated Israeli border kibbutzes; Palestinian refugee camps in Lebanon, Syria, Transjordan and the Gaza strip became the target of Israeli reprisals. At the beginning of June 1967 Nasser again provoked Israel by closing the Gulf of Aqaba to Israeli vessels. The Israeli reaction was swift and ruthless: at dawn on June 5, it launched a series of air attacks destroying Egyptian aircraft in the airports, while tank units commanded by General Moshe Dayan attacked on three fronts: Egypt, Syria and Jordan.

It was a spectacular and victorious offensive, concluded in just six days. Israel had doubled its territory at the expense of its neighboring countries. The victorious nation seized Sinai and the Gaza strip from Egypt, the Golan Heights from Syria and Transjordan from Jordan. In addition, Israel annexed the whole of Jerusalem. The Egyptians lost ten thousand men; Israeli deaths amounted to 300. A further 200,000 Palestinian refugees were forced to flee, although 1.5 million remained in Israel, full of the bitterest resentment towards Jews. This was an impossible basis for shared land and lives.

Israel colonized all the occupied territories, planting agricultural settlements that transformed desert and arid grazing land into flourishing farms exporting produce worldwide. Israel's technical and scientific expertise was second to none. On the domestic front, concern for security precluded any possibility of a softer Israeli stance toward the Palestinians. Despite its brilliant victory in the Six Day War, Israel was to receive many blows at the hands of a new challenger: Yasser Arafat.

In 1969, on becoming president of the PLO, Arafat set up a fully functioning government in exile, although it was more interested in terrorism than diplomacy. During this period the PLO focussed on El-Al, the Israeli national airline. Planes were hi-jacked and exploded in mid-air, killing all passengers, Israelis and others. Arab hatred cost the lives of many innocent people, mainly tourists of German, British, Italian and other nationalities. Arafat's *fedayeen* (warriors) made their most spectacular attack during the Olympic Games in Munich 1972 (although Arafat always denied that he knew anything about it, and there is no proof to the contrary). Eight fedayeen, with the aid of the German left-wing terrorist group Rote Armee Fraktion (which included pro-Communist Jewish students), killed two Israeli athletes and kidnapped nine others. The police attacked in force. All the athletes and five terrorists died, the other three terrorists were arrested. Soon thereafter another Palestinian group hi-jacked a Lufthansa plane and threatened to blow it up if the three Palestinian terrorists were not freed. Germany gave in and freed them.

The men of the Mossad (the Israeli secret service), were able to track down the three released prisoners, and killed in their homes. The Mossad, which devoted significant money and manpower to counter-terrorism, was no less ruthless and cruel than the PLO, but chose its targets more carefully. It generally attacked key executive figures, while the PLO attacked more generally, hitting whole groups of people. The support the Palestinians received from Jordan, Syria, Iraq, Egypt, and Libya was by no means disinterested in that the PLO constituted a destabilizing factor against the western powers. Inter-Arab friction and the overall political tension and misunderstandings came to a head in Jordan in September 1970. King Hussein, tired of being accused of giving in to Israel, sent the troops into the refugee camps where armed rebellion was being organized. Thousands of Palestinians died in what was to become known as "Black September." The survivors had no option but to flee to Lebanon, taking with them the threat of vengeance. Over a decade and a half of bitter civil war followed, in which 70,000 people were killed. Beirut, which had been considered the Paris of the Mediterranean, was reduced to a pile of rubble.

67

291
Israeli infantry and armored vehicles commanded by Moshe Dayan in action in the Sinai. In this extremely short conflict Egypt lost 10,000 men, Israel 300.

292-293
Center: this photo was taken in the morning of June 5, 1967, when Israeli motorized infantry (following Israel's M-46 Patton *tanks) began to attack Egyptian positions in the Sinai. This was the beginning of the third Arab-Israeli war. Top right: an Israeli convoy speeds toward the Sinai desert; center: Egyptian prisoners, at gunpoint, forced to lie supine in the Gaza Strip; bottom: Israeli soldiers, in the Sinai desert, are praying before the battle.*

1967

294-295
Israeli soldiers study Jordanian positions from the Mount of Olives before launching the attack that won them control of Jerusalem in its entirety.

295
Top: Israeli soldiers capture the Temple area: it's a fundamental moment of the battle to win over Jerusalem. Center: Israel takes over a part of Jerusalem near the of the Dung Gate, in the Old City; bottom: Israeli soldiers of both sexes are jubilant when the Tashal's victory is announced.

THE YOM KIPPUR WAR
1973

Nasser died in 1970, his reptuation tarnished by the defeat suffered in the Six Day War. He was succeeded by Anwar Sadat. He loosened Egypt's ties with the USSR and started looking to the USA for support. Sadat even envisioned an agreement under which Egypt could live in peace with Israel. To this end he worked to set up meetings between President Nixon and Leonid Brezhnev. But Sadat thought that a "small war" was needed to convince the two superpowers of the need for peace initiatives; just enough of a war to show that the Arabs too knew how to fight and that, when necessary, they could block oil supplies to pro-Israel nations.

It was an astute but cynical strategy. Sadat first created a unified command for Syria, Egypt and Jordan's armies. Then, on October 6 1973, he launched the Yom Kippur offensive. Yom Kippur, the day of atonement and fasting, was an important religious event in Israel; the Israeli army was taken by surprise and Egypt's initial success seemed to prove Sadat's strategy was right. The United States watched from the sidelines in concern. But the Israeli counter-attack was not long in coming and in a few weeks the Israeli army was only 43.5 miles from Damascus. At the end of October the United Nations assembly ordered the warring factions to cease fire; at the same time it declared the Palestinians' right to have their own country. To demonstrate its good intentions, Israel handed back the Gaza Strip and Transjordan, enabling the refugees to return and settle there. This was a sort of victory for Arafat: he was received at the United Nations with all the pomp reserved for heads of state. This event foreshadowed the Camp David agreements in 1977 between Egypt and Israel, brokered by President Carter. Israel withdrew from Sinai; Egypt in exchange recognized the state of Israel. It was a gesture of détente that Sadat was to pay for with his life, assassinated by hard-line anti-Zionist extremists.

Nevertheless, the conflict was not at an end. In 1982, with the Peace in Galilee, the Begin government ordered the destruction of the PLO bases in Lebanon, from where the fedayeen launched their incursions against Israeli border villages. The operation, which saw Lebanon's Christian Maronites allied with the Jews, ended in the massacres of Sabra and Chatila: hundreds of Palestinians were killed in the two refugee camps. An exodus of the surviving Palestinians followed: 150,000 left war-torn Lebanon and took refuge in the Bekaa, a Lebanese valley controlled by Syrians. Finally, the United Nations intervened in an attempt to bring some peace to Lebanon. It sent a joint American, French and Italian expeditionary force to re-establish peace and harmony. The troops paid a high price in terms of lives lost.

Palestinian hatred of the Jews did not diminish at all, but continued to be expressed through numerous typical operations. The 1990s saw the birth of the Intifada (the Uprising), but this temporarily calmed down with Arafat and Rabin's historic Washington meeting in 1995. But Rabin paid for this action with his life; he was assassinated by an Israeli extremist. In 2000, the conflict re-ignited into an endless chain of violence.

296-297
Scenes from the Yom Kippur War, the fourth Arab-Israeli conflict. It began on October 6, 1973, with Syria, Egypt and Jordan fighting Israel. The Arab forces attacked on Yom Kippur (the Jewish day of atonement and fasting). On the left: Egyptian troops after capturing an Israeli bunker at Bar Lev. Top right: October 1973, Moshe Dayan, then to become Israel's minister of defense, on an observation post in the Golan Heights. Bottom: October 13, 1973 Israeli troops on the road to Damascus.

298
October 17, 1973, during the Yom Kippur War. An Israeli father and son, both in the military, meet and greet each other near the Suez Canal.

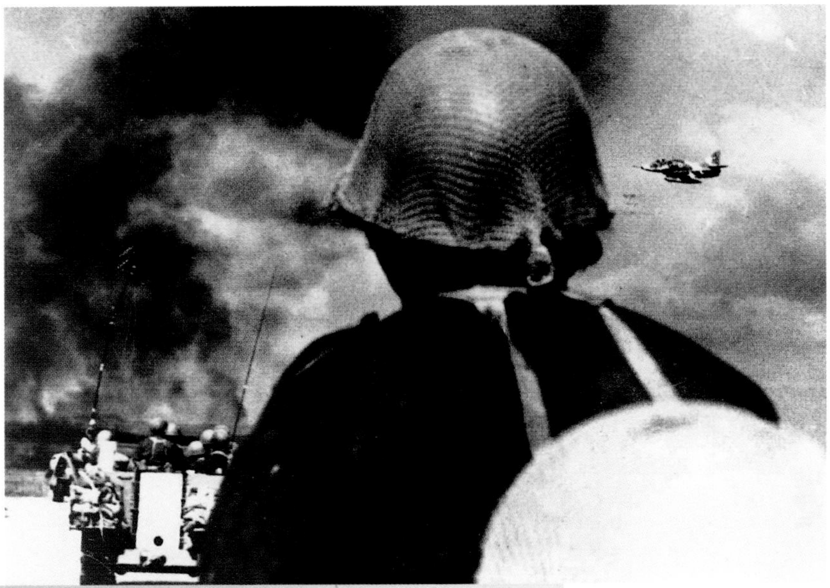

300-301
Two following pages: Life and death in the never-ending Arab-Israeli conflict over Palestine. On the left: An Egyptian tank driver, killed next to his soviet tank T-62. On the right: a wounded Israeli soldier is consoled by a comrade.

1973

299
Top: October 10, 1973, an Israeli soldier fighting on the Golan Heights helped by A-4 Skyhawk *bombers; center and bottom: Israeli armored vehicles transporting a prefabricated steel bridge that will help them cross the Suez Canal.*

1973

THE

KOREAN WAR

THE KOREAN WAR LASTED THREE YEARS. DURING THIS PERIOD, 3 MILLION PEOPLE LOST THEIR LIVES AND MILLIONS OF FAMILIES WERE SEPARATED FOR A HALF-CENTURY. THEN, IN JUNE 2000, THE TWO KIMS (KIM DAE JUNG, PRESIDENT OF SOUTH KOREA, AND KIM JONG, PRESIDENT OF NORTH KOREA) SIGNED A HISTORIC IF UNEXPECTED PEACE AGREEMENT.

The country fell under Japanese influence in 1910, and had been forced to suffer the consequences of World War II (soldiers at the front, cities bombed by the Americans, and an oppressive occupation by Japan). Korea regained its freedom (at least in theory) in August 15, 1945, with Japanese troops, in keeping with the terms of Tokyo's surrender, handing over their arms to the victors. The terms stipulated that soldiers north of the 38th parallel would give up their arms to the Russians; those south, to the Americans. Thus the solemn commitments to restore Korea's freedom and independence, which were made during the Cairo Conference in 1943 (presided over by the Chinese leader, Chiang Kai-shek) and repeated at Potsdam in 1945, were disregarded. In fact, this ancient country, which had no blame at all in starting World War II, was about to share Germany's destiny of being divided into two.

All hopes for the re-unification of Korea came to nothing, in part because times did not favor the agenda. It was the height of the Cold War, with the United States and the USSR at daggers drawn because of events in Greece. There an underground pro-Communist army, which Moscow financed and directed, had tried to upset the Yalta Agreement, which gave Britain and the Soviet Union equal influence in the region. And so in 1948, under the guns of Soviet and American tanks, the two republics of North and South Korea were formed. North Korea had Pyongyang as its capital and Kim Il Sung for president; South Korea had Seoul as its capital and Syngman Rhee for its president. Both states organized their own army, and gradually the occupying Russian and American troops left their respective areas. Then, with the political and diplomatic restraints gone, the two Koreas began to throw their weight around. The first skirmishes took place along the contentious 38th parallel.

The global political balance was now delicate. While Europe tried to heal its World War II wounds, the Americans (who had military bases scattered throughout Europe, Japan, and the Pacific islands), kept Stalin's expansionist desires in check. He, the red tsar, had emerged the true victor of World War II. Churchill, in a famous speech made in the United States, had already accused Russia of drawing "an iron curtain" across Europe.

In the previous year (1949), Mao Tse-tung had finally defeated Chiang Kai-shek in the bloody civil war he had been waging in China for thirty years save for a brief cessation in World War II. Like the Ch'ing (Manchu) dynasty, Chiang Kai-shek's regime had collapsed. The People's Republic of China held sway: six hundred-millions Chinese regimented by a rigid Communist dictatorship. Chiang Kai-shek and his soldiers, accompanied by their families, had fled to Taiwan, where they founded a new state, the Republic of China, with Taipei as its capital. The hope of returning to the mainland and winning back the whole nation of China was ever present.

302
South Korean girl flees the conflict, carrying her brother on her shoulders. Next to her, at Haengju, is a US M-26 vehicle. This picture symbolizes the odyssey forced upon Korea's civilian population.

1950

1953

THE KOREAN WAR

1950-1953

On Sunday, June 25, 1950 at 4.00 a.m. without any warning or declaration of war and in the absence of any serious tensions that could have justified security concerns, seven North Korean infantry divisions and a tank division broke through the 38th parallel's frontier defenses and began overrunning South Korea. It was a massive force of 90,000 men pitted against a weak army of a mere four infantry divisions, with no tanks or planes. Simultaneously with its land attack, North Korea made a series of landings on South Korea's northeastern coast, and also bombarded the outskirts of Seoul.

The world held its breath. "I felt a shiver down my spine," General MacArthur, commander-in-chief of the American forces in the Pacific, was to write later in his memoirs. "I said to myself, 'It can't start again.'" The Communist troops advanced rapidly. In just two days they occupied Seoul, the government barely having time to escape to Pusan, in the far south. Barely a week after the conflict had begun the aggressors broke through the defences along the Han River and headed for Pusan.

The Americans (who had only 600,000 men throughout the Far East, as opposed to 8 million at the end of World War II) had withdrawn from South Korea a year earlier. They were not, however, prepared to accept recent hostile events. President Truman called for an urgent meeting of the UN Security Council, and ordered General MacArthur to supply the South Korean army with weapons. He also ordered the Seventh Fleet to set sail from Japan for Taiwan.

Within two days of the onset of aggression, the UN Security Council issued a heavy condemnation of North Korea. Secretary General Trygve Lie used the expression "bandits" and requested North Korea to withdraw its troops to above the 38th parallel. The Security Council also unanimously voted to supply South Korea with "all the necessary assistance to deal with the aggression." The decision was passed without dissent. The USSR was not present to cast a veto; its delegate had left the meeting in protest because the representative of Mao's China had not been allowed to take part.

Kim Il Sung, the red dictator, had therefore set himself against the world. Within a few days an United Nations international force (the "Blue Helmets") had been formed, and the United States made its first military move. On July 8, 1950 the entire US Eighth Army was airlifted from Tokyo to South Korea and US aircraft began to bomb North Korea's military bases, cities, bridges and streets. That same day General MacArthur was appointed commander-in-chief of the UN force, and found himself at the head of troops from 15 different countries.

Truman, who in a speech to Congress had defined South Korea as "the Greece of the Far East," intended end to any further Soviet attempts to annex free and independent nations. Thus was born the image of America as the "police-force of the world." In fact, the United States felt duty-bound to intervene in Korea primarily on moral and idealistic grounds; the country did not have any strategic value for the United States since it already dominated all of the Far East, including Japan.

MacArthur's first military objective was the defense of Pusan, South Korea's last stronghold. The first bloody battle of the Korean War took place in its vicinity and lasted until September. In the early stages of the war, MacArthur proved to be a clever and daring strategist, outwitting and outflanking the enemy. In ordering the 10th Armed Corps to land at Inchon (Seoul's east coast port), a good 186 miles from the front line, MacArthur went against the opinions of his closest advisers. In particular, he disregarded those of General Omar Bradley, who had expressed serious reservations about the landing, given the topographic obstacles. These principal one was the shallow silted-up waters of the sea channel chosen for launching the operation.

On September 14, 1950, in an operation that recalled the heroic Normandy landings, a fleet of 262 ships landed 40,000 men at Inchon. They easily overpowered the North Korean defenders and started advancing south. Attacked from behind, and caught between the two flanks of the US forces, the North Korean army broke ranks and surrendered: the Americans took tens of thousands of Kim Il Sung's soldiers prisoner. By the end of September, MacArthur's army had reached the 38th parallel.

At this point a choice had to be made: declare a cease-fire and release the UN International Force's units back to their respective countries or try to unite the two Koreas, as had been decided at the Cairo Conference. After a positive vote from the UN Security Council, the second option was chosen.

The US Marines then made two spectacular landings in North Korea: the First Division at Wonsan, the Seventh Division at Iwon. On October 15, 1950, on Wake Island in the mid-Pacific, President Truman met with General MacArthur. Truman was worried: "Are we really sure that China won't intervene?" MacArthur was prepared to bet everything on a "Yes: no intervention," using

THE KOREAN WAR

1950-1953

his famous intuition that had served him so well during World War II and the early stages of the Korean War. "The Chinese," he said confidently, "will not intervene." He then guaranteed that all operations would be finished within the year. The next morning, October 16, 1950, the first Chinese contingents crossed the Yalu River, which marked the Manchurian-Korean frontier, and took up their positions.

On being informed of the Chinese move, President Truman gave orders that any kind of direct retaliation on Chinese territory was to be avoided: he did not want the situation to escalate. MacArthur disobeyed Truman. This marked the start of his stormy relationship with the White House.

The campaign in North Korea continued with ever bloodier fighting, costing the lives of thousands of victims. On October 26, MacArthur granted the South Korean army the honor of liberating Chosan (in the northwest of South Korea) but just 24 hours after the troops entered the city, the North Koreans won it back with the help of hundreds of Mao's Chinese soldiers. They had been signed up as "volunteers" and given North Korean uniforms so that no claim could be made that Mao's Red Army was waging war on the United Nations. On November 21, another landing by US Marines enabled them to reach the Russian border. By this time the North Korean army contained abo,ut 100,000 Chinese soldiers, while between ten and twenty "yellow" divisions were waiting for the signal on the other side of the River Yalu.

On December 12, the Communist launched a fierce and unexpected counter-offensive. The 2nd and 25th US Infantry Divisions, the South Korean 2nd Armed Corps, the British 27th Infantry Brigade and the US 1st Mounted Division were severely hit. Two United Nations' armies had to make a very difficult retreat, made even harder by a harsh weather with temperatures that dropped to -40°C. A senior American officer, General Walker, died on December 23 defending Seoul. Plans were made to evacuate Korea. MacArthur brought 193 ships into Hung Bay, selected as a mustering base for units in retreat. In the east resistance to the Sino-Korean counter-offensive was more effective. This was thanks to the US Eighth Army which, after having retreated in an orderly fashion to Osan, had regrouped and regained its positions along the 38th parallel.

At this stage in the conflict, China had more or less openly entered the war. Mao's premier, Chou En-lai, had already on several occasions threatened direct intervention if UN troops advanced beyond the 38th parallel again. But the causus belli was MacArthur's decision, in direct violation of President Truman's orders, to instruct General Stratmeyer to send up the B-29 Flying Fortresses to bomb the Yalu River bridges.

By the end of March 1951 NATO and US troops had been fighting desperately along the 38th parallel for three months, and many lives had been lost. In an attempt to put an end to the war, MacArthur asked President Truman to authorize three actions:

•to attack Chinese Manchuria with strategic air strikes to destroy the MiG bases;

•to set up a naval and economic blockade of The People's Republic of China;

•to mobilize Taiwan's national army to counter the attacks of Mao's Red Army.

Truman's vetoes were a bitter blow to the old general, one he could never have imagined. Truman feared that if he granted MacArthur's requests, he would be risking a third world war. Truman realized that the old warrior might simply would do what he thought best (as when he bombed theYalu bridges), supported by the enormous popularity he enjoyed among his men. Truman removed MacArthur from his post of commander-in-chief and replaced him with General Matthew B. Ridgway.

The removal of MacArthur caused an uproar in the United States, where the majority of Congress and the media sided with the general. MacArthur himself, on being asked by the Congress to address its members, forcefully defended his thesis. But Truman would not budge. As the American constitution vested the supreme military authority in the president, his orders could not be reversed. From then on the war effort stalled. The Flying Fortress bombers were restricted to bombing only military positions in the North, while artillery skirmishes continued along the 38th parallel between units well protected in underground bunkers. Direct encounters became rare occurrences, and usually only at the regimental level.

Truman had given Ridgway precise orders: Bring about peace. On July 8, 1951, in a teahouse in Kaesong on the 38th parallel, the first conversations between the emissaries of the two sides took place. These were to continue for two years. In the meantime, two events occurred within the two superpowers that were to resolve the Korean question. First General Dwight D. Eisenhower was elected president. He had had a successful military career dur-

THE KOREAN WAR

1950-1953

ing World War II, ending as supreme commander in Europe. He was committed to peace, but also ready to threaten to use the atomic bomb if the Chinese raised any more obstacles to achieving an agreement. Second, Stalin, the real obstacle to agreement, died in the USSR in March 1953. His successors immediately set about introducing less repressive policies. Finally, on July 27 1953, in Panmunjom, the armistice was signed. Under its terms, prisoners of war were to be sent home, and a demilitarized zone created between the two Koreas along the 38th parallel. The war had lasted three years, one month and two days. It cost the lives of 1.5 million Chinese and North Koreans, 300,000 South Koreans, 142,000 Americans, and 25,000 UN troops from 14 different countries. In addition to great military losses, about one million civilians in the war zones had lost their lives in air strikes or in the destruction of their villages.

The Americans called the Korean War "the yo-yo war" because of the way the fighting moved back and forth north and south of the 38th parallel. In reality, it was a ruthless war that caused the combatants, as well as those who had no desire to fight, endless suffering. For two years the opposing armies faced each other along the 38th parallel (not to mention the violent offensives and counter-offensives that dragged on throughout the peninsula), with artillery, machine guns and sometimes even sorties that involved hand-to-hand fighting reminiscent of World War I.

The American forces' weaponry had a devastating effect. In the first 70 days of the war 70 percent of the North Korean arms industry was wiped out. The crews of the B-26 and B-29 Flying Fortresses had orders to destroy railway networks, ports and factories. Though the Americans did not want to repeat the dreadful indiscriminate bombing of cities that had characterized World War II, General Bradley stated his "doctrine" clearly: "We do not want to attack the civilian population, but to us the workers in the arms factories are on a par with the enemy soldiers."

In January 1952 the North Korean radio announced that the United States had used and was still using chemical and biological weapons that could cause epidemics of encephalitis, plague and cholera. The Americans denied this and agreed to the creation of an international commission of doctors to investigate the charges. However, the commission never got to the bottom of the affair and the doubts remained. No less serious were the atrocities attributed to the Communists, who were accused of the mass killing of prisoners. At least two cases were proved: 800 American soldiers were walled up alive in a railway tunnel in Wonsan, and 430 soldiers of the UN multinational force were tied to each other by a steel cable and then electrocuted.

Refugees were another pitiful aspect of the Korean War. The fear of air strikes and the need to escape political reprisals forced thousands of families to keep on the move. They often took refuge in enormous sheds that came to be known as "Little Koreas."

But the Korean War's most surprising and unexpected chapter only surfaced more than half a century late when the Russian flying ace Sergei Kramarenko described it. He revealed that in the early stages of the war the Russian MiGs that engaged the American pilots in fierce duels were flown by Russian crews wearing Chinese uniforms. Had it been known at the time, this information would have been a serious threat to world peace. But the Russian airmen kept their secret. Nor could the Kremlin grant them any form of official recognition as their involvement in the Korean War had to be kept secret for at least fifty years. And that is what happened. During a friendly reunion of former American and Russian airmen, all about eighty years old, it came to light that the Soviet *MiG-15s* were unquestionably superior to the American *F-86s Sabre*. The Russians were clearly the victors of the air battles; they knocked out 1300 of their adversary's planes, losing 335 planes and 135 airmen of their own.

Fifty years of hostility were to pass before a glimmer of hope for future peace and harmony appeared between the two Koreas. On June 14, 2000, the presidents of the two Koreas signed an agreement in which they undertook to work toward national reconciliation. The event was a moment of hope for the 70 million Koreans who live north and south of the 38th parallel, and above all for the 10 million citizens who have been cut off from their families, separated by the 38th parallel border since the 3 year war of 1950-53.

307

Top, troops of the US Infantry's 24th Regiment moving to the front in July 1950; bottom two Marines, in a mopping-up operation in a South Korean village just recaptured from the Communist forces .

1950
1953

308-309

Left: Marines attacking North Korean positions on September 15, 1950, the day after the landing at Inchon. Top right: US Air Force bombs a bridge across the River Han, southwest of Seoul, to block the advance of the Communist troops to the front. Bottom right: the long battle the US Marines fought to liberate Pusan, under siege by the North Koreans.

310-311

Top left, General Douglas MacArthur, with binoculars, observes the July 14, 1950 landing operation at Inchon. At his side, first from the left, Major General James H. Doyle. Center: the second Communist offensive of December 1950, when the US thought seriously about evacuating Korea and sent 193 ships equipped for transferring the US troops. The warship USS Begor *is anchored at the Bay of Hung, while a catastrophic explosion destroys the port area. Right, top, the landing at Inchon. Bottom, a US cruiser shelling the North Korean coast in September 1950, during the UN troop landings.*

1950
1953

127

19 50
1953

1950-1953
The Korean War

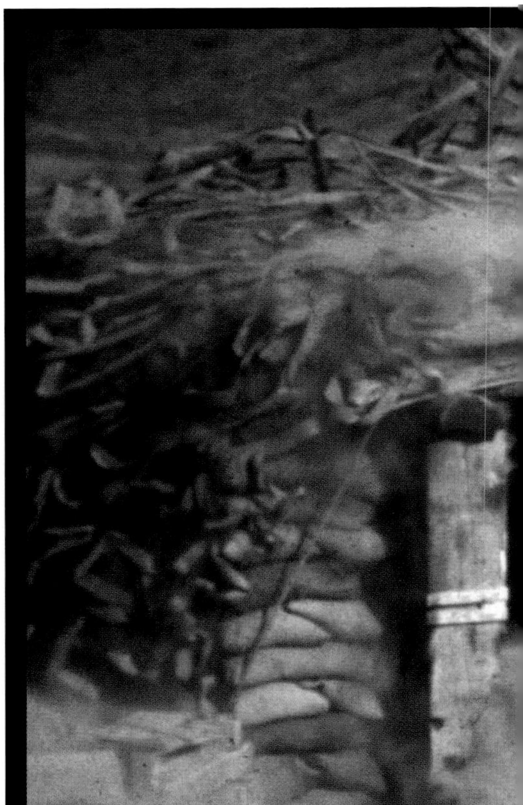

312-313
US planes bombing North Korea. A railway bridge across the River Kum is blown up. A B-29 Superfortress releases bombs on military targets. Napalm destroys military supply warehouses in Hasen Ni, North Korea.

314-315

These pictures depict scenes from the static warfare that began in autumn 1951. Top left, a US infantryman is being taken prisoner by a Chinese soldier. In the center, North Korean soldiers are captured by US Marines. Bottom, the US Infantry's 35th Regiment's 1st Platoon shells the Hun Dung-ni valley. Right, again during the static warfare of 1952, US soldiers shell the enemy lines.

316-317
Dramatic photos capture the terrible offensive launched by the North Korean army and its irregular Chinese allies in the winter of 1950-51. At this stage of the war the UN troops had to face the harsh weather as well as the enemy. Right: a US soldier advances in a snow storm. US soldiers (center) respond to enemy fire. Marines belonging to the 5th and 7th Regiments (top right) rest in the snow during a transfer march. Bottom: a tank belonging to the 25th US Division's 89th Battalion uses a flame thrower against a Chinese straw hut by the Han river.

1950-1953
The Korean War

318-319
The pictures document the suffering that soldiers and civilians underwent during the Korean War. Top left, a tank accompanies a troop of North Korean prisoners. Bottom: the exodus of the civilian population--a phenomenon seen in both North and South Korea, affecting more than 10 million persons. Right: a US concentration camp with hundreds of Chinese and North Korean prisoners. The election of Dwight Eisenhower as President of the United States and the death of Stalin in March 1953 accelerated the peace negotiations, which concluded with the Panmunjom armistice, signed on July 27, 1953. Overall, the war cost the lives of 1.5 million Chinese and North Koreans, 300,000 South Koreans, 142,000 US soldiers, and 25,000 UN Blue Helmets from 14 nations.

1954
1962

THE

ALGERIAN WAR

WHEN THE ALGERIAN UPRISING AGAINST THE FRENCH GOVERNMENT BEGAN ON NOVEMBER 10 1954, NINE MILLION ALGERIANS AND ONE MILLION EUROPEANS WERE LIVING IN THIS FRENCH AFRICAN TERRITORY.

Algeria had become a French colony in 1830 and later had been bound more closely to France when it became a full *département* of France. This was in contrast to Tunisia and Morocco, which were initially colonies and then, after World War II, became French protectorates until they gained their independence.The FLN (Front de libération nationale) was a clandestine Algerian organization seeking independence. Led by a group of young students and graduates, including Ben Bella, the 3000 guerrillas were ready to do anything to get rid of the French (or rather "the Europeans." Over the years, not only the French but immigrants from Italy, Belgium and Spain had arrived and settled in Algeria and had slowly obtained French citizenship. The guerrillas, who in the 1970s were to inspire various terrorist organizations in Germany and Italy (Rote Armée Fraktion and Brigate Rosse), in turn were inspired by the example of Mao Tse-tung, with his ideological fanaticism and ruthlessness in dealing with the enemy. November 10 was just the beginning of seven bloody years. On that day, 30 attacks were carried out across Algeria: an army officer, two soldiers and two policemen were killed. The French authorities were taken by surprise and the FLN's military wing (Armée de libération nationale, or ALN) stepped up the offensive. Its intelligent, ruthless brand of terrorism was carefully targeted: in an effort to create internal divisions, the ALN guerillas were harder on European settlers than on whites born in Algeria, whom they tended to spare. The French reaction was equally harsh. General Massu's paratroopers, charged with repressing terrorism who used equally tough methods: torture, night raids and group executions. An impenetrable electrified barbed wire fence was put up along Algeria's borders with Tunisia and Morocco to prevent the rebels from receiving assistance and supplies. Ben Bella fell into a trap: Massu's agents hijacked the airplane in which he was traveling from Tunisia to Morocco. The plane then landed in Algiers and Bella was taken prisoner. He remained in a French prison for six years only to return in triumph to his native land in 1962 as head of the new independent government. He was later ousted by his defense minister, Boumedienne, and was killed in mysterious circumstances in 1965. In the meantime the ALN's ranks were expanding and a strict military organization created. Algerians who had formerly been officers of the French army headed the various units. Many had fought as lieutenants or captains in Indochina, and they adopted the guerrilla tactics learned from the Viet Minh for use against the French army. The soldiers in uniform were called mujahideen ("fighters for the faith"), the irregulars, who were specially trained in terrorist attacks, fedayeen ("warriors"). In addition to a military commander, each unit had its own political commissar, following the example of Mao's Red Army, which in turn had copied the Soviet army. The political commissar's job was twofold: to ensure the soldiers received the orthodox doctrine and to "educate the masses." The uprising in Algeria was therefore a mixture of Communism and Islam that proved attractive to movements in France with links to

320
Top: two French soldiers next to the body of an Algerian killed by FLN (National Liberation Front) rebels. Center: FLN fighters during exercises on the Ames mountains. Bottom: November 1954 (Ben Bella's rebellion has just begun); a group of French soldiers on a search mission in the desert.

the Communist party. Indeed reactions in Paris, and France as a whole, to the FLN's constant terrorist offensive varied a great deal. While the various governments, from Mendès-France's on, rejected outright any possibility of Algeria separating from France, "a territory," said Mendès-France, "that stretched from Flanders to the Congo." The French opposition fanned the flames of national discontent about a situation that was becoming difficult to control. The soldiers' families wanted to know why their sons had to go and get killed in a foreign land, just to protect the interests of a French minority, which came to be known derogatively as the *pieds noirs*. The military forces sent to Algeria in an effort to stamp out the guerrilla warfare grew to 500,000 soldiers--the number mobilized at the start of World War II. The French government's inability to extract itself from the Algerian question brought down the Fourth Republic. On May 13, 1958 French colonials and soldiers united and rebelled against Paris. A general strike was called and a Committee of Public Safety was formed under the leadership of General Salan, a hero of the Second World War. This was the so-called "Putsch of Algiers." It had dramatic repercussions in France where the Pflimlin government resigned and the president of the Republic, Coty, appointed a new premier: General Charles de Gaulle, who had retired to Colombey-les-deux-Églises after leading the country to a final victory during the World War II. Initially the insurgents in Algiers applauded the choice of de Gaulle, convinced that he would give them his full support. But they soon had to think again. During his first visit to Algeria (in June 1958) de Gaulle disappointed Salan and his supporters by his refusal to take sides in the conflict. Not long after, the National Assembly gave de Gaulle great power to act (a decision confirmed by a referendum). Then, on January 5, 1959, he was elected president of the Republic. At this point, de Gaulle could reveal his intentions without fear. In a radio speech he announced that France would grant the Algerians the right to self-determination. The "European" Algerians felt betrayed. They did not resign themselves to abandonment by France and continued to wage war against the ANL.

This situation continued in Algeria for almost two years, with attacks, bombs, bloody skirmishes and deaths. The "Europeans" in Algiers and the military that fought alongside them created the OAS (Organisation Armée Sécrète), which sowed terror everywhere, including France, planting bombs in cinemas and department stores, and even organizing an attempt (that failed) to assassinate de Gaulle.

The final showdown came with the famous appeal the president made on television in April 1961, during which he condemned the "traitorous generals who have betrayed their country." The prison and death sentences for the rebels were already on the desks of the military judges.The Foreign Legion put an end to the last glimmers of rebellion. The war ended with the Treaty of Evian on March 18, 1962. The Algerians had suffered losses of 158,000 men, the French 33,000. On July 1, 1962 a referendum in Algeria returned a vote of 99.72 per cent in favor of independence. One million *pieds noirs* had to pack their bags, leaving behind their houses, land, schools, and jobs to go and live and rebuild their lives in a hostile France.

322
This photo taken in Algeria in 1961 shows a group of civilians arrested by French soldiers. These soldiers were led by French rebel generals in Paris who wished to continue the bloody war which Charles de Gaulle's government had been attempting to end since 1959.

323
Two dramatic images of the unrest in Algeria after the rebel generals' May 13, 1958 announcement. Top: police rush to the site of an attack. Bottom: soldiers with armored vehicles try to block a road to prevent access for a parade of pieds noirs.

THE VIETNAM WAR

IN 1953, PEACE IN KOREA TEMPORARILY ENDED THE BLOODY CONFRONTATION BETWEEN THE TWO DOMINANT WORLD SYSTEMS: WESTERN CAPITALISM (LED BY THE UNITED STATES) AND COMMUNIST COLLECTIVISM (LED BY THE USSR AND CHINA). THREE YEARS LATER, IN 1956, THE CONFRONTATION RECOMMENCED IN VIETNAM.

The root of this long drawn-out war, for which for many years no end seemed in sight, was once again a face-off between the two superpowers. In Vietnam, as in Korea, the conflict started with the division of the country: into North Vietnam and South Vietnam. The division had been decided at the Conference of Geneva on July 21, 1954, when French colonial rule in Indochina ended.

The Conference split up Indochina: Laos and Cambodia became independent states; Vietnam was divided into two along the 17th parallel. In the North, Ho Chi Minh governed a Communist state where the Viet Minh were in the majority. This party, the the League for the Independence of Vietnam, had fought to drive the French out of Southeast Asia. In the South, emperor Bao Dai headed a state whose citizens had also fought against French colonial dominion and who, like him, did not accept Communist ideology. On July 1st, 1949, with the support of the French, Bao Dai founded the Kingdom of Vietnam, locating the capital in Saigon. In 1957, the United States, under President Truman, having recognized the kingdom, arranged for armaments and military advisers to be sent to Saigon. Historically, this act was America's first involvement in the future tragedy of Vietnam.

The Geneva Accord's provisions required that free elections were to be held within two years to reunite the country under the government chosen by the majority of voters. This project, or rather this dream, was never to be fulfilled.

Shortly before the Communist General Giap's final attack on the French barricaded in Dien Bien Phu, US Secretary of State John Foster Dulles, suggested to President Eisenhower that the United States should intervene on behalf of the French, but received a definite no. Nevertheless, after the Geneva Accord, the United States decided to support the new independent state of South Vietnam, mainly to provide it with a development model different from the Communist one implemented in North Vietman.

First of all, Washington wanted Emperor Bao Dai to appoint its choice of premier, or at least a man they thought was one of "theirs." Ngo Din Diem, who had gone into exile in the United States at the end of the 1930s, was duly made premier. He had a reputation for honesty, but had a paternalistic approach to power, entirely in line with the American view. Diem's arrival coincided Bao Dai's final departure (he had retired from the political stage), and more importantly with the arrival of the first American "military advisers." Some 225 officers and 60 enlisted men arrived in Saigon in the summer of 1964 as instructors to train the local armed forces. According to the Geneva Agreement, neither North nor South Vietnam should have been able to build up its own defenses, still less seek foreign military alliances. Indeed, North Vietnam greatly resented the 60 US soldiers, and responded by sending "advisers" and weapons to the Pathel Lao, the Communist armed movement that was trying to take over in the newly independent state of Laos.

In short, a typical cold-war mechanism had been set in motion. The United States responded to the North Vietnamese provocation in Laos by creating the Southeast Asia Treaty Organization (SEATO), Southeast Asia's NATO, a military defense pact signed by

324
South Vietnamese farmers work in their fields; a few kilometres away a village thought to be a Viet Cong hideout is burned down by napalm bombs. This picture could well symbolize the cruellest war of the 20th century's second half.

1964
1975

the United States, Great Britain, France, Australia, New Zealand, Thailand, Pakistan, the Philippines, and South Vietnam. This action brought protests from China, the USSR and the Western Communist parties, and Soviet fifth columns in Europe. The plans for a referendum on the unification of the two Vietnams came to nothing: both governments opposed it. Diem maintained with good reason that in the North there was no political freedom; the people would therefore vote as their leaders wanted them to. For his part, Ho Chi Minh said that until Saigon pulled out of SEATO, he could not believe in the free vote of the people. In reality, the agricultural reforms that Hanoi had implemented, which brought farmhouses, land, livestock, and even clothes under state control and eliminated every remaining piece of private property, had lost the Lao Dong (North Vietnam's Communist party) a lot of support.

The last Frenchman left Saigon on April 28, 1956. The Americanization of South Vietnam had started some time before: the American dollar had replaced French franc, and English was gradually becoming the nation's second language. Diem was practically unopposed when, in addition to his role of premier, he sought the post of head of state in place of Bao Dai (who after his resignation had retired to the Côte d'Azur), and that of commander-in-chief of the armed forces. Diem was a true dictator, an embarrassment to the Americans who had supported him and now had to watch as he surrounded himself with people such as his sister-in-law Ngo Dinh Nhu. She was a beautiful but ruthless woman, an intransigent Catholic, a mortal enemy of the Communists, and also intolerant of Buddhists. Diem gave the enemies of his regime, the Viet Cong (the Communist Vietnamese) a hard time right from the start. Nonetheless, their treatment was not comparable to the persecutions Ho Chi Minh's régime had meted out to the unwilling peasant conscripts in the North who had tried to escape to the South, abandoning their homes, belongings and families. In addition, the Viet Cong's determination and fighting spirit and their indoctrination by their leaders turned them into an authentic clandestine army. They responded to Diem's repressive measures and his police force by adopting terrorism--a tactic they had already used successfully against the French.

From early in 1959, village chiefs started to disappear at the rate of one a day. Their horribly mutilated bodies turned up in the undergrowth, by the banks of rivers, and in caves. Round their necks was a notice that read "enemy of the people," a throwback to the French Revolution's Jacobin propaganda, assimilated by the Indochinese during the succeeding century and a half. By the end of 1959, political crimes were occurring at the rate of 10 per day; by the end of 1969 they had risen to an average of 25 per day.

Government repression was equally harsh. Special police squads investigated the slightest suspicion; any captured Viet Cong faced certain death, together with his family and friends. Between 1960 and 1961 18,000 Viet Cong were summarily executed, while 14,000 were imprisoned pending trial, which usually returned a death sentence. These figures alone give an indication of how bloody and violent was the civil war in which America found itself involved, first with Truman, then with Eisenhower, and (from January 1961, when he was elected to the White House) with Kennedy. In December 1961, Kennedy solemnly undertook to support the independence of South Vietnam against the continuous attacks of the Viet Cong guerrillas. Tension had grown ever since, a year previously, the North Vietnamese government had openly supported the need to "liberate the South from the yoke of United States imperialism": in actual fact, the North Vietnamese government was declaring a state of war. Kennedy did not hesitate to move from words to facts: he was the first American president to send not just arms and military advisers but also armed forces. The first 400 US soldiers landed in Saigon at the end of December 1961; with a year, this number had increased to 11,200.

With the help of aid and reinforcements from the North, the Viet Cong gradually refined their terrorist approach and moved on to open guerrilla tactics. The United States had no option but to provide similar aid to the South. In 1963 the American "military advisers" grew to 15,000 (including 27 generals); they had also brought their own airplanes and helicopters. The first American casualties occurred during the anti-terrorist operations: 31 in 1962, 77 in 1963. This was only the beginning: the number of lives lost was to grow exponentially over the next few years: 146 in 1964, 1,365 in 1965, 4,896 in 1966. Vietnamese losses were much higher: in the seven-year period from 1960 and 1966, 50,000 South Vietnamese soldiers, policemen and officials lost their live, as did and 157,000 Viet Cong.

The most striking consequences of the bitter conflict were twofold: the South Vietnamese population's fear of becoming victims of Viet Cong vengeance, and the increasing harshness of the Diem government. The government refused to adopt the reforms the American advisers suggested. On the economic side, these would have eased the situation of the laborers; on the religious and political side, the position of the Buddhists.

Diem had his own ideas. Convinced that the Buddhist opposition had secret links with the Viet Cong movement, he banned the display of national flags at the celebrations for Buddha's birthday (his 2,587th). The prohibition gave rise to violent demonstrations, and the police opened fire on the crowd. This was in June 1963, the date when the first Buddhist monks set themselves on fire after pouring petrol over themselves in the streets of Saigon in an act of self-immolation. The harrowing sight of the monks' extreme action, which was to continue until the end of October, was shown on television across the world, giving a very poor image of government in South Vietnam.

The situation was so bad that the US Central Intelligence Agency (CIA) was in favor of the plot being hatched in Saigon to get rid of Diem. On November 1, 1963 a group of South Vietnamese generals decided to strike: Ngo Dinh Diem and his brother Nho were assassinated and a military junta took over. The first thing it did was to ease the Buddhists' situation. Then three weeks later, on November 22, President Kennedy was assassinated in Dallas, for reasons quite unrelated to the Vietnamese conflict. Vice-President Lyndon B. Johnson became president and inherited the Vietnam conflict.

The Viet Cong movement became ever more widespread and powerful. The guerrillas laid booby-traps along the roads and paths and then lured police units and the South Vietnamese army into them. They dug underground tunnels up to 3 miles long into which they escaped, only to reappear behind the enemy. The South Vietnamese Army was in serious difficulty. President Johnson decided to increase the US army's involvement. Open war loomed.

In 1964 the US contingent increased to 24,000 men. It continued to grow from year to year until, by spring 1967, the combined army, navy, air force and marine forces stood at 450,000 men. In addition, there were the B-52 bombers crews, who flew out of the Pacific military base on Guam to bomb North Vietnam, and there were no less than 50,000 sailors aboard Seventh Fleet vessels anchored off Vietnam.

Open warfare began in 1964 with incidents such as the naval battle of August 2, when the Seventh Fleet launched a counter-attack against North Vietnamese units. The North Vietnamese had attacked two American destroyers, sinking one of them, in which 1500 crewmen lost their lives. The US government and the military command immediately spoke of a counterattack in response to the North Vietnamese forces' attack in cold blood. However, the New York Times later confuted this version by revealing (on the basis of correspondence from the Pentagon), that the incident had been a put-up affair to justify the massive attacks on North Vietnam, involving the air force and the bombing of the cities. The war had now become irreversible, with no holds barred.

By the end of 1964, even though the generals' government in Saigon had mobilized 200,000 men, the Viet Cong controlled two-thirds of South Vietnam. North Vietnam launched accusations at the United States for its use of napalm during the air strikes, stirring up anti-American hostility among pro-Communist groups throughout the world. The Communist propaganda hit home above all in Europe, where even Pope Paul VI made a number of appeals for peace. American families with military-service-aged sons experienced hours of anxiety and terror (at the end of 1965 the American army in Vietnam numbered 175,000 men). In the United States, as throughout the world, opposition to the war was growing stronger. A group of famous intellectuals from numerous western nations, led by the English philosopher-historian Bertrand Russell, established a tribunal (afterwards known as the Russell Tribunal), which offered to pass judgment on "American crimes" in Vietnam. In 1967 Che Guevara, another legend in the worldwide opposition to the "American" war, launched the slogan: "Create two, three, thousands of Vietnams," and the United States saw the start of the great demonstrations against the war, with the cry of "Stop the bombing."

However, the bombing raids, with or without napalm, did not produce any practical results, while the American planes continued to be shot down by Russian missiles. By spring 1967, after 26 months of ineffective strikes against North Vietnam, 500 American aircraft had already been destroyed. The war continued to escalate. In 1965 the forces involved in the conflict had reached impressive proportions: 600,000 South Vietnamese, 165,000 Americans, 20,000 South Koreans supporting the American forces, 230,000 Viet Cong, 20,000 regular North Vietnamese soldiers, plus smaller numbers of Australian and New Zealand soldiers as part of SEATO.

The year 1965 was also the first in which major field battles took place involving entire US divisions, while the Phantom fighter-bombers, the fastest in the world (maximum speed of 2,400 km/hour), continued to bomb the North to little strategic effect. The population had taken to living underground although the strikes never targeted heavily populated areas such as cities (a restraint the Americans had not shown in the war with Germany, Italy and Japan). However, this was not enough to prevent the United States being loathed by almost the entire world, in particular by the students of European universities.

It would be difficult to say whether the Viet Cong were more ruthless during the Vietnam War than the Nazis during the Second

World War. John Steinbeck reported instances of men considered not ardent enough Communists being impaled on wooden stakes, or disemboweled and forced to drag themselves through the streets of the villages with their intestines hanging out. Others opposed to the Viet Cong were slowly hacked to pieces in stages (first a finger joint, then a finger, then an arm, then a shoulder) in front of the inhabitants of the village, their children, wives and parents. Nevertheless, by and large the press, including the American media, did not make much mention of these atrocities. Instead papers reported on the criminal action of American commanding officers (one had ordered a village to be burned--the massacre of My Lai). What was it, besides national pride and political faith, that gave the North Vietnamese the strength to offer such a fierce resistance to the air war that had been triggered off against their territory?

The pro-Soviet nations sent aid to North Vietnam, which channeled it to the Viet Cong in the field. The USSR sent trucks, MiG-21 planes, SAM missiles and helicopters; China sent small weaponry, lethal anti-personnel mines and mortars; Czechoslovakia and Poland sent artillery and boats; East Germany cars, motorbikes and bicycles; and Romania medical supplies. Faced with an endless war and the steadily mounting number of lives lost, American public opinion was divided into "eagles" and "doves," the former few and the latter many.

The United States faced the enormous cost of US$ 30 billion per year in waging the war. Wall Street feared a repeat of the 1929 crash. Some Washington strategists thought the friction that had arisen between Russia and China at the time could have harmed Hanoi. But events took a different turn as the USSR undertook to provide the Viet Minh with all the military assistance it needed, leading to a situation whereby China competed with the USSR to see which of them could supply the most equipment and aid to Ho Chi Minh.

In Saigon one military government after another proved ineffective. On July 19, 1965 it was the turn of the 35-year-old air-force general Kao Ky, who presided over government meetings in a leather flying suit and professed his anti-Communist feelings long and loud. But the real Achilles' heel of the anti-Communist front was the hesitation of General William Westmoreland, the American commander-in-chief. A veteran of the WW II Sicilian landings and the Korean War, he had now been transferred from West Point Military Academy (where he was the commanding officer) to the South Vietnamese front. He was above all a theoretician. Instead of launching the heavy, ruthless attack that the situation demanded, he lost time in such tactics as dropping a billion anti-Communist leaflets over Viet Cong bases. This resulted in about 2,000 Viet Cong "desertions" to the South Vietnamese army, not to collaborate with it, but to spy on it and sabotage its actions.

Only the Americans could have found the idea of a repentant Communist plausible. There was probably no such figure anywhere, and certainly not in a situation such as Vietnam's, where the Communists were mostly young men and women, angry and hungry, whose brand of terrorism had been learned from the Bolsheviks.

Of the 14 years of the Vietnam War, 1968 was the most violent. Caused by the emotions created by the bloodshed in that remote southeast Asian country, a world-wide revolutionary movement developed. It was later remembered as "the generation of '68." In 1968, the United States was about to receive one of the most severe blows to its image. It began with the Tet Offensive. South Vietnamese President Van Thieu had announced a 48-hour ceasefire because of the Buddhist New Year, the Tet, which was celebrated at the end of January. At the same time, on January 27, a one-week cease-fire decided by the National Liberation Front began. But on January 30, without prior announcement and in total breach of the cease-fire, the Viet Cong and the North Vietnamese army initiated a gigantic offensive. The majority of the US expeditionary corps was occupied along the 17th parallel and on the Laotian and Cambodian borders, seeking to block the supplies that reached the guerrillas from there. Some 50,000 Viet Cong and regular Viet Minh soldiers simultaneously attacked 140 sites of varying strategic importance: the GHQ of South Vietnam's army in Saigon; 8 of the 11 divisional commands; 30 provincial capitals; and 14 air bases. It was without doubt the largest offensive during the entire Vietnam War. One part of Saigon fell under enemy's control; it even established a provisional revolutionary government there. A Viet Cong commando group that had penetrated the US embassy was pushed back with great losses. This effort was very bloody. Westmoreland ordered the mobilization of all available forces to recover from losses sustained in the previous relaxed period. Regaining control over Saigon and the other towns ended in a bloodbath: at least 30,000 Viet Cong were killed.

The Tet Offensive had been an attempt at an all-out attack. Though a move of great symbolic value, it was not a military success. US troops managed to take back almost all positions that they had lost previously, including Hué, the country's ancient capital. The operation was nevertheless a turning point for the entire war; it demonstrated to American and world public opinion that a US victory was unthinkable. Throughout March the fighting remained heavy. The United

States launched a counteroffensive in the Mekong Delta, which marked the beginning of the so-called "war of the rice fields." In the meantime, the Viet Cong continued to pressure the US base at Khe Sanh. Then the most serious incident of the entire US involvement in the war occurred: the My Lai massacre. At 7.30 a.m. on March 16, 1968, the US 11th Brigade's Charlie Company entered the village of My Lai in the Son My district. Charlie Company was headed by 24-year-old Lieutenant William L. Calley. Captain Ernest Medina, his direct superior, gave Calley orders to "neutralize the enemy by killing them all." But the enemy was not present in the village of My Lai. In fact, there were very few adult civilians, only women, old people, and children. But the order to "kill them all" was carried out to the letter. Lieutenant Calley himself was the first to open fire on a hut of terrorized inhabitants. He ordered his men to follow suit. At 11 o'clock, 347 dead bodies were counted. For many months, no news about the massacre reached the public, until Ronald Ridenhour, a soldier who had finished his military service, heard about the events from some of his comrades. He took the initiative and wrote a letter to a few members of Congress. The letter found its way to the desk of the journalist Seymour Hersh, who investigated the case--and who was later awarded a Pulitzer Prize for his research and report. In June 1969, *Lieutenant Calley* was sent back to the USA and charged with war crimes. On 29 March, at the end of a trial that shocked the entire country, he was convicted and sentenced to life in prison. During the trial, another journalist, John Sack, took the side of the accused and wrote a book entitled *Lieutenant Calley*. In it, the lieutenant claimed that he had done nothing but execute the orders Captain Medina had given him. However, these orders referred to the Viet Cong, who were to be killed up to the last man--no prisoners were to be taken--certainly not to women and children. President Nixon commuted the sentence from life to 20 years. Calley did not serve out his jail term; he was released at the end of 1974, and took up the job of insurance broker. Captain Medina submitted his resignation from the armed forces, as did General Samuel Koster, commander of the America Division. To understand the deep division this incident caused not only within US public opinion but also within the armed forces themselves, one has to look at the story of three soldiers who had tried to resist the massacre. David Egan, a professor at Clemson College (South Carolina) identified the three in 1988, during his research project on My Lai. Their names were Hugh Thompson, Lawrence Colburn, and Glenn Andreotta. They were on board a helicopter, under the command of Thomson (like Lieutenant Calley, he was 24 years old). Thompson's mission was to observe the village My Lai from the air. At mid-morning they distinctly saw an officer shooting at a young girl lying on the ground. He finally killed her with a shot in the neck. Thomson decided to land and he and his crew immediately found numerous bodies of women, old people and children thrown in a ditch. They also observed a group of soldiers directed toward a hut, where an old woman holding a newborn and a child stood still, immobilized by fear. The helicopter crew pulled their pistols in order to defend the civilians. They managed to save about a dozen people. Glenn Andreotta, who had rescued a two-year-old child that was still holding on to its mother's dead body, died three weeks later when his helicopter crashed. Thompson and Colburn submitted a report to their superiors and received awards of honour for their actions: Thompson received a Military Cross, Colburn a Bronze Star.

Although the My Lai massacre was not committed by Special Forces, it would be impossible to tell Vietnam War story--even in a short version--without mention of the mythical "Green Berets." This élite corps was admired by the extreme right (not only in the USA) but hated by the Beatnik-generation and by liberal opinion leaders around the world for its excessive nationalism and brutality. The Green Berets were volunteers who specialized in counter-guerrilla measures and jungle fighting. They acted independently or with MACV-SOG (Military Assistance Command Vietnam/Studies and Observations Group), more commonly known as SOG (Special Operations Group), created in 1964. Initially SOG's task was to provide training and strategic advice for the South Vietnamese. Later, the Green Berets began gradually to develop their own secret military actions. They carried out spy missions to identify the hideouts of the Communist guerrillas, as well as so-called black operations, which included illegal killings, sabotage, psychological warfare and counter- information. The Green Berets had helicopter and boat squadrons at their disposal to take them into enemy territory and back to their bases. The SOG consisted of up to 2000 Americans and 8000 South Vietnamese, who were selected according to strict criteria. Their GHQ was near Saigon, next to the town of Than Nut. Their special missions took off from FOB-bases (Forward Observer Bases) at Ban Me Thuot, Kontum, Ke Shan, and Da Nang. After November 1967, the Green Berets concentrated their forces in three locations: Da Nang for operations in the North, Kontum for central operations and those along the borders with Laos and Cambodia, and Ban Me Thuot for southern operations. Their standard operative units (Spike Recon Team) consisted of three men from the US special forces, and nine locals. They specialized in fighting the

THE VIETNAM WAR

1964-1975

Viet Cong in jungle areas and also the North Vietnamese troops that had crossed the 17th parallel. The Viet Cong paid a high price until it learned that it was difficult to escape the Green Berets, who were hiding in the forest and suddenly appeared with tremendous fire power and physical force and courage.

After the Tet Offensive of mid-1968 and the American counterattacks, the regular North Vietnamese army had to bear the major burden of the war. But the political and military prestige of the United States had been seriously wounded. The government was blamed and Johnson resigned. Richard Nixon, a Republican who had run against Kennedy, became the next president and although he was rightwing, he started peace negotiations in Paris in January 1969.

The United States basically admitted that military victory in Vietnam was an impossibility. But alongside the military defeats it had suffered in Southeast Asia, the Nixon administration had to take into consideration the growing voices of dissent in America. There were some sensational protests, such as that of Cassius Clay, the famous world heavyweight boxing champion, who refused to be drafted into the army. TV war correspondents emphasized the negative images of the war. Even in America Vietnam had become the symbol of the struggle of the poor against imperialism and the affluent society. On university campuses rebellion was rife. At Kent State University, the National Guard used undue force and four students were shot dead during a shoot-out. The unrest quickly spread to European universities, where the term "'68" (from the year in which student protests started in Paris and spread to the other major German and Italian cities), became synonymous with the protest movement. The protests continued in the name of the "great people of Vietnam," supported by intelligent organizational and financial contributions from the KGB, the Soviet Union's security organization.

From 1970 on, the war spread into Cambodia and Laos. In Cambodia a coup d'état had ousted Prince Sihanouk and General Lon Nol seized power in Phnom Penh, the capital. In Laos, the government continued to stand up to the Communist guerrillas. From late 1970 the Americans began to gradually reduce the number of troops in Vietnam in line with the plan Nixon's chief adviser, Henry Kissinger, drew up. The Vietnamese were to take on the major burden of fighting the war: America would limit itself to supplying arms, munitions and medical assistance.

The American troops were gradually sent home. At the end of 1972 only 43,000 US soldiers were left in Vietnam, and they were about to leave. In Paris, on January 27, 1973, the United States finally signed a peace treaty with North Vietnam, having lost 47,000 men to the war. The withdrawal of the US forces allowed the Communists to take their revenge unhindered. The bodies piled up in South Vietnam while the Pathet Lao party also came to power in Laos, conquering the capital Vientiane. In Cambodia, Pol Pot, leader of the Khmer Rouge, overthrew the government of Lon Nol and proceeded to commit one of the most dreadful Communist massacres of the 20th century. In this massacre, three million Cambodians, a third of the population, were killed. South Vietnam, governed by Van Thieu, resisted until April 30, 1975. On that day Ho Chi Minh's soldiers entered Saigon and the whole world watched stunned as the last Americans escaped from the roof of the American embassy in a helicopter. The war that had started twenty years earlier to stop Indochina from becoming Communist ended with the whole of Southeast Asia being handed over to the agents of Moscow and Peking. It was a bitter defeat for the West. For the South Vietnamese it marked the beginning of the trials of the "boat people," the families that tried to escape by sea, in small boats at the mercy of the South Pacific, in the hope of being picked up by a passing American ship. On the Vietnamese side the war resulted in more than two million dead, three million wounded and 12 million refugees. For its part, the United States mourned 57,685 dead and about 153,000 wounded. At the start of the Third Millennium, Vietnam is at peace. Saigon, now Ho Chi Minh City, in memory of the Communist statesman who died in 1969, and the new generations are seeking to rebuild, with love and goodwill, that which their elders destroyed in the folly of hatred.

331

A war photographer's dramatic image captures events in Shan Valley after a battle between US and Viet Cong soldiers. A US soldier mourns for a dead comrade. The ferocious civil war between South and North Vietnam saw the USA caught in the middle; first under President Truman, then under Eisenhower, finally--even more dramatically--under Kennedy. In December 1961, Kennedy solemnly promised to maintain South Vietnamese independence against the continuous attacks of Viet Cong guerrillas.

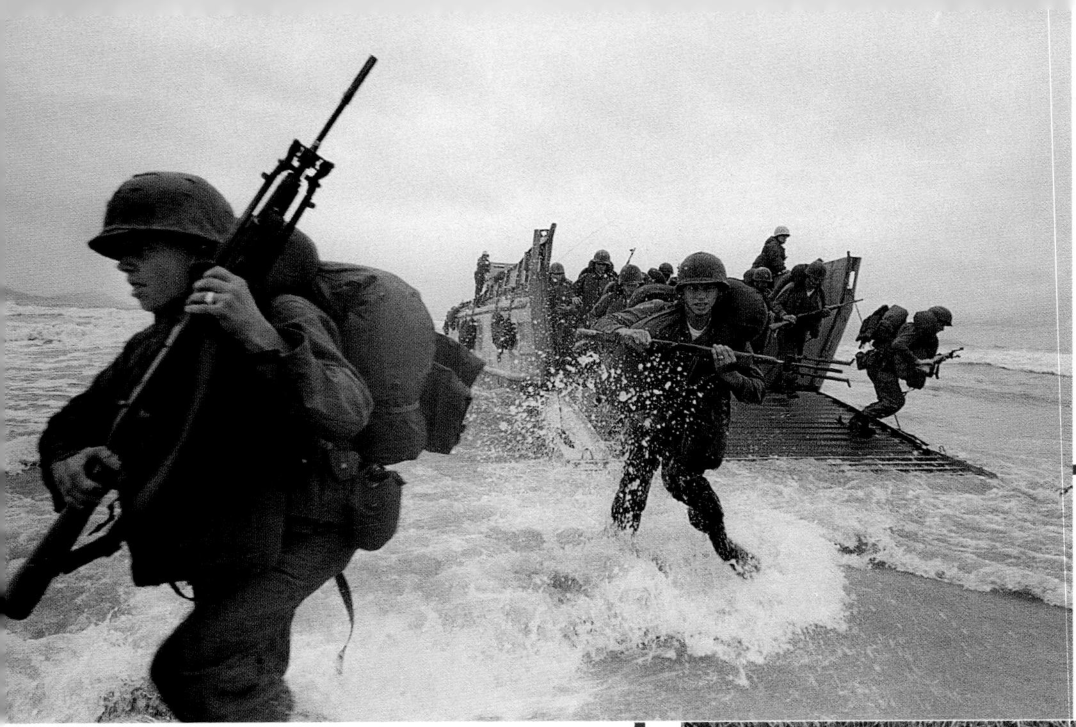

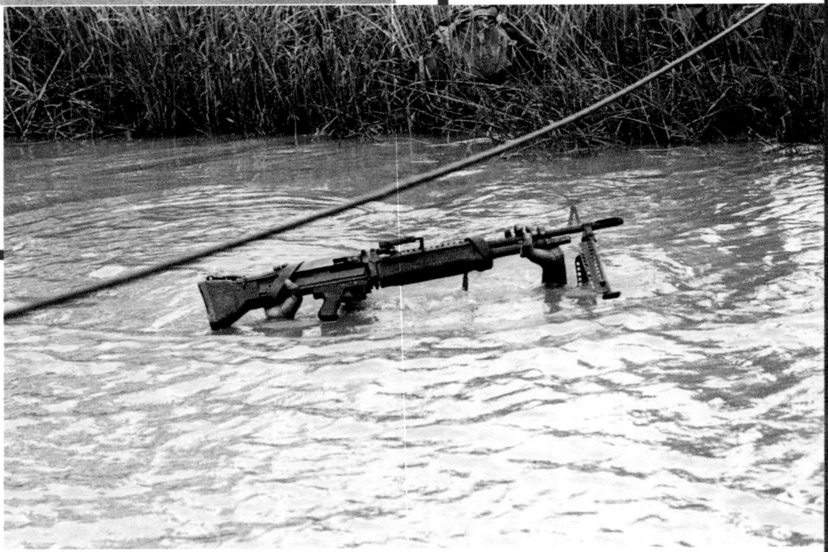

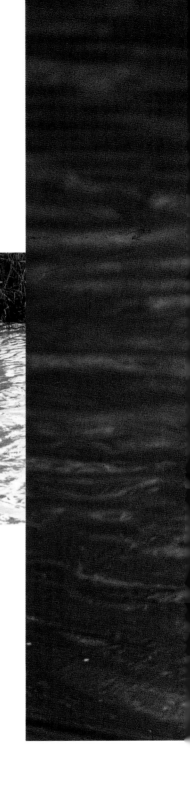

The Vietnam War
1964-1975

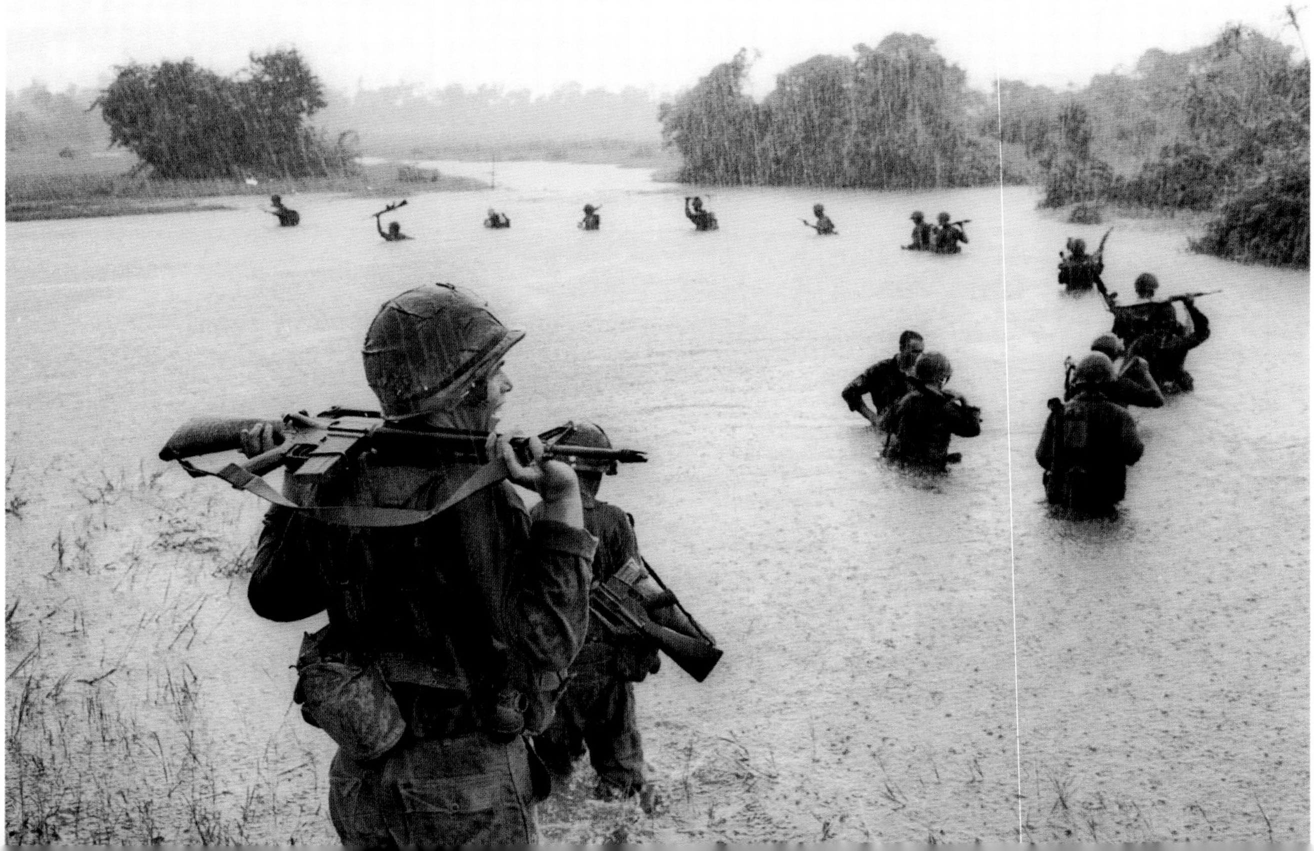

332-333

Top left: US soldiers cross a ditch at Phuo Vinh to fight off a Viet Cong attack launched in the morning of June 13, 1965. The other pictures: the 173rd Airborne Division's 2nd Battalion in operation against Viet Cong positions around Ben Cat. The raid is being carried out in heavy rain, and US infantrymen are attempting to protect their automatic weapons and bazookas against the water.

334-335

The other side of the medal: Viet Cong marching into a "liberated" village (left), preparing an ambush along a river (center), and in action with a potent Soviet-made anti-aircraft artillery gun. At the end of 1964, the Viet Cong controlled two thirds of the South Vietnamese territory, although the "Government of the Generals" in Saigon had mobilised 200,000 men.

1964
1975

The Vietnam War

1964-1975

336-337

Left: paratroopers from the US Air Cavalry's 1st Division on An Thi hill, central South Vietnam, during operation Masher (winter 1965-66). Right: US units in Long Khan are waiting for helicopters to take them to safety (October 1966).
A severely injured soldier needs emergency assistance. The dead soldier has been wrapped in a cloth to protect his dignity.

The Vietnam War

1964-1975

338-339
Dead, wounded and mutilated soldiers. These dramatic images were shot by a war reporter in January 1966 during one of many violent field battles fought in that year between North Vietnamese/Viet Cong troops and US forces.

The photographs express a dramatic tension never fully captured in the numerous feature films made later about the war. These included The Green Berets *(1968),* The Deer Hunter *(1979),* Platoon *(1986), and* Born on the Fourth of July *(1989).*

340-341

Left: US Marines crossing a napalm-charred hill at Da Nang. The picture was taken in March 1968 during a counterattack against the North Vietnamese Tet Offensive, launched on January 30 in violation of a cease-fire agreed upon for the Buddhist New Year's celebrations. Right: US troops use a flame thrower to burn down the remains of an enemy camp at Binh Duong.

342-343

The picture on the right aroused the conscience of the entire world and earned the Associated Press a Pulitzer Prize in 1973. The scene is Trang Bang, 8 June 8, 1972. Little Phan Thi Puc, 9 years old, is running away naked and terrified after ripping off her clothes, set afire by napalm during an attack that South Vietnamese forces carried out in error on her village. First from the left: her brother Phan Yhan Tam. The girl now lives in the United States, is married, has taken the name Kim, and has a son called Huan ("Hope"). Picture on the left: A desperate mother is holding her child, who was terribly burned during the same attack.

1964
1975

346-347

More images from the Tet Offensive. Left and bottom, military surgeon James E. Callaghan assists a comrade hit in the head by a bullet. He also attempts mouth-to-mouth resuscitation of another battle victim. Right: an African-American marine is assisted by a comrade during the battle to hold Saigon's Eastern Gate (February 1968).

344-345

The images on these pages capture the Tet Offensive, launched by the Viet Cong at the beginning of 1968. US soldiers from the 101st Airborne Division are waiting for helicopters to evacuate those injured during the defense of Hué, South Vietnam's ancient capital. The Tet Offensive, an attempt at an all-out attack, had great symbolic value but did not lead to definitive military success. The Viet Cong attackers, in fact, did not succeed in conquering and holding important military targets, neither did they manage to incite insurrections in the cities, as they had hoped.

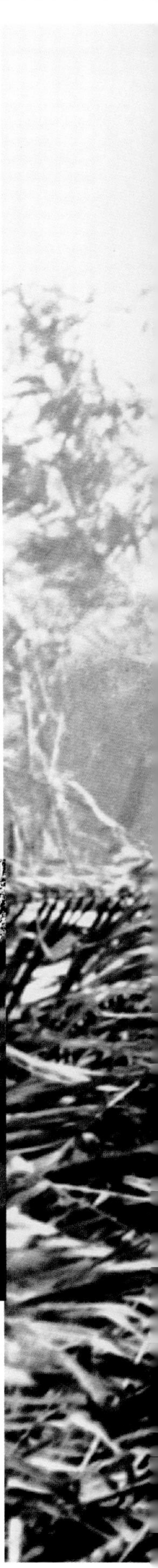

1964
1975

1964
1975

348-349

Left: a South Vietnamese soldier keeps vigil beside his dead comrades in a rice field on Tan Dinh island; he is waiting for helicopters to take away the bodies. On the right, surviving US infantry soldiers after a shoot-out. US casualties during the first six years of the war were high, but South Vietnamese losses were far heavier. Between 1960 and 1966 the Saigon government lost 59,000 soldiers, police and other officials; Vietcong, lost 157,000 fighters.

350-351

The images show the war through Viet Cong eyes. Top left, an American plane, coming back from a raid against Viet Cong is shot down by mistake by an American anti-aircraft. In the other two pictures, a Viet Cong anti-aircraft position and a girl hiding in a underground position.

352-353

In these pages the tragic condition of the Vietnamese population: mothers and children running away during a US air raid in the Mekong Delta. In March 1968, the US launched a counteroffensive in the Mekong Delta, initiating the "War of the Rice Paddies."

1964
1975

1964
1975

1964
1975

354-355

These photographs show counteinsurgency guerrilla operations. Top left: an injured North Vietnamese soldier is captured and pulled out of his bunker by men belonging to the US 1st First Airborne Cavalry Division in Bong Son; bottom: Vietnamese police officer interrogates a Viet Cong guerrilla tided up hands and feet hanging from his feet. Right: US soldiers point their weapons against suspected Viet Cong guerrillas who have been driven out of the jungle.

356-357

Top left: a South Vietnamese police officer interrogates a Viet Cong guerrilla in Mekong Delta; bottom: an american soldier points his M16 rifle at the prisoner's head during an operation conducted by the 101st Airborne Division in Tom Ky, 300 miles north of Saigon. Center: a South Vietnamese officer interrogates a vietcong guerrilla in the wheabouts of Tan Dinh.

The Vietnam War

1964-1975

358-359

On the left, perhaps the most dramatic photo of the entire Vietnam War. General Nguyen Ngoc Loan, the South Vietnamese police chief, executes a Viet Cong prisoner in Saigon (1968). The photographer, Edward T. Adams, won a Pulitzer Prize. The picture did not please the South Vietnamese government or the US command; it contributed to the growing anti-war sentiment that culminated in a series of pacifist initiatives in almost all European nations and in the USA. On the right, a group of Viet Cong guerillas who have just been executed on an island in the Mekong Delta while two US "advisers" look on.

19*64*
1975

1964
1975

360-361

These three images are from Viet Cong sources. They show North Vietnamese soldiers (among them a woman) transporting supplies and participating in a battle. The Communist forces, too, used a powerful propaganda apparatus that influenced the war and also world public opinion. But the US position in the war was weakened most by the explicitness of US reporting in all media. Documentaries and other reports hid nothing about the dehumanising training of recruits and the atrocities that were committed, mainly against civilians.

362-363

The helicopter: for both the South Vietnamese army and later for US forces the helicopter was a very important resource. Lack of roads, numerous swamps, and the existence of traps and ambushes made it difficult for troops to move into the jungle with vehicles or on foot. Therefore, mounting military attacks, supplying fighting units, and post-battle evacuation always required helicopters. The helicopter deserved its description: the weapon "par excellence" of the Vietnam War.

The Vietnam War
1964-1975

The Vietnam War

1964-1975

364-365
Helicopters again: providing air cover for a US infantry advance in a hilly area, in a plain, and in dense, man-high vegetation granting security in a extremely dangerous war field. Helicopters also played a major role in the numerous movies that Hollywood produced about the war. Perhaps the most famous scene is in Apocalypse Now *(Francis Ford Coppola, 1979), starring Robert Duvall as a squadron commander leading a helicopter squadron attack to the music of Richard Wagner.*

366-367
These are not scenes taken from a movie but pictures take by Larry Burrows, one of the most famous war reporter, and published by Life *magazine. Soldier James Farley, holding onto the door of his helicopter, fires his M-60 submachine gun at the enemy . Shortly thereafter, Farley is dismayed by the death of two comrades, hit by Viet Cong anti-aircraft fire. Finally, back at base, he weeps desperately for the loss of his two friends.*

19*64*
1975

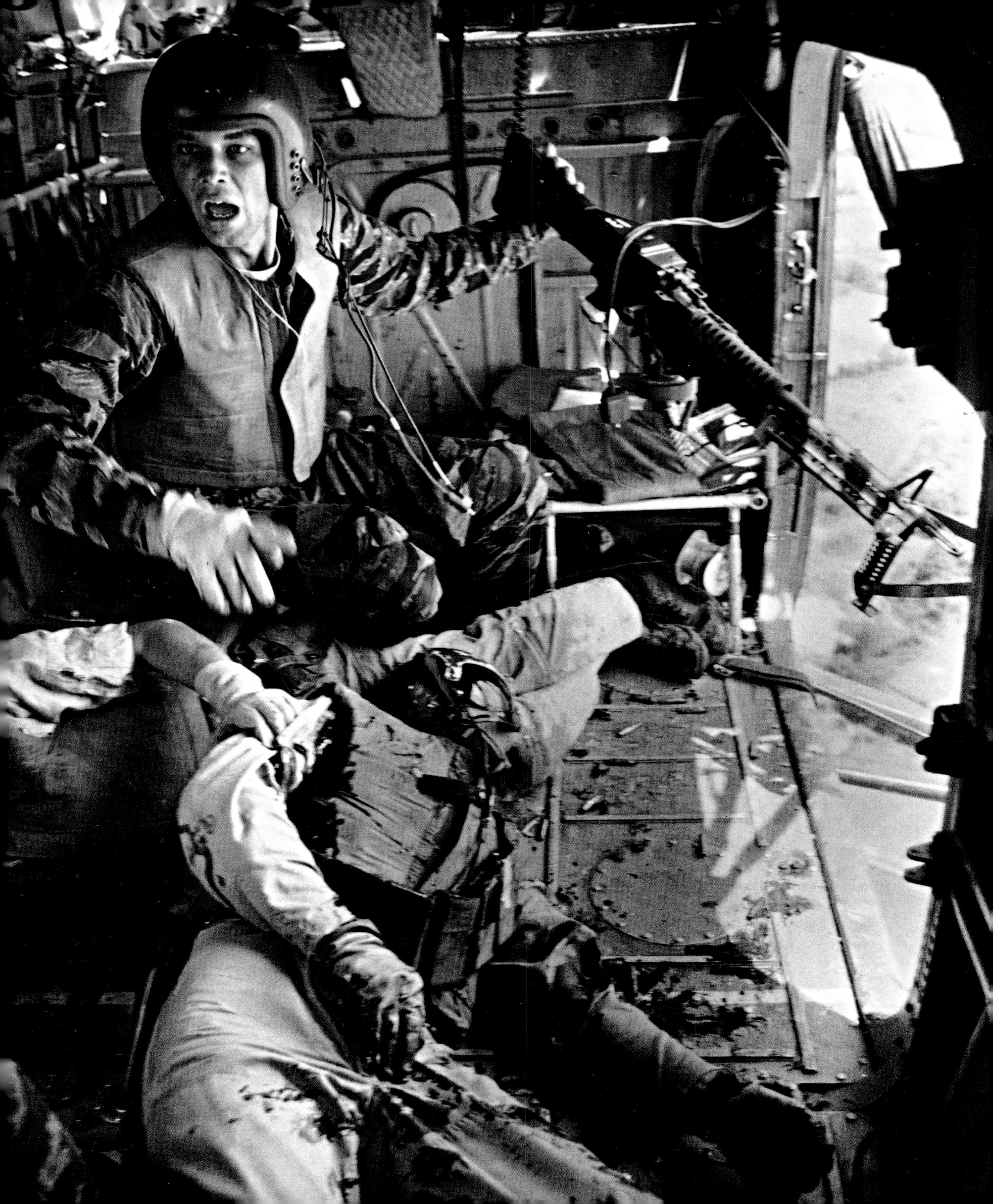

1964
1975

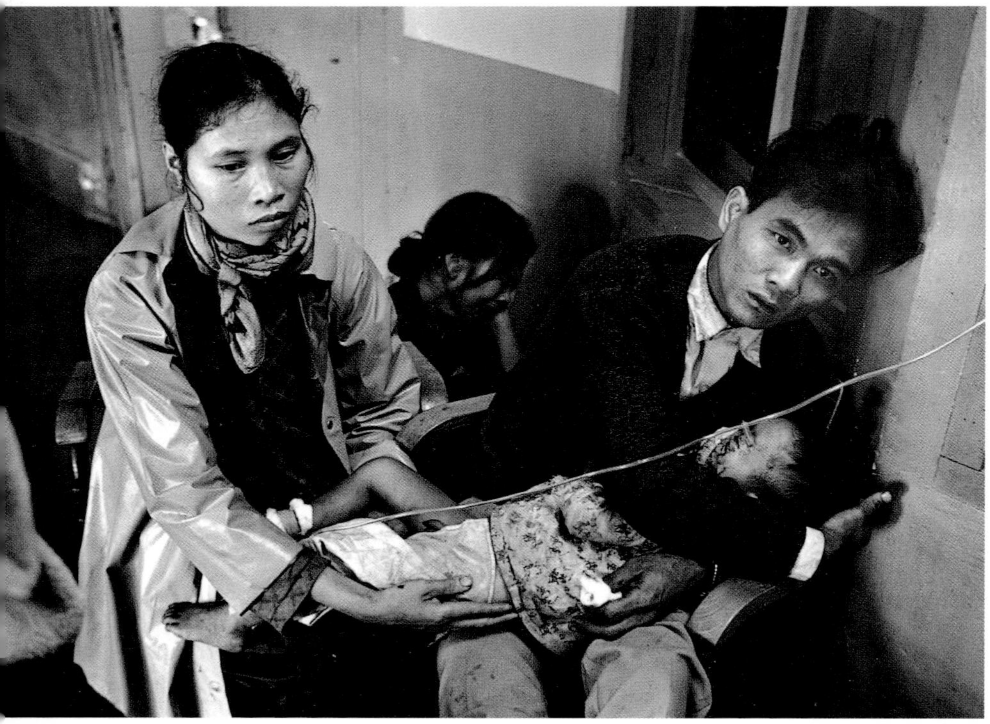

The Vietnam War

1964-1975

368-369

A US unit is wiped out in an ambush in 1969, near Saigon. The bodies are loaded on a tank while the crew wait for transport helicopters.

370-371

Dramatic pictures of the "Battle for the Citadel" fought to gain control of Hué, in 1968. US infantry units take shelter behind tanks or trees. Bottom left: the suffering of the civilian population caught up in the battle.

372-373
Dramatic scenes shot in the course of the evacuation of Saigon during the North Vietnamese/Viet Cong Tet Offensive. After months of fighting and thousands of victims, US troops succeeded in recapturing almost all the lost positions. Nevertheless, the Test Offensive made it clear that a US battlefield victory was unthinkable in the short term and probably impossible in the long run.

374-375
These heart-rending photgraphs capture the war-caused suffering of the civilian population, above all of children. Children were the main victms of the bombing raids that hit villages merely suspected of harboring Viet Cong guerillas. Surviving to napalm or to bombs it was even worse than death. Many of the children had no parents, house, or place to go. Left to themselves, they had to live in a world without pity.

1964
1975

376-377
These photos taken on April 30, 1975 show the end of the Vietnam War and the helicopter evacuation of US Embassy personnel. That same day Hanoi's troops overcame the final resistance offered by the South Vietnamese army and entered Saigon. Thereafter, the city's name was changed to Ho Chi Minh City.

378-379
Tens of thousands of people killed; hundreds of thousands injured and mutilated; a country destroyed by defoliating agents and napalm. Another country assailed by its conscience; its people wrestling with shame. Such was the outcome of this most senseless war. At the end of every conflict, the world witnesses the dramatic and long-lasting pain of those who survived.

The
Vietnam War

19 64
1975

B
A

THE AFGHANISTAN WAR

FOR ALMOST A DECADE, FROM DECEMBER 1979 TO FEBRUARY 1989, AFGHANISTAN, THE CENTURIES-OLD NORTHERN ASIAN MUSLIM NATION OF STRATEGIC IMPORTANCE SINCE ALEXANDER THE GREAT'S TIME, WAS "RUSSIA'S VIETNAM."

In the Afghanistan War some 14,000 Soviet soldiers lost their lives; while many more Afghans were killed, at least half a million. The war, which was as bitterly fought as the Americans' war in Vietnam, marked the separation and irreconcilable contrasts between the world of Islam and the Soviet empire, contributing in no small way to the collapse of the latter. Afghanistan, enshrined in the tales of the English writer and journalist Rudyard Kipling, had been the unbending adversary of British imperialism throughout the 19th century and for the first years of the 20th. After conquering India, Britain thought it would be equally easy to take this harsh country. In the south, the Khyber Pass (on the borders of modern Pakistan) offered a tortuous entry route. From the Khyber, the harsh terrain rolls on north to the old tsarist region of Russian Central Asia. Afghanistan had become an independent emirate in 1747, with Kabul as its capital, with rulers of Pathan descent. But Afghans were not as amenable as the Indians were. They resented being given orders by others. Throughout the 18th century they had taken up arms and used guerrilla tactics against tsarist attempts to subjugate their country. They gave the British no quarter during the three Afghan wars, 1839-42, 1878-80 and 1919.

At the Bolshevik coup of 1917, Afghanistan had been the first nation to recognize the new Russia of the Soviets, but in the 1930s, during Stalin's savage repression of the Central Asia peoples, Afghanistan had offered hospitality and assistance to the refugees, saving tens of thousands from the Bolshevik massacres. Nor did the Afghans think twice about clashing with the vanguard of the Red Army along the border routes.

In 1947, with the end of British rule in India came the end of British influence in north central Asia. Keen to keep its independence, Afghanistan settled its border dispute with the USSR, with whom it signed a military aid agreement in 1955. The mullahs, the Muslim religious leaders who had always sustained the independent spirit of the population, continued to exert their influence on the Kabul government. On April 27 1978 a military coup ousted Prince Mohammad Daud and installed Mohammad Taraki, a strong leader who did not, however, please the religious hierarchy. This marked the end of a long period of political stability for Afghanistan and the start of clashes between Islamic factions.

At this stage, with Leonid Brezhnev in the Kremlin, the "Afghan question" once more came to the fore in Soviet policy. Brezhnev had been carrying out aggressive expansionist policies in the Horn of Africa (supported by the local dictator Haile Mariam Mengistu). In Mozambique and the former Portuguese colonies, the USSR backed various puppet-governments; the task of providing them with military support fell to Fidel Castro's Cuban mercenaries. Brezhnev was in a strong position since the United States, whose vigilance had been decisive in Southeast Asian matters, was now embroiled in the highly politicized, much reported Nixon Watergate scandal. The United States was in a weak posi-

380
A Mujaheddin ("Fighters for Faith") guerrilla's child checks a revolver. During the long Afghan resistance against the Soviet invaders, children as young as 12 to 13 fought side by side with 80-year-olds who had participated in Afghanistan's last war of independence against the English in 1919.

1979 1989

tion, while the USSR gathered strength. Given this situation, Brezhnev decided to intervene in the feuding that had divided Kabul. First, in he signed an alliance with the government of Mohammad Taraki. Then in September 1979, he betrayed his stopgap dictator, ousting him and installing an old Communist diehard, Hafizullah Amin. Kabul was full of Soviet paratroopers who had been airlifted into the city. The government buildings were swarming with Russian "advisors." One of these, a general, was assassinated in December 1979 as a result of a conspiracy. This was the pretext for the invasion.

At dawn on December 27 1979 a division-sized Soviet armed unit occupied Kabul's public buildings. The soldiers mercilessly killed President Amin, who had dared to disagree with the Kremlin advisers' suggestions. The loyal Babrak Karmal, who had been living in exile in Czechoslovakia, replaced Amin and was to remain in power until May 4, 1986. The Soviet paratroopers shot on sight anyone, whether soldier or civilian, who put up any resistance. This execrable act of brutality horrified all the peoples of Central Asia and Caucasus, who had been observing hopefully what was happening in Iran, where Khomeini, with his ayatollahs, had driven the Shah into exile. Iran and Pakistan therefore became the supply bases for the Afghan *mujahideen* ("fighters for the faith"), who had decided to resist the Soviet tyranny.

In a matter of days the Soviet invasion force rose to 90,000 men. Having occupied Kabul and other major towns in the country, the Red Army headed toward the legendary Khyber Pass and the other routes connecting Afghanistan with Peshawar and Rawalpindi, where Pakistan had made bases available to the mujahideen. The Soviet intention of closing the roads and thus creating an impenetrable border failed because many Soviet soldiers were Muslims and refused to open fire on fellow-Muslims. The Afghan soldiers guarding the passes, pending the arrival of fresh troops from the Soviet Union, proved an easy target for the guerrillas. The first of nine offensives launched by the Soviet troops and those loyal to the Kabul puppet-government failed. The rebels attacked swiftly and ruthlessly. At Herat they shattered a Russian tank regiment. They were armed with Kalashnikov AK-47s they had stolen from the regular army's barracks. After the early months of guerrilla fighting, the resistance fighters no longer restricted themselves to defending the passes to Pakistan but, under the leadership of Ahmed Shah Masoud (the most popular of the leaders surfacing in the rebellion's first days), they now attacked the Salang Pass. This was to the north, on the road from Kabul to the Russian border.

At this stage the Russians started to wage chemical warfare against the mujahideen and their supporters. The Russians used both poisonous and nerve gases, and also mycotoxins and lethal "yellow rain." Concurrently, in the United States reports that the US Air Force was using napalm against the Viet Cong were causing demonstrations and protests on university campuses. They provoked much discussion as to the morality of the military action. However, the atrocities attributed to the Red Army did not have the same effect, not only in Soviet Union where they were in any case ignored, but among student bodies in the West, which tended to sympathize with "true Communism." This tendency was helped along by propaganda in the media, which had been much infiltrated by journalists in the pay of the KGB.

As so the United States in Vietnam, so for the Soviet Union in Afghanistan. The conflict was soon to become an enervating war of attrition. Typical of the Soviet military problems in 1981 were the mujahideen victory in the battle of Paghman (12.5 miles south of Kabul), and the failure of the Soviet offensives in June and September. In following year, 1982, Sergei Sokolov, the Soviet deputy minister of defense, entered the fray. He brought in fresh troops for a series of major land operations supported by aircraft and helicopters. But a further four Russian offensives failed in the face of an enemy that couldn't be pinned down and that used the guerrilla tactics of swift attacks and retreats the Viet Cong had earlier used against the Americans.

The mujahideen appeared neither to sleep nor eat; they lived in remote mountain caves, and used daggers and hand grenades. The Red Army had no option but to copy the American strategy in Vietnam: air strikes, villages razed to the ground, accompanied by the mass exodus of the people.

An attempt to split the enemy front by offering an armistice to Masoud, the fiercest of the mujahideen leaders, lasted only a few months. The agreement was respected only until the spring of 1984 when pressure from the other mujahideen groups forced Masoud to return to the fighting. Two years of constant defeats followed for the Russians. Although Soviet paratroopers repulsed many of the guerrilla attacks on Kabul it was at the cost of heavy losses. A contributing factor was that there was little or no collaboration on the part of the local government army, leading the occupying Russians to remove the inept Karmal and install the more dynamic Najibullah as president.

The core Soviet force was the Fortieth Army, initially commanded by Lieutenant-General Mikhailov, and later in 1985 by General Zaitsev. His strategy was designed to limit losses as much as possible in order to avoid repercussions in Russia. The Red Army's war was therefore paradoxically one of "resistance" against the true resistance fighters who, on the contrary, were constantly on the attack. Indeed, the mujahideen virtually controlled 80 percent of Afghanistan, while the occupying forces held control of the roads and airports, according to some rumors, to ensure that they could pull out at any time with as little damage as possible. The limitations of the Soviet strategy were also manifest in the cost of the war. This was a fraction of what the United States had spent in Vietnam, and never more than $4 billion per year.

A major player in the strange Afghan war was the Hind helicopter, a vital Soviet weapon, more important even than the supersonic MiG-27s and SU-25s. In particular, the Hind MI-24 combat helicopters dropped poisonous gas, decimating the ranks of the guerrillas and wreaking havoc among the survivors. Soldiers arrived from all points of the Soviet empire, from Cuba, East Germany, Bulgaria, Vietnam and Syria, to fight alongside their Russian comrades.

By contrast, the Kabul government's army suffered very heavy losses, in the region of 50 percent of its men. At least 10,000 men were killed, wounded or deserted every year. There were many deserters; the soldiers not only had to shoot at fellow Muslims but also lacked training. They had not undertaken any training courses offered by the Russians as they felt a built-in resistance to helping the infidel create efficient fighting divisions. There was a heavy backlash, however. A significant percentage of Afghanistan's youth was deported to the USSR to undergo Marxist-Leninist training.

This plan failed too; Marxist-Leninist ideas were not compatible with the religious beliefs of Islam that were an integral part of the Afghan family tradition.

As opposed to the Afghan army, the Resistance, although made up of seven political parties ranging from traditionalists to fundamentalists, was nevertheless solidly united in its hatred of the USSR. The most outstanding figure of the Resistance, and not only for his military skills, was Ahmed Shah Masoud, dubbed "The Lion of Panishar" after the name of the valley where, at the head of his mujahideen, he had repulsed dozens of Soviet offensives.

The guerillas and their strategy repay examination They were the most disparate group imaginable: they ranged from very young adolescents (it was not unusual to find boys of 12 or 13 years old fighting) to wrinkled veterans of the Third Afghan War of Independence, octogenarians who way back in 1919 had faced and beaten the British. Theirs was a rare example of national pride with very few precedents in the world. They suffered great losses: at least 500,000 killed in ten years of war. To this must be added an incalculable number of wounded and mutilated, also 4 million civilians (out of a total population of 9 million) who were forced to leave their homeland and seek shelter in Pakistan (2 million) and Iran (1 million).

From 1985, when Mikhail Gorbachev came to power in the Soviet Union, events of the war in Afghanistan were closely linked to the historic events unfolding in Russia. Leonid Brezhnev, the true author of the conflict in Afghanistan, had succeeded Khrushchev in 1964 and governed jointly with Kosygin and Podgorny until the day he died on November 10, 1982. He was followed by Yuri Andropov, a former chief of the KGB who was unwilling to abandon Afghanistan but equally unprepared to commit men and resources. When, on Andropov's early death on March 11, 1985, Gorbachev became general-secretary of the USSR, he faced political corruption and a bankrupt economy. These factors was to lead to the fall of the Berlin Wall in December 1989 and, on Christmas day 1991, to the end of the USSR in its post-World War II form.

After studying the deteriorating Soviet situation, Gorbachev decided to introduce reforms of a type and extent that had never been carried out before in post-war Russia. He announced his *perestroika* ('restructuring') at the Communist Party of the Soviet Union's (CPSU) 27th Conference, held February 26 - March 6 1986). Gorbachev's other watchword was *glasnost* or openness: to be applied to the behavior of government functionaries, in relations between the state and its citizens, and in the distribution of senior posts.

In line with his program, Gorbachev dismissed 70 percent of the senior technocrats and replaced them with honest democratically oriented people. That essentially was what perestroika was about. He allowed famous dissidents such as Andrei Sakharov to return home, he admitted the state's responsibility for the nuclear catastrophe of Chernobyl, and at the end of 1987 he called for an enquiry into Stalin's crimes. In brief, Communism was already imploding.

With regard to foreign policy, Gorbachev from the outset had set himself the task of establishing peaceful relations with the West, giving up the dream of strategic parity with the United States. He had three meetings with President Reagan: in Geneva (November 1985), Reykjavik (October 1986) and Washington (December 1987). The outcome was that both superpowers agreed to dismantle some of their nuclear missiles, while missile silos were to be gradually destroyed. The disarmament was ratified during the CPSU's 29th conference in the summer of 1988, when the old Stalinist Andrei Gromyko had to hand over the running of Soviet foreign policy to the moderate and democratic Edward Shevardnadze. Just a few months earlier, during an official visit to Belgrade, Gorbachev had publicly denounced the so-called theory of the "limited sovereignty"' of countries that after the Yalta Conference (1944) fell within the Russian sphere of influence.

The new course of events was officially confirmed at the United Nations in December 1988. There Gorbachev announced to the world that the Soviet Union would no longer come to the military aid of other Communist regimes. It was the end of the "Brezhnev doctrine" that had justified aggression towards Czechoslovakia; the end of Soviet meddling in the domestic affairs of Communist countries. In fact, it was the end of USSR imperialism.

Such radical changes could not but have immediate repercussions on the war in Afghanistan. And indeed the new leader at the Kremlin had no second thoughts about acting in keeping with the USSR's new foreign policy. He ordered the unilateral withdrawal of Soveit troops from Afghanistan. The evacuation started unobtrusively at the end of the month of October 1986 and was completed on February 15 1989, when the last Russian soldier climbed aboard the Tupolev on the runway at Kabul airport and closed the hatch.

384-385

This image is emblematic of the spirit within the Afghan mujaheddin ("Fighters for Faith") struggle. The Afghan people's resistance was fueled by national pride combined with their Islamic faith.

386-387

The mujahedding groups who were fighting against the Russian invasion, found hideouts in the mountainous area of Afghanistan: from there they used to organize ambushes and raids, prepare themselves to war thanks to their faith and their yearning to freedom.

388-389

Top left and right: BM-13 rocket launchers and machine guns now in the hands of mujaheddin open fire against the enemy. Bottom left: mine-clearing Soviet tanks ready to clean up an area once held by the mujaheddin.

1979

1989

1979
1989

390-391
On the left: two mujaheddin in a hideout observe the movements of a Soviet motorized column. Center: Islamic fighters take some time off after an ambush.

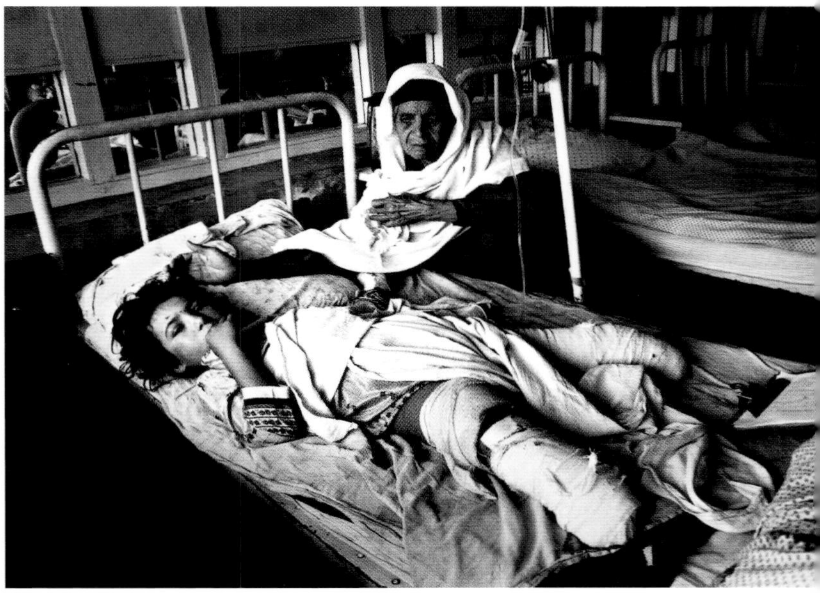

391

Top right: Children receiving weapons training from the mujaheddin. Thousands of Afghan youths were taken to Russia for the entire duration of the war. They were subjected to political indoctrination programs. These failed totally: meaningful dialog between Islam and Marxism-Leninism proved to be impossible. Bottom: an 12-year-old Afghan who lost both legs after jumping on a Russian anti-personnel mine placed close to her village, is nursed by her mother.

982

THE

FALKLANDS WAR

IT WAS GREAT BRITAIN'S LAST CHANCE TO SHOW ITS CLAWS IN THE 20TH CENTURY.

This happened in April 1982, when the Argentine president, General Galtieri, decided to take back the Falkland Islands, a small archipelago in the south Atlantic, to the south east of Argentina. The islands, known as the Malvinas by the Argentinians, had been under Great Britain's ownership since the 17th century, but Britain's claims of sovereignty had been long contested. Galtieri's move may have been a tactic to deflect the country's attention from its domestic policies (the controversy over the *desaparecidos* showed no signs of abating; indeed it was getting worse).

On April 2, 1982, 20,000 Argentinian soldiers landed on the East Island and forced the garrison of 22 British commandos to surrender. The only valid reason Galtieri could have had for his aggressive act was to gain control of the Cape Horn routes; this had been the reason why Britain had originally planted the Union Jack on the uninhabited islands. While the assault troops occupied all of the remote colony's islands, first Perez de Cuellar, secretary-general of the United Nations, and then the US president, Ronald Reagan, tried to reason with Argentina. But it was to no avail: Galtieri was not going to take anyone's advice.

At this stage Britain showed the world what it was still capable of. Prime minister Margaret Thatcher ordered Admiral John Woodward to muster and send a task force to the Falklands to drive out the Argentinians. In a very few days two aircraft carriers (*Hermes* and *Invincible*), 2 cruisers, 6 frigates, 6 torpedo-boats, 2 amphibious assault vessels, 4 nuclear submarines, 38 fighter-bombers, and 52 helicopters were ready to depart. The weaponry was impressive: rapid-fire cannon, missile launchers, missiles and anti-missile missiles. The armed force had a high proportion of volunteers; many were veterans, now professionals, civil servants, and ordinary working people prepared to leave their families and their work to defend the interests of their country.

On April 25 the first British landed on Georgia Island, where the Argentinian units that had captured the island surrendered. On May 2 a British nuclear submarine sank an Argentinian cruiser *Belgrano*, causing the deaths of 368 sailors. On May 21 British commandos and paratroopers commanded by General Jeremy Moore attacked Porto San Carlos, where 1500 Argentinian conscripts surrendered without even attempting to resist. On May 25, to avenge the sinking of the *Belgrano*, the Argentinian air force attacked two British destroyers, killing about 40 men. On May 28 and 29, the toughest battle was fought. Colonel Herbert Jones led 450 British paratroopers in an attack on Port Darwin and Goose Green. British won, taking 1400 prisoners. The Argentinians lost 250 men, the British 17. Among these was Colonel Jones.

On June 8 the Argentinian air force launched a violent attack on the British fleet, sinking two frigates and hitting many planes. British losses amounted to more than 50. This was the last Argentinian offensive. On June 11, British forces headed toward Port Stanley, the Falklands' capital, capturing hundreds of enemy soldiers on the way. On June 14, after assessing the situation and realizing that a battle would have resulted in a bloodbath, General Menendez, the Argentinian commander, surrendered, ordering his troops to evacuate the Malvinas. The archipelago to all intents and purposes once more became the Falklands. The final losses were estimated at 700 Argentinians and 256 British dead. President Galtieri resigned.

392-393

Top left, above, Royal Commandos land on the Falkland Islands. Bottom: attacking Mount Kent. Small picture: Right: the Union Jack flies above a captured hill.

394

Harrier GR.Mk3 *RAF fighters planes take off from* HMS Invincible. *In the conflict British forces lost two torpedo boats, two frigates, ten fighter-bomber planes, 24 helicopters and other minor units, in spite of their technical superiority.*

1982

395
An Argentinian soldier surrenders (top right), but many of his comrades are lying dead in a mass grave (top left). Bottom: HMS Antelope *hit by Argentinian fire in the Bay of San Carlos (Eastern Falklands).*

THE GULF WAR

IN 1988, MIKHAIL GORBACHEV DECIDED TO WITHDRAW THE RED ARMY FROM AFGHANISTAN.

Russian imperialism was on the decline; Khrushchev's policy, which had supported the invasion of Hungary, and Brezhnev's policy, which had supported that of Czechoslovakia, were denounced. The world's second superpower had started its process of disengagement, at the same time calling for an end to the arms race. On the other side of the world, the United States was emerging with difficulty from a period in which its international prestige had plummeted. First there had been the defeat in Vietnam, then the embarrassment of the Johnson administration after the North Koreans boarded the *USS Pueblo*, taking the crew prisoner, putting them through a humiliating trial and a verdict that was broadcast on television the world over. Finally at Christmas 1979, there was the occupation of the US embassy in Teheran by Khomeini militants. They took the entire American diplomatic group hostage and held them prisoner for more than a year, with all the humiliations imaginable in such a situation. President Carter, after an unfortunate attempt to storm the embassy had failed, had to negotiate an agreement for the Americans' release. The unwillingness of a series of Democratic administrations to undertake any kind of military action in reaction to the attacks on the prestige and dignity of the nation finally made the Americans choose the Republican party. Although Nixon's presidency, brought to a premature end by the Watergate scandal, was not long enough to achieve the foreign policy plans of the right, his successor, Ronald Reagan (1981-1989), did not encounter any further obstacles in re-establishing American prestige in the world. In March 1986 he did not hesitate to launch an air strike against the headquarters of the Libyan leader Ghaddafi, accused of being a key player in Islamic international terrorism. One of Ghaddafi's daughters died in the attack. But by March 23, 1983, with his famous speech on the Strategic Defense Initiative, Reagan had outlined the new American military strategy. The newspapers had coined the term "star wars" at the time, an appropriate term given the major role computers were now to have in the management of war. Traditional strategy and tactics suddenly appeared to be very old-fashioned. In the war of the future the head of the armed forces would only need to choose a given plan from among the various plans prepared by military headquarters. Once chosen, computer software would take over and see to its execution. Computers would control the weapons. This technique also made it possible to create the Missile Defense Shield, designed to intercept enemy missiles and destroy them with laser beams from satellites orbiting the Earth. Naturally all this cost vast sums of money: between 1984 and 1990 the United States invested thousands of billions of dollars in hi-tech military research. The arms industry became an increasingly important source of employment and business in the country. The overall American-European-Soviet balance of power now contrasted sharply with that which had successively followed the Yalta Conference (1944) and the fall of the Berlin Wall (1989). Maintaining the new balance demanded a frenetic arms race with ever larger budget allocations. After the fall of the Berlin Wall and the end of aggressive Communism, the world looked forward to a long period of peace and prosperity, with no more wars. The hope soon vanished. After the Camp David Accords between the Egyptian president Anwar Sadat and the Israeli premier Menachem Begin, Egypt gave up its guiding role in the Arab world. This role devolved upon the Iraqi leader, Saddam Hussein. The western powers

396
At least four million Iraqi men and women served voluntarily in the army of Saddam Hussein – the rais (leader) whose portrait was omnipresent among them. Iraq paid an extremely high price in the war: 150,000 dead compared to Allied casualties of 165 dead.

1991

THE GULF WAR

1991

had not grudged him arms and credits as long as he combated the Islamic fundamentalism that Iran supported. Iran was a strategic country, both because of its mineral deposits and control of the oil routes. After Shah Reza Pahlevi, a firm ally of the United State, was forced to abdicate and escape into exile (January 1979), Iran fell prey to the fanaticism of the imams, the Shi'ite religious leaders. Ayatollah ("Sign of God") Ruhollah Khomeini assumed power. He was anti-Western and in favor of the most rigidly literal application of the Koran: the stoning to death of adulterers, the wearing of the chador to be obligatory for women, the hands of thieves to be cut off, and public execution for "enemies" of the state. The fanaticism of Khomeini and his imams did not sit well, particularly with the more secular Arab countries, for which Saddam Hussein acted as spokesman. He was the first to challenge the Iranian fundamentalists, in 1980 occupying Basra and the surrounding oil zone. In May 1980 Hussein started a war that he thought he could quickly finish with economic and military aid from the Gulf emirates and the West. Instead, the war lasted for nine years. It was an exhausting war of attrition; a front was established at Shatt-el-Arab, and the Iraqi positions were constantly attacked by the *pasdaran*, the young Iranian fundametalists, ready to die in their thousands in the name of Allah, sure of their eternal reward in Paradise. In 1988, when a UN-brokered truce ended the conflict, more than a million had died, the vast majority Iranian. Throughout the Iran-Iraq war, the West had stood by looking on, while a lively market in arms (mainly American) developed. Only in 1987, when Iran had threatened to paralyze shipping in the Persian Gulf, did a Western fleet intervene to take control of the shipping lanes.

At the end of the war with Iran (the First Gulf War), Iraq was armed to the teeth and possessed hi-tech weaponry too (such as Scud missiles). However, the nation was burdened with debt. Given his economic situation, Saddam set his sights on the neighboring oil-rich Kuwait, which until 1917 had been an integral part of Mesopotamia. This Greek word, meaning "between the [Tigris and Euphrates] rivers," was the historic name for modern Iraq. On August 2, 1990, accusing the Emir of Kuwait of having authorized the "theft" of crude oil from the wells on the two nations' border, and trusting in America's neutrality, Saddam ordered the invasion of Kuwait. He claimed Iraq's ancient right to the territory, according to the old borders. The name he gave to the operation was to become legendary: "The Mother of All Battles." With the invasion, Saddam Hussein, who was certainly an able, astute and unscrupulous man, hoped to solve all the economic problems of his country, prostrated by the war with Iran. He would have access to the oil wells in Kuwait, be able to pay off all his debts and guarantee his people a good standard of living. But it was no joking matter when oil was involved. The day after the invasion (August 3) the USA and the USSR released joint statements inviting Saddam to withdraw his troops immediately. Two days later, on August 5, President Bush delivered a warning ("the invasion will not be tolerated") to the man who, until recently, had been his strongest ally in the Middle East. He also sent his defense minister, Richard Cheney, to Saudi Arabia to show King Fahd the secret service reports revealing Iraqi intentions of invading his country. Bush thus obtained the king's agreement to send American and allied troops and planes to Saudi Arabia. In very little time the United States formed a coalition of 33 countries, including Arab League countries such as Syria, Egypt and Morocco. Within six months, 500,000 soldiers, 300,000 Americans, the rest British and moderate Arabs, were positioned along the Saudi-Arbian border with Iraq, equipped with the most modern and sophisticated weaponry. In the meantime the Iraqi leaders demonization was taking place in the international press. Bush's accusation ("Saddam is worse than Hitler") prompted Saddam to close his frontiers, taking 10,000 Westerners hostage (including the diplomatic corps stationed in Kuwait) and exhorting the Arab world to join his Jihad. The situation escalated during the heat of August 1990. On one hand, Saddam, having reached a rapid and unexpected agreement with Iran, was able to transfer 300,000 men to the border with Saudi Arabia and gave orders that the foreigners belonging to enemy nations be transported to strategic targets to act as "human shields." But on the other hand, Germany, Italy, Spain, Greece, The Netherlands and Belgium sent war ships to the Gulf, as well as planes and soldiers, to support the Anglo-American forces. Saddam was taking a big risk. Not one to miss a media opportunity, he had himself filmed on television while stroking the hair of some British children being held hostage (Great Britain and the rest of the world were horrified by these images, which they interpreted as a threat to kill Western families being held hostage). On the same day, he ordered the release of fifteen French hostages, a clear sign of friendship towards the only Western country that had not sent either war ships or soldiers. He was a skillful operator. But these intimidatory or propagandistic maneuvers did not help Saddam Hussein at all.

On August 25 the UN Security Council approved the use of force in the Gulf; a few days later Bush and Gorbachev released another joint statement exhorting Saddam to withdraw unconditionally from Kuwait. At this stage, since he was getting nowhere with threats, the Iraqi dictator decided to adopt a more conciliatory approach. First, he announced that he was freeing foreign women and children; then he said he was prepared to free all the hostages in exchange for a guarantee that he would not be attacked.

It was a wasted effort. The American reply was to send a further 100,000 soldiers to the Gulf, while Great Britain sent a second armored brigade. On January 12, 1991 the United States Congress authorized President Bush to use "all necessary means" to force Saddam to leave Kuwait. With the failure of UN Secretary General Perez de Cuellar's mission to Baghdad, the last attempt to avoid the conflict failed. Weapon replaced words.

On January 17, 1991, at 03.00 local time, five successive waves of bombers armed with Harm and Cruise missiles launched the first attack on Iraq. However, the British and American missiles (and soon those of Italy and other countries involved in the war) hit not only the sand dunes in the desert but also the center and outskirts of Baghdad, killing hundreds of people. The Tomahawk missiles fired at the Iraqi ships wreaked terrible destruction. The commander-in-chief of the international coalition was General Norman Schwarzkopf, an American general and Vietnam veteran, known as the "Desert Bear" because of his robust physique (6 feet and 2 inches in height, about 220 lbs in weight). He was committed to driving back Saddam Hussein with the minimum loss of life to the Allied and American forces, but with no such regard for the enemy. Schwarzkopf fulfilled his mandate. On January 17 Iraq started launching Scud missiles at Tel Aviv and Haifa. Saddam had a very precise reason for such a direct provocation of Israel, which had kept itself out of the conflict. He was counting on the fact that the Israeli government would react and enter the war alongside the coalition commanded by the United States. In this case, given the Arabs' hatred of the Jews, he hoped to incite the whole of Islam to join him in a sort Jihad. But the maneuver failed. On one hand, Israel's Patriot anti-missile missiles were intercepted and destroyed the Scuds in mid-flight. On the other, the Jewish state was very careful not to react to the provocation and did not declare war on the aggressive Iraqi leader.

Every move Saddam made failed. His last attempt was on January 23 when the Iraqi soldiers set three Kuwaiti oil wells on fire and hundreds of thousands of tons of burning oil flooded the Persian Gulf, creating an ecological disaster. The effect of this was to bring down on Saddam the disapproval of the whole world. The moment had come for the West to carry out its final punishment of the Iraqi tribal leader-cum-head of state. The first land battle between the Allies and the Iraqi army took place on January 30 near Khafji, on the border between Saudi Arabia and Kuwait. This was followed by a cease-fire to enable Gorbachev's spokesman, deputy foreign minister Evgeny Primakov to make a last attempt at mediation. Bush decided the negotiations were dragging on too long and took action. On February 21 he gave Saddam an ultimatum: to pull out of Kuwait within two days, or Iraq would be invaded and his army routed. In light of Baghdad's silence, at 04.00 on February 24, the coalition's armored forces crossed the border and attacked the enemy positions. Within a short space of time the assault claimed 100,000 dead, an incalculable number of wounded, and 90,000 prisoners. The retreating Iraqis were killed by the Allies very advanced weapons, some of which were being tried out for the first time. The journalists who followed the Allied troops were not allowed to film the corpses (these were quickly buried by mechanized diggers), but only the shells of thousands of lorries and tanks that had been blown to bits during the vain attempt to escape. On February 26 the coalition forces entered Kuwait City. The occupation of Kuwait had lasted for 211 days, the Gulf War 42 days. A total of 60,000 tons of bombs had been dropped. Iraqi losses were staggering: 150,000 soldiers killed; 175,000 captured; 141 planes downed; 3,700 armored tanks destroyed; and 73 ships sunk. Allied losses were minimal: 175 soldiers; 106 prisoners; 37 planes; 2 tanks; no ships. The figures speak for themselves.

Some have marveled at the fact that, after such a show of strength, the United States left Saddam Hussein in power, instead of taking him prisoner and trying him before an international tribunal based on the Nuremberg or Tokyo models. Saddam Hussein wasted no time in taking advantage of the Americans' liberality. He ordered the bloody repression of the insurrectionist movements that flared up a few days after the end of the war, on March 3 1991, in Basra, where the soldiers faithful to the their tribal leader killed 60,000 civilians in a matter of days. Operation Desert Storm marked a new phase in world affairs in which there would only be one superpower, a power that was prepared to put its military deterrent to use to dissuade any country attempting to upset the world order. All the other countries, including the Russian Federated State (successor to the USSR), would be subordinate to it. It is clearly not plausible that every flare-up in a far corner of Asia or in an African desert poses a threat to American national security. Overreaction, that historical constant, is not always held in check. The case of Peter Arnett (the most famous American war correspondent) is proof that the force can be misapplied. Arnett was the only Western journalist left in Baghdad during the Allied air strikes and CNN, for whom he worked, was able to broadcast images of the bombs falling. When Arnett broadcast images of a dairy destroyed by Tomahawk missiles, the Allied command accused him of getting his facts wrong, maintaining it was a center for testing biological weapons. Control of information (whether by denial or by misinformation) is common to all possessors of superior might. New weapons often miss their targets. This historical truism was proved in the war in Kosovo and in almost every conflict. Military powers therefore seek to test weapons systems in "real conditions" from time to time. The prevalent theory, as of the 1990s, is that military power is necessary to safeguard and develop the affluence and well-being of the "developed" world (described more often as the "most developed countries"). Hence the need to keep the arsenals constantly updated. Justifiable use is a valuable means of testing efficiency, so often a target has to be identified. Saddam Hussein self-identified as a justifiable target. In the ten years since the end of the Gulf War he has not paused for a moment in his attempts to breach the terms of the armistice. He has constantly offered provocations to the UN and the United States. On a number of occasions he has refused the UN inspectors permission to enter his country to destroy his chemical weapons' factories. On December 16, 1998 the United States and Great Britain once more bombed Iraq to punish Saddam. Naturally, it was not Saddam but a few dozen shepherds, peasant farmers or school children that were killed. Finally, dictators such as Saddam Hussein have a part to play in the strategy of the "new world order." In September 2000, Saddam once more accused Kuwait of stealing oil from the wells on the border (350,000 barrels per day, he claimed, with the approbation of the United States). "Watch your step. We are ready to react at a moment's notice," came the reply from William Cohen, then heading the department of defense in Washington. Nobody can have any doubt that the United States is.

400-401
Flames and smoke rise above a Kuwait oil field after Iraqi forces blew it up; in the foreground a T-82 Iraqi tank destroyed by the Allies. During the conflict's final phase, Saddam Hussein ordered the firing of more than 950 oil wells and related installations. He hoped to destroy Kuwait's economy and hinder Allied bombing.

402-403
On the left, two images that well exemplify the high-level of technology used in contemporary wars; top: a US F-15 plane launches a Sparrow *missile. Bottom, a load of 227 mm rockets is launched by a* MLRS *tracked tank. Right: Allied preparations for war after Saddam Hussein invaded Kuwait. Within a few months, the anti-Saddam coalition landed 500,000 troops in neighboring Saudi Arabia.*

1991

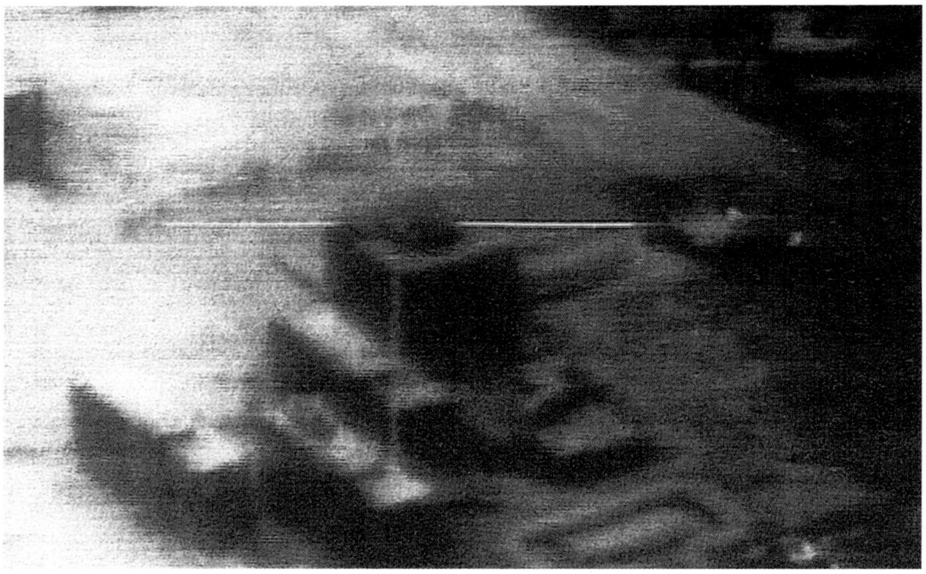

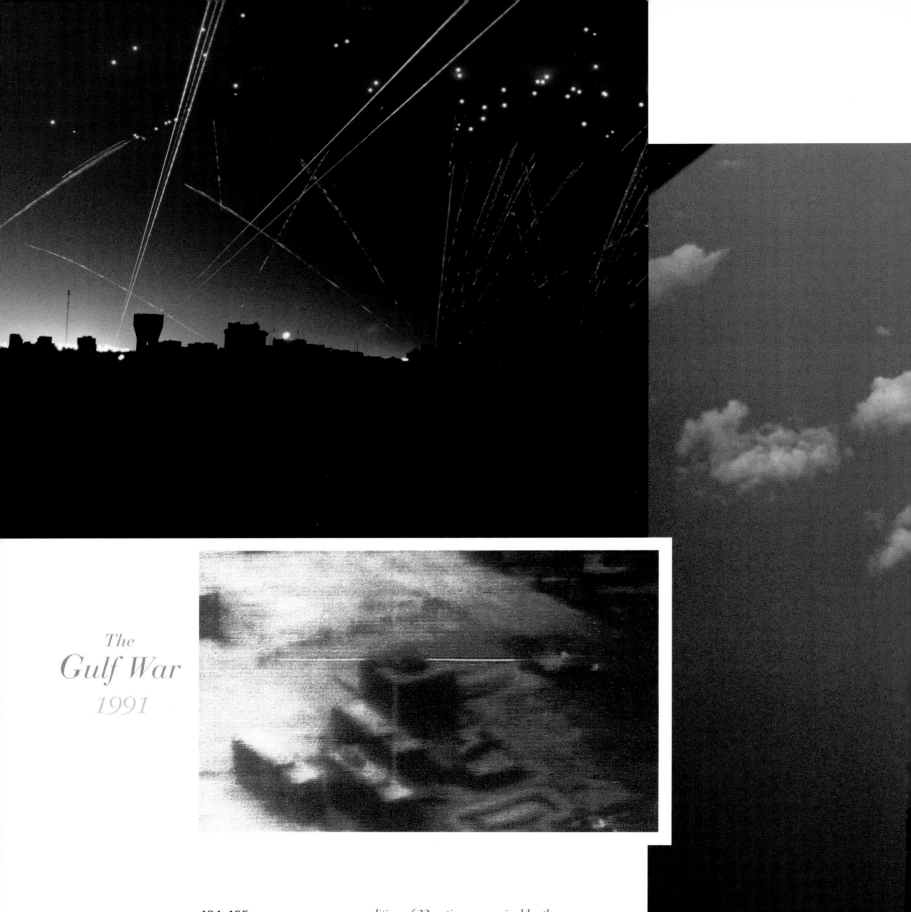

The
Gulf War
1991

404-405

Allied air raids on Baghdad, started at 3.00 a.m. on January 17, 1991. From the onset they were intense, and firestorm conditions often enveloped the Iraqi capital. Operation Desert Storm was carried out by the armed forces of six western countries, supported by an anti-Iraq coalition of 33 nations, organised by the USA. Bottom left: this image was taken by a Stealth pilot during an air attack, using an infrared ray system: in few seconds the telecommunication building will be blown up. Right: the unique profile of a F-117, the "invisible" bomber, sharply etched in the sky.

406-407
Scenes from the air war against Iraq, baptised by the media as history's first "Star War." Right: a technician wearing a heavy amiantus suit takes a moment off on the carrier USS Saratoga. *On the background "old"* A-7 Corsair II *bombers ready for take-off. Top right: an Italian Air Force* Tornado *jet refuelling in mid-air while continuing its 684-mile journey toward the target. Center:* F/A-18 Hornet *fighters ready to lift off from the* USS Saratoga. *Bottom: two British* Westland Sea King *helicopters have just taken off from their carrier for a surveillance mission.*

The *Gulf War* 1991

408-409

Left, the American battleship USS Missouri, *a "veteran" of the Second World War, bombards Iraqi positions in Kuwait with its 406 mm cannons; the pictures to the right illustrate the launch of a* Tomahawk *missile from a destroyer (top) and the firing of a volley from the battleship* USS Wisconsin *(bottom) during the first phase of Operation Desert Storm.*

1991

410-411

On these two pages scenes from the final and bloodiest phase of the Gulf War. This began on February 24, 1991 when Allied tanks, supported by bombers and helicopters, broke through the Kuwaiti border, 'till then controlled by Iraqi troops. Within a few days, the Allied coalition killed 100,000 enemy soldiers and took 90,000 prisoners. During this operation, the Allies tested high-tech munitions, including bullets with depleted uranium, with devastating effects.

The *Gulf War*

1991

1991

412-413
Dramatic pictures of the mass killing of Iraqi soldiers during the final offensive, begun on February 24, 1991. Top left: Two Marines involved in the battle of Khafji. Bottom: a Saudi soldier in the anti-Iraqi coalition looks at the remains of an Iraqi tank driver, who died in his burning vehicle. Right: Iraqi soldiers taken prisoners by US Marines on the road to Kuwait City, liberated on February 26, after only two days of fighting.

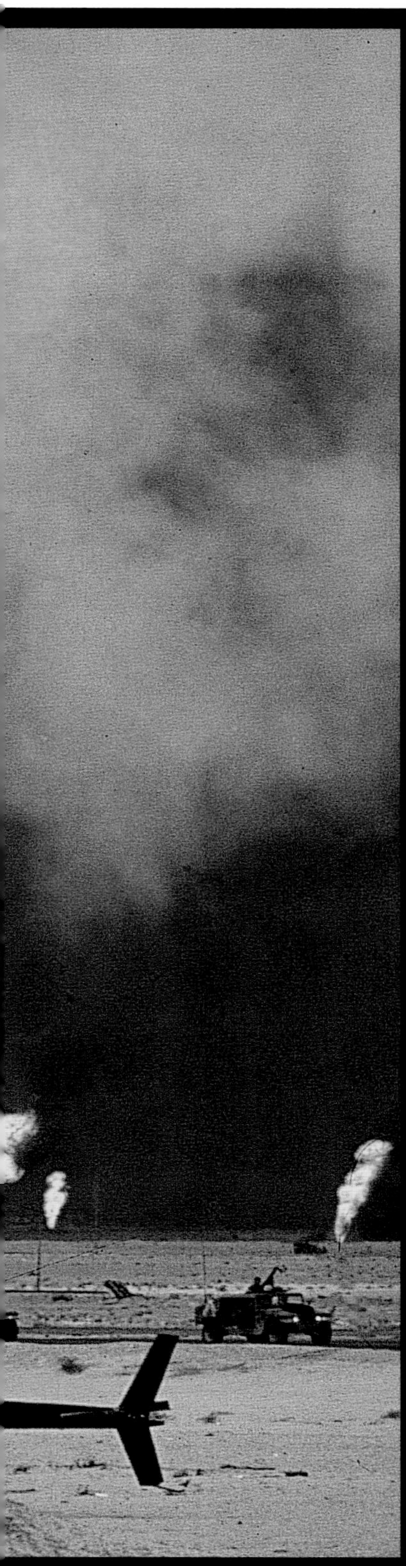

1991 The Gulf War

414-415

Left, after the allied attack on Iraqi occupied Kuwait, military bases were established near the Iraqi border in just a few hours; the picture at the left shows an extemporaneous heliport in which American assault helicopters are defended by a ring of armored vehicles.To the right, we see two pictures of the apocalyptic atmosphere following the Iraqi retreat from Kuwait. The flight of Baghdad's troops towards the north assumed strongly dramatic overtones; to Western observers, the road to Basra appears obstructed by transport vehicles of every type, destroyed by allied aviation or abandoned, while the air was contaminated by the smoke of oil wells set on fire on the orders of the Iraqi leader.

416-417
The war is over. Bottom: American General Norman Schwarzkopf, commander of allied forces in the gulf, is surrounded by his celebrating, victorious men. Schwarzkopf, who is much loved by his soldiers, planned and won a lightening-war, taking care to limit his own losses as much as possible. The numbers tell the whole story: Iraqi tanks destroyed 3,700, allied 2; Iraqi ships sunk 73, allied none. The photograph in the center shows part of the enormous mass of Iraqi prisoners (175.000) that fell into allied hands. Top right: Saddam Hussein's soldiers, defeated, resigned, ragged and tired, surrender to coalition troops. Bottom: Arab allies sing praises of the victory in a ghostly light. Alongside the Euro-Americans, thousands of soldiers from the Arab League fought against Saddam Hussein, who had hoped in vain to unleash a "Jihad" or "Holy War" against the West.

418-419
In these pages, two pictures stand out for their harshness: they well testify the useless ferocity of war and the capacity for destruction of today's war apparatus.

420-421
These dramatic Gulf War pictures document the consequences of Saddam Hussein's criminal decision to set fire to Kuwaiti oil wells (January 23, 1991) and to order the discharge of two milliards of litres of crude oil from Mina al-Hamadi wells into the sea (January 25, 1991). This caused a gigantic oil carpet to spread into the Persian Gulf, resulting in an ecological disaster without precedent. The image of oil-drenched cormorants remains a powerful reminder of the event.

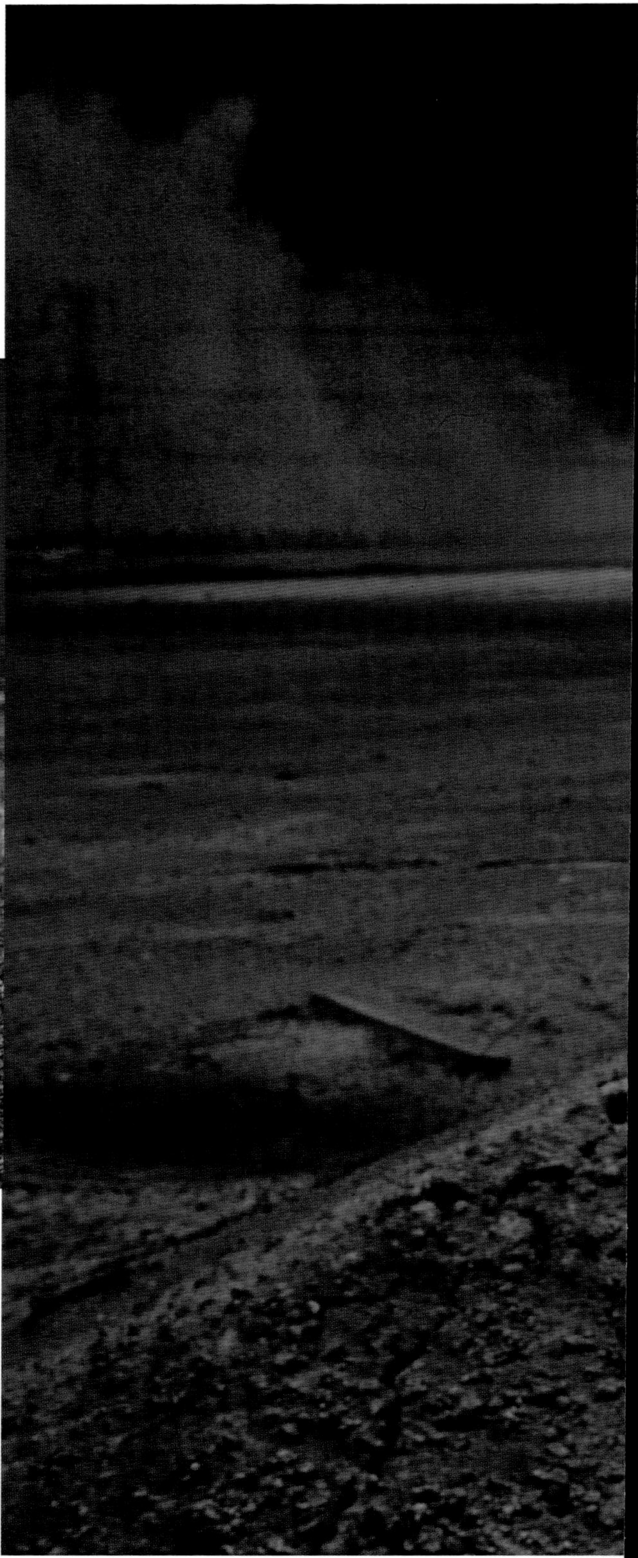

1991

1991

1991
1994

THE

WAR AT THE HORN OF AFRICA

THE FORMER ITALIAN COLONIES HAVE ENJOYED NO PEACE IN THE SECOND HALF OF THE 20TH CENTURY.

In 1952, Ethiopia finally gained a coastal outlet by annexing Eritrea. This nation has never accepted Ethiopian domination, as proved by a creeping civil war that is continues to this day.

On December 13, 1960, a young official named Haile Mariam Mengistu, leading a group of conspirators, while emperor Haile Selassie was visiting Brazil, attempted a military coup crushed by the Air Force. On his return, the emperor had 475 men of the imperial guard hanged. Mengistu managed to flee. Eritrea became a continuous source of trouble. There was no break in the guerrilla warfare. Starting in 1962, the emperor responded to the attacks of dissidents with savage suppression. By the early 1970s, Ethiopia's situation was of extreme backwardness. The famine in 1973 killed over 100,000 people in the country and set off a rebellion against the emperor. Mengistu came out of hiding and took up his struggle again, this time with the assistance of Soviet "advisers. "He "deposed" Haile Selassie on September 12, 1973, and imprisoned him. On March 21 of the following year, he proclaimed the country a republic with an openly Communist program. Haile Selassie died at the age of 83 on August 27, 1974, in a small refuge on the hill overlooking Addis Ababa, where the dictator Mengistu had placed him under house arrest. The colonel linked with Moscow became a ruthless dictator and ruled the country untill 1991, when after thirty years of guerrilla fighting, the Eritrean separatist army occupied Asmara (in northern Eritrea) and threatened to advance to Addis Ababa (Ethiopia's capital) and oust Mengistu. He allowed a coalition government to take over while he fled to Kenya, but the guerrilla fighting was to drag on for years. The USSR also supported the government of Siad Barre, the dictator who ruled Somalia, which extends around the Horn of Africa, to the south of Eritrea. In addition, Barre received financial and other aid from the Italian government. In 1991, after the collapse of the USSR and the new Russian state's declaration that it was no longer interested in Africa, civil war escalated between the numerous Somali clans. Siad Barre then lost control of the situation and fled to Kenya. The guerrilla war spread and thousands were killed, forcing the United Nations to intervene in March 1994, when it send an international expeditionary force to the troubled country. While humanity enters the third millennium, Somalia probably is the world region where people suffer the most. There are hunger, floods, and epidemics that kill thousands of children and old people. All power lies in the hands of tribal chiefs. The population is fleeing to Kenya. After over 12 years of civil war, more than one million people have fled the country. About 400,000 Somalis are criss-crossing the country without homes. The World Health Organisation continues to send physicians and emergency helpers with vaccines against polio and cholera into the country. At the end of the 20th century, hell has a name: Somalia.

Ethiopia and Eritrea are heavily involved in a debilitating border war that seems to have no end in sight. Throughout 2000, ferocious fighting continued along the Barentu-to-Mendefera highway and for the conquest of the town of Zalambessa. The fighting caused many hundreds of deaths. Foreign journalists were not allowed into the war zone. Consequent-ly the exact number of victims remained unknown. Local papers-- which have little credibility--reported absurdly high numbers of deaths. Addis Ababa claimed to have killed 60,000 Eritreans in just a few months; Asmara talked of having killed 25,000 Ethiopian soldiers in the same period. Some more reliable estimates are in broad agreement that between the beginning of the conflict (May 1998) and the end of 2000, the two sides have lost a combined total of 50,000 soldiers. While the Ethiopian prime minister Melles Zenawi criticized the USA and Great Britain for not supporting the hypothesis that Ethiopia was the victim of Eritrean aggression, Gebu Maskel, the spokesperson for the Eritrean government, claimed the exact opposite: the aggressors were the Ethiopians.

422

Scenes from the interminable war between Eritrea and Ethiopia. Top and center: Eritrean soldiers in action. Bottom: Ethiopian soldiers in a hideout at Tsorona, on the Eritrean-Ethiopian border.

424
Bodies of Ethiopian soldiers lie next to the burnt-out remains of a tank at Tsorona, 62 miles from Asmara, the Eritrean capital. The picture, taken on March 18, 1999, marks the ninth year of this war without end.

425
More images of war and atrocities in Eritrea: corpses left on the streets and by the enemy positions. The situation is no better in Somalia, the other country at the Horn of Africa. The ferocious civil war between Somali clans and tribes has been going on since 1994. A United Nations force tried in vain to stop this conflict. Famine and violence spread ever more widely.

Horn of Africa 1991-1994

THE

BALKAN WAR

TITO'S DEATH (1980) MARKED THE BEGINNING OF THE DISINTEGRATION OF YUGOSLAVIA. IN REALITY IT HAD NEVER BEEN A TRUE NATION, HAVING BEEN ARTIFICIALLY CREATED AND HELD TOGETHER BY THE COMMUNIST DICTATOR'S POWERFUL PERSONALITY AND THE STRICTNESS OF HIS REGIME.

After Tito's death, the Serbian Communists, led by Slobodan Milosevic, hoped to play a leading role among the ethnic groups that comprised Yugolsavia. However, in spite of all its efforts, which often gave rise to violent clashes, the Communist party was unable to quell the desire for independence in the other states in the federation. One by one, Slovenia, Croatia, Macedonia, and Bosnia-Herzegovina left the "Federal Republic" to establish their own sovereign, independent nations. Milosevic was left with Montenegro, which he duly integrated into the Yugoslav Federation, proclaimed in March 1992. From Belgrade, Milosevic was able to do very little to Slovenia or Croatia.

He did, however, finance and arm the Bosnian Serbs, thus contributing to the outbreak of a bitter three-year ethnic war that from 1992 to 1995 tore Sarajevo (the Bosnian capital) and other Bosnian cities apart. It was a tragic settling of old accounts between the Orthodox Christian Serbian population and the mainly Muslim Bosnians. The religious factor was by no means insignificant, indeed, perhaps at a subconscious level it was crucial, at least with regard to the ferocity of the conflict.

In August 1995, NATO finally decided to put an end to the slaughter and bombed the Serbo-Bosnian armies led by General Ratko Mladic and his political ally, Radovan Karadzic. Concurrently, the International War Crimes Tribunal, based in The Hague, issued warrants for the arrest of the two. To date, it has not proved possible to make the arrests. However, the Yugoslav crisis marks the first time in the late 20th century that NATO launched a military intervention on its own initiative, sending its own expeditionary force (the KFOR) into a war zone.

Having rediscovered nationalism and realizing that it could easily replace a failing Communism as an instrument of mass control, Milosevic decided to continue with the strategy he had already adopted in Bosnia. Instead of using the clenched left fist, demonstrating workers and students could just as easily raise their right hands in the traditional Christian and monarchist salute, their thumbs, index and middle fingers extended. They were probably unaware that the three extended fingers stood for God, Country and King. For Milosevic it was power that counted; he was prepared to use it to create an enemy (the Bosnian Muslims) to serve up to his Serbian compatriots. Having finished with Bosnia, Milosovevic turned to Kosovo. For centuries, this buffer region between Serbia and Albania had been a great enclave of the Orthodox faith (the sacred city of Polje testifies to this) and a region of endless skirmishes between the Serbs and their historic Turkish Muslim aggressors. During the 20th century, Kosovo increasingly became an area into which illegal immigrants from Albania arrived, looking for work and food. Peaceful and obedient to Belgrade's orders until Tito's death and the subsequent slow collapse of the Yugoslav Federal Republic, the Kosovars of Albanian origin became restless, demanding independence and equal rights with the Bosnians and Macedonians. This gave rise to a bitter clash, with ever more violent episodes, and the mass arrests of opponents of Milosevic's government, with trials, and sentences. Finally a state of latent civil war

426
Sarajevo 1992: A Bosnian girl, holding the remains of the Serbian grenade that destroyed her house. This is only the beginning of a ferocious ethnic and religious war, which until 1999 ripped apart the multi-state nation known as Yugoslavia.

1992
2000

broke out between the Yugoslav army and the "Kosovo Liberation Army" (the UCK), made up of Kosovars of Albanian ethnic origin.

On January 15, 1999, the situation suddenly deteriorated. The bodies of 45 people of Albanian extraction were found in Rakak, southern Kosovo. William Walker, the American ambassador who headed OSCE (Organization for Security and Cooperation in Europe), was there at the time. He asked the War Crimes Tribunal in The Hague, which was already looking for the Bosnian Serbs Mladic and Karadzic, to send its inspectors to Kosovo. Milosevic's reaction was harsh. On January 18, Serbian troops started bombing some rebel Kosovar villages, and the Belgrade government issued a decree expelling the OSCE observers and ordering the border police to prevent the inspectors from the Hague from entering the country. The Yugoslav president then refused to meet General Wesley Clark, commander in chief of the NATO forces, as he suspected the general's sympathies already lay with the UCK. Belgrade saw the situation as one in which the major powers, led by the United States, were blatantly meddling in their domestic affairs--those of a sovereign nation.

Belgrade refused to yield. Perhaps Milosevic's advisers were under the illusion that the leaders of the impressive US arms industry (which represented 40 percent of US industrial production) would reflect carefully before giving the go-ahead for testing the new aircraft, targeting mechanisms and helicopters in an area such as the Balkans. The slogan in Belgrade in those days was "When Serbia goes to war the whole world does." This was a clear reference to the events in 1914. But in 1999 Russia was no longer able to support and sustain the policy of supporting its traditional ally, Serbia. On January 29, at the end of an armed struggle between Yugoslav and UCK units, 24 UCK separatists were killed. The event gave the President Clinton; a pretext for issuing Serbia with an ultimatum: an agreement had to be reached to ensure peace in Kosovo, if not military action would be taken. In the past, such a threat would have definitely risked starting another world war. But not in 1999, with the United States as the world's unrivalled superpower, and with NATO largely dependent on the American armaments industry for its aircraft and weapons systems. In addition, most Europeans nations had center-leftist leaders (Schröder in Germany, D'Alema in Italy, Jospin in France, Blair in the UK). These nations had strong economic and financial ties to the United States, and were also ideologically close to its Democratic Party. As self-proclaimed mediator between the two sides, NATO followed Clinton's ultimatum with an official invitation to Milosevic to take part in a peace conference. This was held at the Château de Rambouillet (near Paris), and had the aim of giving Kosovo some kind of autonomy that would respect both the Serbian and the Albanian ethnic groups. On January 30 the ambassadors of NATO's 16 member nations, invested the secretary general, Javier Solana, with the authority to order air attacks on Yugoslav territory in the event that no peace agreement was reached at Rambouillet. This was clearly another provocative measure which might have persuaded a more realistic and aware president than Milosevic to be more prudent and come to some agreement.

Negotiations began on April 6. The UCK called for a referendum in Kosovo, but the Yugoslav delegation rejected the proposal saying that hundreds of thousands of illegal immigrants had crossed the Albanian border and entered Kosovo, putting the Albanians and Muslims in the majority. The Yugoslavs also imposed a condition, which was unacceptable to the UCK, that the territorial integrity of the Yugoslav Federation had to be maintained. In the meantime, 20,000 Albanians had gathered in front of Château de Rambouillet, demanding independence for Kosovo. Questions arose as to who had paid for their journey and accommodation Some journalists suspected the American armaments industry, but no proof was found. The meetings had already started when Madeleine Albright, the American secretary of state, turned up at Rambouillet. The two delegations met for the first time in her presence. But their positions were irreconcilable: the UCK, wanting an independent Kosovo, insisted on a referendum, knowing it could count on the majority of the population; the Serbs, knowing they would lose, were unwilling to authorize one. In addition they did not want to accept NATO troops on Federation territory. In the meantime, the international press continued to publish accounts of Serbian massacres of Muslim Kosovars. The initial negotiations thus ended in failure. Further sessions were postponed until March 15, while at the international level tensions rose, and the media in America and the NATO countries prepared the public at large for the inevitability of war. When negotiations resumed the two sides had adopted even more entrenched positions. On March 20. As the Rambouillet farce came to an end, the Serbian army launched a series of attacks on UCK positions throughout Kosovo. President Clinton immediately called a meeting of the UN Security Council, and on March, 22 the American special envoy, Richard Holbrooke, flew to Belgrade in one last futile attempt to avert war.

On March 23 Javier Solana decided to delay no longer and gave orders to the NATO troops to attack the following day. A few hours later, in a climate of high tension, the Belgrade government declared a state of emergency and general mobilization, while Montenegro distanced itself from Serbia. Yevgeny Primakov, premier of the RFSR, who was on his way to Washington for a meeting with Clinton, ordered his plane to turn around and go back to Moscow. It was clear that the American position, which was decisive within NATO, could not be influenced. On 24 March, 1999, at 19.20 local time, the first Cruise missiles were launched by squadrons of American B-52s from bases in Italy and from American battleships cruising in the Adriatic. The targets were the ten principal cities of the Yugoslav Federation, including Belgrade, Pristina and Podgorica, therefore sparing neither Kosovo nor Montenegro. Airports, radar stations, military barracks and telecommunications masts were targeted. Among the victims were many civilians; the timing of the air strike had coincided with the end of the working day when people were on their way home. When informed of the attack, President Yeltsin telephoned President Clinton and had a 20-minute conversation with him. But Yeltsin could do little apart from make an official protest since the two leaders had previously made clear their respective positions. All Yeltsin could do in a face-saving exercise was to request that the UN Security Council be convened as a matter of urgency and to withdraw the Russian representatives from the OSCE delegation in Yugoslavia. The next day, March 25, the fury of the attack was redoubled. The NATO forces held clear technical and military superiority. Every attempt the Serbian MiGs made to counterattack was thwarted almost before it started, and any planes that managed to take off from the few military airports still functioning were ruthlessly shot down. Safe in an underground bunker, the Belgrade government pathetically announced that it was breaking off of diplomatic relations with the United States, France, Great Britain and Germany, but curiously did not mention Italy, where the B-52s took off from the NATO air-base at Aviano, in the Veneto. Yugoslavia's imports of raw materials and foodstuffs from neighbouring Italy were too important for Yugoslavia's survival for it to antagonize Italy.

The smallest spark of common sense and a realistic view of the situation should have induced Milosevic to cede. In fact the opposite occurred. While the Belgrade government exhorted the army and the population to resist, NATO propaganda continued to disseminate the news of terrible massacres of blameless civilians carried out in Kosovo by Serbian soldiers. But at the end of the conflict almost no trace was to be found of these mass killings. What did prove to be true was that most of Kosovo's ethnic Albanians had fled into Albania, fearing violent Serbian reprisals if they remained in Kosovo. The Belgrade government proposed a cease-fire at about the time of the Orthodox feast of Easter but President Clinton refused. Given the battered state of the Yugoslav infrastructure and the mounting human and economic losses, Milosevic had no realistic option but to surrender. Pope John Paul II had even sent his foreign minister, Jean Louis Tauran, to Belgrade, to urge Milosevic to surrender, but to no avail. On April 2, two days before Easter, NATO launched an air attack on the parliament and government buildings in Belgrade. The ministry of domestic affairs and the armed forces' GHQ were hit. No minister or general was among the victims; all were safe were in underground bunkers or away in their country houses. The April 2 strike was merely the forerunner of a series of new and violent raids that did not spare the civilian population. In the following days bridges, tunnels and railway lines were destroyed; on April 12 a missile hit the Belgrade-Salonika train at Bistrica, killing dozens of civilians. A few days later two trains packed with Kosovar Albanian refugees were destroyed at Djacovica in Kosovo, causing 75 deaths.

These incidents were followed by expressions of NATO's "apologies" and "deep regrets." The new missiles' electronic targeting systems had clearly mistaken the two trains for military transports. War, as ever, was proving to be the opportunity to try out, test and fine-tune the efficiency of new military technology, in this case the e-weapons of an e-war, in which e=electronic. Unfortunately, in another rendering, e=error. When the town of Aleksinac was hit (60 houses destroyed and dozens of people killed), the military command talked in terms of an "error." The May 8 1999 bombing of the Chinese Embassy in Belgrade (four killed, including two journalists, and 20 wounded) was also described as an "error." It can be argued that the only people who believed this were the Chinese themselves; they would otherwise have been forced to take steps they did not want to take and for which they were not prepared. It can also be argued that the bombing of the Chinese embassy was a way of dissuading Beijing from offering any assistance to the overwhelmed Serbs.

In April, Cruise missiles targeted and hit the headquarters of Serbian TV "because it was an instrument of propaganda and repression." At this point Boris Yeltsin suddenly woke up and became threatening: "Be careful, Americans! You are risking a third world war!" Fortunately, however, in the Russian Federal Republic and in America and Europe, his words were interpreted as the consequence of one of his alcoholic-gastronomic binges. On April 13 General Wesley Clark asked for a further 300 bomber aircraft, and on April 16 the United States called up 33,000 reserves in preparation for a possible land campaign in Serbia. On the 19th, Clinton and Yeltsin had an hour-long telephone conversation, but nothing was achieved. At military level the NATO allies were increasing the pressure. While the first Apaches (a new American combat helicopter) landed in Tirana, Albania's capital city, other important events were occurring. On the Kosovo-Albanian border, the first battle between Serbian and Albanian regular army troops was being fought. The battle lasted 7 hours, with heavy casualties on both sides. For the first time, there was a real risk of the conflict spreading. In response, NATO applied the oil embargo authorized by the European Union, and intensified the bombing of Belgrade. Buildings were destroyed in the following order: first, the Belgrade skyscraper that housed Milosevic's political party HQ, then the premier's family home (empty at the time of the attack), then the six-story Serbian radio and television building (then broadcasting a interview with Milosevic). In this particular hit, 31 journalists and technicians were killed and 20 wounded. On April 23 and 24, NATO air strikes destroyed all the bridges over the Danube and all Serbia's power stations. Also destroyed were Serbia's water and electricity distribution systems. Finally, because of the bombing of the Danube rail and road bridges, Serbia was effectively divided into two separate regions with no easy access between them. Serbia's determination now showed the first signs of weakening and having leadership problems: Serbia had a premier stubborn enough to allow his people to be massacred without having any possibility of this policy being vindicated.

The Serbian government agreed to allow the International Red Cross into Kosovo to verify that no mass massacres of ethnic Albanians had occurred, in contrast to widespread television and press accounts. Simultaneously, the deputy premier, Draskovic, was even considering allowing NATO forces into Kosovo, if accompanied by UN soldiers. Draskovic, however, had gone too far; Milosevic forced him to resign. Milo Djuganovic, the Montenegrin president, then decided to distance himself from the despotic Serb. He threatened secession if Milosevic did not end his futile resistance to NATO demands. In the meantime, the NATO airforce's macabre "errors" continued to occur. In southern Serbia, the village of Surdulica was destroyed, with 20 children killed in their school. A bus on the Pristina-Nis road was hit and burned out (47 dead), as was another in Pec, Kosovo (17 dead); the hospital in Nis was bombed (15 killed and 70 wounded); a refugee camp was bombed in Koriza (southern Kosovo), with 87 dead. The prison in Istok, Kosovo, was hit; of the prisoners and staff, 19 were killed and 10 wounded. On May 10, two days after the bombing of the Chinese Embassy in Belgrade, and following demonstrations in front of the American Embassy in Beijing, Clinton officially apologized to the Chinese government.

The embassy bombing probably helped to end the Serbian-NATO conflict. The first meetings between Kofi Annan (the UN Secretary-General) and Viktor Chernomyrdin (Yeltsin's special envoy) took place at about this time. The agenda was to discuss bringing a UN peace force into the war zone. Finally on May 19, after an eight-hour meeting with Milosevic, Chernomyrdin (clearly, the mediator in this war) managed to obtain the Serbian leader's agreement to a political solution to the conflict. KFOR--a NATO peace force under UN control--was then formed. A total of 60,000 men, including Russian contingents, was to be deployed in Kosovo. The Serbs would withdraw in exchange for an end to the raids on Yugoslavia, and KFOR would oversee the peaceful return of the refugees of Albanian extraction (over one million people) to their homes and land. The agreement for the withdrawal of Serbian troops from Kosovo and KFOR's entry into the war-torn region was signed on June 9, 1999, in Kumanovo, Macedonia. It followed 79 days of bombing that had caused appalling devastation and an unknown number of deaths. The next day, Javier Solana called a halt to the raids on Serbia. One small incident marred the KFOR occupation of Kosovo. The Russian contingent stationed in Bosnia quickly crossed Serbian territory and was the first to enter Pristina on June 11, to the great irritation of Javier Solana and General Wesley Clarke. The refusal of General Jackson (UK) to stop the Russian contingent's 10 tanks and 30 trucks cost him his post. In retrospect this incident, involving as it did, the representatives of the world superpower and the successor of what had in the past been its greatest rival, seems rather puerile.

The war in the Balkans (the last war of the 20th century, also marked the end of Milosevic's long dictatorship in what was left of the Federal Republic of Yugoslavia. On August 19, 1999, 200,000 Serbs marched through the streets of Belgrade shouting "Get out, Slobo!" This was just the beginning of a power struggle that after much maneuvering behind the scenes, led to the defeat of Milosevic's party in the autumn of 2000, the rise of the new leader, Vojislav Kostunica, and Montenegro's continuing moves toward independence. Though here and there in the Kosovo countryside, KFOR troops uncovered the hastily buried bodies of both Serbian and Albanian war victims, they have yet to find proof of the reported mass slaughters underpinning NATO's intervention. The Hague Tribunal issued new warrants of arrest for war crimes in the names of Milosevic, his generals and ministers.

431

March 30, 1999. A woman weeps in the ruins of house in Montenegro. At 17.00 on March 24, B-52 bombers launched the first waves of Cruise missiles on Belgrade, Pristina, and eight other cities in Serbia, Kosovo, and Montenegro. Bombers flying from airbases in Italy and US ships in the Adriatic launched almost daily missile attacks on these regions.

432-433
In 1991, the first period of the Balkan civil war, the newly formed Croatian military fought to defend Croatian independence against Belgrade's federal troops, fighting in vain to preserve Yugoslav unity under Milosevic. On the left: scenes of destruction in Croatia (top, Yukovar; bottom, Lipik). Right: a view of Nustar after fighting between Serbs and Croats.

434-435

The Croat-Serb civil war. Left: Croatian anti-terrorist forces. In the center: and top right: Bjelovar (Croatia), two soldiers firing a machine gun in response to a Serb air attack. Bottom: a "federal" (Serb) soldier killed during the successful Croat attack on the barracks in Vojnovic. In 1992, after Croatia's secession from the Yugoslav Federation of Croatia, Slovenia, Macedonia, and Bosnia-Herzegovina (which began disintegrating after Tito's death), Milosevic proclaimed a new Yugoslav Federation, composed of Serbia and Montenegro, the two remaining states.

The Balkan War 1992-2000

436-437

A changing scenario. Top left and bottom: Serb soldiers in action with artillery and tanks against KLA (the clandestine Kosovo Liberation Army) positions. Center: The Yugoslav conflict becomes internationalized with the deployment of UN-blue helmets in the Bosnian civil war and US and Russian tanks in Bosnia in 1997--the first US-Russian military collaboration since World War II. Right: a British Challenger *tank near Skopje (Macedonia) during training exercises.*

SFOR 946

439
The dramatic cruelty of the war recently fought in the Balkans: the lacerated bodies of a peasant family killed during a NATO bombardment in Djakovica
lie in the street beside the cart on which they had loaded their meager belongings.

440-441
Ethnic Albanians fleeing Kosovo for Albania and independent Macedonia, to escape the indiscriminate violence of the bombing.

442-443
Kosovar refugees are housed and fed in camps set up by the International Red Cross on the Albanian-Macedonian border.

438
More effects of the NATO bombing of Yugoslavia. Top and bottom: The Ministry of the Interior and the Police HQ complex is on fire. Right: Serb anti-aircraft fire during a missile attack on April 13, 1999.

1992

2000

1992
2000

AFGHANISTAN

GUERRILLA WARFARE WITHOUT END

AFGHANISTAN – THE SOURCE OF 90 PERCENT OF THE WORLD'S HEROINE, GROWN THROUGH THE NATURAL CULTIVATION OF OPIUM – IS A "BUFFER STATE" THAT HAS ALWAYS BEEN AT THE CENTER OF INVASIONS, WARS AND BATTLES.

Bordered by Pakistan and Iraq to the south, southeast and southwest, and by Turkmenistan, Uzbekistan and Tajikistan to the north, Afghanistan was occupied for ten years, between 1979 and 1989, by Soviet troops against whom the *mujahideen* unleashed a bloody guerrilla war. This war compelled the second world power, at the time on the brink of political collapse (the so-called "implosion" after the fall of the Berlin Wall), to leave Afghanistan on February 15, 1989. A long, bloody civil war followed between the Tajik and Uzbek ethnic groups, and the Taliban (students of the Qur'an) movement emerged, which originated in the Sunni schools in Pakistan. Their spiritual leader was and still is Mullah Omar, who has close ties to Osama bin Laden's terrorist group al-Qaeda. His men, who fought fiercely against the government forces, conquered Herat in 1995, Kandahar in '96 and finally, the capital, Kabul in '98, thereby forcing President Hamid Karzai to flee.

They then instituted throughout the country the *sharìa*, the Islamic law code that provided (and continues to provide) for, among other things, the prohibition of listening to music, of projecting and watching films, and the obligation for women to wear the *burqa*; in addition women were not allowed to work or study. In 2001 in the mountains of Bamyan, began the systematic destruction of the ancient, enormous statues of Buddha, one of the wonders of the world.

Since 1997, Osama bin Laden, having resided in Saudi Arabia after the retreat of the USSR, returned to Afghanistan for the express purpose of organizing anti-American training camps. The first terrorist acts were carried out on August 7, 1998, when al-Qaeda members attacked the United States' embassies in Kenya and Tanzania, killing dozens of people. The American reaction was not long in coming, with United States airplanes bombing al-Qaeda training camps near the border of Pakistan. It was after this attack that Osama bin Laden prepared the terrible response occurring on September 11, 2001 in which the assaults on New York and Washington, D.C. resulted in both the destruction of the World Trade Center, leaving 2950 dead, and damage to the Pentagon when a plane, one of four hijacked by terrorists, piloted by Mohamed Atta, crashing into the building. The date chosen for the attack of the Twin Towers, the symbol of the modern West, was significant: September 11 was the anniversary of the 1683 expulsion of Muslims from Vienna at the hands of Prince Eugène of Savoy's men, who were acting under orders from Jan Sobieski, the king of Poland.

444
The north tower of the World Trade Center photographed 30 seconds before its catastrophic collapse on September 11, 2001. This al-Qaeda terrorist attack claimed almost 3000 victims.

445
An American soldier watches the border between Afghanistan and Pakistan, a vast and unexplored region where al-Qaeda volunteers hide.

AFGHANISTAN GUERRILLA WARFARE WITHOUT END
2003

The immediate response of the United States to the worst terrorist attack in history was the launching of air strikes against the Afghanistan Taliban, who were accused of harboring the Saudi sheik. The raids began on October 7, 2001, as Afghan troops from the anti-Taliban "Northern Alliance," who were armed and instructed by American agents, simultaneously advanced on Kabul, which fell into their hands on November 17, and thereby allowed Hamid Karzai's return to power. At the beginning of December it was Kandahar's turn; meanwhile, the Taliban took cover in the mountains of the southeast, protected, aided, and financed by Pakistan, a nation against which it was not advisable for the Americans to intervene militarily since – as is well known – they have atomic weapons. At that point, a coalition formed by NATO entered into action and engaged in heavy fighting against bands of Taliban who attempted to descend from the mountains. Hamid Karzai launched continual accusations against the government of Islamabad, which was reputedly responsible for financing, and in any case of giving free rein to Osama bin Laden and Mullah Omar's terrorists along its borders. During a press conference, the CIA Director John Negroponte also accused Pakistan of aiding and sheltering the head of al-Qaeda, but this accusation was never pursued for the reasons mentioned above. Moreover the border between Pakistan and Afghanistan is over 1490 miles (2400 km) long: an area too large to be kept under control.

Among the most combative Taliban exponents of that period, and today as well, is Gulbuddin Hekmatyar, the former leader of the *mujahideen*, who was previously a threat to the Russians, and is now one to the Americans. Like Mullah Omar, Gulbuddin Hekmatyar is a member of the Pashtun ethnic group, which has for decades been one of the most powerful groups in Afghanistan. Karzai himself is also Pashtun, but he is considered to be a traitor by his kinsmen, and therefore requires close protective surveillance by American mercenaries.

The state of perennial military alert that characterizes Afghanistan has created for its population severe survival issues, which include a scarcity of potable water and an agricultural crisis resulting primarily from the danger of land mines that, over the years, American forces have placed throughout the area, and which result in the mutilation and death of elderly and children every day. An area of Afghanistan completely under Taliban control is Waziristan, which runs along the Pakistan border and is impenetrable by NATO troops; thousands of militant Muslims from all of the Arab world arrive here to enlist with al-Qaeda in an anti-Western and anti-infidel capacity. While the American and British forces, 27,000 and 6000 strong respectively, have their base in Kandahar, NATO has sent 20,000 troops to Afghanistan for the alleged purpose of "reconstruction and aid," but, in reality, for fighting together with the British and American troops to counter the terrorist actions of the Taliban; the following examples, in addition to the continual capturing of Western hostages, should suffice to convey the full magnitude of these actions: 50 percent of the schools have been burned down, the chiefs of police have been systematically assassinated, the imams (local spiritual leaders) are decapitated if they are too "liberal" with women, and women are stoned and have their throats cut if they study not only in a school but also in their own homes.

There is a total of 27 NATO countries taking part in the International Security Assistance Force in Afghanistan. Among these, the countries most involved are Germany, Canada, Holland, Italy, Australia, and France. Switzerland is also present with a minimal contingent of a few volunteers. Meanwhile, from the time of the war with the USSR until today, Afghanistan has become a graveyard for one million people. The current head of the militants is Mullah Dadullh, who has announced that he has 6000 volunteers ready to sacrifice their own lives for the jihad, or holy war.

In June of 2007, President Hamid Karzai, pushed by the continuous and rapid growth of innocent victims in the villages as well as the cities, launched a harsh accusation against "indiscriminate military operations" by NATO that kill "a disproportionate number of innocent victims." In fact, in a period of only 10 days – this was the event which convinced Karzai to make his appeal – 90 civilians, including women and children, lost their lives "due to an extreme lack of coordination among Afghani forces, NATO forces and the international coalition led by the Americans."

447
The photo shows a destroyed street in central Kabul after American forces launched raids in 2001 to eliminate the Taliban emplacements linked to al-Qaeda and to put President Hamid Karzai back in power.

448
The photo (top) shows an American observation point at Gardez. An American soldier (bottom) checks a shepherds' camp in the mountains of Afghanistan.

Afghanistan 2004

448-449, 450 and 451
Even a boy's pocket can hide a bomb. This photo exemplifies the tensions that have characterized the political-military situation in Afghanistan for years, well illustrated in the photos on the following two pages.

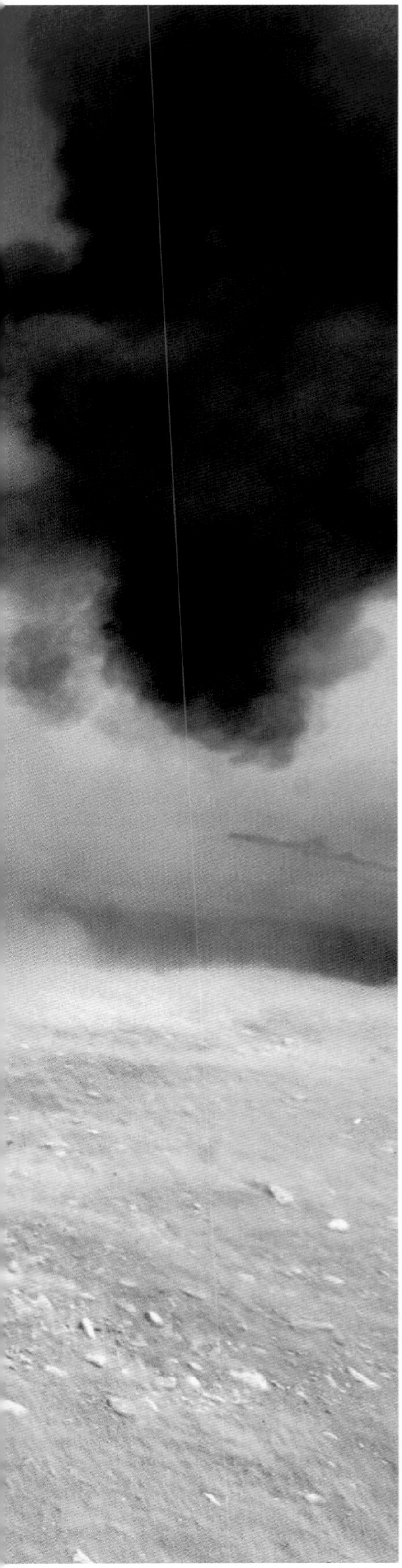

452-453

Canadian artillerymen from the NATO mission open fire on April 18, 2007 against zones occupied by the Taliban in Helmand province. Bin Laden's men can also count on the support of fundamentalists who are active within the Pakistan borders.

453

Two soldiers from the British contingent in Afghanistan (above) are shown in action. Below, American soldiers are intent on placing mines in the territory controlled by al- Qaeda.

Afghanistan 2007

454-455

British soldiers from the 2nd Royal Fusiliers Regiment move inside a destroyed market after a battle between Taliban and NATO troops, which ended on April 22, 2007 in Sangin, in Helmand province.

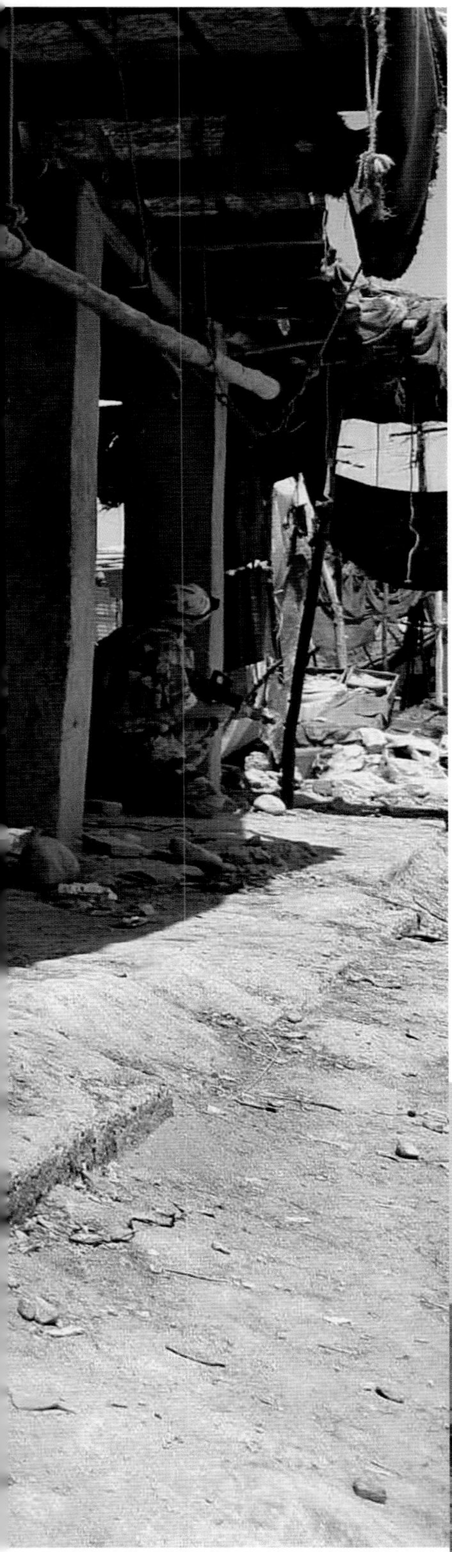

455
American soldiers (top) shown in action in the village of Loy Kariz, just after the Taliban left. Center, a British soldier photographed during the operation in Sangin (April, 2007).

456 and 457
While the conflicts intensify along the borders, in cities such as Islamabad groups of fundamentalist students continue to sing the praises of Osama bin Laden.

ASAMA BIN LADIN
OSAMA
OUR HERROW
Coca-Cola

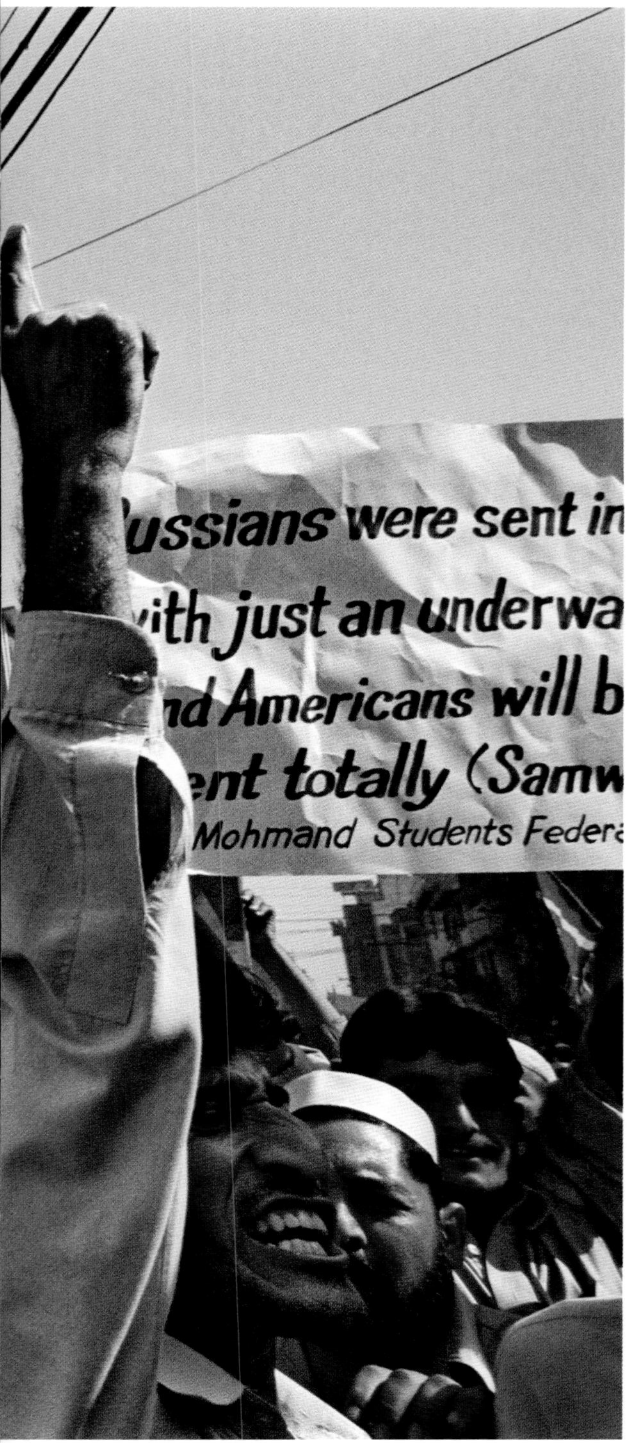
ussians were sent i
ith just an underwa
nd Americans will b
ent totally (Samw
Mohmand Students Federa

AL-Jazeera
Exclusive
خاص
بالجزيرة

2001

HQ/II

THE SECOND

GULF WAR

AND THE END OF SADDAM HUSSEIN

ON FEBRUARY 27, 1991 THE FIRST GULF WAR BETWEEN THE UNITED STATES AND IRAQ CAME TO AN END WITH THE LIBERATION OF KUWAIT AND THE REINSTATEMENT OF THE EMIR.

However, the embargo the UN imposed on Iraq resulted in thousands of victims, especially children, who were left without medicine. Saddam Hussein's reaction consisted of hindering the disarmament inspections until, in October of 1998, American President Bill Clinton launched operation "Desert Fox" with the intent of neutralizing factories and storage facilities for the weapons of mass destruction that Hussein Saddam was accused of possessing and developing. The campaign bore the motto "Shock and Awe." The premise consisted of a sort of media war between "embedded" American information providers and the aggressive Muslim television station al-Jazeera, which transmitted from Qatar. To compete with this station, a group of Saudi, Kuwaiti and Lebanese billionaires – Saddam Hussein's petroleum-interest rivals – created al-Arabiya, a television station based in Dubai, which quickly failed to meet the expectations of the "editors," thereby irritating the Americans. In reality, in the Muslim world religion comes before everything else, and this fact resulted in an anti-American sentiment that was also apparent on al-Arabiya.

The media war was followed by a real war that was initiated after the new Republican President George W. Bush took office on January 20, 2001, and more importantly, after the September 11 attack on the Twin Towers that same year. After the attack, Washington publicly asserted its belief that Iraq was associated with Osama bin Laden, and openly threatened a preventive war. In the 18 months prior to the commencement of hostilities, diplomatic maneuvers were undertaken to determine the stance of the other world powers, which were divided on their assessment of events, as well as the appropriate measures to take. While France, Russia and China, members of the UN Permanent Security Council, declared that they were opposed to military intervention, Great Britain quickly committed itself to intervening alongside the United States. Italy, Spain, Denmark, Portugal and Holland later aligned themselves with Washington, pledging their support.

The military operation, called "Iraqi Freedom," began at dawn on March 20, 2003; it would be concluded in just three weeks, due to the overwhelming superiority of American military technology when compared to that of an army whose weapons had not been updated since the first Gulf War.

An enormous ground force of approximately 300,000 American and British soldiers entered Iraqi territory from Kuwait, heading for Basra. The following day, March 21, the first bombardment of Baghdad by American planes, which received permission to fly over Turkey, resulted in hundreds of deaths and was accompanied by the harsh declaration of Bush: "No half-measures." Nassiriya was conquered by the Americans on March 22, while Basra would resist for weeks a British siege. Meanwhile, the first American paratroopers leaving from Italy's Vicenza air base landed in the north, and fighting continued to rage in the south where Iraqi resistance, mostly by Sunnis, extremely loyal to Saddam, urged Peter Arnett, the famous CNN journalist from the time of the first Gulf War, to stage a dramatic scene. During an interview on al-Jazeera, he harshly criticized the heads of the American military, accusing

458
An American marine faces the principal mosque of Baghdad. It is a photo symbolic of the conflict that started on March 20, 2003 as the definitive settling of accounts between the United States and Saddam Hussein's regime.

2003

them of incompetence, and was immediately dismissed from his position at NBC. His reaction was to move to Baghdad to live.

In the meantime, dozens of Iraqi civilians, accused of terrorist acts against the Anglo-American forces, were transferred to Guantanamo Bay detention center where they were tortured. This was a highly polemic issue for the now divided American public, many of whom had also begun to consider the accusation that Saddam Hussein had accumulated weapons of mass destruction a fabrication; in fact, such weapons would never be found.

While in Baghdad the slaughter of innocent people by Sunni terrorists multiplied (a bus full of children exploded, the maternity ward of a hospital was attacked) and two girls sacrificed themselves by using trinitrotoluene to blow up a unit of Marines, on April 6 Basra fell and the Americans took control of the Baghdad airport after a battle which left thousands of Iraqis dead. The United States followed with an offensive against the respective television station headquarters and the hotels occupied by journalists. This operation resulted in the deaths of many Arab columnists, as well as a Spanish and a Ukrainian correspondent. Baghdad finally fell on April 9, with the famous scene of the bronze statue of Saddam Hussein knocked down in Paradise Square. While groups of looters commenced a devastating plundering of the city, Jay Gardner, a retired general who was director of a company that specialized in the production of missiles and was a supplier to the Pentagon, was nominated governor. Controversy was inevitable, and after just a month he was replaced by a civilian, Paul Bremer. While a few Iraqi politicians who were enemies of Saddam formed an interim government, American Vice President Cheney took charge of ensuring the restoration of petroleum production. By the end of the year production reached 2.5 million barrels a day, thanks to strict American control of all of the oil fields.

Unfortunately, groups of vandals destroyed the National Museum, which contained artifacts dating back to 7000 BCE, and set fire to the National Library, as the Mongols had done one thousand years before, resulting in an incalculable and unrecoverable loss of cultural heritage. The Shiites, tired of submitting to constant aggression, divided into moderates and radicals, the latter being led by Muqtada al- Sadr and having the motto: "Yes to Islam, no to America, no to Saddam."

On April 15, 2003 Italy sent 2500 military personnel to Baghdad for the purpose of providing humanitarian aid, while law and order were privatized and placed in the hands of companies composed of mercenaries, in effect creating a third occupying force in addition to those of the British and of the Americans. Massacres that were promoted and organized by the terrorist group al-Qaeda, founded by Osama bin Laden and with al-Zarkawi as its head in Iraq, continued without pause in Falluja, Mosul, Najaf, and wherever anti-American protests were held, especially after the declaration by the Donald Rumsfeld, the United States' Secretary of Defense: "We will stay as long as necessary."

On May 1, 2003 George W. Bush descended from a helicopter onto the aircraft carrier USS *Abraham Lincoln* and solemnly declared that the war was over. He also stated that 50,000 soldiers would suffice to guarantee the security of Iraq. By the end of 2004, however, that number had already risen to 150,000. It was at this point that the horrible and interminable series of terrorist attacks began (a typical example: a vehicle loaded with explosives driven by a suicide bomber into a predetermined target) which, on November 12, 2003, involved the Italian contingent in Nassiriya, causing 28 deaths (later the Italians, still in Nassiriya, were the object of other deadly attacks, always at the hands of al-Qaeda militants).

In January 2005, Iraq's first democratic elections were, which were characterized by irreconcilable differences between the Shiites and Sunnis, while Saddam Hussein met his fate. Captured on December 13, 2003 in a hiding place near his native city of Tikrit, the dictator – who rose to power in 1979 and then embroiled the nation in the bloody war against Iran from 1980 to 1988 over dominance of the Persian Gulf – was condemned to death on November 5, 2006 and hanged at 6 am on December 30. He was 69 years old. During these wars he lost two sons in combat: Uday and Qusay. Fifteen days later, Hussein's stepbrother Barzan al-Tikriti was hanged in a horrifying scene in which his head became detached from his body and rolled on the ground.

On April 6, 2007 the *Washington Post* revealed the content of a Pentagon report which concluded that the evidence of a presumed link between the terrorist organization al-Qaeda and the regime of Saddam Hussein was tenuous.

461
Ex-dictator Saddam Hussein laughs in scorn while listening to the prosecution's witnesses during his trial in the spring of 2007, which also included seven of his closest collaborators (in the photo, behind him, Mizer Abdullah al-Rowed and Taha Ramadan). He was later condemned to death.

462
Paul Sakala (top), special infantryman of the American First Infantry Division destroys with fire some mortars recovered to the north of Baghdad. It is November 29, 2004, and the war has been over for some time, but fierce attacks by the Sunnis against the occupying forces continue. In that month alone, the American forces lost 134 soldiers.In a cloud of dust (bottom), American troops lead a group of recently captured Sunni terrorists to a helicopter that will take them to the base in Al Qaim, during an operation called "Steel Curtain," which began in November 2005.

462-463
American Sargent John McDonald, of the 158th Airborne Regiment, lands at the periphery of Baghdad in a cloud of sand. The war has just ended, but reinforcements are needed to counter violent attacks by Sunnis who are extremely loyal to Saddam Hussein.

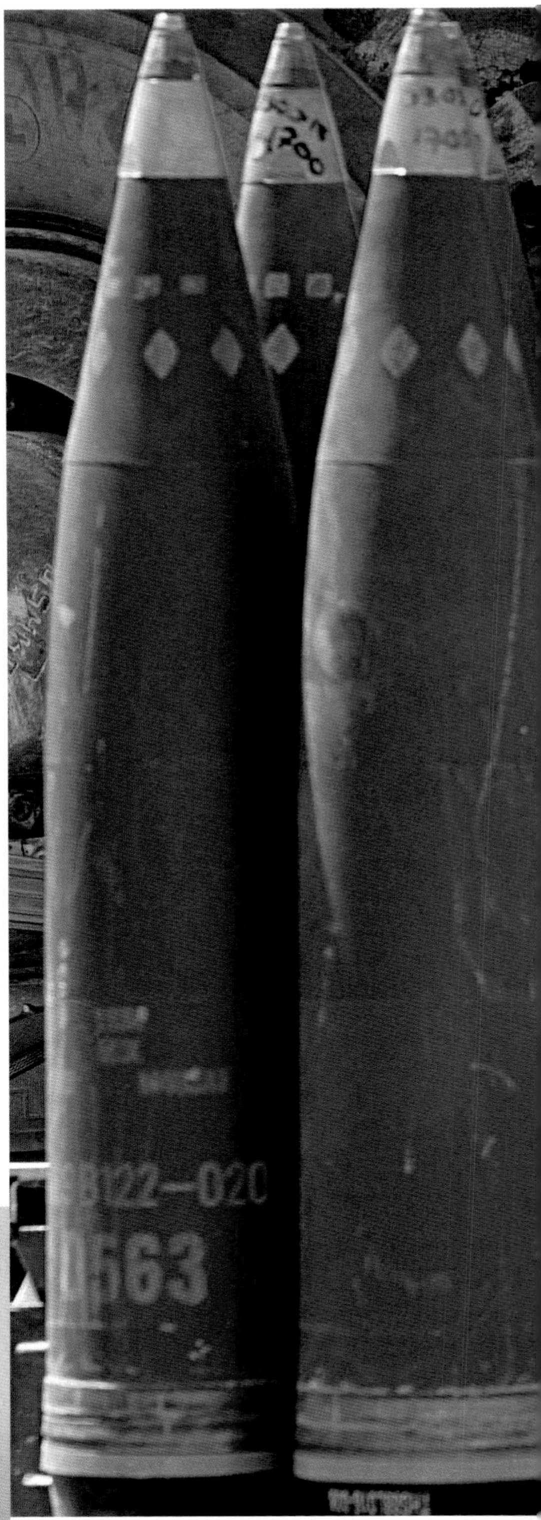

In Karbala (top), five days after the Anglo-American offensive left from Kuwait on March 20, 2003, infantrymen from the American 7th Infantry Regiment are immobilized by an intense sand storm. The storm hindered the advance of tanks (center) from the 64th Armored Regiment. Bottom, the sand storm has died down. It is now the helicopters' turn to continue the offensive and occupy the country.

2003

464-465

A young artilleryman dozes off next to some 155-mm projectiles destined to clear the way for the Marines.

466

This photo shows the horrifying effect of an American air bombardment in the center of Baghdad on March 31, 2003, eleven days after the operation began.

467

This scene, a year after the capture of Baghdad, has been immortalized: a group of rescuers attempts to carry an elderly man to safety amidst the rubble of a building destroyed by a "suicide" truck that was filled with trinitrotoluene and driven by Sunni terrorists.

468-469
Baghdad, April 10, 2003. The capital fell the day before, and a passerby throws a rock at a huge poster of Saddam Hussein, which someone had already set on fire.

469
Just after the news of Saddam Hussein's surrender and flight, the Iraqi people's rage exploded (top) and the work of pulling down the statue of the dictator began. The crowd praises the Americans (bottom) and shakes hands with Sergeant Richard Heglund, of Wilmington, Delaware, with the 101st Airborne Division.

Baghdad

IRAQ
On Patrol in Najaf

470 and 471
These images captured by photographers from the Associated Press won the Pulitzer Prize for best photos of the Iraq conflict. To the left, two American infantrymen seek shelter from enemy gunfire in Najaf. To the right, a marine from the First Division advances, with a toy dressed in uniform hanging from his backpack.

472
These two dramatic scenes are from the terrorist attack launched by the Sunnis against the Marine base in Falluja on November 15, 2004.

472-473
This image, in contrast, is from the battle for the capture of Baghdad – honoring a fallen American.

474-475
The sorrow of two fellow soldiers at the death of Gregory Huxley, 19 years old, from Forest Port, New York, killed in combat on August 6, 2003, three days before the fall of Baghdad.

Baghdad

476
Operation "Phantom Fury" was initiated to drive the terrorists loyal to Saddam Hussein from their hiding places in the southern section of Baghdad (top). Many Americans have lost their lives during such operations because of mines laid by the Iraqis. The cage (bottom), destined for Iraqi terrorists, was placed near the Abu Ghraib prison in the suburbs of Baghdad.

477
A marine drags by the collar a terrorist who has just been captured in the center of Falluja on November 12, 2004.

478-479
A fire-bomb has just been thrown at a group of British soldiers in Basra on March 22, 2004. The action was taken in retaliation for the killing in Gaza of Sheik Ahmed Yassin, founder of Hamas.

479
American Marines (top) reach the center of Baghdad, where terrorists have just launched an attack on the Ministry of Energy and on two hotels occupied by businessmen and Western journalists.

Two photos (bottom) taken during a bloody battle between marines and terrorists in Falluja.

480 and 481
These atrocious scenes document the violence of the military actions that continued for years after the official end of hostilities: the despair of the mother of young Samah Hussein, killed during a suicide attack in Baghdad along with eleven other innocents; a group of terrorists using a mortar against the American emplacements in Falluja; and finally, a survivor from a vehicle that was just destroyed by a mine hidden in the asphalt.

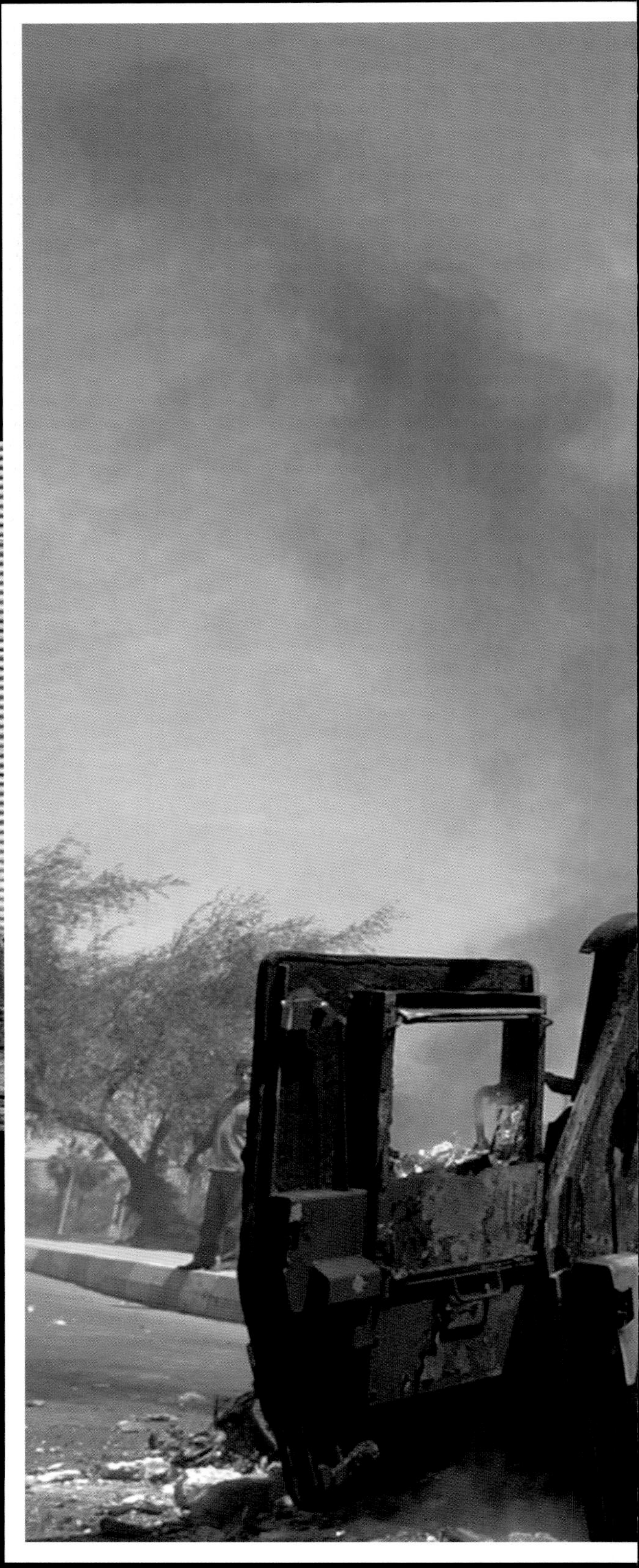

2004

Saddam

Concealment and Capture

482-483

Washington, D.C., December 15, 2003. On an improvised bulletin board, someone has glued the first three pages of the main newspapers containing stories of the capture of the ex-tyrant of Iraq, Saddam Hussein, which occurred on the 13th. The man who was considered, until the fall of his dictatorship, the worst enemy of the United States, had taken refuge in a damp, subterranean cave in his native city Tikrit, located to the north of Baghdad, where he was discovered by soldiers from of the 4th Infantry Division.

American General Ray Odierno, during a press conference on December 14, 2003, told reporters from around the world the details of the capture of Saddam Hussein. Immediately after his arrest (bottom), the ex-dictator underwent a humiliating medical exam, recorded by television cameramen. He would later be hanged on December 30, 2006, after a detention that lasted three years.

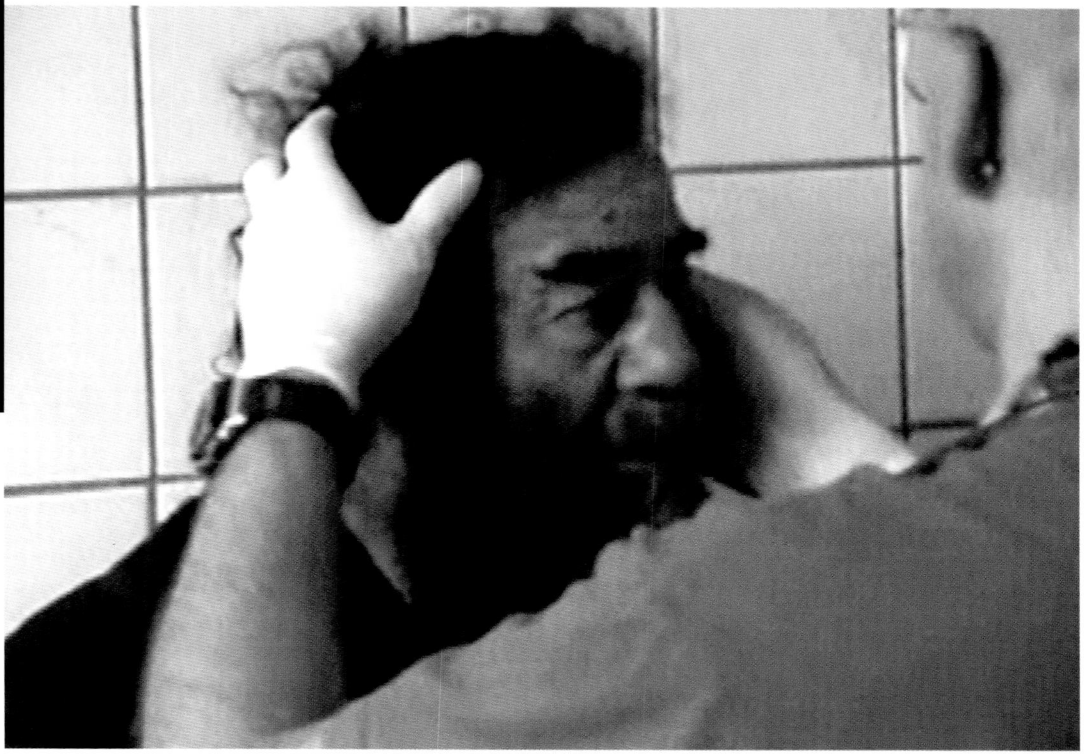

Down with USA
امام حسین (ع) :
امام حسین (ع) :
۲۲ بهمن
همبستگی ملی
مهرورزی
حزب موتلفه اسلامی

THE ETERNAL CONFLICT IN

MIDDLE EAST

THERE IS NO PEACE FOR ISRAEL

THE WAR HAS NOT YET HAPPENED AND PERHAPS (AS EVERYONE HOPES) IT NEVER WILL. HOWEVER, THAT SEEMS TO BE THE CURRENT ATMOSPHERE.

The young Iranian president Mahmoud Ahmadinejad, after having declared on more than one occasion that "Israel should be wiped off the map," proclaimed during a speech to the nation on Sunday, February 25, 2007: "We are proceeding with our nuclear program! We are ready even for war!" Thus, the official program of Iran (a new sort of Hitler era Germany, at least with respect to its anti-Semitism) seeks to develop atomic weapons, which could endanger Israel's continued existence. In reality, Shah Reza Pahlavi had already shown an interest in nuclear weapons, but the matter was not pursued after his fall – until that is, the ambitious project received the declared support of Russia and China, and was then reinstated. On July 31, 2006 the UN threatened Iran with sanctions if it did not suspend its uranium enrichment program. Ahmadinejad responded with a flat refusal, and sanctions, including an embargo on the sale of conventional weapons, were imposed. Israel, for its part, has officially stated that as soon as its secret service indicates that the production of enriched uranium in Iran has reached the "point of no return" (that is, when it has the capacity to create nuclear bombs), it will launch an air raid comprising at least fifty F16s and F15s capable of destroying the nuclear plants in Natanz, Isfahan and Arak. The countries bordering Iran on the western coast of the Persian Gulf (Kuwait, Bahrain, Qatar, United Arab Emirates and Oman) have stated that they would allow Israeli planes to fly over their countries in the event of an attack on Iran. The position of Saudi Arabia is similar. With this potential war in the background, the United States continues to maintain up-to-date plans for the attack and invasion of Iran. The response of the Foreign Minister in Tehran, Manouchehr Mottaki, was harsh: We do not believe that the United States is in a position to force upon its taxpayers another war in the Middle East. However, we are ready to face whatever choice America makes." At this time, hopes for peace rest on Ahmadinejad, who does not have the semblance of a fierce dictator and who allowed the pacifist movement to freely express itself, giving rise to demonstrations that were at times violent. Serious clashes with the police, organized by thousands of university students and their leader Ali Nesbati, took place, for example, in June 2006. Also, in the summer of 2007 a revolt broke out in the streets of Tehran due to a rationing of gasoline imposed on the people of Iran, whose petroleum production is the fourth largest in the world; evidently the country's abundance of this natural resource had been diverted to other objectives.

There exists in Iran an elite politico-military formed by the *pasdaran* which has always been very powerful. The *pasdaran* gave rise in 1979 to the Ayatollah Khomeini, who was called the "guardian of the revolution," and today this body comprises 150,000 militants. Several Islamic leaders with extremist positions regarding Israel, including Ahmadinejad, Rafsanjani and Ali Khamenei, rose from the ranks of the pasdaran. Members of this force had been protagonists of the bloody Iranian war against Iraq, but when the conflict was over they did not demobilize, but instead continued fighting in the mountains on the Afghanistan border. After a time, they came to control Iran's entire energy industry (including nuclear energy). Their current leader is General Yahya Rahim Safavi, who commands150,000 soldiers, and can rely on at least an additional 10 million volunteers. The *pasdaran* have been the authors of some of the most daring international provocations, including the intermittent capture of British patrols in the Persian Gulf, to both see what kind of reaction would occur and to prove that Great Britain was no longer that it once had been.

484
Tehran, February 11, 2006. Demonstrators burn the flags of Denmark and Israel on the 27th Anniversary of the Khomeini Revolution in a show of protest against the blasphemous cartoons of Muhammad published in Copenhagen.

2006

2006

The Eternal Conflict

486 and 487

Village of Har Dov, Israel, July 12, 2006. Israeli artillery (above) open fire toward the Lebanese border after a group of Hezbollah captured two Israeli soldiers. The Minister of Defense Amir Peretz requested their immediate release. When nothing happened, Tel Aviv (bottom) intensified the bombardment of Lebanese territory, while Israeli paratroopers (right) prepared for a possible invasion of southern Lebanon.

488 and 489

When the two Israeli soldiers were not freed, Israel decided not to accept the UN plan for a cease-fire, and the violent bombardment recommenced. An elderly woman (above left) is carried to safety by the photojournalist Wael Ladiki, while the inhabitants of Chiah, on the periphery of Beirut, hold funerals for the 41 victims of the bombardments, and a woman (bottom) cries in front of the ruins of her house. To the right, a view of the southern suburbs of Beirut one day after a cease-fire was declared on August 14, 2006.

It was the Iranian *pasdaran* who created in Lebanon the first cell of "Hezbollah" in 1982. The following year, Hezbollah attacked the general headquarters of the American Marines and the French troops in Beirut, causing over 300 deaths and forcing the retreat of the multinational force. In the following two decades, the movement strengthened to the point that it dictated the country's political policy, and inflamed the border situation with Israel after the attack in which rockets were launched at an Israeli reservists' barracks in Galilee on July 11, 2006. Just a few hours later, while the bodies of the twelve soldiers who were killed were still being recovered, Haifa was hit by an indiscriminate bombardment that killed three civilians and wounded sixty more. The response from Israel was extremely harsh: a series of long-range bombardments that caused dozens of deaths in Beirut. From that moment, and for the next 26 days, Israeli air raids and artillery fire claimed an additional 900 victims, while fierce battles took place between Israeli soldiers and Hezbollah militia led by Hassan Nasrallah. At the end of the conflict, the Israelis created a security strip approximately 4 miles (7 km) wide inside Lebanese territory. A truce was signed on August 13, 2006.

A conflict practically without end, the war between Israel and Lebanon began in 1982, when General Ariel Sharon (the future prime minister of Israel) mobilized his troops and commenced the operation that would be known historically as "Peace of the Galilee." The objective of this operation was to attack groups of Palestinians belonging to the PLO (Palestinian Liberation Organization) who had taken refuge there after the "Black September" operation in Jordan, and to erase the Syrian military threat present in Lebanon since 1976.

After the Six-Day War in 1967, the refugee camps in the southern area of Lebanon sheltered no fewer than 300,000 Palestinians, and gave rise to the Shiite militia led by Amal, which was created to attack Israel. Alongside them, the Christian militia the "Falange" was also formed, thereby providing the origin of the civil war between Christians and Muslims in Lebanon.

The conflicts lasted until 1985, when Israel decided to withdraw from Lebanon, but they maintained a presence in the security strip until 2000. The war, which claimed 15,000 lives between 1982 and 2000, thousands of whom were Israeli, erupted again on July 11, 2006 when a Hezbollah commando attacked and destroyed a military unit in Israeli territory.

FROM WEST BANK TO
GAZA

490 and 490-491
A Palestinian woman walks along the 26 ft (8 m) high wall, built by Ariel Sharon to impede direct contact between Israel and the West Bank and to put an end to the attacks. To the right, an evocative image of a female hand (of a mother?) extended towards a child on the other side of the wall, upon which are written protests. It is possible that a photojournalist staged this, but it still manages to convey the idea of the difficulty that has been created within the Palestinian community.

The Arabs of West Bank and Gaza took to the streets to praise Hezbollah when they heard news of the attack launched from Nasrallah on Galilee on July 11, 2006. The friction, exchange of gunfire, and attacks did not cease despite the erection of the wall between Israel and West Bank by Ariel Sharon. Even the death of Yassir Arafat, on November 11, 2004, did not assuage the situation. On the contrary, the tension began to rise in 2006, when Hamas took power in the Gaza strip. A long war began in 1948 when the territory to the west of the Jordan River, assigned to Jordan, was claimed by the new State of Israel, who subsequently took possession of it in 1968 after the Six-Day War. From that point on, the West Bank and the Gaza Strip, which faces the Mediterranean, comprise the so-called "Palestinian territory" which is at the center of the interminable Arab-Israeli conflict, and the subject of negotiations, terrorist acts and war. The UN has defined the West Bank and the Gaza Strip as "territory occupied by Israel."

However, Tel Aviv does not agree and maintains that the eastern border of the Jewish State has never been defined by anyone. In addition, thousands of Jews have settled permanently in the territory. The issue therefore remains as undecided as ever.

الذكرى
لانطلاقة
فتح

c = caption